Critical Acting Pedagogy

Critical Acting Pedagogy invites readers to think about pedagogy in actor training as a research field in its own right: to sit with the complex challenges, risks, and rewards of the acting studio; to recognise the shared vulnerability, courage, and love that defines our field and underpins our practices.

This collection of chapters, from a diverse group of acting teachers at different points in their careers, working in conservatoires and universities, illuminates current developments in decolonising studios to foreground multiple and intersecting identities in the pedagogic exchange. In acknowledging how their positionality affects their practices and materials, 20 acting teachers from the United Kingdom, the United States, Europe, and Oceania offer practical tools for the social justice acting classroom, with rich insights for developing critical acting pedagogies. Authors test and develop research approaches, drawn from social sciences, to tackle dominant ideologies in organisation, curriculum, and methodologies of actor training.

This collection frames current efforts to promote equality, diversity, and inclusivity in the studio. It contributes to the collective movement to improve current educational practice in acting, prioritising well-being, and centring the student experience.

Lisa Peck is Senior Lecturer in Theatre and Performance Practice at the University of Sussex. Her research interests include actor training, theatre-making pedagogies, women in theatre, critical pedagogies, and site-based performance.

Evi Stamatiou is Senior Lecturer and Course Leader of the MA/MFA Acting for Stage and Screen at the University of East London. She is a practitioner-researcher of actor training with two decades of international experience as an actor and creative.

Routledge Advances in Theatre & Performance Studies

This series is our home for cutting-edge, upper-level scholarly studies and edited collections. Considering theatre and performance alongside topics such as religion, politics, gender, race, ecology, and the avant-garde, titles are characterized by dynamic interventions into established subjects and innovative studies on emerging topics.

The Art and Occupation of Stage Design in Finnish Theatres
The Rise and Fall of a Professional Community
Laura Gröndahl

The Human Touch
Redefining the Art of British Contemporary Improvisational Theatre
Chloé Arros

Black Queer Dance
Gay Men and the Politics of Passing for Almost Straight
Mark Broomfield

The Rise and Fall of Rape on the English Stage
1660–1720
Anne Greenfield

Theatre and Human Rights
The Politics of Dramatic Form
Gary M. English

Who Is In the Room?
Queer Strategies for Redefining the Role of the Theater Director
Brooke O'Harra

Arabs, Politics, and Performance
George Potter, Roaa Ali, and Samer Al-Saber

For more information about this series, please visit: www.routledge.com/Routledge-Advances-in-Theatre-Performance-Studies/book-series/RATPS

Critical Acting Pedagogy

Intersectional Approaches

Edited by Lisa Peck and Evi Stamatiou

Foreword by Josette Bushell-Mingo
Afterword by Amy Mihyang Ginther

Routledge
Taylor & Francis Group

LONDON AND NEW YORK

Designed cover image: Nathaniel Noir/Alamy Stock Photo

First published 2025
by Routledge
4 Park Square, Milton Park, Abingdon, Oxon OX14 4RN

and by Routledge
605 Third Avenue, New York, NY 10158

Routledge is an imprint of the Taylor & Francis Group, an informa business

British Library Cataloguing-in-Publication Data
A catalogue record for this book is available from the British Library

ISBN: 978-1-032-49408-1 (hbk)
ISBN: 978-1-032-49414-2 (pbk)
ISBN: 978-1-003-39367-2 (ebk)

DOI: 10.4324/9781003393672

Typeset in Sabon
by Apex CoVantage, LLC

In memory of Sarah Davey-Hull. A friend, colleague, and educator who embraced acting students and teachers holistically and inspired affection, enthusiasm, and critical generosity.

Contents

Contributors

Editors

Lisa Peck is Senior Lecturer in Theatre and Performance Practice at the University of Sussex. Her research interests include actor training, theatre-making pedagogies, women in theatre, critical pedagogies, and site-based performance. Her most recent publication, *Emma Rice's Feminist Acts of Love*, was published by Cambridge Elements in 2023. *Act as a Feminist: Towards a Critical Acting Pedagogy* was published by Routledge in 2021. She is Associate Editor of *Theatre, Dance and Performance Training* where she curates an open-access blog on Critical Pedagogy.

Evi Stamatiou is Senior Lecturer and Course Leader of the MA/MFA Acting for Stage and Screen at the University of East London. She is a practitioner-researcher of actor training with two decades of international experience as an actor and a creative. She recently published *Bourdieu in the Studio: Decolonising and Decentering Actor Training through 'Ludic Activism'* (Routledge 2023). She has a PhD from The Royal Central School of Speech and Drama. She is Senior Fellow of the Higher Education Academy. She chairs the Acting Program at the Association for Theater in Higher Education and co-convenes the Performer Training Focus Group at the Theatre and Performance Research Association.

Contributors

Joelle Ré Arp-Dunham (PhD, MFA) is Teaching Assistant Professor at Kansas State University. She is a director, actor, consent and staged sexual intimacy professional, scholar, and educator in both theatre and film. She also serves on the editorial board of *The Journal of Consent-based Performance* and recently released the edited collection, *Stanislavsky and Intimacy* (Routledge).

Electa Behrens (USA/Norway) leads the BA in Acting at the Norwegian Theatre Academy. She is a performer, mother, theorist, and teacher. She holds a PhD from Kent University. Her work explores voice as a way to be in, build, and deconstruct worlds. She has written on voice and touch, darkness, composition, decomposition, presence, action, intersectionality, agency, ethics, and space. She has worked with, among others, Odin Teatret (DK), Richard Schechner (USA), Marina Abramovic (Serbia), Dah Theatre (Serbia), and the Centre for Performance Research (Wales).

Stan Brown is the Inaugural W. Rockwell Wirtz Professor and Director of Graduate Studies in the MFA in Acting Program at the School of Communication. He has an extensive acting career and holds an MFA in Acting from the University of South Carolina. He received classical training at the Shakespeare Theatre in Washington, DC, and started teaching at the University of Warwick in Coventry, England. He collaborated with voice expert Cicely Berry, influencing his exploration of cultural impacts on actor training.

Josette Bushell-Mingo OBE is Principal and CEO at The Royal Central School of Speech and Drama and Artistic Director for The National Black Theatre of Sweden. She is an award-winning actor and director, and an active spokesperson for inclusive arts and politics. Josette continues to travel internationally, giving lectures and workshops in the creation of sign language theatre, cultural diversity challenges, and inclusion.

Elizabeth M. Cizmar is Assistant Professor of acting and directing and an affiliate faculty member of African American and Diaspora Studies at Vanderbilt University. She holds a PhD and an MFA. She is an artist-scholar whose research centres on Black diasporic performance and acting theory. Her most recent book, *Ernie McClintock and the Jazz Actors Family* (Routledge), was published in 2023.

Denis Cryer-Lennon is a part-time lecturer in Theatre, Drama and Performance at the University of South Wales. He researches inclusive voice pedagogies, breath training, and critical thinking. His PhD thesis is titled '"Speake, Breathe, Discusse": Towards a Critical Breath Pedagogy for Speaking Shakespeare'. He has co-authored a manifesto for performer training: 'Undisciplined discipline: performer training for a new generation' published in *Theatre, Dance and Performance Training* in 2020.

Niamh Dowling is Principal at the Royal Academy of Dramatic Art, London, and has worked as a movement practitioner in the United States, Asia, and Central and South America. She is a Cultural Advocacy Research Fellow at Queen Mary University of London and on the Editorial Board of Theatre Dance and Performance Training.

Øystein Elle, associate professor at Østfold University College, is a multidisciplinary artist, singer, and composer. Elle is a classically trained countertenor with a further specialisation in extended vocal techniques. His research and performance spans baroque, Dadaism, Western avant-garde traditions, and intercultural and transdisciplinary projects. He has toured over 30 productions in Europe, Asia, and the Americas. In addition to art productions for a general audience, he has been for the past 12 years active as a creator, performer, and researcher in art experiences and performances for the youngest children's audience on which he recently co-edited an anthology.

Amy Mihyang Ginther (she/they) is an associate professor in the Department of Performance, Play & Design at UC Santa Cruz. She is a queer, transracially adopted theatre maker, accent designer, and theorist who publishes and performs around themes of identity, embodied trauma, power, and representation. They are a Master Teacher of Acting and Singing with Archetypes and a certified teacher of Knight-Thompson Speechwork and the Tectonic Theater Project's Moment Work devising method. Amy is currently working on a musical, No Danger of Winning, and a virtual reality experience about reproductive justice, Mountains after Mountains (산 넘어 산).

Zoë Glen is a neurodivergent theatre practitioner, actor-trainer, and researcher. Her research interests include inclusive practice, neurodiversity, and access in actor training; neuroqueer performance; and how phenomenology can be used in acting. She is currently undertaking a PhD at the University of Kent, investigating the needs and experiences of autistic student-actors in BA acting programmes.

Sherrill Gow is Joint Head of Postgraduate Training and co-head of MA Performance (acting and musical theatre pathways) at Mountview Academy of Theatre Arts. She holds a PhD from the Royal Central School of Speech and Drama. Before her appointment at Mountview, Sherrill worked as a freelance director on several off-West End, fringe, and touring productions, as well as a visiting teaching artist for various drama schools, universities, and youth theatre programmes.

Jessica Hartley is Course Leader of the MA/MFA in Actor Training and Coaching at the Royal Central School of Speech and Drama. Her recent publications have highlighted the urgent need for critically conscious training, one that maximises the agency and uniqueness of each actor to shape their work, identity, and careers.

Chris Hay is Professor of Drama at Flinders Drama Centre in the College of Humanities, Arts and Social Sciences at Flinders University, where he is also the research section head for Creative and Performing Arts. He has published on early Australian actor training and serves as Associate Editor of *Theatre, Dance and Performance Training*, for which he co-edited a special issue on Actor Training in Australia in 2021.

Amy Rebecca King is Visiting Assistant Professor of Acting at Southwestern University in Georgetown, Texas. She teaches movement, theatre dance, playwriting, directing, clown and devising, as well as theatre history. Recent productions at Southwestern include *Witch* (director), *Ride the Cyclone* (choreographer), and *Stage Kiss* (director). She received her BFA from New York University, and her MFA from California State University at Long Beach. She is a designated Meisner teacher at The Meisner Institute.

Kristine Landon-Smith is a theatre practitioner and lecturer in higher education. Credits include Senior Lecturer in Acting at the National Institute of Dramatic Art, Australia; Artistic Director of Tamasha Theatre Company, UK; Senior Producer for BBC Radio Drama; and freelance appointments as a director and lecturer within industry and HE settings. Kristine focuses on artist training using a multilingual intracultural theatre practice and the creation of new work using the headphone verbatim tool in applied theatre settings.

Tara McAllister-Viel is Head of Voice and Speech at East 15's Southend campus. Her research areas include intercultural approaches to voice pedagogy, Korean pansori, and Anglo-American approaches to training actor's voices. She wrote *Training Actors' Voices: Towards an Intercultural/Interdisciplinary Approach* (Routledge, 2019). She has been Associate Editor-in-Chief of the Voice and Speech Review (2011–2017) and currently sits on the Board of the Korean Association for Voice of Performing Arts.

Valerie Clayman Pye is Associate Professor of Theatre (Long Island University, Post). Her research focuses on actor training pedagogy, theatrical intimacy (TIE), Shakespeare's Globe, Shakespeare tourism, and practice-as-research (PaR). She is the author/co-editor of four books with Routledge. Her essays have appeared in collections and journals.

Jennifer Smolos Steele is the Dean of the School of Visual & Performing Arts/Artistic Director of the Santa Clarita Performing Arts Center at College of the Canyons in Los Angeles, CA. She holds a PhD in Educational Leadership and Administration from New York University. Her experience in universities, conservatories, and community colleges inspires her scholarship regarding how post-secondary performing arts programmes balance traditional technique and innovative practice, with important implications for theory and praxis.

Robert Torigoe is Manager at the Lincoln Center for the Performing Arts Education Initiatives. He served as a Graduate Assistant for the Department of Theatre and Dance at the University of Hawai'i at Mānoa. Born and raised in Hawai'i, Robert is now based in New York City, where he has performed Off-Broadway and Off–Off Broadway. Credits include *Honor* (Prospect Theatre), *Sundown* (Yara Arts), *Fan Tan King* (Pan Asian Rep), *Numbness 2* (One-Eight Theater), and *Dissecting Civil Rights* (The Tank).

Peter Zazzali is Professor of Theatre and Director of the School of Theatre and Dance at James Madison University in the United States. Before that, he was the director of the BA (Hons) Acting Programme at the University of the Arts Singapore (LASALLE). His research on performance training has appeared in numerous journals and edited volumes. He received high praise for his books *Acting in the Academy: The History of Professional Actor Training in US Higher Education* (Routledge 2016) and *Actor Training in Anglophone Countries: Past, Present and Future* (Routledge 2021).

Acknowledgements

Thanks to our students who continue to teach and inspire us.

This project would not have been possible without the members of the Acting Program at the Association for Theatre in Higher Education (ATHE) and the members of the Performer Training Working Group at the Theatre and Performance Research Association (TaPRA).

Foreword

The world remains complicated. Our existence requires reflection and constant navigation. Understanding who we are, what this life is and how, through the arts, we can find a kind of map; where signposts of practice can help us to navigate. These spaces we hold are ones destined for challenge and provocation, brushing the edges of our infallibility.

This book looks at the spaces we hold, or more to the point, the people who hold them. The irony I have found in my brief time within the Higher Education sector, but over 40 years in the arts both as actress, performer, director, and mentor, is wanting to create a space of challenge and openness, while simultaneously clinging to what *I* know, what *I* think is the best way, what *I* believe is the way forward.

In this book two things are happening: the practitioners offer provocations and insight into how to navigate these spaces and the questions we should ask; and in doing so they give insight into the person themselves. The reader can place themselves in between at the intersection of that, to feel its fluidity, the living undulation of diversity.

No one owns anything. The ossification within some practices can only end with silence and emptiness. The 'positivity of difference' also backfires when we ask who it is that needs to see it as positive, and when? Therefore, I am mindful of the intersection within each contributors' practice. How do the practices shared on these pages open up and simultaneously expose assumptions of knowledge, new ways of being and letting go.

What I believe binds them is the rigour and acceptance that this is the most profound and necessary thinking and practice, fundamental for our humanity. If birth and death are the book ends, this book offers a timely middle space to the ongoing conversation of how to transform traditional practices in between; that equity, inclusion, equality, and diversity is the foundation.

I realise that I understand less and less about notions of identity: Who defines it? Whose reference is it? How does this manifest in the room? To be inclusive, we must place each person at the nexus of intersectionalism. The chapters in this volume pursue this, seeking fluidity in thought and action.

One of the curiosities I have is how to transfer policy to practice so that this work meets the participant. How are these questions answered? How do we establish spaces that can understand and hold on tightly, yet be ready to let go of what no longer serves?

The contributors to this book provide a wealth of information for educators to rethink their teaching practices from a place of humility, respect, and genuine interest in fostering equitable, just, and inclusive spaces of learning. In doing so, this book will undoubtedly challenge brave educators, seeking innovative approaches to revolutionise traditional ways of teaching and learning, to go beyond the superficial 'celebration' of diversity.

Inclusion and equity are the cardinal principles of social justice and key priorities for education. The practical advice and knowledge gained from this book are essential for educators at all levels to implement more inclusive and equitable pedagogies, integrating decolonised practices that can help us build more respectful and caring relationships with students.

Therefore, I conclude, with subtexts and vulnerability, the world remains complicated. Our existence requires reflection and constant navigation. Understanding who we are, what this life is, and how, through the arts, we can find a kind of map to navigate – signposts of practice. How will you the reader find your way?

Josette Bushell-Mingo

Introduction

Lisa Peck and Evi Stamatiou

Pedagogy and Acting

> Talking about pedagogy, thinking about it critically, is not something most folks think is hip and cool.
>
> (hooks, 1994, p. 204)

It's time to talk about (and celebrate) pedagogy in acting – to dive deep into the processes of teaching and learning. Who are we teaching? What are we teaching? Why? And, most importantly, how?

It's likely that you have come to this book grappling with these questions. As bell hooks notes, too often pedagogic research is sidelined. At this time of seismic cultural change, when social and ecological injustices are being called to account perhaps, more than ever, we need to invest in our processes. This book seeks to recognise and reposition acting pedagogy – uniting theory and praxis – as a research field in its own right and invites a community of practice to gather in.

Changes in the terrain sharpen the senses as we navigate new directions. We'd like to start by noticing how key coordinates have shifted the positionality of actor training in Higher Education. In mapping our route, we are alert to changes in discourse; terms that once sounded faintly in the field now reverberate across the landscape. Constructs once seen to be anathema to technique, 'dirty words' in acting, 'criticality' and 'identity politics', are now essential to advancing the organisational structures and ethics, epistemologies, and pedagogies of the landscape.

It's curious that, when its teaching and learning practices are so distinct, multivarious, and potentially transformative, acting pedagogy hasn't been more widely shared and disseminated. Perhaps its truncated history throughout the twenty-first century, the grafting of two different approaches to pedagogy – conservatoire and university – has stymied its potential momentum. In the United Kingdom, vocational actor training in conservatoires has been allied to 'training' or 'coaching' as opposed to 'teaching', seen to be the domain of universities. Actor training maintained a familial passing-on of knowledges, usually taught by actors replicating their own experience (Prior, 2012). When drama schools were affiliated with universities in 2002, with degree-awarding status, distinctions purposefully blurred, allowing universities to benefit from the actor training market and conservatoires to acquire educational status. The growth of the study of acting at university meant that practitioner/researchers, increasingly with PhDs, and sometimes working across both institutions, started to push the boundaries of scholarship in the field. Conservatoires had to work with learning outcomes, assessment modes, and criteria. In university, with less contact hours,

DOI: 10.4324/9781003393672-1

without the pressure of serving the industry, and responding to Performance Studies as a discipline, pedagogy became more critically orientated to the politics of acting, as opposed to, or alongside, teaching technique. Different institutions were doing different things with different goals and acting – what it is, who it is for, how it is taught – was understood differently. Not making space to better understand and disseminate pedagogies between and across the sectors has, perhaps, stymied progression and we are now playing catch up. As we seek out new ways of teaching acting, it seems important not to lose the best of the old ways and to recognise pedagogies as contextual and contingent to their environment. The 15 chapters in this collected edition, international in scope, from conservatoire and university training grounds, attest to this.

The knowledge of acting may be constantly changing but one constant for many students is the desire to work as an actor. The neoliberal economy that swelled the number of acting graduates throughout the twenty-first century has resulted in wide-scale unemployment. In the United States, after the unprecedented expansion of theatre programmes from the mid-1960s, employability prospects became an increasing cause for concern (Zazzali, 2016, p. 9). To ethically balance the diminished return between the economic growth of actor training and industry employment, there has been a move towards facilitating actor-entrepreneurs who create and manage their own work (ibid, p. 159). Actors are taught to know 'one's brand' and be able to '"pitch" it' during 'grant writing and approaching investors' (Zazzali, 2021, p. 186). There is an orientation towards transferable skills that promote an awareness of individualised and relational aptitudes – communication, leadership, flexibility, problem-solving, empathy, creativity, cultural competence – linked to the mission of Higher Education to boost employability (National Careers Service, 2023). While these competences can be seen to serve the contemporary demand for managerialism, efficiency, and market liberalism (for some, anathema to art-making), this new landscape offers fertile terrain for acting pedagogies, highly attuned to these knowledges and skills.

Developing a critically embodied practice is at the heart of this. The idea of criticality, inherent in a university education, has increasingly infiltrated actor training. In the context of this book, criticality means critiquing and working to solve issues of social injustice, drawn from social movements for equity and freedom – anti-colonialism, women's rights, sexual freedom, gender inclusivity, anti-ableism, and racial desegregation. In its essence, criticality questions the way that mechanisms of power operate to better understand how value systems can maintain and perpetuate oppression and exclusion. Being critical requires self-reflexivity, curiosity, openness, and humility. One could surmise that actor training resisted the critical imperative because it ran counter to the discipline and self-negation required to serve the industry. At drama school in the United Kingdom in the early 2000s, we were told not to question a practitioner about their approach; a silencing that, on reflection, worked to inscribe an accepted status quo in an industry where one 'suffered for the art'. This lack of criticality which fed into the common trope, 'Don't think about it, just do it', perpetuated the de-intellectualizing and de-politicising of acting. By curtailing students' freedom to question and express concerns well-being suffered, fuelling oppressive cultures (Ginther, 2023; Freeman, 2019; Luckett & Shaffer, 2017; Margolis & Renaud, 2011).

The political landscape of the last decade with its explosion of 'identity politics' alongside the COVID-19 pandemic has changed the field forever, bringing complex questions of power and well-being to the fore in every aspect of the teaching and learning exchange. As Amy Mihyang Ginther notes, 'actor training programs . . . must be able to comprehensively understand their students' identities in relation to power so they can fully support them'

(2023, p. 3). Acting is a discipline where exploration of added representational identity is key and vulnerability is required, with inherent tensions between self and other, acting and not acting, character and actor. However, considering the ways that sociopolitical identity is met and formed in acting has, until recently, been secondary to technique. This reorientation has meant we've had to grapple with the slipperiness of 'identity' as a term.

Many see identity politics, its categorisation and labelling, as separatist and fragmentary. Stuart Hall cautions:

> [I]dentity is not a set of fixed attributes, the unchanging essence of the inner self, but a constantly shifting process of positioning. We tend to think of identity as taking us back to our roots, the part of ourselves which remains essentially the same across time. In fact, identity is always a never completed process of becoming – a process of shifting identifications, rather than a singular complete, finished state of being.
>
> (2017, p. 16)

Critics argue that, by creating endless categories of difference, identity politics feeds speciality markets to become currency in global capital (Ahmed, 2012; Bilge, 2013). Others claim that it values cultural recognition over economic redistribution, fostering victimhood politics where people chase their own narrow interests rather than being committed to the social good (Nash, 2019; Carastathis, 2016). Marxists and postmodernists deride the ways that identity politics perpetuates a compulsive repetition of dramatic events that hold people captive of their oppression (Hall, 2017; Collins, 2019). From our perspective, the recent scholarship in actor training that brings questions of identity to the fore does vital social justice and cultural activist work. It challenges outmoded power dynamics of training and gives voice to those who have previously been unheard – through race and antiracist practices (Ginther, 2023; Luckett &Shaffer, 2017), feminist (Blair, 1992; Malague, 2011; Alexandrowicz, 2012; Peck, 2021), queer (Spatz, 2015; Pearlman & McLaughlin, 2020), and dis/abled positions (Sandahl, 2009; Whitfield et al., 2022). These welcome interventions are essential in centring questions of difference in training grounds. The complexity of actor training studios has recently prompted intersectional approaches to address dominant ideologies in actor training (Stamatiou, 2022, 2023). This book picks up on Ginther's recognition at the end of her edited collection *Stages of Reckoning: Antiracist and Decolonial Actor Training*. She reflects that no identity category lives 'in a vacuum', that we must teach from our 'full selves', and that 'future conversations will incorporate more explicit intersectionality' (2023, p. 249). Responding to this, this collection of chapters, from practitioners working in the United States, United Kingdom, Australasia, and Europe, contributes to this developing field of knowledge and community of practice, offering ways to advance acting through intersectional critical pedagogies.

Intersectionality and Actor Training

We were delighted to come across Ginther's challenge as it spoke to our evolving position. Originally, responding to the current scholarship, we worked with identity categories – sex, gender, disability, race, age, class – as organising structures for critical pedagogic enquiry. However, we became increasingly cognisant that this approach might reaffirm boundaries in exclusionary ways, rather than working with the transformative possibilities of difference for everyone in the room, recognising multiple axes of identity and our constant states of becoming.

It feels like we are living at a time where we are split between listing categories of difference that define us and collapsing them to seek a place of shared humanity. The chapters in this book, in distinct and particular ways, work with intersectionality to respond to this challenge. One could argue that non-intersectional approaches lack the nuances and complexity of social structures and subjective experiences. Instead of seeing categories as oppositional – the differences *between* – intersectionality examines their interconnections, with an individual's identities as intersecting and performative. Identity is not something one *has* as much as something one *does*, differentially performed from one context to the next. This feels closely allied to the knowledge of acting and how the actor steps in and out of identities, both themselves and themselves performing the character or role. As actor Willem Dafoe explains: 'I'm a guy given a character, a performing persona, and I'm going through these little structures and how I field them is how I live in this piece' (cited by Auslander in Zarrilli, 1995, p. 305). If, as twenty-first-century acting practices attest, rather than some kind of mystical transformation, the actor is discovering the specificity of their tasks within a particular context, they are acutely aware of the multiple and simultaneously intersecting identities fielding the structures of representation moment-to-moment. From this perspective, offering actors an intersectional approach to questions of identity seems vital. We are not suggesting that it should replace the vital approaches that foreground specific work – anti-racist, feminist, or anti-ableist – but that it might work as an umbrella for, and in relation to, identity-informed pedagogies.

Intersectionality is a slippery term. The construct has a long history in Black feminism, mostly attributed to the work of Black feminist legal scholar Kimberlé Crenshaw ([1989] 1997, 1991) yet emerging through a long lineage of Black scholarship, including, but not limited to, Combahee River Collective ([1982] 2015), Anna Julia Cooper (1988), and Deborah King (1988). One concern is the way it has been co-opted by feminism as a political solution to one of its most pressing problems – 'the long and painful legacy of its exclusions' – while sidelining its origins (Davis, 2008, p. 70). Crenshaw herself reflects on the term's changing iterations: a synonym for oppression without specifying what that oppression is, a metaphor for demarginalising, a provisional concept demonstrating the inadequacy of approaches which separate systems of oppression, focusing on one, while eluding others. She notes how intersectionality has had a 'wide reach, but not [a] very deep one', 'it is both over and under used' (interview quoted in Berger & Guidroz, 2009, pp. 65, 76). Perhaps though, as Kathy Davis suggests, 'its vagueness and open ended-ness is the secret to its success' (2008, p. 69).

This open-endedness has led us to wrangle with the term. Part of the problem is that the word 'intersecting' suggests discrete systems whose paths cross. This promotes the idea of tidy, separate, and binary categories of identity, when each is always in relation with another. This, invertedly, can suggest that certain differences are more important than others, or that differences are fixed states that can be seen or named. Responding to the ambiguity of the intersectional, Rosi Braidotti suggests that instead of drawing attention to the differences *between* women, we should consider the differences *within* every woman (2011, p. 148). Like Braidotti, we are mindful that intersectionality might perform a retrograde form of identity politics that builds walls around categories as opposed to doing the work of dismantling them. In conflating intersectionality with identity, it can be seen as a type of identity studies which perpetuates certain problems: an alleged attachment to essentialised identity categories, a focus on categories which some deem too exclusionary, a lack of aspiration to celebrate diversity. Scholars continue to question if the term is fit for purpose. Jennifer Nash problematises how, in US colleges, through its 'citational ubiquity', intersectionality is conflated with 'terms that are imagined to be allied: "diversity" and "inclusion" 'which intersectional scholars critique as performative' (2019, pp. 15, 22). She highlights the ways that difference and diversity have been co-opted and intersectionality appropriated as part of the false promise of neoliberal education, where cultural currency is marketable (ibid, pp. 22–26). As Ginther cautions, '[a]n educational space can espouse notions of multiculturalism and diversity and still centre whiteness' (2023, p. 7).

Mindful of the above concerns, we are drawn to think about cultural competence, used in various fields, including healthcare, psychology, and education, as a key material in developing acting knowledges. Initiated by Geert Hofstede's cultural dimensions theory (1983), and sometimes named the 3 c's (cross-cultural competence), cultural competence involves a life-long journey of self-critique and reflection (Frawley et al., 2020, p. 3). Cultural competence has been described as 'set of behaviours, attitudes and/or policies that come together in the higher education sector or among professional and academic staff, and students enabling them to operate efficiently in intercultural contexts' (Cross et al., 1989, p. iv). Often discussed along the terms 'diversity competence' (Chun & Evans, 2016, pp. 131, 136) and 'culturally responsive pedagogy' (ibid, p. 353), cultural competence works to develop respect for each individual in the room and their differences, aiming to promote non-judgementalism, tolerance for ambiguity, cognitive and behavioural flexibility, and cross-cultural empathy (Deardorff, 2009). This speaks loudly to Paulo Freire's conscientisation in its fight against ethnocentrism towards ethno-relativism and, of course, to the knowledges of acting. As actors embody the stories that might reshape culture, such knowledge seems vital. Making 3c knowledge explicit in our teaching might be a way to scaffold identity politics and reposition actors as cultural agents. In this collection, we invite readers to notice this emergent strand of thinking. Examples include Tara McAllister-Veil and Stan Brown's Chapter 5 on voice teaching, Sherrill Gow's approach in Chapter 6 to scene study, or Kristine Landon-Smith and Chris Hay's methodology in Chapter 2 for playing with difference in training.

Returning to the problem of the intersectional, while Patricia Collins' 'interlocking' might be more apposite to the state of simultaneously juggling many parts of ourselves – a state particularly pertinent to acting – whatever way you look at it, intersectionality is the word that has stuck. Sirma Bilge and Collins' pragmatic definition has informed our approach:

> Intersectionality investigates how intersecting power relations influence social relations across diverse societies as well as individual experiences in everyday life. As an analytic tool, intersectionality views categories of race, class, gender, sexuality, nation, ability, ethnicity, and age – among others – as interrelated and mutually shaping one another. Intersectionality is a way of understanding and explaining complexity in a world, in people, and in human experiences.
>
> (2020, p. 2)

This recognises that in any given society, place, and time, multiple power relations work on each other in specific ways for each individual, shaping experience. When used as an analytical tool, intersectionality can serve social justice projects. At the end of *Mapping the Margins*, Crenshaw suggests that we think of identity-based groups as coalitions constituted by internal differences as much as by commonalities (1991). This harnesses a more expansive idea of identity politics, connecting the individual to collective empowerment where the structural, cultural, and disciplinary domains shape individual identity but, most importantly, the individual, as part of the group, has the ability to affect change in these domains. This image can be seen to reflect the acting studio, where individual uniqueness is separate, yet connected to the plurality of the group. Bilge and Collins note the potential activism of this work – where a transformed identity can be long-lasting: 'Once people are changed on the individual level through political consciousness-raising, they are also likely to become actors for collective change' (2020, p. 187). This idea politicises group formation and points to the social justice and cultural activist potential of actor training practices when informed by intersectionality.

From this position, we are motivated to think of intersectionality as a way of thinking and doing. We consider intersectional analysis *beside* praxis so that critical enquiry *becomes* intersectional praxis. In critical education scholarship, intersectional praxis is a form of activism – shaping work on social inequalities in curriculum, institutional structures, pedagogical methodologies, and interpersonal exchanges. Collins and Bilge identify four interconnected domains of power which we have used to inform the curation of this book: the cultural domain of power, the disciplinary domain, the fundamental structures of institutions, and the interpersonal domain (2020, pp. 31–36). In the case of acting, the cultural domain of power concerns the politics of representation and identity, and how intersectional methodologies respond to this, which is explored in Part One of this book. The disciplinary domain helps us understand how rules and regulations affect groups of people with differing identity characteristics, as seen in casting or assessment in acting, which is considered in Part Two. The fundamental structures of institutions that relate to actor training combine education and the industry, which is explored in Part Three. The interpersonal domain, or how individuals experience these convergences and how they affect social interactions, including pedagogic exchange, is examined in Part Four. In curating the chapters in this volume, we have used these frameworks as organisational structures to focus our thinking about intersectionally informed critical acting pedagogy.

(Post)Critical Pedagogies and Acting

Over the last decade, there has been a steady move to reconsider the practice of teaching and learning in acting as critical pedagogy (Luckett & Shaffer, 2017; Peck, 2021; Ginther, 2023; Stamatiou, 2023). Critical pedagogy is an umbrella term that draws on the work developed by Freire, first in Brazil with oppressed communities, which paved the way for teaching approaches that foreground marginalised groups, including, but not limited to, feminist, queer, and race pedagogies. Freire maintained that pedagogy as 'a political act' was never 'neutral' (Freire & Shor, 1987, p. 13). When we fail to bring questions of context, positionality, and the mechanisms of power into the pedagogic exchange, we comply with oppression. Freire's humanising praxis is 'reflection and action upon the world in order to transform it' and this happens through 'conscientization', which means recognising and critiquing oppressive power structures in order to activate alternative ways of being ([1970] 1996, p. 33). Conscientisation is a common spine that runs through all the chapters in this collection.

Certain tenets can be seen to characterise this learning exchange: through dialogue, students critique the ways that power works in language, behaviour and representation to understand how oppressive marginal positions are constructed, and to reimagine the status quo; the students' personal experiences and lived histories are privileged; the negative view of 'the other' is challenged to seek empowerment where there is difference; *how* you teach something is as important as *what* you teach; there is the aim to flatten power structures; a commitment to develop the individual's political, personal, and social awareness; to recognise the complexities of problems as opposed to seeking conclusions; to take notions of difference and particularity as productive sites for resistance. In acting, when we combine ideas of technique in training with the personal and social knowledges, or dispositional qualities produced *beside* technique, then the developmental learning exchange of performer training can be reconsidered as critical pedagogy (Peck, 2021). Recent collections of anti-racist, feminist, and inclusive actor training approaches have implicitly or explicitly drawn on precepts of critical pedagogies. In *Bourdieu in the Studio: Decolonising and Decentering Actor Training through 'Ludic Activism'*, Stamatiou offers a comprehensive intersectional pedagogy that invites critical consciousness and critical praxis in *authorial acting* (2023).

Critical pedagogy is aligned with intersectionality in both enquiry and practice. Both draw on broader philosophical traditions of participatory democracy and are located in an institutional framework, pursuing equity and concerned with constructs of difference. Collins and Bilge state:

> [C]ritical education's emphasis on dialogical pedagogy and intersectionality's focus on relationality speak to a similar theme, namely that navigating difference is an important part of developing critical consciousness both for individuals and for forms of knowledge.
> (2020, p. 197)

Navigating difference – asking difficult questions about power and privilege, oppression and shame – is challenging and complicated. It is rooted in the belief that difference, like the dialectic, can spark creative and transformational action. Through difference, interdependency can become unthreatening; we recognise how different strengths, acknowledged and equal, can open up new sustainable and courageous ways of being in the world (Lorde, 1984, pp. 111–112).

Critical pedagogy has evolved since Freire. Educationalists Naomi Hodgson, Joris Vlieghe, and Piotra Zamojski call for a post-critical pedagogy that moves from cruel optimism (Berlant, 2011) to hope in the present, shifting from education to citizenship and to love for the world (Hodgson et al., 2018, pp. 19–20). Their position challenges Freirean critical pedagogy to reflect feminist concerns. These include the lack of space it gives to questions of difference *between* and *within* participants (Brady, 1994); the way it professes to shift the status quo of teacher–student hierarchy without acknowledging the intersectional complexity of this (Ellsworth, 1989); its rather fixed understanding of the states of oppressor and oppressed (Weiler, 1995; Jackson, 1997); and the absence of embodiment in the process of conscientisation (Shapiro, [1999] 2015). It is in feminist approaches that we can find embedded and embodied convergence between intersectionality and critical pedagogy. hooks' 'engaged pedagogy' foregrounds transformation for both the teacher and student, with an ethics of care as its process, centred on hope and love in the pedagogic exchange: 'When we teach with love, combining care, commitment, knowledge, responsibility, respect and trust, we often are able to enter the classroom and go straight to the heart of the matter' (2010, p. 161). This openness to love as a material can be seen repeatedly in the discourse of theatre-making and acting pedagogy (Bogart, 2021; Wangh, 2013), in particular through Black and indigenous practices (Luckett & Shaffer, 2017; Mackiestephenson, 2022).

In thinking through an intersectional praxis for critical acting pedagogies, Nash's framework for a reorientating intersectionality is generative. In challenging what she refers to as the 'black defensiveness' that has territorialised intersectionality, she, like hooks, returns to features that have been central to Black feminism: witnessing (the ability to stand witness to injustices with and for each other) and love (working with vulnerability and compassion to enact change) (2019, p. 3). Constructs of witnessing and love, as actants for social justice and cultural activism, can be traced, implicitly or explicitly throughout the chapters in this collection.

Pedagogy-informed Actor Training

To situate actor training pedagogy as a research field in its own right, we need to develop research methodologies that are fit for purpose. Recent scholarship has started to harness educational approaches and concepts such as Bloom's taxonomy (McNamara, 2021), action research (Aujla, 2021), critical pedagogy (Mircev, 2021), and critical participatory action research (Stamatiou, 2023). Recognising that, in the scope of this introduction, we can only indicate approaches, here we propose formative methodologies, drawn from education and social sciences, responding to an imagined teaching challenge: decolonising Stanislavski-informed text-based acting in Higher Education. These qualitative and ethnographic research methodologies include case study, discourse analysis, and action research.

A qualitative research approach is appropriate for acting pedagogy as it foregrounds human participation. It usually starts with 'broad assumptions' and 'a theoretical lens that shapes the study' (Creswell & Poth, 2018, p. 61). Actor training scholarship increasingly draws on critical theories (feminist, race, queer, disability, class, intersectional) as theoretical lenses through which to investigate equality. The acting tutor can utilise critical theories as part of mixed methodologies that prioritise the embodied knowledge of all participants in the acting studio, driving the research questions that will shape the project. For example, in our imagined text-based acting class, if Judith Butler's concept of 'gender performativity' is the lens, a set of questions might include the following: How is gender relevant to the warm-ups of the class? How does the use of Anton Chekhov's *Three Sisters* as the key text invite stereotypical manifestations of femininity in the students' physical scores? How do Stanislavskian techniques reinforce or resist stereotypical representations of women? How do feedback processes reproduce/expose/tackle expectations of how female characters should be performed? Such research questions can be illuminated through multiple data, such as interviews, observations, documents, and audiovisual or digital materials such as emails and private blogs (Creswell & Poth, 2018, pp. 98, 163). In the acting studio, data might include artefacts, such as recorded showings of improvisations or workshop performances, schemes of work and lesson plans, actors' logbooks, the acting tutor's reflections, and group reflective discussions and email interviews. The ethics of involving participants should be at the centre of the practice and research narrative (ibid, p. 44).

According to health researcher John Creswell and educational researcher Cheryl Poth (2018, pp. 42, 43), the characteristics of a 'good' qualitative study include the following:

- Starting with a single focus.
- Using 'pure' qualitative inquiry or adopting qualitative research methodologies that have been successfully tried by the social sciences, such as ethnography and case study, with the researcher as an instrument of data collection, and with a focus on participants' views.
- Writing that makes the reader feel that they are present in the study.
- Including reflection on the history, culture, and personal experiences of the researcher.
- Adopting an ethical approach to research beyond obtaining formal permission.
- Enacting rigorous data collection procedures involving multiple forms of data collection, data analysis, and report writing, including triangulation of data.
- Analysis of data, moving from particulars to general levels of abstraction.

Recent actor training efforts to decolonise the studio have been flexibly working with these approaches according to the needs of the specific research project.

Qualitative approaches often draw on ethnography, which involves the researcher's immersion in a community to observe their practices and understand them better through interviews and relevant documents. Returning to our teaching challenge, an ethnographic approach might situate our decolonising effort within the course and the institution: observing classes across courses, reviewing schemes of work and policy documents, discussing with students and staff to question the extent to which dominant ideologies persist or resist decolonising efforts.

In working with ethnographic and other qualitative approaches, we should be mindful of potential shortcomings. Martyn Hammersley questions 'whether ethnography is, as it were, theoretically neutral'. And how, when 'what informants say in interview contexts is always socio-discursively constructed in a context-sensitive fashion', it can be 'considered without biographical context' (2006, pp. 5, 9). In our pedagogic research, we need to be clear about our critical frameworks and remain self-reflexive, recognising how positionality and unconscious bias might affect analysis.

We might approach our pedagogic enquiry as a case study. Case study research answers questions that 'require an extensive and "in-depth" description of some social phenomenon' (Yin, 2018, p. 4). This resonates with the actor trainer's aim to investigate how social power works in their studio. As 'an empirical method that investigates a contemporary phenomenon – the "case" – in depth and within its real-world context, especially when the boundaries between phenomenon and context may not be clearly evident', case study embraces the complexity of the actor training environment, where multiple and intersecting axes of oppression are surreptitiously reproduced. As used in social sciences, case study research highlights the importance of developing 'theoretical propositions to guide the design, data collection, and analysis', employing 'multiple sources of evidence, with data needing to converge in a triangulating fashion' (ibid, p. 15). For actor training, this suggests a theoretically informed hypothesis. In the case of our imagined acting class, this might be to use multiple texts, instead of only working with Chekhov's *Three Sisters* as key text, in order to resist the reproduction of historical stereotypes that oppress women. This would form the critical lens through which to examine and compare multiple data, such as schemes of work, lesson plans, documentation from practice, and participant observations, all of which should be analysed and evaluated against the hypothesis.

We might choose to focus on the ways that discourse plays out in the teaching and learning exchange through discourse analysis (Clark et al., 2021, p. 477). The methodology's variation known as critical discourse analysis is particularly useful for actor training research that aims to tackle social power. Critical discourse analysis 'emphasizes the role that power has within texts and how particular ideologies are embedded within particular discourses. The "critical" emphasis of critical discourse analysis reveals an interest in how these ideas are often implicit rather than explicitly expressed' (Gee, 2011, p. 492). To understand how this can be useful in our imagined project, the acting tutor-researcher might consider how the language choices in student interviews, or even the textual choices in *Three Sisters*, indicate biases that perpetuate patriarchy and white supremacy. Critical discourse analysis could be used as a secondary analysis of case studies and ethnographic research, investigating the interviews of key actor training agents/institutions concerning their decolonising efforts more closely. It can highlight how, in the context of discussing solutions for decolonising actor training, such agents might be unknowingly surrendering to oppressive structures.

Arguably, the most useful methodology for analysing the teaching and learning exchange is action research. Action research, which can be broadly applied across educational frameworks, including higher education (Norton, 2019), is described by the educational researchers Jean McNiff and Jack Whitehead as follows:

> [A] form of enquiry that enables practitioners in every job and walk of life to investigate and evaluate their work. They ask, 'What am I doing? Do I need to improve anything? If so, what? How do I improve it?' They produce their accounts of practice to show: 1. how they are trying to improve what they are doing, which involves first thinking about and learning how to do it better; and 2. how they try to influence others to do the same thing. These accounts stand as their own practical theories of practice, from which others can learn if they wish.
>
> (2011, p. 7)

An action research process, contextualised through our imagined example within the brackets, adopts the following structure:

1. Identify and clarify the general idea (such as 'my class surreptitiously oppresses women').
2. Describe and explain the facts of the situation (for example, classical scripts portray female stereotypes and acting choices often reproduce limiting dispositions about women because of students' learnt behaviours through a patriarchal society).
3. Construct the general plan of action (such as adapting my scheme of work/lesson plans to avoid classical scripts and invite critical discussions around how acting choices might surreptitiously reproduce stereotypes).
4. Develop the next action steps through monitoring techniques that test the effectiveness of the action plan against intended and unintended effects and also from more than one perspective (for example, 'I apply the adapted scheme of work/lesson plans and evaluate how it decolonised from patriarchy the versions that I applied in earlier teaching').
5. Implement the next action steps (around the lines of 'this worked but that didn't' and 'from this learning, I re-adapt my scheme of work/lesson plans for further testing'). (Elliott, 1991, pp. 72–76)

Such an iterative process can be useful for the acting tutor, aware of the structural resistances that might perpetuate social inequalities despite decolonising interventions. The effectiveness of all methods can be maximised through a recurring action research process with a minimum of three or four cycles (ibid, p. 85). Each cycle involves planning, acting, observing, reflecting, planning, and so on (McNiff, 2013, p. 42). The acting tutor who employs action research sees their pedagogy as a work in progress where the methodology sustains their engagement with finding solutions and making improvements. However, action researchers need to maintain their flexibility rather than follow a methodological orthodoxy (Somekh, 2006, p. 2).

Techniques and methods for gathering evidence for action research include but are not limited to personal accounts of feelings and reflections about the implemented actions; outlines of sessions; analysis of documents, such as schemes of work and exam papers; photographic evidence and artefacts, including performances and dramatic works; videos and transcripts of lessons; observations and interviews; mobile digital technologies; running commentary, which involves stopping at key points in the process to document one's observations; shadow study, which involves following a specific participant for a certain time and documenting their actions and reactions; checklists and questionnaires; inventories that involve both close and open questions and can quantify responses; triangulation, which compares and contrasts the various sets of evidence (ibid, pp. 77–83).

A useful strand of action research that acknowledges the role of the students in developing new materials is critical participatory action research, which involves both teachers and students as active research partners (Reason & Bradbury, 2013). The contributors in this collection that engaged with critical participatory action research include Denis Cryer-Lennon, who works with breath, Stamatiou, who explores liminal casting, and Joelle Ré Arp-Dunham, who develops consent and intimacy in the acting classroom. Similar to action research but with a greater focus on the students, participatory action research involves the following stages: Reconnaissance, which identifies the problem in educational practice; Planning, which plans an intervention that addresses the problem; Enacting and Observing, which applies the intervention with participants and all participants share observations; Evaluation and Reflection, which critically reflects on the application of the intervention and relevant observations, aiming at modifying the educational practice (Kemmis et al., 2013, p. 89). As with action research, the findings from the last stage lead to replanning and enacting the new plan, and so on, in a manner that enacts cyclical explorations and improvements in teaching practice, with the student voice at the centre.

Recent scholarship in actor training that tackles the inequalities in its structures draws on many of the above characteristics but does not necessarily work explicitly with these methodologies. This book seeks to draw attention to these useful approaches, welcoming methodological rigour in our pedagogic research. In this way, we can maximise our research impact, discover new methodologies tailored to the specific needs of our field, and improve the quality of experience for our students. Our belief in the values of educational research methodologies challenged the contributors of this book to look outside of current practice research approaches to apply research designs from social sciences and education and some accepted the invitation. However, and importantly, these chapters offer a range of approaches, reflecting the exciting variety and potential of this field to seek out new research methodologies that embrace the embodied complexities of our discipline. We hope this collection might inspire others to take up this challenge.

Overview of Sections

As noted, we have worked with Collins and Bilge's intersectional domains of power (2020, pp. 31–36) as curatorial structures to organise these chapters. However, we should note that the content of some chapters transverses sections. For example, Zoë Glen's chapter might be equally at home in the section on methodologies and Stamatiou's essay could be considered in relation to institutional practice. Each of the 15 contributions, from scholars/practitioners, all working in acting and performance programmes in the United States, Australasia, the United Kingdom, and Europe, approach the intersection between critical pedagogy and intersectional praxis from a particular context and positionality. Each teases out, problematises, and responds to a specific problem in actor training. Most contributors presented their work at conferences in 2023: in the United States at the Association for Theatre in High Education (ATHE) and in the United Kingdom at Theatre and Performance Research Association (TaPRA).

Part One: Intersectional Methodologies and Critical Acting Pedagogies points to ways of training that centres the actor and their intersectional identities. Separately and in conversation, the chapters apply conscientisation, to scaffold choice and positionality through dialogic practices.

Chapter 1 by Peter Zazzali introduces key aspects of Freire's approach as the foundation for a potentially liberatory acting pedagogy. Zazzali's ethnographic research draws on examples of Australasian acting programmes to investigate how critical approaches can 'honor equity and inclusion'. Chapter 2 by Kristine Landon-Smith and Chris Hay offers a case study from Landon-Smith's original actor training method. She invites actors to play with their native or second language, harnessing their 'intersectionally subordinate identities' as a superpower. Overviewing a critically reflexive methodology, Chapter 3 by Valerie Clayman Pye investigates how the introduction of a framework for journaling helps educators to 'flatten the hierarchy and promote student agency'. The last two chapters in this section focus on voice teaching. In the participatory-action-research-informed Chapter 4, Denis Cryer-Lennon collaborates with his students to interrogate the politics of breath concerning decolonising approaches to voicing Shakespeare. Finally, in Chapter 5, Stan Brown and Tara McAllister-Veil open a cross-Atlantic conversation about the reductionist effect of universal approaches to voice training. Their chapter revisions voice teaching to work from 'the unique intersectional identities' of students to explore the voice as cultural material, challenging voice trainers to develop curricula through co-authorship between students and teachers.

Part Two: Approaches to Scene Study as Cultural Intersectionality explores alternative approaches to casting and scene work with the potential to reshape the cultural domain through approaches to representation and casting. These chapters evidence cross-cultural competence in action, scaffolding choice to foreground intersectional identities.

In Chapter 6, Sherrill Gow works with a feminist paradigm to develop a robust critical framework for scene study. Chapter 7 by Amy Rebecca King and Robert Torigoe contributes to conversations about racial oppression in actor training, focusing on how to approach acting students with multiple ethnicities. In Chapter 8, Stamatiou applies action research and case study to explore intersectional approaches to casting and how student evaluations might serve to decolonise the studio.

Part Three: Structural Intersectionality in Values and Assessment thinks through the architectures that underpin pedagogical approaches. In developing progressive pedagogies, we need to address inequitable structures that foreclose change, such as the values and mission statements that frame ideologies and feed systems that can allow or disallow equity, and also function as the disciplining structures that measure and ascribe value.

The first two chapters offer case studies from elite institutions working to activate institutional change. Jennifer Smolos Steele's Chapter 9 uses organisational saga and self-designing systems to assess the effectiveness of Yale's decolonising mission and practices, drawing on public-facing documents and interviews. Chapter 10 by Niamh Dowling considers RADA's first stage of rewriting its core values and mission statement through a process of co-authoring. Dowling maps the process through a blended methodology, where the leadership model meets somatic practices. Both chapters show the importance of the words that we choose to define our identities and orientate us, and that '[h]ow we identify, both as individuals and institutions, in relation to our students frames the ways we approach decolonial practices' (Ginther, 2023, p. 9). The next two chapters focus on the disciplining structures of assessment as an integral part of the acting curriculum. In Chapter 11, Elizabeth M. Cizmar explores how assessment might respond to her students' shifting intersectional identities. In Chapter 12, Electa Behrens and Øystein Elle challenge systems of value in both its polyplural form and content, agitating against academic conventions. Through case study research, the authors reflect on a module that challenged exclusionary structures of value that define notions of quality in the singing curriculum, advocating for 'intersectional vocal expression'.

Part Four: Interpersonal Intersectionality: Learning Edges turns to the ways that critical and intersectional pedagogy works in the teaching exchange between tutor and student and between students. Each chapter tackles a particular relational challenge, centring on ethics of care and well-being to enable greater personal and collective safety. In this way, they enable the chance for greater risk-taking, through a process of conscientisation.

Jessica Hartley's Chapter 13 is an insightful critical reflection from a teacher of actor trainers drawing on attachment theory, to remodel and redirect the complex teacher–student power exchange. Joelle Ré Arp-Dunham's Chapter 14 applies an action research model to inform intimacy and consent exercises with neuroscience and student observations. In Chapter 15, Zoë Glen draws on the neurodiverse paradigm to highlight exclusionary systems in actor training, working with students to improve materials for multiple and intersecting neurodiverse populations.

In relation with and through each other, these chapters test, trial, and map intersectional praxis, through structural, cultural, and relational interventions. Many utilise or draw on educational research methodologies, with some teasing out new possibilities. This collection speaks to a challenging yet exciting time: when '"we"-who-are-not-one-and-the-same-but-are-in-*this*-together' (Braidotti, 2022, p. 8); when actors explore themselves as the curriculum; when actor training finds new orientations, new possibilities, its embodied critical pedagogy realising its potential resonance in research and praxis. All contributions, in specific and distinct ways, reflect the messy, humbling, emotional demands of enacting change that embraces difference and yet, throughout, you can feel the beating heart of our discipline, its courage, creativity, and, above all, aptitude and willingness to evolve, transform, and move forward.

References

Ahmed, S. (2012). *On being included: Racism and diversity in institutional life*. Duke University Press.

Alexandrowicz, C. (2012). Pretty/sexy: Impacts of the sexualisation of young women on theatre pedagogy. *Theatre, Dance and Performance Training*, 3(3), 288–301. https://doi.org/10.1080/1944392 7.2012.711130

Aujla, I. (2021). Opening pathways to training for young disabled dancers: An action research approach. *Theatre, Dance and Performance Training*, 12(4), 482–498. https://doi.org/10.1080/1 9443927.2021.1877805

Berger, M. T., & Guidroz, K. (Eds.). (2009). *The intersectional approach: Transforming the academy through race, class, and gender*. University of North Carolina Press.

Berlant, L. G. (2011). *Cruel optimism*. Duke University Press.

Bilge, S. (2013). Intersectionality undone: Saving intersectionality from feminist intersectionality studies. *Du Bois Review: Social Science Research on Race*, 10(2), 405–424. https://doi.org/10.1017/ S1742058X13000283

Blair, R. (1992). Liberating the young actor: Feminist pedagogy and performance. *Theatre Topics*, 2(1), 13–23. https://doi.org/10.1353/tt.2010.0042

Bogart, A. (2021). *The art of resonance*. Methuen Drama.

Brady, J. (1994). Critical literacy, feminism, and a politics of representation. In P. McLaren & C. Lankshear (Eds.), *Politics of liberation: Paths from Freire* (pp. 162–173). Routledge.

Braidotti, R. (2011). *Nomadic theory: The portable Rosi Braidotti*. Columbia University Press.

Braidotti, R. (2022). *Posthuman feminism*. Polity.

Carastathis, A. (2016). *Intersectionality: Origins, contestations, horizons*. University of Nebraska Press.

Chun, E. B., & Evans, A. (2016). *Rethinking cultural competence in higher education: An ecological framework for student development*. Wiley Subscription Services, Inc., A Wiley Company, at Jossey-Bass.

Clark, T., Foster, L., Sloan, L., & Bryman, A. (2021). *Bryman's social research methods* (6th ed.). Oxford University Press.

Collins, H. P. (2019). *Intersectionality as critical social theory*. Durham. Duke University Press.

Collins, H. P., & Bilge, S. (2020). *Intersectionality* (2nd ed.). Polity Press.

Combahee River Collective. ([1982] 2015). A Black feminist statement. In G. T. Hull, P. B. Scott, & B. Smith (Eds.), *All the women are white, all the Blacks are men, but some of us are brave: Black women's studies* (2nd ed., pp. 13–22). The Feminist Press at the City University of New York.

Cooper, A. J. (1988). *A voice from the South*. Oxford University Press.

Crenshaw, K. ([1989] 1997). Demarginalizing the intersection of race and sex: A Black feminist critique of antidiscrimination doctrine, feminist theory and antiracist politics. In K. Maschke (Ed.), *Gender and American law: Feminist legal theories* (pp. 23–52). Routledge.

Crenshaw, K. (1991). Mapping the margins: Intersectionality, identity politics, and violence against women of color. *Stanford Law Review*, 43(6), 1241. https://doi.org/10.2307/1229039

Creswell, J. W., & Poth, C. N. (2018). *Qualitative inquiry & research design: Choosing among five approaches* (4th ed.). SAGE.

Cross, T., Bazron, B. J., Dennis, K. W., & Isaacs, M. R. (1989). *Towards a culturally competent system of care: A monograph on effective services for minority children who are severely emotion- ally disturbed*. Child and Adolescent Service System Program Technical Assistance Center, Georgetown University Child Development Center.

Davis, K. (2008). Intersectionality as buzzword: A sociology of science perspective on what makes a feminist theory successful. *Feminist Theory*, 9(1), 67–85. https://doi.org/10.1177/1464700108086364

Deardorff, D. K. (Ed.). (2009). *The Sage handbook of intercultural competence*. Sage Publications.

Elliott, J. (1991). *Action research for educational change*. Open University Press.

Ellsworth, E. (1989). Why doesn't this feel empowering? Working through the repressive myths of critical pedagogy. *Harvard Educational Review*, 59(3), 297–325. https://doi.org/10.17763/haer.59.3.058342114k266250

Frawley, J., Russell, G., & Sherwood, J. (Eds.). (2020). *Cultural competence and the higher education sector: Australian perspectives, policies and practice*. Springer Singapore. https://doi.org/10.1007/978-981-15-5362-2

Freeman, J. (Ed.). (2019). *Approaches to actor training: International perspectives*. Methuen Drama, Bloomsbury Publishing Plc.

Freire, P. ([1970] 1996). *Pedagogy of the oppressed* (Rev. ed.) (M. B. Ramos, Trans.). Penguin.

Freire, P., & Shor, I. (1987). *A pedagogy for liberation: Dialogues on transforming education* (1st published). Macmillan.

Gee, J. P. (2011). *How to do discourse analysis: A toolkit*. Routledge.

Ginther, A. M. (Ed.). (2023). *Stages of reckoning: Antiracist and decolonial actor training*. Routledge.

Hall, S. (2017). *Familiar stranger: A life between two islands*. Duke University Press.

Hammersley, M. (2006). Ethnography: Problems and prospects. *Ethnography and Education*, 1(1). https://doi.org/10.1080/17457820500512697

Hodgson, N., Vlieghe, J., & Zamojski, P. (2018). Education and the love for the world: Articulating a post-critical educational philosophy. *Foro de Educación*, 16(24), 7–20.

Hofstede, G. (1983). National cultures in four dimensions: A research-based theory of cultural differences among nations. *International Studies of Management & Organization*, 13(1–2), 46–74. https://doi.org/10.1080/00208825.1983.11656358

hooks, b. (1994). *Teaching to transgress: Education as the practice of freedom*. Routledge.

hooks, b. (2010). *Teaching critical thinking: Practical wisdom*. Routledge.

Jackson, S. (1997). Crossing borders and changing pedagogies: From Giroux and Freire to feminist theories of education. *Gender and Education*, 9(4), 457–468. https://doi.org/10.1080/09540259721196

Kemmis, S., McTaggart, R., & Nixon, R. (2013). *The action research planner*. Springer.

King, D. K. (1988). Multiple jeopardy, multiple consciousness: The context of a Black feminist ideology. *Signs: Journal of Women in Culture and Society*, 14(1), 42–72. https://doi.org/10.1086/494491

Lorde, A. (1984). *Sister outsider: Essays and speeches*. Crossing Press.

Luckett, S. D., & Shaffer, T. M. (Eds.). (2017). *Black acting methods: Critical approaches*. Routledge, Taylor & Francis Group.

Mackiestephenson, A. (2022). Resist & rise: The one love method and human rights performance. *Theatre Topics*, *32*(3), 139–148. https://doi.org/10.1353/tt.2022.0027

Malague, R. (2011). *An actress prepares: Women and 'the method'*. Routledge.

Margolis, E., & Renaud, L. T. (Eds.). (2011). *The politics of American actor training* (1st issued in paperback). Routledge.

McNamara, A. (2021). Flipping the creative conservatoire classroom. *Theatre, Dance and Performance Training*, *12*(4), 528–539. https://doi.org/10.1080/19443927.2020.1864462

McNiff, J. (2013). *Action research: Principles and practice* (3rd ed.). Routledge.

McNiff, J., & Whitehead, J. (2011). *All you need to know about action research* (2nd ed.). SAGE.

Mircev, A. (2021). Reenacting pedagogies of socialism: Auto-analysis of a critical practice. *Theatre, Dance and Performance Training*, *12*(4), 540–553. https://doi.org/10.1080/19443927.2021.1877806

Nash, J. C. (2019). *Black feminism reimagined: After intersectionality*. Duke University Press.

National Careers Service. (2023). *Develop your soft skills* [Government services]. Careers Advice. https://nationalcareers.service.gov.uk/careers-advice/how-to-develop-your-soft-skills

Norton, L. (2019). *Action research in teaching & learning: A practical guide to conducting pedagogical research in universities* (2nd ed.). Routledge.

Pearlman, L., & McLaughlin, D. (2020). If you want to kiss her, kiss her! Gender and queer time in modern Meisner training. *Theatre, Dance and Performance Training*, *11*(3), 310–323.

Peck, L. (2021). *Act as a feminist! Towards a critical acting pedagogy*. Routledge/Taylor & Francis Group.

Prior, R. W. (2012). *Teaching actors: Knowledge transfer in actor training*. Intellect.

Reason, P., & Bradbury, H. (Eds.). (2013). *The SAGE handbook of action research: Participative inquiry and practice* (2nd ed., paperback ed.). SAGE.

Sandahl, C. (2009). The tyranny of neutral: Disability and actor training. In P. Auslander & C. Sandahl (Eds.), *Bodies in commotion: Disability and performance.* (pp. 255–268). University of Michigan Press.

Shapiro, S. B. ([1999] 2015). *Pedagogy and the politics of the body: A critical praxis*. Routledge.

Somekh, B. (2006). *Action research: A methodology for change and development*. Open University Press.

Spatz, B. (2015). *What a body can do: Technique as knowledge, practice as research*. Routledge.

Stamatiou, E. (2022). Pierre Bourdieu and actor training: Towards decolonising and decentering actor training pedagogies. *Theatre, Dance and Performance Training*, *13*(1), 96–114. https://doi.org/10.1080/19443927.2021.1943509

Stamatiou, E. (2023). *Bourdieu in the studio: Decolonising and decentering actor training through ludic activism*. Routledge.

Wangh, S. (2013). *Heart of teaching: Empowering students in the performing arts*. Routledge, Taylor & Francis Group.

Weiler, K. (1995). Freire and a feminist pedagogy of difference. In J. Holland, M. Blair, & S. Sheldon (Eds.), *Debates and issues in feminist research and pedagogy: A reader* (pp. 23–44). Multilingual Matters in association with the Open University.

Whitfield, P. (Ed.). (2022). *Inclusivity and equality in performance training: Teaching and learning for neuro and physical diversity* (1st published). Routledge.

Yin, R. K. (2018). *Case study research and applications: Design and methods* (6th ed.). SAGE.

Zarrilli, P. (Ed.). (1995). *Acting reconsidered: Theories and practices*. Routledge.

Zazzali, P. (2016). *Acting in the academy: The history of professional actor training in US higher education*. Routledge.

Zazzali, P. (2021). *Actor training in anglophone countries: Past, present and future*. Routledge.

Part One

Intersectional Methodologies and Critical Acting Pedagogies

1   Oppression and the Actor

Locating Freire's Pedagogy in the Training Space

Peter Zazzali

Introduction

Paolo Freire depicts education as a power struggle within which those in positions of authority objectify and exploit those who are vulnerable. His *Pedagogy of the Oppressed* disrupts conventional education models that have historically shunned shared governance while favouring hierarchies that privilege a few individuals at the expense of everyone else.[1] Freire offers hope for the oppressed through unified resistance against authoritarian pedagogies and systemic formulations of knowledge. Tradition and culture can be understood as weaponising forces that uphold hegemonic social orders. His goal is to challenge these systems in support of a just and inclusive approach to teaching and learning. He accentuates the fluidity and instability of power structures, thereby prompting us to seek ways to replace oppression with critical consciousness. Nothing is a fixed entity. Everything is and always will be subject to interrogation, self-reflection, and change. An equitable distribution of agency is foundational to a diverse and inclusive pedagogy, the likes of which can appreciably define training in the twenty-first century. Freire invites us to rethink our teaching by centring students and fostering joy in their careers, their artistry, and their lives.

How does Freire's *Pedagogy of the Oppressed* apply to drama schools and more specifically the training of actors? In what ways do history, tradition, and culture colonise curricula? How can trainers disrupt these practices and develop epistemologies that honour equity and inclusion? This chapter addresses these questions by exploring acting programmes throughout Australasia. Relying on primary and secondary research, I use an ethnographic methodology drawn from onsite visits at leading drama schools in Southeast Asia and Oceania. In doing so, I acknowledge my positionality as a white, able-bodied, straight, cisgender male who is a citizen of both the United States and European Union and understand how these characteristics frame my perspective. As a scholar exploring cultural practices and traditions different from my own, I conduct my research with humbleness and care while recognising the limitations – and uniqueness – of its scope.

My study extends from observing classwork and rehearsals to interviewing staff/students and reviewing archives. My aim is to ethnographically investigate a school and its training. Southeast Asian acting programmes present an under-researched and apt case study given their postcolonial context relative to curricula that could be understood as Freirean. Thus, I position his pedagogy alongside my fieldwork to offer best – and better – practices on behalf of diverse and inclusive training models.

DOI: 10.4324/9781003393672-3

Freire and the Pedagogy of the Oppressed: An Overview and Context

The basis of Freire's pedagogy is *conscientização*, or conscious raising, a Hegelian and Gramscian practice exploring the contradictions of a given topic. Thus, fulsome dialogue and dialectical reasoning become foundational to the ways in which teachers and students communicate and collaborate in creating a learning environment. Conscientização compels the oppressed to become aware of the mechanisms of the sociopolitical systems subjugating them and respond by 'fighting to [restore] their humanity' (2017, p. 19). Grounded in knowledge acquisition and critical thinking, it invites dialectically '[unveiling] reality and [getting] at the phenomenic essence' of a given object of study. An 'awakening of critical consciousness', conscientização is a sensibility – a way of being – that causes the oppressed to act on behalf of their self-interest (1974, p. 26). It can manifest in the acting studio and rehearsal hall in numerous ways. Imagine a classroom in which actors and their instructors dialogically engage the craft and exchange ideas instead of a perceived guru parroting techniques from bygone eras. What may have been commonplace 10/15/20 years ago is most likely outdated and in need of recontextualisation. The values and praxis of diversity, equity, and inclusion (DEI) are germane to any course of study in academia nowadays, and actor training is no exception. Freire's theory of conscientização can likewise help stage directors to collaborate with their cast and members of the design team. Crafting individual moments and making character choices can and should be a shared process wherein ideas are jointly vetted, explored, and implemented. Such an approach invites different offers and opinions, which is precisely the reason to undertake it.

Freire argues critical reflection and informed action empower the oppressed to engage their subjugators in a constructive struggle towards achieving liberation – and this is key – for both parties of an educational exchange. The pursuit of fuller humanity for all is the pedagogy's goal: 'The great humanistic and historical task of the oppressed [is to] liberate themselves and their oppressors as well' (Freire, 2017, p. 18). Following Hegel and Gramsci, Freire argues that struggle humanises the oppressed and empowers them to dialectically expose the causes of their disenfranchisement. Authoritarians maintain their power by trafficking in prescriptivism and false charity to construct hegemonic social orders through conscious and unconscious bias. History and tradition are weaponised to shape the superstructure through its constituent elements: legal, governmental, and educational systems – to name just a few. The privileged are the powerbrokers, the proverbial 'haves' in a capitalist setting wherein agency is 'determined' through acquiring material goods, money, and influence. Changing this hegemonic model depends on the oppressed mobilising against their rulers through a contradictory praxis of reflection and action towards dismantling 'mythical remnants of the old society' (2017, p. 132). Conscientização can thus be seen as a salve for those of us undertaking a critical pedagogy and reimagining twenty-first actor training through the multivalence of DEI.

We have seen such resistance in drama schools throughout the United Kingdom/United States and Australia over the past five years, as the predominance of white and Western authorities and education systems have come under criticism and in some instances revolt.[2] Acting programmes from RADA and Central to Juilliard and Sydney's National Institute of Dramatic Art have been forced to reconcile biases that have been baked into their training for generations. History and tradition have reified positions of power such that those coming from privileged backgrounds stand to gain at the expense of those who are marginalised and underrepresented. This is evidenced in curricula ranging from the materials chosen for scene work and productions to pedagogical deliverables and the identities of teachers and their students. Efforts to adopt antiracist policies have begun at Western drama schools, but considerable work remains before their oppressive systems are dismantled and replaced with an equitable and just alternative.

Freire provides a blueprint for addressing this problem. He argues that meaningful change occurs through critical discourse and negotiation alongside personal reflection and non-violent resistance. If we are to achieve liberation for all – to live in a space of fairness and social justice – it is necessary to *dialectically* identify and dislodge the root causes of pedagogical oppression. Thus, acting students should be encouraged to take ownership of their positionality to access agency and counter discrimination. Described as 'human and libertarian', a pedagogy of the oppressed necessitates accountability and compassion alongside consciousness and courage (2017, p. 40).

Influenced in part by the neo-Marxist theories of Gramsci, yet also bound by the pacifist work of Gandhi, Freire's dialecticism disrupts hegemony through a combination of action and self-awareness.[3] Discourse is foundational to the *Pedagogy of the Oppressed*. Through dialogue, students and teachers form a unique bond of shared learning. It is a dynamic process marked by reciprocity and respect, whereby instructors are not positioned as gurus dispensing knowledge, but as a partner collaborating with students while encouraging their curiosity and sharing in their discoveries. It is a process fuelled and facilitated by critical thinking, self-reflection, and an abiding generosity towards others. While independent thought and acknowledging one's voice are crucial, it is equally important to meet ideological and cultural differences with a sense of possibility without cynicism or self-aggrandising judgements. Dialogical reasoning is the stuff of courage and motivates educational leaders to regard their privileged status with humbleness and humility (2017, pp. 25–35).

Freire uses a banking metaphor to make his case for a dialogical model: 'the banking approach [turns] women and men into automatons – the very negation of their ontological vocation to be more fully human' (2017, p. 47). In describing students as containers into which teachers 'deposit' their knowledge, he exposes paternalist arrangements wherein the former have no agency in the learning process. He rejects paternalist structures that locate students as passive 'receptacles' instead of fostering independent learners who are encouraged to think critically and self-reflect (Gottlieb & La Belle, 1990, p. 7). The banking model depicts a hierarchy that has plagued higher education – and by extension actor training – for decades. If our students are to identify their artistic voice, we must enter a dialogue with them within a community of reciprocal learning and mutual growth. As Freire states, '[teachers] are no longer merely the-one-who-teaches', but an active contributor to a dialogic exchange by which they are 'in turn being taught' (2017, p. 53).

In Western contexts, we have seen some progress in this direction since the era of the so-called master teacher, when instructors deployed their symbolic capital to justify breaking down and subsequently rebuilding acting students into products for consumption defined by the dictums of the industry.[4] This Pygmalion complex of sorts has been evident in training programmes throughout the United Kingdom/United States/Australia since their inception and is finally being interrogated as students meet the profession on their own terms towards transcending and reshaping it.[5]

The banking approach minimises students while reinforcing an instructor's authority. A decidedly hierarchical model, it reduces the teacher–student relationship into top-down dispensations of knowledge instead of inviting a learning experience defined by partnership and collaboration. Contrarily, the *Pedagogy of the Oppressed* is contingent on proactive struggle whereby power is exposed and questioned in favour of just and equitable outcomes. Such resistance can cause the classroom to become a site of even-handed exchanges that lend to critical discourse and shared discovery. This result requires rethinking curricula that sustain canonical models and tropes, and instead create opportunities where students can cultivate their artistic voice and celebrate their personal identity. By centring students and student-directed projects, as is currently occurring in a handful of acting courses in Southeast Asia and Oceania, drama schools can adopt best and better practices to prepare performers for twenty-first-century careers.

Debunking oppressive learning environments requires a concerted effort from within educational systems. Students, teachers, and administrators must undertake difficult and uncomfortable work to cause meaningful change. The former have little recourse to exercise their agency and often take a significant risk when challenging authority figures and the systems that extol them with superlatives like expert and luminary. Titles such as professor, dean, or doctor often coincide with these lofty characterisations – drama schools operating under the auspices of universities have especially adopted this nomenclature. While distinctions of rank are generally earned, professional designations represent a system attempting to sustain positions of power and influence. This institutional practice might be worthily questioned if not outrightly dismantled. It has historically favoured white men and been evident in postcolonial settings, wherein the training and cultural traditions of Western societies are favoured when compared to non-Western ones. This dynamic is present in the examples I explore in the second section of this chapter, insofar as each acting programme is attempting to balance Western and non-Western traditions without surrendering its own cultural identity. Schools in economically advanced countries in the West – namely the United Kingdom and America – generally do not have to consider such culturally sensitive matters given their comparative privilege and corresponding myopia.

While the *Pedagogy of the Oppressed* criticises hierarchical models, Freire acknowledges the importance of proficient teaching and learning in acknowledging that inspiring students is directly related to authoritative instruction. 'Freedom and authority cannot be isolated', he states, as the two are intertwined within a dialogical transference of ideas and praxis (2017, p. 151). It is of course necessary to respect instructors and their requisite authority per a given subject area. Freire summates this point as a chiasmus: 'There is no freedom without authority, but there is also no authority without freedom' (ibid). It is important for students to openly express their ideas and pose questions in the context of such an exchange. To echo the banking metaphor, they are not entities into which one deposits knowledge but a group of individuals learning in partnership with their instructor.

Freire counters the banking method with what he terms a *problem-posing* approach. In what could be likened to the flipped classroom of contemporary parlance, he encourages students and teachers to learn from one another in an equitable process that champions critical thinking.[6] If hierarchical models shut down self-expression, Freire's problem-posing method recognises the teacher–student relationship as one of mutual enlightenment, wherein both participants are 'jointly responsible for [the] process' in which they grow in their mind and spirit (2017, p. 53). This dynamic lives in dialogues more so than lecturing, active listening as opposed to docile absorption, resistant reading instead of dutiful acceptance. Students have agency and are inspired by their teachers, who in turn humbly embrace their own knowledge gaps as part of a shared learning experience. Freire's problem-posing method prompts us to reimagine actor training in the twenty-first century, which like his other strategies can be seen in many acting programmes throughout Southeast Asia and Oceania.

Locating Freire's Pedagogy in Practice: Training in Southeast Asia and Oceania

With the emergence of BlackLivesMatter and #MeToo, theatre departments and performance programmes throughout Western and Australasian societies have been addressing

the values and praxis of DEI. Though he penned *Pedagogy of the Oppressed* several generations ago, Freire's manifesto coincides with this triad of values. Indeed, DEI constitute his
writing and inform his professional practice. Social justice and empowering underrepresented members of society define his life's work as a pedagogue, a writer, and an administrator. His approach can thus be a useful resource for acting teachers throughout the world, as
we train artist citizens with the confidence and know-how to create their own career paths.

Freire stresses the need for students and educators to 'become restorers of humanity'
as part of a 'cooperative' process where the demarcations between subject and object are
erased. This is not to suggest that he dismissed the importance of authority, which 'affirms'
the 'freedom' Freire associates with sound pedagogical practice (2017, pp. 18, 140). There is
a distinction between the guru who takes a hierarchical stance in the classroom and locates
students as mere receptacles of knowledge and someone overseeing a learning community
of shared discovery. The guru relies on the traditions and conceits of bygone eras. As acting
teachers, we are responsible for keeping abreast of current pedagogies and sociopolitical
trends in preparing our students for the profession. Therefore, I argue for an entrepreneurial
approach that gives students a nimble skillset steeped in critical thinking and self-awareness
towards meeting and transcending the industry's expectations while understanding the artist's role in society. I am not referencing entrepreneurism in the capitalistic use of the word,
but instead suggesting a student-centred environment with actors identifying their artistic
voice and how they want to deploy it professionally or otherwise. At the centre of this ethos
is the practice of theatre-making/devising, insofar as the creative process lends to critical
thinking and self-reflection in the context of making discoveries – a strategy aligned with
Freire's premise.

Theatre scholars and others writing in the Humanities have been positioning entrepreneurism as a strategy for educating student artists for over a decade. Linda Essig was among
the first to do so, as evidenced in her 2009 *Theatre Topics* article, wherein she coalesces
the concepts and practice of 'risk' and 'opportunity' alongside 'creativity' and 'innovation'
(2009, p. 118). These criteria are applicable to actor training and envisioning a career as
such. Essig defends entrepreneurship as a basis for theatre education, claiming that 'it is
not a dirty word', but a way to provide 'the next generation of theatre artists and scholars [the] skills to harness an entrepreneurial spirit to further artistic goals' (2009, p. 124).
More recently, Theatre scholars like Broderick D.V. Chow and James D. Hart have made
convincing cases for linking skills associated with entrepreneurism to actor training. In
the former instance, Chow assumes a dialectical investigation of the actor as an entrepre-
neur by positioning 'acting as labour' in the Marxist sense of the word, while arguing that
actors need to take responsibility for their craft and careers through organisational management towards achieving artistic/professional agency (2014). His theory can be likened to
Hart's work in that both consciously echo Stanislavski in attempting to encourage actors to
become entrepreneurs who choose 'actions' in pursuit of 'objectives' to realise their artistic
and professional goals (Chow, 2014; Hart, 2020, pp. 7–11). Hart has written extensively
on arts entrepreneurship and is the founder and director of Southern Methodist University's
Division of Arts Management and Arts Entrepreneurship. An erstwhile actor and graduate
of the Yale School of Drama, he does not define the term as blithely capitalist but instead
leans into its etymological root – *entreprendre* – meaning to undertake an enterprise that
invites a degree of risk and investment. Perhaps this is most evident for actors through
devising – theatre-making – wherein students 'create' and explore 'new opportunities' by
utilising their imaginations, working in group settings, engaging sociopolitical themes, and
moving across disciplines towards affirming their identity as an individual and an artist
(Hart, 2020, p. 19).

Theatre programmes throughout Southeast Asia and Oceania are currently teaching theatre-making in entrepreneurial ways.[7] In the Philippines, the national university and Ateneo de Manila University have student-centred initiatives to support their actors. The University of the Philippines Diliman (UP) is a public research institution with a diverse socio-economic range of students, whereas Ateneo is a Jesuit university with a largely middle-class enrolment. Both offer four-year courses in performance towards a bachelor's degree in Theatre Arts.[8] The UP's Head of Acting/Performance Olivia D. Nieto oversees a devised unit called Dulaang Laboratoryo (Play Laboratory) that culminates with either an individual or small ensemble creating a piece that addresses sociopolitical themes. For instance, UP student Ela Figura devised a work dealing with sexual assault for her capstone project in 2022. Entitled *Still Awesome* and presented bilingually in Tagalog and English, she rendered a poignantly personal account of the trauma that rape victims endure. Figura commanded the stage through a combination of song and spoken word, thereby demonstrating her skill as a trained actor who can work in both musical theatre and acting, sectors of the industry well-practised in the Philippines. She wrote both the music and the script for *Still Awesome* with compelling numbers such as 'A Little Bit Crazy', a fist-pumping anthem with the refrain 'What can't they understand? No means No means No means No means No!' The song's completion prompts a reflection in which Figura responsibly explores the nuance of sexual violence. She states, 'How and why it started I honestly don't know. The problems piled up and it felt like the physical manifestation of the pain made sense. I started hating myself . . . But I'd rather transfer the emotional pain into something tangible' (Figura, 2022a). Because the subject matter was so personal, Figura and Nieto accounted for her emotional well-being throughout the process. Figura felt affirmed as an artist who took a traumatic experience from her past and transformed it into a powerful piece that responsibly accounted for her pain and deployed it to help others by prompting greater awareness of sexual assault, something that she claims is lacking in the Philippines. She states:

> The training has pushed me out of my comfort zone. I have found confidence in my speaking voice. Naturally, as an indigenous woman having a strong and present literal voice has been important. I am learning how to fully express and stand up for myself.
>
> (Figura, 2022)

The result was a 90-minute work that was her creation in every way: writer, composer, and performer. Most importantly, it was a clear and resonant portrayal of her identity as an artist.

Figura's achievement is consistent with what Freire calls teaching to a student's *untested feasibility*, or 'the possibility of doing something that has not been tried before', an approach that places them at the centre of what can be accomplished (Freire, 2002, p. 8). It is 'not a meaningless idiom', but a dynamic practice prompting 'change steered at a more humane future' (Freire, 2002, p. 9). Untested feasibility taps into a student's potential for success, which for actors participating in the Dulaang Laboratoryo means telling stories that are personal and sociopolitically relevant. Figura's narrative is her own. She developed her craft while training with empathic teachers dedicated to her personal and artistic development. The feat of creating *Still Awesome* exemplifies her artistic voice in ways that cannot be reached through traditional training methods, namely assuming a role in text-based theatrical productions. While producing plays (and musicals) will – and should – continue to be an important part of acting programmes, as Figura's case demonstrates, providing students with the space and encouragement to create independent work is also important.

Figura was coached by both Nieto and a guest lecturer, Missy Maramara, who leads the acting course at Ateneo; it is impressive to see such collegial exchanges between the two institutions. Maramara was trained in the United States, a path that many Filipino theatre artists working in higher education take. Indeed, most instructors at the UP and Ateneo did their graduate work overseas. This practice invites questions regarding the nexus of artistic, cultural, and national identities. Why don't Filipino theatre artists study at home? Why are they compelled to go abroad to earn their credential? Maramara (2022) claims that 'the identity of the Filipino actor is complex because of our colonial history. We are very good at adjusting and remaining open to foreign influence – especially from America'. Filipino theatre artists have been training in the United States for decades and then returning home to work professionally and/or enter higher education.[9] Maramara earned her MFA at the University of Arkansas while on a Fulbright, whereas her mentor Ricardo Abad and his teacher – Rolando Tinio – were, respectively, educated at Fordham University and the University of Iowa. Tinio became one of the Philippines' most celebrated poets and theatre professionals of the twentieth century and Abad is internationally recognised for his Tagalog productions of Shakespeare. His *Merchant of Venice* and *Taming of the Shrew*, for instance, deftly appropriated and subverted the postcolonial imprimatur the United States has had in the Philippines since 1898 when it annexed the archipelago after the Spanish–American War. In *Merchant of Venice,* Abad had the Christians speak in Shakespeare's English, whereas the Jewish characters' lines were in Tagalog. This choice underscored how 'Americans imposed a new order in colonial Philippines just as the Christians seek to make Shylock subordinate to Christian law' (Abad, 2009, p. 6). Similarly, Abad coercively appropriated *Taming of the Shrew* by depicting Petruchio as an American soldier attempting 'to tame his native subject' (Katherine), who juxtaposes her rival's English by speaking in Tagalog (2009, p. 7). Yet in the final scene when she delivers her iconic speech vowing servitude to Petruchio, Abad had her shift to English and assume a declamatory style befitting 'elocution contests', thereby undermining the language to 'suggest resistance'. Despite his subversive use of appropriation, like Shakespeare's Katherine, Abad claims that 'the Filipino of colonial and postcolonial times has only managed to negotiate her space in the world' and continues to search for an unequivocal national identity (2009, p. 11).

One of Abad's former students, Guelan Luarca credits him for 'repurposing Western texts to support Filipino actors and audiences' by translating Shakespeare into Tagalog and then 'staging it so it becomes localized for Filipinos' (Luarca, 2022). As such, Abad appropriates 'canonical' texts to facilitate a learning process by which students are empowered to embrace their artistic and cultural identities. His approach can be likened to Freire's theories of conscientização and cultural synthesis to disrupt postcolonial tropes that persist in the Philippines and elsewhere. Abad's work is steeped in critical analysis towards challenging systems of power through a dialogic investigation of sociopolitical conditions and contexts to address differences between Western and non-Western identities. Negotiation is crucial to this process, as Freire dialectically insinuates in describing cultural synthesis: 'In cultural synthesis – and only cultural synthesis – it is possible to resolve the contradiction between the world view of the leaders and that of the people to the enrichment of both' (2017, p. 154). In sum, Abad and his Filipino colleagues are working in ways consistent with a pedagogy of the oppressed.

Negotiating cultural and national identities in postcolonial settings is exemplified by other Australasian theatre departments and drama schools. Perhaps the most advanced practice is that of New Zealand's Toi Whakaari, which balances Western and indigenous pedagogies and traditions towards empowering students to develop and celebrate who they are as artists. Like most conservatoires that follow a British model, the curriculum is three years with the bulk of training focused on the actor's craft. Toi distinguishes itself as a bicultural institution and therein reflects New Zealand/Aotearoa's national character. Māori principles and traditions (tikanga) comprise the pedagogy. The Acting Program – for instance – contextualises the curriculum according to the values of Tūranga, Raranga, and Waewae. Each represents a distinct practice that results in a student fostering their personal/cultural identity (tū) and positionality (mana) before weaving (raranga) these attributes to form their artistic voice (waewae).[10] The essence of the praxis – and its consistency with Māoridom – is to invite a diverse range of perspectives throughout the training.[11] Engaging difference is a vital part of the process. Whether addressing decisions in rehearsal or conferring over opinions and/or sharing identities, Toi embraces difference by making and responding to offers from individuals and groups alike. Students nurture their tū while owning their artistic/personal identity in relationship to that of their co-collaborators. Hierarchies are minimised – if not erased – as multiple perspectives intersect and are negotiated. Toi's understanding of difference is an extension of New Zealand/Aotearoa's commitment to a society of belonging, insofar as it has implemented policies and laws to establish equity among its citizens, albeit within a postcolonial and oftentimes controversial context. The Treaty of Waitangi is one such example. It symbolises the country's bicultural identity as a decree constituting Pākehā and indigenous rights, yet it has been met with mixed perspectives and opinions since being established in 1840 (Godfery, 2022).[12]

Toi's faculty, staff, and students regard difference as a resource for personal and pedagogical growth. Perhaps the best example is the school's annual retreat to an *iwi* (indigenous tribe) and its *marae* (dwelling house) on the north island, a 530-km journey from Wellington that results in an exploration of artistic praxis in coordination with indigenous values, traditions, and philosophy. Referred to as *Noho Marae*, a guest's multi-night stay at an iwi, the week-long endeavour is an important part of Toi's training. The Noho Marae allows students to undertake Māori principles and traditions through self-discovery and devising original content (Figure 1.1).

During the residency Toi's third-year actors share content from an Independent Practice module, for instance, generating short pieces that include solo acts and group work to digital performances and lectures. The experience demonstrates cross-culturalism and intersectionality. The learning methods throughout the Noho Marae consist of collaboration, listening, self-empowerment, and negotiation – all values aligning with Maoridom (Zazzali, 2021, pp. 163–165). The approach enriches and vitalises the learning community, thereby distinguishing Toi's cultivation of artistic entrepreneurs fit for the twenty-first century.[13] Toi alumni are self-producers keen to create their own opportunities, a skill rendering them ever-present throughout New Zealand's creative industries. (ibid, pp. 167–169).

A cross-cultural approach to actor training defines the pedagogy at LASALLE College of the Arts. Recognised as Singapore's National University of the Arts, it is a racially diverse and multinational institution preparing students for professional careers in their chosen métier. The BA (Hons) in Acting is among the college's most prestigious courses with 90% of its graduates employed in the profession at any given time. In addition to performing at Singapore's numerous professional theatres, they regularly find employment doing TV programmes and adverts. Alumni also create job opportunities by applying the hard and soft skills they learned in school to produce their own projects as well as by working as teachers, directors, and dramaturges.[14]

LASALLE's Acting Programme has a curriculum of Asian and Western pedagogies and traditions. Kathakali and Silat, for instance, are balanced alongside European movement systems such as corporeal mime and Grotowski's approach to physical theatre. The content

Figure 1.1 Toi Whakaari students and staff arriving for Noho Marae (2020). *Photo credit:* With permission from Toi Whakaari (New Zealand Drama School).

for productions and classroom instruction likewise reflects the programme's cross-cultural ethos, as texts from the United Kingdom and United States are aligned with those from Asian traditions – most especially Singapore. In March of 2022, for instance, the Acting Programme produced Chay Yew's mash-up of *The Cherry Orchard* and *Three Sisters* (Figure 1.2).

A Singapore national who has relocated to the United States, Yew's *A Winter People* is set during the Maoist uprising in the 1940s, a clear shift from Chekhov's pre-revolutionary Russia. He rewrote the likes of Ranevskaya and Lopakhin into a cast of Chinese characters, while also including figures inspired by *Three Sisters*, all of which gave LASALLE's students an experience that aligned with the Acting Programme's cross-cultural curriculum. Somewhat like Abad's reappropriation of Shakespeare, Yew's recontextualisation of a classical work invited critical engagement of the so-called canon while empowering the predominantly Asian group of student actors.[15] Its inclusion in LASALLE's curriculum occurred alongside other Singaporean plays by Alfian Sáat, Kuo Pao Kun, Joel Tan, and Haresh Sharma.[16]

Like Toi Whakaari and some of the other examples presented in this chapter, LASALLE's Acting Programme honours indigenous voices and engages narratives relevant to and reflective of its student population, which largely mirrors Singapore's predominance of three racial groups (Malay, Chinese, and Indian). In addition to text-based work, similar to their counterparts at Toi and the Filipino programmes, LASALLE's actors are trained as theatre-makers capable of devising and self-producing original work. One such example is a unit in Forum Theatre, a practice founded by Brazil's Augusto Boal as part of his *Theatre of*

Figure 1.2 LASALLE College of the Arts production of Chay Yew's *A Winter People* (2022); pictured in the foreground (Roshini Periyachi), in the immediate background (Miza Syazwina) seated at the table (Fandy Ahmed). *Photo credit:* Crispian Chan.

the Oppressed (1985), which was inspired by Freire's pedagogy.[17] Under the guidance of a specialist in Boal's techniques, third-year students create and develop a piece that addresses sociopolitical themes and topics they deem significant. Graduates from the Acting Programme's 2021 and 2022 cohorts undertook topics ranging from sexual harassment in the workplace and systemic racism to socio-economic inequality and gender identity. Alumna Indumathi Tamilselvan describes how the experience informed her work as an actor and teacher in stating Forum Theatre 'taught [her] the importance of representation and to listen to the needs of [her] students and value their voices' (2023).

Tamilselvan and her fellow actors created stories that were significant to their locality, an approach consistent with Freire's pedagogy. A city-state known for its authoritarianism and sociopolitical conservatism, especially pertaining to matters of gender identity and racial equality, Singapore proved to be a fitting – if risky – place to undertake Forum Theatre. Shrouded by improvisation and the praxis of devising, thereby escaping the Orwellian oversight of government-sanctioned censorship, the project facilitated a rigorous interrogation of topics that were important to LASALLE's students and their audience. As part of what Boal describes as a game with specific rules, the actors applied skills in devising and improvisation alongside an abiding commitment to critical thinking as part of a multivalent exercise with multiple learning outcomes.

The Forum Theatre Project invited LASALLE's actors to think critically and reflect personally. In collaboration with their peers, they chose what they wanted to say as artists. They became liberated in their learning precisely because the educational environment was one of dialogue and shared discovery as opposed to a hierarchy steeped in paternalist tropes. The actors took responsibility for their training and were given the space and support to do so. Such an arrangement requires continual negotiation while collaborating within a community where everyone's identity and perspectives are valued (Freire, 2017, pp. 22, 23).

The praxis of negotiation is consistent with what Freire terms a problem-posing approach. Based on dialogue and critical thinking, participants are encouraged to ask questions and problematise topics in the context of instruction. The relationship between teachers and students is not dichotomous, but a mutual exchange of discoveries that permeate the learning process. As Freire states: 'The teacher is no longer merely the one-who-teaches, but one who is himself taught in dialogue with the students, who in turn while being taught also teach' (2017, p. 53).

The Acting Programme at Hong Kong's Academy for Performing Arts (APA) operates in the School of Drama and has recently been undertaking a problem-posing strategy. Exalted by the QS World Ranking of Higher Education as Asia's foremost performing arts school, the APA has a rich tradition of excellence, most especially its Acting Programme, which has been under the leadership of Chan Suk Yi since the 1990s (Hong Kong Academy, p. 4). He claims their training has assumed a more socially engaged ethos over the past three years, as demonstrated by a curricular initiative called the Hong Kong Theatre Artist, whereby students spend a semester researching a topic relevant to the city state's cultural history towards developing an original piece. As Chan states, 'students learn about their own country's history and have a point of view about it' (2022). They are responsible for generating interviews and otherwise researching their chosen topic in conjunction with rehearsing the devised piece. This initiative is consistent with the School of Drama's overarching goal to become more intradisciplinary and socially engaged – if not politically active, given the vulnerable situation Hong Kongese are currently experiencing at the behest of Beijing. As faculty member Li Wing-Hong asserts: '[W]e must be careful in the ways we resist. Delivering the training in Cantonese is one way that we try to preserve our identity' (Wing-Hong, 2022). The APA's students and faculty are proud to be the only conservatoire in the world delivering training in Cantonese, an inviting choice for stage actors given the language's lyrical elegance and tonal complexity.[18]

The School of Drama launched an Applied Theatre Program during the 2022–2023 academic year and hopes to weave it into cognate courses like Acting and Directing. They have also introduced a module called Theatre and Society, which invites students to consider their personal and cultural identities relative to their artistry within a 'holistic training environment' (Wong, 2022). An important part of this new direction for the school, and by extension its Acting Programme, is creating original work. As APA faculty member Billy Sy asserts: 'We believe that the future of theatre and performing arts in Hong Kong requires being skilled in many areas. Apart from training them as professional actors, we want our actors to be theatre-makers' (2022). Thus, devising original work that is socially conscious is one of the many ways that students can be empowered to identify their artistic voice.

Devising lends to decolonising training and is consistent with Freire's pedagogy. It affords participants comparative flexibility because concepts and corresponding prompts invite an explorative process that is less possible in text-based creative processes. As seen by LASALLE's use of Forum Theatre and Toi's Independent Practice module, devising/theatre-making allows an individual or ensemble to engage with an innovative process towards a clearer understanding of themselves, their culture, and the world they inhabit (Oddey, 1994, p. 1). It should be part of any responsible curriculum preparing actors for the twenty-first century. Devising liberates students from becoming beholden to extant texts and traditions, which in the case of the Oceanic examples presented here, are commonly Western in their scope and purview. While a case can be made for utilising works such as Shakespeare and Chekhov in classes and productions, it makes good sense to include writing from non-Western cultural traditions, especially when working with students from the Global South. Devising invites students to claim their own histories and identities through a creative process that aligns with Freire's teaching strategies. Critical analysis (conscientição), posing questions, engaging sociopolitically, and student-centred learning, each aligns with theatre-making and therefore represents a pedagogy of the oppressed.

Ideally, devising is positioned as an important part of the curriculum complementing its other elements (e.g. technique/script analysis/movement). While it is often a source of student empowerment and social justice, devising does have limitations and should not be seen as a panacea for all challenges pertinent to equity and fairness in the acting studio. Likewise, it is not the only approach for achieving innovative and forward-facing learning outcomes. Indeed, artist-scholars who have spent their careers devising have recently articulated these limitations in the context of Title IX policies at US universities, insofar as the work can be deeply personal and oftentimes revealing (Bowles, 2016, p. 261). Nonetheless, giving students the opportunity to envision and realise original content causes them to identify their artistic voice and use skills that are related to yet distinct from other facets of their training.

Like the other examples presented in this chapter, devising is evident in the acting curriculum at the Western Australian Academy of the Performing Arts (WAAPA). Students practice it in each of the BA Acting Programme's three years, with the first having them create a solo piece drawn from their life experience. In the second year, they create a physical theatre project under the direction of faculty member Sam Chester, who specialises in devising and sees it as a means for 'inventing and reinventing' oneself as a performing artist (Lewis Smith, 2023, p. 38). Chester is an alumna of Australia's other major conservatoire, the National Institute of Dramatic Arts (NIDA), which has also begun incorporating theatre-making into its Acting Programme. NIDA students thus undertake projects in their first and second years, with the former introducing ensemble-based initiatives and the latter – like WAAPA – resulting in a devised piece referred to as *Embody* (Lewis Smith, 45). Despite the Australian schools' relatively recent inclusion of theatre-making in their curriculum, they both focus on postcolonial pedagogies, texts, and practices. As a result, there is virtually no attempt to explore the country's rich indigenous history or address its national character. While NIDA and WAAPA's students are quite skilled and have the highest employment rates among Australia's acting conservatoires, there seems to be a lack of investment in cultural inclusivity and racial diversity within their respective curricula. Perhaps the cross-cultural work of this volume's fellow contributors, Kristine Landon-Smith and Chris Hay, will help their Australian colleagues consider such a change. The presence of devising in WAAPA and NIDA's curriculum suggests an interest in addressing DEI. More work appears to be needed, however, before one could argue their training is consistent with Freire's pedagogy.

The Pedagogy of the Oppressed: A Blueprint for Twenty-first-Century Actor Training

Freire's work can tangibly and theoretically inform the training of actors, as seen by the examples presented in this chapter. Acting Programmes throughout Southeast Asia and Oceania are reimagining curricula and creating learning environments that invite actors to think independently and embrace their cultural/personal identity. Within processes marked by self-reflection and critical thinking (conscientição) alongside problem-posing and dialogic strategies, students are afforded the agency to question their institution and its training traditions towards developing their artistic voice. Freire describes such an interrogation as decoding the 'limit situations' that systemically perpetuate the status quo and its correlative positionalities, thereby inhibiting personal and pedagogical growth (Freire, 2017, p. 77). Limit situations hegemonically reduce participants to 'things' by which they naively contribute to their own oppression while submissively going about their quotidian experience (2017, p. 76). Acknowledging and disrupting these daily practices and the machinations contextualising and causing them is the first step to becoming aware of the sociopolitical forces determining our learning environments.

A dialogic partnership between students and teachers is foundational to Freire's call for *cultural synthesis* and making a positive impact on society. Interestingly, he describes this process much like devising/theatre-making. Likening reformers to actors, he describes cultural synthesis as a 'co-authorship of action [whereby] both perform onto the world' (2017, p. 153). Through openness and cooperation, students/teachers are encouraged to investigate the training relative to their sociopolitical surroundings. Embracing and negotiating difference(s) are therefore essential. Doing so responsibly can not only achieve a given course's learning outcomes but also invite possibilities to extend the 'communion' forged in the studio to the social sphere (2017, p. 102). For example, this was evident in LASALLE's Forum Theatre exercise in that students and their instructors collaborated to bring their work to the local community.

Freire's *Pedagogy of the Oppressed* prompts us to reimagine actor training in the twenty-first century. It is an approach that bears merit and untold potential. From the student-centred praxis of the Filipino schools to how indigeneity shapes curricula at Hong Kong's APA and Toi Whakaari, conservatoires throughout Southeast Asia and Oceania show how Freirean principles can inform our field's future. Students are empowered to speak their minds and practice self-reflection while collaborating with their teachers to interdependently engage in the learning process. Everyone deepens their personhood and artistic voice. Perhaps these outcomes are best seen in the devised work undertaken in each of the cases cited, as it addresses sociopolitical topics through a creative process that is grounded in dialogism. As such, these acting programmes disrupt oppressive histories and shortsighted pedagogies in favour of forward-facing strategies steeped in critical analysis and self-expression.

The Pedagogy of the Oppressed is as relevant today as it was when Freire proposed it some fifty years ago. It invites students to grow as individuals through group learning wherein the teacher is a responsible authority collaborating alongside their students. Eschewing the guru model of yesteryear in favour of an entrepreneurial and just approach, as demonstrated by our Australasian colleagues and their students, Freire's system can guide us in decolonising curricula towards realising a more diverse and inclusive training experience for teachers and students. From dialogical praxis and conscientição to problem-posing strategies and dismantling educational hierarchies, his strategies can help nurture actors who are artist citizens and entrepreneurs every bit as much as they are technically proficient in their craft. Students are invited to find personal and professional fulfilment through expressing their minds, fostering their artistic identity, and making a positive difference in the world.

Notes

1 While Freire's Pedagogy of the Oppressed is explained in his book bearing the same title, I am presenting his pedagogy as a system and therefore will not put the term in italics except when specifically referencing the book.
2 RADA, Central, Julliard, NIDA and other conservatoires/acting programmes have been the site of student protests since the middle 2010s. This movement started in conjunction with #MeToo

and Black Lives Matter and escalated after the murder of George Floyd in 2020. Perhaps the most salient example occurred at Central in 2019 when its principal at the time (Gavin Henderson) proclaimed to staff and students that admitting applicants from underrepresented and marginalised communities would 'reduce the quality' of training (Hemley 2018).

3 For information on Gramsci and Gandhi's influence on Freire, respectively, see P. Allman (1988). Gramsci, Freire, and Illich: Their contributions to education for socialism. In T. Lovett (Ed.), *Radical approaches to adult education* (pp. 85–113). Routledge; and B. Mann (1995). *The pedagogical and political concepts of Mahatma Gandhi and Paolo Freire: A comparative study on developmental and strategic political education in the third world*. Krämer.

4 For more on the commodification of actors in training, see P. Zazzali (2016). *Acting in the academy: The history of professional actor training in US higher education*. Routledge.

5 The Pygmalion complex is a psychological term pertaining to a teaching situation when an expert – commonly assumed to be an older white male – transforms someone from a lower social class to achieve perfection through authoritative and draconian training methods.

6 The 'flipped classroom' connotes a fundamental change in teaching and learning that began in the United States during the 1990s. It was initially used in Humanities courses and undertook a synthesised approach through peer review, dialogue and debate, group work, creative problem-solving, and out-of-class learning. It was a move away from lecture-based learning and became the basis for other progressive methods like the 'inverted classroom'.

7 My fieldwork involved onsite visits at each of the drama schools exemplified throughout this chapter. I was generously funded by three institutions as such (University of Kansas, LASALLE College of the Arts, and James Madison University) and the recipient of a Fulbright in 2019 that facilitated a six-month residency at Toi Whakaari. My research methods consisted of interviewing staff/faculty/students/alumni/theatre professionals as well as observing coursework, analysing curricula, attending performances, and investigating archives whenever possible. Ever mindful of being a Westerner conducting work in non-Western contexts, my approach was and continues to include awareness of my own conscious and unconscious cultural biases, thereby requiring a rigorous and humble respect for the institutions and people supporting this and other projects of mine.

8 Ateneo's Theater Department is spelled with an 'er' ending, whereas the University of the Philippines chooses to do so with the British 're'. For more on both departments, see their respective websites: http://2012.ateneo.edu/ls/soh/finearts/bachelor-fine-arts-major-theater-arts; and www.dscta.kal.upd.edu.ph/bachelor-of-arts-speech-communication-copy.

9 MFAs earned in the United States predominate the faculties of Ateneo. Britain and its former colonies are also sometimes selected, as is the case with the UP's Theatre Department's current director, Sir Anril P. Titatco, who earned his PhD from the National University of Singapore.

10 For an overview of these practices and their implementation into Toi's curriculum, see the Acting Programme's webpage at retrieved May 29, 2022, from www.toiwhakaari.ac.nz/course/acting.

11 Māoridom is a noun referring to the customs, traditions, and practices of the Māori. For more on the subject, see H. M. Mead (2003). *Tikanga Māori: Living by Māori values*. Huia Publishers.

12 The term Pākehā is a Te Reo word signifying someone of European descent.

13 For comprehensive accounts of Toi Whakaari and its bicultural pedagogy, see B. Guest (2011). *Transitions: Four decades of Toi Whakaari New Zealand national drama school*. Victoria University Press; and P. Zazzali (2021). *Actor training in anglophone countries: Past, present, and future*. Routledge.

14 I was the Director of LASALLE's Acting Programme from 2019 to 2022, during which time we implemented much of the curricular praxis detailed in this chapter. The 90% employment statistic was furnished by the college's alumni officer.

15 All but one member of the cast of 12 actors identified as Asian.

16 Between 2020 and 2022, LASALLE's Acting Programme began producing Singaporean plays as part of its mainstage season for the first time since the college was founded in 1984.

17 Boal claims Forum Theatre 'produces a stimulant for our desire to change the world', a remark that conveys his indebtedness to Freire, whose pedagogy of the oppressed clearly inspired him (Boal 2002: 274).

18 There are nine tones in Cantonese, the manipulation of which ascribes meaning to a given word. By contrast, Mandarin has only four tones and is less nuanced and lyrical.

References

Abad, R. (2009). Appropriating Shakespeare and resisting colonialism: Reflections of a stage director. In H. Nagai & T. Valiente (Eds.), *Transnationalizing culture in Asia: Dramas, music, and tourism*. Ateneo University.

Boal, A. (1985). *Theatre of the oppressed* (C. A. McBride & M.-O. Leal McBride, Trans.). TCG.

Bowles, N. (2016, July). Devising and mandatory reporting: An update from the field. *Theatre Topics, 26*(2), 261.

Chan Suk Yi (2022, June 1). Interview with Peter Zazzali.

Chow, B. D. (2014). An actor manages: Actor training and managerial ideology. *Theatre, Dance and Performance Training, 5*(2), 131–143.

Essig, L. (2009). Suffusing entrepreneurship education throughout the theatre curriculum. *Theatre Topics, 19*(2), 117–124.

Figura, E. (2022a). Sill awesome. *YouTube Video*, 1:38. Retrieved May 18, 2022, from www.youtube.com/watch?v=YpDc1iiALOC

Figura, E. (2022b, June 17). Interview with Peter Zazzali.

Freire, A. (2002). Paulo Freire and the untested feasibility. *Counterpoints, 209*, 8.

Freire, P. (1974, Spring). Concientisiation. *Crosscurrents, 24*(1), 26.

Freire, P. (2017). *Pedagogy of the oppressed* (M. B. Ramos, Trans.). Penguin Books.

Godfery, M. (2022, February 3). Māori might be the 'Luckiest' Indigenous people-but that's not down to New Zealand exceptionalism. *The Guardian*. Retrieved May 30, 2023, from www.theguardian.com/world/commentisfree/2022/feb/04/maori-might-be-the-luckiest-indigenous-people-but-thats-not-down-to-new-zealand-exceptionalism

Gottleib, E., & Thomas, B. (1990, March). Ethnographic contextualization of Freire's discourse: Conscious-raising, theory and practice. *Anthology & Education Quarterly, 21*(1), 3–18.

Hart, J. (2020, January). Utilizing the Stanislavski system and core acting skills to teach actors in arts entrepreneurship courses. *Journal of Arts Entrepreneurship Education, 2*(1), 2–31.

Hemley, M. (2018, April 27). Central school principal, 'Quotas Would Reduce the Quality of Our Student Intake'. *The Stage*.

Hong Kong Academy for Performing Arts Website. *Undergraduate and post-secondary programme prospectus 2022/23*. Retrieved June 4, 2022, from www.hkapa.edu/file/upload/54323/2022-23_UG&PS_Prospectus-17SEP2021.pdf

Indumathi, T. (2023, January 31). Email exchange with Peter Zazzali.

Lewis Smith, A. (2023). *Devising and collective creation in actor training* [PhD dissertation, Edith Cowan University].

Luarca, G. (2022, May 5). Interview with Peter Zazzali.

Maramara, M. (2022, May 2). Interview with Peter Zazzali.

Oddey, A. (1994). *Devising theatre: A practical and theoretical handbook*. Routledge.

Sy, B. (2022, June 1). Interview with Peter Zazzali.

Wing Hong, L. (2022, May 31). Interview with Peter Zazzali.

Wong, E. (2022, June 1). Interview with Peter Zazzali.

Zazzali, P. (2021). *Actor training in anglophone countries: Past, present, and future*. Routledge.

2 Playing with Difference in Actor Training

A Method to Transform Policy into Pedagogy

Kristine Landon-Smith and Chris Hay

Introduction

> When Kristine and I worked together I struggled a lot. My character was a chief detective and was questioning a murderer, which meant I had to be assertive and tough. I thought it was so far from me that I would have to do a lot of character work and practices to get to that place, which not only prevented me from listening and staying active and alive in rehearsal but made me doubt my talent and ability greatly, so instead Kristine asked me to speak the text in Arabic which is the language I speak at home and therefore the language where I am probably my truest self.
>
> When I spoke the text in Arabic, I found the strength needed to play that character. I had strength all along and I didn't need some elaborate acting technique to get there. All I had to do was speak in my mother tongue. I now improvise all my texts in Arabic and see what comes from it. I've learnt that acting shouldn't be so hard. It's all you and you don't need to discard yourself and especially your culture and language in order to play someone else. In fact, I've discovered it's a superpower.
>
> Actor 1[1]

This quote is from an actor in her third year of a British conservatoire training programme, who was introduced to our method through rehearsing a workshop performance. The year group was working on a contemporary text about a police investigation into a murder case, and the actor was playing a Detective Inspector. She is of Arabic heritage although brought up in the United Kingdom, speaking only English in her professional life – but only speaking Arabic when at home with her family. When the work began, this actor had never considered that her own being-in-the-world could, and should, be an integral ingredient in the creation of her role. In this way, Actor 1's experience reflects what we identify as the gap between policy and pedagogy in the contemporary conservatoire. While institutions are pursuing official policies of diversity and decolonising, they are not often following through with intersectional training pedagogies that empower what Valerie Purdie-Vaughns and Richard Eibach call the 'intersectionally subordinate identities' (2008, p. 384), of those not regularly depicted in mainstream cultural representations.

Across the last few years, thanks in large part to the extraordinary labour of the Black Lives Matter movement and its global analogues, theatre training institutions have enacted a range of overdue policy changes that 'honour difference', in phrasing drawn from the Equity Safe Spaces Statement, which is referenced in the RADA Students Anti-Racism Action Plan (2020). Amy Mihyang Ginther, who wrote the Afterword to this volume, summarises this and other welcome recent developments in her 2023 edited collection *Stages of*

DOI: 10.4324/9781003393672-4

Reckoning (2023, pp. 2–5). Institutions now seek to create safer and braver rehearsal rooms for all actors; many have followed Brian Arao and Kristi Clemens in 'shifting away from the concept of safety and emphasizing the importance of bravery instead, to help students better understand – and rise to – the challenges of genuine dialogue on diversity and social justice issues' (2013, p. 136). However, we argue that the pedagogy in their rehearsal rooms has not always kept pace with these policy aspirations, stranding actors and paralysing trainers in a desert of good intentions. Honouring difference is a necessary first step: the following step is to play with and through that difference, igniting the unique identity positions of the many actors of diverse and intersectional identities who make up our cohorts.

Kristine has been working in this gap for decades, first through the work of Tamasha Developing Artists (TDA) from 2000 onwards,[2] where she noticed that many students would come to sessions with no understanding of how to bring their cultural heritage and native languages to their training. Even in this initiative led by a global majority company, they often left aspects of their subordinate identities outside the door. When Kristine was appointed to Australia's National Institute of Dramatic Art (NIDA), she began to formalise her TDA investigation into an articulated training pedagogy. Elsewhere in the NIDA building, Chris was interrogating what Conrad Alexandrowicz has identified as 'effemiphobia' in actor training (2017), thinking through gender dissidence and its implications for pedagogies and performance practices historically invested in a binary view of gender. Recognising this was an intersectional enquiry, we joined forces to articulate the de-centring potential of Kristine's distinctive approach to actor training in an academic form. Elsewhere, we have referred to this approach as an 'intracultural methodology', acknowledging its debt to Rustom Bharucha's approach of working '*through* one's difference as it is constituted through social and cultural specificities, angularities, quirks, imperfections, and limitations' (1996, p. 38). Recently, though, our students have pushed back against this framing, arguing that overlap of intracultural with ethnicity could limit their engagement with the method. This perception prompted an important moment of reflection for us: although ethnicity was and continues to be our starting point, we expand our vocabulary here to refer to Kristine's work as 'unique identity practice'. This highlights that we are working through difference across multiple axes of identity, and that the search to ignite the actor traverses all parts of the unique identity they bring to the floor.

To that end, we offer in this chapter a detailed account of a single rehearsal process, following the actor with whose words we began as she was guided on how to utilise her cultural and linguistic context in her work, and describing the freedom and power this afforded her. Helping actors bring their multiple identities to any work is a complex and subtle endeavour that lies at the heart of many actor training pedagogies. A method is required that always puts the actor at the centre, not just in the creation of a character, but without allowing the world of the play to dominate in such a way that an actor forgets the power of their unique being-in-the-world. The method we describe here does not advocate that the actor only ever plays themselves; rather, it is focused on the revelatory moment when an actor wholly feels that their unique cultural and linguistic context is what will enrich and enhance their work. Like any method, it is not straightforward – we have outlined its key steps elsewhere (Landon-Smith & Hay, 2023; Hay & Landon-Smith, 2018) – but here we follow a single rehearsal process with its twists and difficulties, and outline the adaptations that must be made each day on the floor as we work to provide the actors with access to their unique power in performance.

Across this chapter, we follow the rehearsal process as framed through the experience of a performer who is struggling to connect with her material. This is a familiar challenge for trainers, whose expertise is in large part focused on guiding actors around roadblocks in rehearsal. Our contention here, however, is that solutions can be found *inside* the actor, in their unique cultural background and being-in-the-world. This claim is supported by Kaja Amado Dunn, who insists that *all* 'students should be encouraged to incorporate themselves into each of their characters and be offered the tools to do this' (2019, p. 77). Our method offers one such set of tools, by focusing consistently on what is intrinsic to the actor, rather than reaching for what is extrinsic. Rehearsing with a diverse cohort in this way allows them all 'to see the assets their body brings to the canon of theatre. It reinforces that the work is about showing up and being present in one's body instead of disappearing one's self' (Dunn, 2019, p. 77). This offers an opportunity for students to mobilise their 'intersectionally subordinate identities' (Purdie-Vaughns & Eibach, 2008, p. 384) as a superpower, to access ease and pleasure to play from which they are often alienated by mainstream pedagogies. Careful and detailed work is required to re-centre the actor and unlock the power of their own being-in-the-world, and in this chapter, we set out that work as we undertake it in three broad steps: accessing unique identities, holding onto power, and playing with headphones.

Accessing Unique Identities

As the vocabulary we have used so far suggests, the method is indebted, particularly to the work of Philippe Gaulier, who advocates that 'all play must be engaged in with pleasure – demonstrably so' (Kendrick, 2011, p. 73). This is particularly critical to our work, because encouraging actors to come to the rehearsal room floor ready to play as themselves 'points out the idiosyncrasies of everybody in the class and does not explicitly compare these to a dominant normative figure' (Amsden, 2016, p. 11). This is the first step towards freeing actors of subordinate identities of the expectations of an imagined mainstream and conceiving of their unique identities as a strength to be embraced rather than a weakness to be overcome. The main goal of our work is to unlock pleasure and confidence in actors of subordinate identities; like Gaulier, we lead actors through truthful steps towards being themselves as they begin their work together. We seek to push further, though, in holding the actor's power and pleasure to play as themselves at the centre of the pedagogy throughout the rehearsal process and into performance.

Rehearsing with our method, then, always begins in the same way: with exercises that ask actors to be seen, and to show themselves to each other. The aim is to lay down the vocabulary of the rehearsal room, and to establish the parameters of the process that will be employed throughout. So, in those first moments together, we eschew reading the text – we aim to not even discuss it, and instead put the focus on the actors. Before any work on the text is done, the actors have a sense of themselves in the process, and they understand that this emphasis will carry throughout. There is some resonance here with the work of trainers like Yevgeny Vakhtangov, who argued that an actor must live with their own passion. According to Vakhtangov, 'we must hear your own voice, your blood, your nerves . . . No characterisation, you are playing yourselves or rather, as we say, you 'proceed from yourselves"' (in Malaev-Babel, 2011, p. 103). We begin by taking actors through a series of games and improvisations that all aim to develop a sense of complicité and a pleasure to play with each other, the specific details of which we have described elsewhere (Landon-Smith & Motta, 2022; Landon-Smith, 2020). Once the actor has accessed the pleasure to play *as themselves*, we encourage them to sit with that feeling, to recognise it and to prize it, so that they can return to it throughout the process.

To begin the movement towards the performance text, the last game on day 1 of the introductory workshop is an emotionally charged improvisation – working with consciously emotive stakes such as a relationship breakdown, or a passionate dispute – in which two student actors are asked to play a scene using only the individual letters of the alphabet. By not being able to use full words, the actors must listen very deeply to each other, and their focus must be strongly on each other for the improvisation to build and maintain complicité. To extend this exercise, the next improvisation draws on all of the languages that the cohort possesses, and instead of using the alphabet the trainer invites actors to improvise in the different languages present, including e/English in its many vernacular forms.[3] In this process, we are 'interested in making visible whatever subordinated aspects of self the participants' desire to reveal (Powers & Duffy, 2015, p. 62); that is, we invite the students to offer up a subordinated identity with which they are comfortable experimenting, rather than insisting they do so. In most cases, this results in an improvisation where both actors do not understand the other, and instead must rely on their connection and the emotional contours of the scene. This early step in the method firmly de-centres English and establishes a multilingual rehearsal room from day 1. These early multilingual exercises can function to empower actors who have never used a first or home language in the professional space.

On day 1 of rehearsals, Kristine took the actors through this process and invited Actor 1 to improvise in Arabic, a language she usually reserved for home. The actor approached Kristine after the class and expressed her bewilderment at the confidence, fluency, and power that she had found when working in Arabic. She confessed that while her language had not been utilised before in her training in her British drama school, she could not yet see how this was going to be employed in the rehearsal process as she created her role of the Detective Inspector, an English-speaking character whose cultural context was not specified in the performance text. This speaks to two factors that must be overcome in the early stages of working with our method. Firstly, throughout their training, actors have internalised a disregard for their home languages, which they often see as insufficiently professional for the training environment. This resonates with what Evi Stamatiou identifies as 'the importance of developing actors to decolonise themselves through interventions that can be applied by all and target all' (2022, p. 97). Secondly, the actor's confusion speaks to the stranglehold of Stanislavski-inspired given circumstances on the actor's imagination, and the extent to which this curtails their engagement with their unique identities when they perceive it to be distant from their character. This acts as another barrier to finding the pleasure to play.

Each day begins with a repeat of some of the games from the previous, to further emphasise that finding complicité and the pleasure of playing together will firmly underpin the whole rehearsal process. On day 2 after the games, we began to read very small sections of the play with the actors. This is not a full table read but rather functions to connect the work from day 1 to day 2 as we move to text. The movement from the perceived freedom of improvisation to the text is a very difficult moment for the actor and is often the moment they lose all sense of self and become paralysed by what they deem to be the demands of the play. In that moment, we have found that they can start to second guess what might be being asked of them, often mimicking the centre rather than holding the pleasure to play they found in the improvisations, as all too often 'the only way for somatic "others" to succeed is to engage in a process of "mimicry"' (Friedman & O'Brien, 2017, p. 6). The task of our method thus becomes to build a bridge from the actor to the text, allowing them to bring the power they discovered from playing with and through their cultural context to the performance text.

In the process we are recounting here, Actor 1 was asked to read her first scene: an interrogation of a convicted criminal that she and her team had pulled out of prison to ask him some questions about a murder to which he had not previously been connected. There were two other performers in the scene: Actor 2, playing the convicted criminal, who is Italian; and Actor 3, playing the second detective, who is White British – an official census term we use to indicate those 'for whom citizenship and national belonging are relatively secure and taken-for-granted' (Clarke, 2023, p. 1770). The White British actor is also an integral part of this unique identity practice; they bring their own vernacular English to the work, and they too are being taken through the process of working intrinsically rather than extrinsically without mimicry. The three actors began to read together with little connection, and it was clear they were falling into the trap of playing a stereotypical interview situation without nuance. They were mimicking what they thought might be a way to play an interview interrogation for the stage, and in so doing lost any sense of who they were and what they could particularly bring to this scene. Kristine therefore stopped them quite quickly and asked the actors to set aside the text and return to improvisation. This new exercise aimed to move the actors as far away from the stock situation of police interrogation while maintaining the emotional undercurrents of the scene and encouraging them to reclaim the pleasure of playing.

To do so required a situation that would allow the actors to play with and through their unique differences, rather than allowing the situation to get in the way and prevent them from so doing. The specific situation Kristine chose was this: three actors at drama school have recently been cast in a play. However, last minute a casting change was announced and the two actors (Actor 1 and Actor 3, who in our rehearsal process are playing the detectives) suspect that Actor 2 (playing the criminal) had a hand in the casting change so he would benefit. This emotionally charged situation is close to the lived experience of actors; they can fully understand it and play *as themselves* without hesitation. To fully inhabit the power that they had found in the previous non-text-based improvisations, Kristine also asked that the actors perform this scenario multilingually, with Actor 1 working in Arabic, Actor 2 in Italian, and Actor 3 in English. All actors play as though they understand what each other is saying, and because there is little literal understanding, the actors are forced to listen very deeply to each other for the flow of the improvisation to make sense.

In this process, the actors began the improvisation, and the onlooking cohort immediately felt a palpable sense of confidence, ease, and fluency from each actor. The actors were listening deeply, and the concentration was off themselves and onto the other with the sensitivity required to make this multilingual improvisation make sense. All three actors seemed in flow and tune with each other, and the improvisation thrilled the onlookers. Once Kristine stopped the improvisation, she took the actors quickly to the next phase of the exercise, asking them to improvise again multilingually but adjusting the narrative to that of the performance text. She was emphatic that the only thing to change was the narrative, and that the performance quality should feel precisely the same as it did in the previous improvisation – even at this moment the performance quality can drop the moment actors start to construct their improvisations to meet a particular scenario, rather than just allowing an uncensored improvisation to flow easily between them. It is therefore imperative that if there is the slightest shift in performance quality, the trainer should stop the improvisation, remind the actors of what they created before, and emphasise that holding the pleasure to play remains the priority for this second improvisation. Once the second improvisation had maintained the performance quality from the first, from that point all the actors were at liberty to switch to English without losing any of the complicité established between them when working multilingually. This is where the real work begins.

Holding onto Power

Revisiting my mother tongue in improvs initially took me by surprise: I am fluent in both Urdu and Punjabi, however, being in a rehearsal space and suddenly having to use these languages without the safety net of a script was something I didn't anticipate being such a dive in the deep end, and I found myself suddenly forgetting how to communicate in these languages, which was bizarre as I am conversational-level fluent in both. The significance of the experience lies in the fact that I felt totally present in that moment – with the inner fire that Punjabi has – and the rehearsal was no longer about the English words written on a page. Taking this into scene work was helpful and also the audience hasn't the faintest idea what 'chal apna pind chalte hain' means!

Actor 4

Trying to help actors retain and utilise what they find when working in a first language or vernacular can be complex. If they have never used a language other than English in their training, they find it hard to understand how this could translate to their ultimate performance. A lot of persuasion is required, as well as the reassurance of the trainer that the power afforded by activating this superpower will be legible to audiences. The trainer must look very carefully at each actor and needs not only to recognise when the freedom often afforded by utilising a home language slips away but also to have the language and tools to encourage and assist them in this journey – which at first can feel intangible and very unfamiliar. Despite the unfamiliarity of multiple languages in the rehearsal room, and the potential lack of literal understanding, our method demands that the trainer is confident in recognising and supporting complicité between performers, even when they are speaking languages the trainer does not understand. Of course, we recognise this sounds challenging, but we reiterate here that 'it is not enough merely to recognize that students are comprised of multiple identities – even subordinated ones' (Powers & Duffy, 2015, p. 63). Trainers must take meaningful steps towards action, and we emphasise that colleagues are expert in recognising performance quality, and the power and ease that accompanies it, and it is this that our method is seeking to unlock.

In this rehearsal process, we observed that Actor 1 had real power, confidence, and size when speaking Arabic, but when she returned to her British English, her voice and demeanour were cowed and at times she was hardly audible. Kristine noticed, for example, that she moved her mouth more: in English, her mouth was very static, barely open; in Arabic, her mouth and lips were fully in play. Her volume in Arabic was instantly louder; in English, she had hardly been audible. The actors worked for some time between Arabic, Italian, and English with Kristine's side coaching, trying to help them hold on to discoveries made while not in English. The last step of this session was to return actors to the text, giving them the instruction to be guided by the confidence and pleasure already achieved rather than being pulled in another direction by what they deemed to be the demands of the text. In this approach, the trainer is very active throughout – here Kristine instructed the actors 'go to Arabic, now English, now Italian, stronger accent, now Arabic, loud Arabic voice', using crude instructions that aimed to help them keep hold of what she recognised as their pleasure to play. The actor is privileged above the text throughout the rehearsal process, not merely in early improvisation and explorations as in the late Stanislavskian practice of Active Analysis, but also in continuing deep into performance.

This first phase of rehearsal was surprising and confusing for all the actors: the three participating and their onlooking peers. Many commented on what was revealed in all three who had improvised, drawing attention to the confidence, power, and fluency in the work. It is then critical to take time at this point in the rehearsal to discuss the process, listen to reflections, and try to explain very clearly what is happening, where it is travelling, and how important it is for every single actor to have permission to utilise and experiment with everything to which they have access in their cultural context while working on the floor. In the post-session discussion here, Actor 1 recognised her freedom and strength when working in Arabic. She revealed that in her training she often received the same note of being too cowed, too small, too light, and she had tried several extrinsic exercises to address this to no success. These will be familiar to many readers: undertaking an animal study, adopting a male gender position, and wearing a costume including a suit and heavy shoes. The moment she was invited to play with something intrinsic – that is, something coming from inside herself – she felt the transformation was instant. By utilising a language from her cultural context that she usually reserved for home and not the stage, Actor 1 found ease and a unique delivery that guided her through the session and on through the rehearsal process.

What is required here is both permission and ignition, in Rustom Bharucha's terms: 'to ignite what has been submerged so that the critical consciousness of the actors can be heightened' (2001, p. 136). Through the course of rehearsals, the guiding intention of our method remains the same: taking actors to a place where fluency, strength, and freedom have been found by utilising their unique identities as one of the crucial ingredients in the making of the work. To do so necessitates not moving forward to the next scene unless that is in place, which can render it a slow process when the pedagogy seems so unfamiliar to actors. Our goal is to utilise the intrinsic rather than the extrinsic to shape a role for performance; to engage and ignite the actor's unique identities rather than to disavow differences. This is at the heart of the de-centring potential of unique identity practice because it exploits the potential for the expressive means accessed via first languages and vernacular English to become a superpower for actors with intersectionally subordinate identities working in English.

This particular rehearsal period required slow and steady work. Actor 1 took a long time to understand how to hold a sense of the expressive means available to her in Arabic when she came to perform the text in English – but more crucially she took even longer to be convinced that it was a legitimate way of working. We would take steps forward, followed by more steps back, and there were many points in the rehearsals where we had to put the performance text down in favour of multilingual improvisations. The actors often wanted to push forward and rehearse the text, but Kristine emphasised that they should permit themselves to do this only once they had accessed the confidence and pleasure to play. Because care has been taken from the beginning of the process to show them what this ease looks and feels like, they can recognise it in their work and in that of others. This, in turn, allows them to appreciate when progress is being made – and when further troubleshooting is required. The whole company thus takes ownership for maintaining complicité, and for celebrating the moments when the pleasure to play returns to the work. This also helps guard against the perception that individual actors are receiving the trainer's attention at the expense of others in the group.

As we travelled through rehearsals, for example, Actor 1 was making great progress and by the start of week three, we hoped that the rehearsals of the text would be quite straightforward. Actor 1 had found and held a size, weight, and fluency through her rehearsals in improvisation and text, and Kristine anticipated that she would move to rehearse the text quite effortlessly. However, when we began the rehearsals, she had slipped right back to a size where she almost disappeared when on the stage. Kristine asked why that was and what was happening, and she was genuinely unable to answer; she was lost, and it was impossible to continue the text rehearsals. We went back to the guiding exercise – a multilingual improvisation which engaged her cultural context – and hoped that this would bring back the size, the confidence, and the fluency that was constantly eluding us. This was a difficult moment, as the company were keen to get on and rehearse the play, but Kristine needed to ignite the actor before any further progress could be made.

This time, Kristine set up a new improvisation between Actor 1, Actor 2, and another who we will call Actor 4, who is from a Punjabi background and speaks both Urdu and Punjabi. Using the length of the rehearsal room to try to encourage size in Actor 1's performance, Kristine set up another emotive situation: Actors 1 and 4 were sisters selling their old family mansion, and Actor 2 had come to buy it. He was wily and, thinking he could beat them down, had come to negotiate the price, offering way below what they were wanting; the two women looked down on him and were rude to him, but they still needed to sell. Actor 1 worked in Arabic, Actor 2 in Italian, and Actor 4 in Urdu. The improvisation immediately took off: the size, the confidence, the fluency were fully present in all three actors. Kristine let the improvisation run for a while – all had found complicité, and their onlooking peers were entertained, so it was beneficial for everyone to play so well together for a while – it fed the confidence of the room. Once they completed the improvisation, Kristine immediately invited them to simply sit a distance from each other, maintaining the feel of the large mansion, and then play the lines from the text with the pleasure and complicité they had found in the improvisation. It began to work, but there was still a hesitancy to Actor 1's performance that acted as a barrier to complicité. A more interventionist approach would be required, drawn from the latter stages of our method.

Playing with Headphones

When Kristine and I had settled on my character having an Arabic accent, to ignite myself in the role she suggested that I use headphone verbatim to perfect the accent. I used a clip of an Egyptian woman talking about the revolution who had a thick accent that was very guttural. My accent in English is very soft and light, which was not aiding me in the interrogation scene. Using headphone verbatim meant that I was not second guessing myself or judging my voice imitating hers as I couldn't hear myself talking. This was amazing to me and did not make me feel like I was trying to actualise a character far from myself because I had the guttural thick strong accent within me – it was just ignited through headphone verbatim.

Actor 1

We have recently begun to utilise headphone verbatim as a technique in training, as it helps actors free themselves from their perceived ideas about a text and it helps them position themselves firmly in the endeavour of creating a role. In headphone verbatim, the actor works with the voice of a real person, they listen to the voice through headphones, and they speak that voice as accurately as they can at the same time as they are listening to the voice. As Caroline Wake describes it, 'in both rehearsal and performance the actors wear headphones, through which they hear the audio script. They then repeat that script as immediately and exactly as possible, including . . . every stammer, pause, and repetition' (2013, p. 323). They reach for the accent, the weight, and the rhythm of the recorded person with no exaggeration or approximation and no judgement. Crucially, the actor does not learn the text, nor do they seek to disappear into character; so the actor and the voice are always held in simultaneous view, with the headphones 'serving as a constant reminder that the actors are presenting the material rather than identifying with it' (Luckhurst, 2008, p. 215). Elsewhere in our professional practice, we use headphone verbatim as a method for generating creative material; here, it is a rehearsal room tool that can break actors away from a constricting focus on text. The actor only plays with the pleasure of finding the voice they are listening to; they are not building or exploring character, and so stay present as themselves.

To reclaim the pleasure of play that was proving elusive when moving back to the performance text, Kristine asked Actor 1 to find a voice which would help her in her rehearsal journey, simply specifying it had to be a voice that she would take pleasure in performing for the company. Actor 1 chose a middle-aged woman speaking English with an Arabic accent: a very full, big, rich voice, which she enjoyed presenting. This points to the power of this way of working for actors of intersectionally subordinate identities, too: the vernacular and the gender identity of the speaker were key to the student's pleasure in performing the voice. She showed great skill in capturing the voice exactly – much to the thrill of the onlooking actors. Once Actor 1 had performed the voice as she had heard it according to the tenets of headphone verbatim, Kristine then asked her to continue to play the voice on headphones and listen to it, but as she was speaking lines of the performance text in which she was playing the Detective Inspector. The emphasis, therefore, is not on the specifics of the voice itself, but on the student gaining an embodied understanding of the pleasure of playing through intersectionally subordinate identities. This understanding is developed through deep listening: using headphones makes it impossible for the actor to do anything *but* listen and repeat.

Drawing on headphone verbatim in training can be an effective tool, as it emphasises the actor and their skill in the same way our method does. In our rehearsal rooms, actors are encouraged to use a full range of expressive means sourced from first languages, vernacular languages, and English through a process of deep listening, all while developing and privileging complicité as a guiding light. Throughout, the actor is privileged above the text, and no work is done on the text until the actor has been ignited. Headphone verbatim works in a similar way and our work with these techniques is particularly inspired by groups like Nature Theater of Oklahoma, whose performers often take 'charismatic pleasure' (Anderson-Rabern, 2010, p. 89) in the words they are speaking. In the rehearsal room, as the actor reaches towards rhythms and idiosyncratic details that are not their own, they often look unsure – but when using headphones, they are not afraid to display their uncertainty, and in witnessing this the current between actor and audience is alive. The actor's focus is off themselves and off the text, and they prioritise their connection and complicité with the audience as they share with pleasure the voice they are reaching for.

As rehearsals progressed, whenever Actor 1's pleasure to play wavered, Kristine returned to the headphone technique, encouraging her to find the confidence she unlocked through the recorded voice alongside the performance text. This also served to reclaim the power she had found when playing through her unique identities: the voice she had recorded was from a world with which she is intimately familiar, and she is the expert when she presents it to us. This was particularly helpful in the context of her role as the Detective Inspector, which required the same effortless authority that she found pleasure in working with the recording. As actors move back to the performance text, constant reinforcement is a necessary step in our method, otherwise they can slip back and lose confidence in the idea that the solution often lies within them rather than outside them. As the actor reflections throughout this chapter attest, the unfamiliarity of working with a multi-vernacular approach means that constant persuasion and reinforcement is required from the director leading the process. However, once they experience the power of fully igniting their individual being in the process of role development, the discovery not only anchors them throughout the rehearsal process but also grounds them in something they can always rely on in any rehearsal room.

Conclusion

As an international drama school student in my last year of training I have been thinking a lot about my accent in relation to the industry I am about to enter. During these last three years my natural accent has shifted a lot and part of that is linked to the idea of a 'correct way of speaking' that I have developed, which led me to consciously try and reduce my accent as much as I could. Working without having to think about the way that I sound was such a relief. I believe that the work on this detective narrative was some of the best I've done. I felt very connected and alive, and I found it easier to draw from my personal and cultural experiences.

Finally, integrating my first language into the rehearsal process was an important breakthrough for me, I had never done it before. It allowed me to be aware of the shift in the way I express myself while speaking my native language and encouraged me to use that unique expressiveness in my performance.

Actor 2

Dunn refers to the actor-in-training's experience as 'mandatory self-erasure and negative stereotyping' (2019, p. 69), describing how the individual personalities are trained out of actors in a traumatic process of self-abnegation. In our work, we continue to see this in many actor training programmes – as the quote that opens this section attests, the validation, and the integration of a first language and the ability to use an uncensored vernacular in training provide welcome relief. In this process, the actor can be exactly who they are, their own personality is given validity, they are asked to bring their cultural heritage to the process of acting, and they are asked not to hide themselves in that process. All too often, the world of the play is the overriding concern and exercises are favoured that look at extrinsic rather than intrinsic solutions. In our method as shown above, we cannot move forward until the actor is ignited, where her rhythms and idiosyncratic details are fully in play, where her ears are alert to the inherent rhythms in a text, and where her own rhythms are allowed to merge with those rhythms in the text.

For this to happen, trainers and directors must give up a sense of certainty and be ready to play with the uncertain encounter of the rehearsal room, in which 'as vulnerabilities infiltrate our imagined modes of expertise, we have no other choice but to acknowledge our distance' (Bharucha, 2001, p. 136). Trainers must be ready for the actor to be the expert – the expert of their own voice, and their unique identities, whether they are working in a first language, a vernacular, or English. The trainer needs to be ready to shift their position from one where they are always imparting knowledge to one where they are rather looking to nurture and capture the individual and their particularities and peculiarities and then help them merge these qualities with the given text. Crucially, this does not mean the trainer has no role in our method – as we have reiterated throughout, the trainer must guide and shape the improvisations, and use their expertise to recognise and encourage complicité and pleasure when they recognise them in the actors. No trainer can be fluent in every language in the rehearsal room or appreciate the unique identities of every actor: this is not required. The first step is simply to embrace the expertise in the room, and then get to work. The time has come to embrace pedagogies that can fully support and exploit the diverse actor cohorts with the multiple and intersecting, protected and unprotected, visible and invisible identities that are in every room. Only then can the practice in our rehearsal rooms match the aspirations on institutional websites; only then will our pedagogy offer the equity that our policy statements profess.

Notes

1 All of the actors we interviewed for this chapter are enrolled in full-time conservatoire training at a British drama school, and worked with Kristine on a performance project that utilised our unique identity practice throughout rehearsals.
2 Tamasha Theatre Company was founded by Sudha Bhuchar and Kristine Landon-Smith in 1989. A global majority-led company, Tamasha was set up to create opportunities for British Asian performers. As well as producing noted productions including "East is East" and "The Tainted Dawn", Tamasha has also led training and professional development activities for theatre artists under the banner of Tamasha Developing Artists.
3 We adapt the work of Bill Ashcroft, Gareth Griffiths, and Helen Tiffin in using this contraction to indicate both English, 'the language of the erstwhile imperial centre' (2002, p. 8), and English, its vernacular subversions throughout the world.

References

Alexandrowicz, C. (2017). Straight-looking, straight-acting: Countering Effemiphobia in Actor Training. *Theatre, Dance and Performance Training*, 8(1), 5–18.

Amsden, L. (2016). When they laugh your clown is coming': Learning to be ridiculous in Philippe Gaulier's pedagogy of spectatorship. *Theatre, Dance and Performance Training*, 7(1), 4–16.

Anderson-Rabern, R. (2010). The nature theater of Oklahoma's aesthetics of fun. *TDR: The Drama Review*, 54(4), 81–98.

Arao, B., & Clemens, K. (2013). From safe spaces to brave spaces: A new way to frame dialogue around diversity and social justice. In L. M. Landerman (Ed.), *The art of effective facilitation: Reflections from social justice educators* (pp. 135–150). Stylus Publishing.

Ashcroft, B., Griffiths, G., & Tiffin, H. (2002). *The empire writes back: Theory and practice in post-colonial literature*. Routledge.

Bharucha, R. (1996). Under the sign of the onion: Intracultural negotiations in theatre. *New Theatre Quarterly*, 12(46), 116–129.

Bharucha, R. (2001). *The politics of cultural practice: Thinking through theatre in an age of globalisation*. Oxford University Press.

Clarke, A. (2023). The (in)significance of citizenship in White British citizens' narratives of national belonging. *Journal of Ethnic and Migration Studies*, 49(7), 1768–1785.

Dunn, K. A. (2019). Hidden damage: When uninformed casting and actor training disregard the effect of character embodiment on students of color. *Theatre Symposium*, 27, 68–79.

Friedman, S., & O'Brien, D. (2017). Resistance and resignation: Responses to typecasting in British acting. *Cultural Sociology*, 11(3), 359–376.

Ginther, A. M. (2023). Introduction: Why this book now? In A. M. Ginther (Ed.), *Stages of reckoning: Antiracist and decolonial actor training* (pp. 1–19). Routledge.

Hay, C., & Landon-Smith, K. (2018). The intracultural actor: Embracing difference in theatre arts teaching. In A. Fliotsos & G. S. Medford (Eds.), *New directions in teaching theatre arts* (pp. 157–173). Palgrave Macmillan.

Kendrick, L. (2011). A *Paidic* aesthetic: An analysis of games in the ludic pedagogy of Philippe Gaulier. *Theatre, Dance and Performance Training*, 2(1), 72–85.

Landon-Smith, K. (2020). A pedagogy for twenty-first century actor training: Intracultural theatre practice which embraces pluralistic identity and plays with difference. *Theatre, Dance and Performance Training*, 11(3), 343–350.

Landon-Smith, K., & Hay, C. (2023). Empowering the somatically-othered actor through multilingual improvisation in training. In A. M. Ginther (Ed.), *Stages of reckoning: Antiracist and decolonial actor training* (pp. 149–163). Routledge.

Landon-Smith, K., & Motta, F. (2022). Seeking complicité, the pleasure to play and clown state as an integral part of actor training in the work of Kristine Landon-Smith and Fabio Motta. *Theatre, Dance and Performance Training*, 13(1), 159–161.

Luckhurst, M. (2008). Verbatim theatre, media relations and ethics. In M. Luckhurst & N. Holdsworth (Eds.), *A concise companion to contemporary British and Irish drama* (pp. 200–222). Blackwell.

Malaev-Babel, A. (Ed.). (2011). *The Vakhtangov sourcebook*. Routledge.

Powers, B., & Duffy, P. B. (2015). Making invisible intersectionality visible through theatre of the oppressed in teacher education. *Journal of Teacher Education, 67*(1), 61–73.

Purdie-Vaughns, V., & Eibach, R. P. (2008). Intersectional invisibility: The distinctive advantages and disadvantages of multiple subordinate-group identities. *Sex Roles, 59*, 377–391.

RADA students anti-racism action plan. (2020). RADA Student Council. www.change.org/p/rada-leadership-sign-in-support-of-rada-students-anti-racism-action-plan.

Stamatiou, E. (2022). Pierre Bourdieu and actor training: Towards decolonising and decentering actor training pedagogies. *Theatre, Dance and Performance Training, 13*(1), 96–114.

Wake, C. (2013). Headphone verbatim theatre: Methods, histories, genres, theories. *New Theatre Quarterly, 29*(4), 321–335.

3 Cultivating the Reflexive Practitioner in the Performance Studio

An Intersectional Approach

Valerie Clayman Pye

Introduction

As a young actor in training, I had excellent teachers who understood the craft of acting and instilled in me a strong foundation of the actor's tools. Under their tutelage, I could identify and articulate discipline-specific vocabulary and the elements of the craft, and I could embody those with increasing success as I developed greater proficiency as an actor. I was not trained, however, in the ability to deepen my own understanding of my relationship to my craft through a repeatable reflective practice. This was, for me and others like me, an assumed skill, an inherent trait that would support my learning as an actor and amplify the nuance with which I could execute the craft – if only the means to access it was articulated as clearly as the steps to identify active ways of playing an objective. Instead, my teachers offered little more than a directive to 'journal' about what happened in class and during my rehearsals and share what I learned/thought about it as if the act of writing would yield the desired result. While any thought or consideration about what happened is better than none, my teachers' best-intended directives relied on my possessing a skill that I may, or may not, have formally acquired.

'What if reflexivity is a feature not only of the individual but of the system?,' asks Maria Kapsali in her essay 'Psychophysical Disciplines and the Development of Reflexivity' (2014, p. 165). Kapsali inquires '[h]ow could a reflexive attitude transcend the moment/period of training and rather equip the trainee with an interpretive capacity that is operative beyond the moment of training?' (ibid, p. 163). What if, as actor trainers, we simultaneously trained actors both in the craft of acting and in practical reflexive processes that support their growth as critical thinkers? How might we draw from educational theories and the fields of other reflexive practitioners, such as education and healthcare, to support our discipline-specific embodied actor training? How can we develop a system for reflection that simultaneously amplifies and empowers student agency? In this chapter, I draw from the fields of practice-as-research, henceforth PaR, and experiential learning to introduce a framework that models a reflection process that can be integrated into an existing training pedagogy. By providing students with a process that helps them learn *how* to reflect, students can simultaneously amplify their ability to assess and understand their own moments of practice. Additionally, under these defining principles, reflexion is simultaneously physical and cognitive, as it occurs in real time. The following paragraphs illustrate my understanding of how the two terms 'reflection' and 'reflexion' are different.

Reflection is a critical practice for all learning, but especially so for experiential learning, where theory, as Robin Nelson notes, 'is not prior to practice, functioning to inform it, but theory and practice are rather 'imbricated within each other' in praxis' (2013, p. 62). From

DOI: 10.4324/9781003393672-5

its Latin origin *reflectere*, which means to 'bend back', the notion of turning back, thinking deeply, or embodying are all central concepts to the Action Research Model, which follows some generalised form of *plan > act > evaluate/observe > reflect*.[1] Reflexivity can be articulated as a 'form of self-criticism that identifies the principles used to generate knowledge and recognises these principles as constituting an interpretive framework' (Berdayes et al., 2004 in Kapsali, 2014, p. 157). This act of knowledge generation is dependent on and enhanced by the 'form of self-criticism' one employs, and this chapter is especially interested in the nexus of self-criticism to develop a systematic framework that advances the practice of and enhances meaning for actors in training.

Actors, like athletes, are simultaneously the player and the instrument, and the duality inherent within those roles demands that they are engaged in conversation with the situation (Schön, 1983, p. 76). These conversations happen in two distinct ways: reflection-in-action, what Schön classifies as an 'epistemology of practice' (1983, p. 49), and reflection-on-action, which is a post-practice event that seeks to capture the tacit knowledge of the practitioner. Reflection-in-action occurs within a phase Schön identifies as the 'action-present' when action can still impact the event itself (1983, p. 63). To be better equipped for those situational conversations 'in-action' (Schön, 1983, p. 50) however, practitioners bolster and refine their knowing-in-action, their 'doing thinking' (Nelson, 2013, p. 29) by interrogating a particular moment through a reflexive practice after the event's conclusion. This cycle of reflective action helps the practitioner to understand and respond through the expertise of their tacit knowledge within a situation.

Conceptual Framework

To construct a conceptual framework that can work in conjunction with my Action Research Model, I drew on the Kolb cycle and the Cowan diagram, which offer dynamic models that are useful for understanding process. John Cowan identifies the distinctions between his own diagram and that of David Kolb's cycle, which he identifies is based on Lewin's 1951 work, despite most often being attributed directly to Kolb (Cowan, 2006, p. 46). The Kolb cycle features a four-sequence rotation that can be entered at any point, but most often is read like the face of an analogue clock with *Experience* at the top in the 12:00 position, and circling round to *Reflection, Generalisation*, and finally what Kolb calls *Active Experimentation* (Kolb, 1984 in Cowan, 2006, p. 46),[2] as illustrated in Figure 3.1. Reflection serves as a bridge to generalisation (ibid, p. 47), or what I would consider *understanding* in Kolb's model. Cowan's own diagram, on the other hand, stretches out the cycle to insert three different phases of the reflection process so that there are points of reflection for, in, and on action, as illustrated in Figure 3.2. While its diagram is more challenging to read, it reflects the complex network that a learner experiences. Cowan's loop-to-loop coil offers the following trajectory: beginning with *prior experience*, it then moves to *reflection-for-learning, exploratory activity, reflection-in-action, consolidation*, and, finally, *reflection-on-action* (ibid, pp. 53–55). Cowan's 'reflection-for-learning', which he uses interchangeably with 'reflection-for-action', builds on to Schön's reflections – in and – on action to deliberately expand how the practitioner engages in the cycle. *Reflection-for-action* identifies the 'needs, aspirations and objectives which will subsequently be prominent in the learner's mind' (ibid, p. 51).

Within the field of reflective/reflexive practices, the two terms are often used interchangeably. Here, I use the term 'reflection' when the emphasis is rooted strongly in *reflectere* or looking back, and 'reflexive' when there is a broader reflective response to a given moment

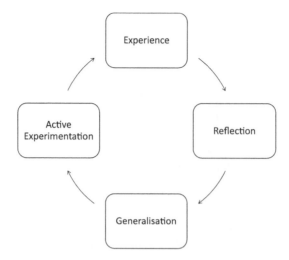

Figure 3.1 Cowan's articulation of the Kolb cycle.

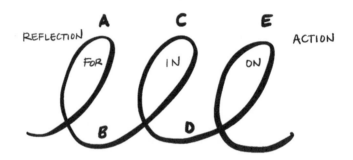

Figure 3.2 The Cowan diagram.

in action, where the act of reflecting – either deliberately or intuitively – can inform and shape a given moment.

Most of the scholarship around critical reflexive practice for practitioners comes from the fields of healthcare, social work, and teaching (Hatton & Smith, 1995; Moon, 2001; Ryan & Murphy, 2018; Ryan & Walsh, 2018; Smith, 2011; Thompson & Pascal, 2012; Wlodarsky, 2014). Creative practitioners can adapt the existing paradigms and frameworks to suit their needs by teasing out parallel elements. As practitioners and teachers of practice, we can undertake reflexive practices to develop not only our own understanding of our tacit knowledge and embodied experiences but also to allow those reflexive practices to deliberately inform our teaching. By encouraging actors in training to develop their own critical reflexive practices, actor trainers can support the moments of active learning which correspond to the markers identified in the cycles above.

In supporting actors in training to develop as reflexive practitioners, or more specifically, *reflexive actors*, we simultaneously train reflexivity alongside the particular acting pedagogy of our studios – we are engaged in what Lev Vygotsky defines as the Zone of Proximal Development (henceforth ZPD). ZPD can be defined as the scope, or 'zone', of possibility between what one is capable of at the outset and what one can potentially achieve under the guidance of a more capable individual. This creates a cycle whereby the novice internalises the learned content that subsequently forms the basis for the next phase of development (Eun, 2019, p. 20). 'Within this conception of the ZPD', Barohny Eun states, 'instruction has to focus on the functions that are ready to develop with the appropriate support from the more knowledgeable other' (ibid, p. 20). These developing functions, in turn, will be internalised and used by the learner independently after the support is withdrawn' (ibid, p. 20). Eun's description of Vygotsky's concept in the final sentence of that quotation recalls learning to ride a bike, which David Pears popularised as an example of understanding embodied knowledge. Pears' well-known example illuminates the duality between intellectual and embodied knowledge by pointing out that one may know how to ride a bike because of the embodied experience of learning to ride, and riding, a bike, but have no understanding of the physics behind why they can do so, and conversely, one might understand the physics that allows one to ride without actually being able to undertake the task (1971, pp. 26, 27). Eun's description ignites images of learning to ride a bike, where learners are often supported by 'training wheels' (the United States) or 'stabilisers' (the United Kingdom). The semantics between these two terms reveal much; the American phrase indicates what the wheels intend to do (train), while the British phrase articulates what is done (stabilise). This is a useful metaphor to reinforce the concept of ZPD, and the idea of modelling or loaning knowledge, to both 'train' and 'support' (or stabilise), will feature prominently in the second half of this chapter.

'The teaching of critical reflective skills in HE offers a way for practitioners to gain insight into their own professionalism' writes Elizabeth Smith (Larrivee, 2000; Schön, 1991), who notes that it is unusual for critical [reflection] theory and practice to be taught explicitly in healthcare higher education (2011, pp. 211, 212). The same may be said of performance training. If education is about 'finding pathways to what we do not know we know' (Bolton, 2014, p. 13), and good teaching makes explicit the implicit, how can we train actors to be reflexive practitioners as we simultaneously train them in the performance pedagogy of our studios?

To maximise the learning potential, we need to understand *how* to think about the thinking we undertake. If we ask actors in training to consider moments of practice, we should enter their ZPD and empower them with the tools to do so effectively and efficiently. Considering that '[r]eflective practice is purposeful, not the musing one slips into while driving home' (Bolton, 2014, p. 16 drawing on Fogel, 2009), acting teachers can model cognitive reflective processes for students to adopt so that they may 'train' and 'stabilise' their ability to reflect.

Jenny Moon identifies the 'frequent' observation that not all students find reflection an easy task when it is a requirement, and that 'it is important to recognise that some staff will not understand reflection either' (2001, p. 9). This may be due to a misunderstanding of the goals and purpose of reflexive writing as something that is exclusively a recollection or record of the recent past for posterity. In *Reflective Practice: Writing and Professional Development*, Gillie Bolton writes that '[r]eflective writing *is* the reflective process, rather than recording what has been thought' (2014, p. 115, italics original to the author). As acting pedagogues, we specialise in teaching processes, which involve systematic ways to create a theatrical experience. This may include elements of working with audience, body, partner, text, and space, but systems of reflexivity are not necessarily associated with the necessary components of theatre training. Reflexive practice is inherently a part of the acting process, but there is little evidence that this ancillary skill is addressed directly as a part of actor training. Through deliberately designed structured reflection frameworks, actors in train-ing can learn not only about their own expertise with regard to the craft of acting but also about the critical metacognition – the 'thinking about thinking' (Martinez, 2006, p. 696).

One of the most crucial components of actor training is the process by which the player engages in ongoing dialogue with their instrument and their audience to reflect-in-action on the process of executing a given performance. We may trace this back to what Konstantin Stanislavsky called 'experiencing', or *perezhivanie*, what Sharon Marie Carnicke calls the 'lost term' (2009, pp. 129–147), which directly relates to Schön's notion of being in conver-sation with. The principle of 'experiencing' is prised in the Western world as 'moment-to-moment' work, popularised by the Americanisation of Stanislavski's work by Lee Strasberg, Stella Adler, and Sanford Meisner, whose methodology centres around responding to impulses and circumstances 'in the moment' (Meisner & Longwell, 1987). Schön illustrates this principle with the practices of jazz musicians, who draw upon theoretical frameworks as they reflect-in-action (1983, p. 55) in the 'action present' (1983, p. 62).³ These moment-to-moment in-action conversations demonstrate the organic, improvisatory qualities we associate with jazz. In his essay for *Twentieth Century Actor Training*, 'Strasberg, Adler, and Meisner', David Krasner identifies that Meisner's focus on ensemble behaviour creates a 'jazz-like atmosphere of action and reaction' (p. 146). The ability to respond to, and in, the moment of performance requires the actor to possess high-level processing capabilities, which echoes what Stanislavsky called *samochuvstivie*, or 'performer's sense of self' (Car-nicke, 2009, pp. 142, 143), and what Michael Chekhov referred to as a 'dual conscious-ness' (1991, p. 155), a concept also discussed in more recent scholarship (Carnicke, 2009, pp. 142, 143), so that they may engage in the type of 'conversation' that Schön identifies.

An actor undergoes complex associations as they navigate through moments of perfor-mance. Philip Zarilli identifies:

> The actor [has] to negotiate between his own understanding/expectations of what acting is or is not, and the demands of this particular production. He [has] to develop a network of relationships-in-action between three sets of demands which any production poten-tially places on the actor's approach: (1) the structural, dramaturgical demands of the dramatic text and/or the particular genre of performance (happenings, performance art, etc.); (2) the structural demands of the performance text – how the director (or whoever is shaping the work) determines the *specific* structure of *this* particular performance text; and (3) the relationship between the actor and what the actor does, i.e., the qualitative, psychophysiological dimension of the actor's engagement in the task-at-hand.
>
> (2002, p. 17)

The ability to assess, understand, and execute a variety of tasks in action requires the actor to cultivate a sense of trust in their own abilities to undertake the task of performance, to identify within themselves the components which must be engaged in the forefront of the experience to respond-in-action. Bolton identifies *trust* as the core of meaningful reflex-ive practice. She writes that '[c]ritical reflexive practice requires: **Trust** in the processes of our practice and reflection upon it' and that '[t]his trust enables us to examine, question, explore and experiment: to be critical. We are the primary authority on our own experience; believing this requires trust, at least initially' (Bolton, 2014, p. 23, original emphasis).

Studio practice is, ultimately, a form of practice as research as the conversation in action and practice has a cyclical, non-sequential lineage that, like jazz musicians, engages theo-retical frameworks and schemas. At times, theory precedes and informs practice (Nelson,

2013, p. 62), a model most often engaged in the acting studio, where there is a methodological approach to a variety of investigations. But theory also emerges from moments of practice for the keen practitioner who can theorise their embodied experience. In her essay 'Toward the Practice of Theory in Practice', Sharon Grady states that '[t]he use of various critical theories allows us to *intentionally* place our attention and bring assumptions to the foreground instead of keeping them in the background' (1996, p. 60). She continues with '[w]hat differentiates a critical theory from a commonplace set of assumptions is the degree of reflexivity involved. Theory and theorise "happens" whether one is paying attention or not' (Grady, 1996, p. 60). As instructors, we can offer actors the means to focus their attention to expand the vocabulary of potential dialogue so that those conversations in and on action enhance growth. In doing so, we follow the tenets of ZPD.

Because '[k]nowing what incident to reflect upon is not straightforward' (Bolton, 2014, p. 13), it is useful to offer clear guidance in this area in a way that supports students' individual needs rather than an overarching approach that ignores the multiple hierarchies embedded in formal higher education and students' intersecting social identities. In this approach, you may apply the structures of ZPD not only to the craft of acting but also to the reflective process. Much in the same way that we acquire language and effective communication skills through modelling, strategies for learning to reflect on moments of practice can be acquired through deliberate practice.

As an instructor, I use my understanding of these various research cycles, principles of reflection and reflexive practices, and Vygotsky's Zone of Proximal Development to intercalate models that work flexibly alongside systems of actor training. In doing so, I aim to shift existing epistemologies of auxiliary reflective training practices to promote critical actor training that urges student actors to interrogate what and how their system of training intersects with their identities as emergent artists, creative practitioners, critical thinkers, and informed citizens.

Designing a System for Student Reflection

I teach in a pre-professional training programme that offers conservatory-style training within a liberal arts university setting. We aim to prepare undergraduate students for entering the profession. The system of reflection I will share with you was implemented with second-year BFA[4] Acting and Musical Theatre students at Long Island University (LIU Post) beginning in the fall of 2018, in a course devoted to scene study work.[5] We met biweekly over 15 weeks and reflective writing was submitted at the second meeting of each week and returned to them the subsequent class meeting which allowed me to remain in dialogue with my students as they were learning. In addition to individualised feedback, each written reflection was assessed as a part of the student's overall grade in the course.

In examining my own ZPD experience – first, as an actor in training, and then as a specialist in actor training – I realised that being a highly skilled practitioner was not enough for undertaking and articulating practice-as-research (PaR). My skills as a practice-based researcher developed over time. Reflecting on that experience, I became curious about how I could create more effective reflexive practices in the studio to optimise my students' potential for learning. I suspected that doing so would both deepen my students' critical enquiry into the studio practice and help them transcend that moment and develop the means to think critically in other areas of their lives as well.

As an instructor, I assume the role of the capable expert in the ZPD model to my novice students and offer proleptic instruction that assumes they already possess the competence to complete the tasks I require of them (Eun, 2019, pp. 20, 21). I model for them how to begin to write, but on a larger scale, I model how to *think* about the writing, and over time that enhances both the reflections-in as well as the reflections-on-action.

I used my familiarity with the cycles of action research and principles of backwards design to determine how I could identify what makes a moment of reflection effective. What would an ideal reflection look like? What would need to be included so that the student could effectively demonstrate the learning that has been asked of them? Moon notes that it is important to acknowledge that instructors may not always be able to 'see' that learning has occurred (2001, p. 6) and we can argue that this may be especially true with students of embodied practice. To help identify the 'representation of learning' Moon offers the following taxonomy, which escalates from basic to complex representations: noticing > making sense > making meaning > working with meaning and, finally, transformative learning (ibid). Coincidentally, this aligns with the model I offer students to shape their reflections.

I created a scaffolded system that mirrors Moon's taxonomy. For my students, I suggest things for them to address, which satisfies Bolton's identification that the focus of reflection is not always apparent. I may offer prompts to identify a challenge that they are facing in their scene, such as a moment that was successful for them in a particular week; a question that they will bring to the subsequent week's work; a specific aspect of the craft, or something that they are curious about exploring further. These prompts are suggested before reflection happens, which enables students to enter moments of their practice with a framework established that informs the way that they think about their work as they are working. This begins to shape the reflexive process even before moments of practice commence by activating all the potential reflection networks that might occur.

Although required, these prompts also provide an opportunity for transparency, which promotes agency that empowers actors in training. They know from the outset the types of reflection that I expect to observe in this component of the classwork so that they understand how to execute the assignment to their fullest capacity. After I offer suggested prompts,[6] I then provide a tiered model of reflection and offer suggestions to further empower students and flatten the inherent hierarchy in the classroom.

Three-part Model for Reflexive Writing

The primary level of this reflection model begins with the facts: what happened in the given moment of practice? At the basic level, we must record what transpired for understanding and theorise to begin. At this first level, it's helpful to record the facts in detail, which offers opportunities for moments of realisation to occur. This is the level that students find relatively easy; it's the 'here's what I did' section. Without further guidance, many student reflections end here, with a record of the events. This first level may look like this:[7]

> We began by coming into the space and walking the floor, noticing how our feet encounter the floor, and then slowly placing attention on the breath and where we hold various points of tension in the body (the belly, the jaw, the tongue, etc). We used three breaths to locate a radiant centre and try to expand that image (using colour or not). Then we made eye contact as we passed each other in space,[8] before stopping opposite a partner to share a connecting breath.

The secondary level makes observations about the facts that were recorded in level one. When we consider what we notice about a series of events, we promote reflection. As we create a habit of awareness around the events we are engaged in, we become adept at entering dialogue and heightening our awareness around our experiences. I would even say that the habit of layering how we note our experiences leads us to a deeper recognition of the event itself. We can think about this section as the 'here's what I think about it' section. At the undergraduate level, many fine reflections on action end here: what happened, and what I observed. This level would build on the example above:

> As I focused my attention, I realised that I was holding tension I wasn't even aware of before. I thought I was feeling just fine but realised that my teeth were touching, and my jaw was clenched, I was sucking in everything (my belly, my bottom), and it took time for me to consciously connect to the centre of energy to expand it. I didn't notice any colour for the first breath, but then I could envision the breath as a faint, pale blue, which helped me to expand the release of that energy further. By the end, I felt much more focused and ready to work.

The third level leads to the greatest possible depth of understanding: inquiry. This final level leads the student-practitioner to question what the observations of the facts mean, prompting the reflector to strive to understand not only their relationship to their body instrument, their craft, and their connection to their partner(s) but also their role in the theatrical event. Advanced practitioners may begin to theorise moments of practice, a necessary component of the evolution of our field. This may be the 'here's what I'm curious about' section. This level may build on the previous two like this:

> I notice a big difference in my ability to focus and the ease with which I work when I take time to release all that excess tension and focus specifically on my breath and coming into the present moment. I wonder what might happen if I borrow some of this and take a moment to have one single breath that connects to my radiant centre and expands throughout my body before I start my scene. If it helps me to focus on being in class, can it help me enter the scene with a greater presence?

Advanced-level work should move beyond observation alone; inquiry leads to moments of inspiration. To support this, I offer the acronym FOI, which corresponds to the three levels of reflection: Facts, Observations, and Inquiry. These three levels are modelled for the student in a sample that is embedded within the syllabus, found below, and remains available for them digitally.

Even the beginning level student is capable of advanced reflection when given a model which they can follow. To adapt Vygotsky's model, I am targeting the functions that are ready to develop (Eun, 2019, p. 23). As I explain the process of developing a comprehensive reflection that maximises their growth potential, I do so by moving from the foundation of factual events to observations, then to the FOI model of inquiry as I explained above, but as I demonstrate the model in practice, I offer models that move from the complex to the basic. This mimics the inside-out/outside-in dialogue that actors in training are accustomed to and provides a model that demonstrates how accessible the aspirational version can be. I begin with the most fully realised version of the model to demonstrate what students should aim for to maximise potential reflection capabilities. This allows students to observe the fully developed reflection and, subsequently, to see how it is pared back to its more basic elements.

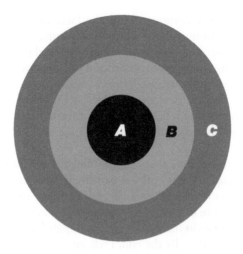

Figure 3.3 Writing target.

Drawing on Neville Hatton and David Smith, Moon identifies that student reflection can be 'superficial and little more than descriptive', and that it may be difficult to get students to reflect with greater depth (2001, p. 10). I offer students a model of what in-depth reflection looks like. I provide a transparent means to achieve it, and I offer students the opportunity to assess for themselves how complex their written reflection is. In doing so, I hope to invite new ways for students to engage while simultaneously dispelling the feelings of vulnerability that students may feel when reflection is compulsory (Hatton & Smith, 1995, p. 37; Wildman & Niles, 1987).

Assessment is an important component of my teaching because I am situated within a university. Once I identify the *Facts > Observations > Inquiry* model, I assign grade levels or assessment ranges to each corresponding point: A, B, and C.[9] I articulate what distinguishes each grade level from another, so the expectations are clear. I often use the model of a bullseye and ask students to visualise writing to the 'target', as illustrated in Figure 3.3. I provide very rudimentary examples of what each level of reflection looks like. This helps to model the distinctions between the levels and helps students prepare to remove their 'training wheels'. This model also keeps student reflections focused on the work and their relationship to it by minimising more general, personal observations that are unrelated to the training or a student's engagement with it.

'A' **Reflections** will address and consider the student's relationship to the subject critically. These reflections indicate the student's degree of understanding of their own function within the practical explorations. As a result, a reflection at this level serves as a record of the student's progress and growth and identifies any challenges the student is facing, as well as how the student aims to address the issue (where applicable).

'A' **Reflection Example**

'As we explored _____, I noticed that I felt _____. Normally, I would expect to react by _____. I'm not sure where this response is coming from – is this just a new thing? Or, have I begun to make the connection between _____ and _____? And, if so, what does that mean? I thought I had already addressed this earlier in the semester, but now I see that I've only scratched the surface and this will be more of an ongoing process that I need to adjust to. I even notice this creeping up in other classes.'

'B' Reflections provide some insight into the student's process but do not cover the subject matter with enough depth so that the student can better understand their own habitual tendencies, and thereby miss the opportunity to improve on those habits.

'B' Reflection Example

'When we did _____ I noticed I was hoping that I wouldn't be picked.'

(There is no further elaboration to understand *why* they felt this way – which would lead to greater self-awareness and growth.)

'C' Reflections provide a record of what was covered but do not consider the student's personal experience of the work in class.

'C' Reflection Example

'We played _____. It was fun.'

(Provides no information about what the student learned or what the exercise aimed to do.)

I then ask students to 'write to the grade': which level do they aim to reach? Because the reflection scaffolding is transparent, students can assess for themselves how deeply they are reflecting on the event, how to improve their reflexive capabilities and, as a result, their grades.

I urge students to consider these guiding questions to tap into their 'FOI':

- What happened? (FACTS)
- How did it happen? (OBSERVATIONS)
- What do I think about what happened and how it happened? (INQUIRY)

I flatten the hierarchy in the studio even further by asking the students to grade their own reflections. I always reserve the right to override their self-assessed grades, but I ask them to use the *FOI* template as a rubric for assessing the grades that they have earned. In doing so, I ask them to engage in meta-reflection, to reflect on their reflections. Have they included all three levels of reflection? If so, the grade is apparent, and we will agree that they have earned the 'A'. If not, it is possible for them to go deeper and expand on what was originally written. Or they may realise that this level is all they are able to contribute to a reflection at a given time, and they are satisfied submitting it for a 'B' or 'C' grade. That is also perfectly fine because they have the agency to act further or not, which is still a form of taking action, but *they* are responsible for overseeing that process. I stress to them that there is no value judgement if they don't achieve all three levels of reflection. I acknowledge that some days, and some reflections, are just like that. What it eliminates, however, is the notion that the instructor 'gives' grades. As a community, we agree that these guidelines are the parameters for reflection, which also means that students cannot write a 'C' level reflection, label it an 'A' and then transfer the responsibility to the instructor to dispute their point.

By relocating the responsibility of assessment to the student, I am dismantling the power differential between professor and student, which helps to encourage students to interrogate other systems, beliefs, expectations, and even potential biases they may have.

In the beginning, creating the pathways for reflection can be self-conscious, but like many skills, with practice, it can become effortless and second nature. Our focus becomes the message we aim to communicate, not how our thoughts are scribed. The same is true of reflection: with guidance, our students can learn how to consider the relationship between themselves and their body instrument, and, even further, practice expanding the art of how they think. This begins the next phase of Vygotsky's ZPD cycle.

Conclusion

Although this chapter is not necessarily a piece of reflective writing, it follows the FOI model. I began the chapter with a statement of facts: reflection is valuable to learning. Next, we moved to observation: certain theories of reflexive practice align with actor training. Finally, we examined the inquiry: how can we intentionally create a model for reflexive writing that encourages optimal learning in the acting studio?

Since developing this method, I have observed that students' reflections have deeper, more complex foci and illuminate a greater understanding of the training. Students' attitudes towards their assessments have improved; grade contestation rarely occurs, and when it does, we have a clear framework to refer to – it becomes a teachable moment where student agency is re-established, and responsibility is confirmed. I have also noticed that students recognise my investment in their learning beyond the training module at hand. I lend my expertise so that students leave my studio with skills that are applicable far beyond the learning outcomes of the course. It is rewarding for them and me.

I am now adapting the FOI model for use with my third year undergraduate Advanced Acting students learning Shakespeare. Fluency in the FOI model has helped me design reflective assignments with greater clarity; I use the structure to promote scaffolded instruction that aligns with a three-tiered level of inquiry. It has also allowed me to interrogate potential work for equitable practices as I can now assess whether the outcomes that I expect have inherent bias. I ask myself: can students apply this framework from their own lived experience? Does the assignment hold space for their agency? Does it help them learn beyond the specific exercise or module to consider their own lived experience more fully?

As is the case with ZPD learning, I hope that by lending this model of systems thinking to you, you may not only borrow the specific FOI system for student reflections but also take on the role of expert by transforming it further to meet your own needs. When you do, I hope that the cycle inverts so I may borrow your expertise as I continue to grow.

Notes

1 The Action Research Model (ARM) is attributed to Kurt Lewin, a social scientist, in the early half of the 1940s. It has been adopted and adapted to meet the needs of many groups, so much so that Lewin is not always credited for the model. For an overview of Lewin's work, 50 years after its inception, see 'Action Research: Rethinking Lewin' (Dickens & Watkins, 1999).

2 While Cowan identifies the Kolb cycle as experience > reflection > generalisation > active experimentation; Kolb's work identifies the cycle as concrete experience > reflective observation > abstract conceptualisation > active experimentation (in Svinicki & Dixon, 1987). I am choosing to use Cowan's terms in order to highlight the distinction between Kolb's cycle (1984) and Cowan's (2006).

3 I explore this example in greater detail in 'On the Page: A Practical Guide to Writing About Practice' (Pye, 2018).

4 Bachelor of Fine Arts degree; akin to a BA Honors degree in the United Kingdom.

5 This course (Intermediate Acting I and Intermediate Acting II) is a two-semester trajectory that begins with the 'classic' American theatrical canon beginning with the mid-twentieth century in the first term, followed by an exploration of naturalism and realism, predominately the work of Anton Chekhov and Henrik Ibsen.

6 Each prompt can interface with the three-part reflection model so that once students understand the process for examining a moment of practice, the aspects to be examined can change and progress according to the trajectory of the training system.
7 I will use the exercise 'Connecting Breath' as a model for this type of reflection and the various levels of engagement (Pye, 2017, pp. 106–109).
8 Please be sure to offer students the option to approximate eye contact, for those students who are neurodivergent or find it difficult to make eye contact with others.
9 In higher education in the United States, there is a 4.0 numeric scale that corresponds to letter grades: A (4.0/4.0), B (3.0/4.0), C (2.0/4.0), which descends to a letter grade of F, or an earned 0 out of 4.0. This grade range can be amended to suit the grading scale at your institution, with the idea that you are moving from the highest achievable level, which may be 'distinction' or 'mastery', to 'proficient' or 'consistent' as a high mid-level point that corresponds to consistently strong work, and finally a 'developing' level that recognises that work was accomplished, but it was not of a complex nature.

References

Berdayes, V., Esposito, L., & Murphy, W. J. (2004). Introduction. In V. Berdayes, L. Esposito, & W. J. Murphy (Eds.), *The body in human enquiry* (pp. 1–20). Hampton Press.
Bolton, G. (2014). *Reflective practice: Writing and professional development* (4th ed.). Sage Publications.
Carnicke, S. M. (2009). *Stanislavsky in focus: An acting master for the twenty-first century* (2nd ed.). Routledge, Taylor and Francis Group.
Chekhov, M. (1991). *On the technique of acting*. Harper Perennial.
Cowan, J. (2006). *On becoming an innovative university teacher: Reflection in action* (2nd ed.) Open University Press.
Dickens, L., & Watkins, K. (1999). Action research: Rethinking Lewin. *Management Learning, 30*(2), 127–140. https://doi.org/10.1177/1350507699302002
Eun, B. (2019). The zone of proximal development as an overarching concept: A framework for synthesizing Vygotsky's theories. *Educational Philosophy and Theory, 51*(1), 18–30. https://doi.org/1 0.1080/00131857.2017.1421941.
Fogel, A. (2009). *The psychophysiology of self-awareness*. Norton.
Grady, S. (1996). Toward the practice of theory in practice. In P. Taylor (Ed.), *Researching drama and arts education: Paradigms and possibilities*. Routledge, Taylor and Francis Group.
Hatton, N., & Smith, D. (1995). Reflection in teacher education: Towards definition and implementation. *Teaching and Teacher Education, 11*(1), 33–49. https://doi.org/10.1016/0742-051X(94)00012-U
Hodge, A. (2012). *Twentieth-century actor training*. Routledge, Taylor and Francis Group.
Kapsali, M. (2014). Psychophysical disciplines and the development of reflexivity. *Theatre, Dance and Performance Training, 5*(2), 157–168. https://doi.org/10.1080/19443927.2014.914968
Kolb, D. A. (1984). *Experiential learning: Experience as the source of learning and development*. Prentice-Hall, Inc.
Krasner, D. (2012). Strasberg, Adler and Meisner: Method acting. In A. Hodge (Ed.), *Twentieth-century actor training* (pp. 147–168). Routledge, Taylor and Francis Group.
Larrivee, B. (2000). Transforming teacher practice: Becoming the critically reflective teacher. *Reflective Practice, 1*(3). 293–307.
Martinez, M. E. (2006). What is metacognition? *Phi Delta Kappan, 87*(9), 696–699. https://doi. org/10.1177/003172170608700916
Meisner, S., & Longwell, D. (1987). *Sanford Meisner on acting*. Vintage.
Moon, J. (2001). PDP working paper 4: Reflection in higher education learning. *Higher Education Academy*, 1–25.
Nelson, R. (2013). *Practice as research in the arts: Principles, protocols, pedagogies, resistances*. Palgrave Macmillan.
Pears, D. (1971). *What is knowledge?* Allen & Unwin.
Pye, V. C. (2017). *Unearthing Shakespeare: Embodied performance and the globe*. Routledge, Taylor and Francis Group.

Pye, V. C. (2018). On the page: A practical guide to writing about practice. *Methods: A Journal of Acting Pedagogy, 4*, 13–32.

Ryan, A., & Murphy, C. (2018). Reflexive practice and transformational learning. In A. Ryan & T. Walsh (Eds.), *Reflexivity and critical pedagogy*. Brill.

Ryan, A., & Walsh, T. (Eds.). (2018). *Reflexivity and critical pedagogy*. Brill.

Schön, D. (1983). *The reflective practitioner*. Basic Books.

Schön, D. (1991). *Educating the reflective practitioner: Toward a new design for teaching and learning in the professions*. Jossey-Bass Inc., Publishers.

Smith, E. (2011). Teaching critical reflection. *Teaching in Higher Education, 16*(2). 211–223. https://doi.org/10.1080/13562517.2010.515022

Svinicki, M. D., & Dixon, N. M. (1987). The Kolb model modified for classroom activities. *College Teaching, 35*(4), 141–146. https://doi.org/10.1080/87567555.1987.9925469

Thompson, N., & Pascal, J. (2012). Developing critically reflective practice. *Reflective Practice, 13*(2), 311–325. https://doi.org/10.1080/14623943.2012.657795

Wildman, T. M., & Niles, J. A. (1987). Reflective teachers: Tensions between abstractions and realities. *Journal of Teacher Education, 38*(4), 25–31. https://doi.org/10.1177/002248718703800405

Wlodarsky, R. (2014). *Reflection and the college teacher: A solution for higher education*. Information Age Publishing.

Zarilli, P. B. (2002). *Acting (re)considered: A theoretical and practical guide* (2nd ed.). Routledge, Taylor and Francis Group.

4 Critiquing from the Centre

Challenging Breath Pedagogies within Dominant British-centric Voice Training

Denis Cryer-Lennon

Introduction

Critiquing from the centre in this research relates to the idea that when a student is in training, they are central to the processes and practices they are asked to explore. The 'centre' can cover disparate factors in voice training, performance, and theory on critical pedagogy and practice. However, this chapter's primary notion of 'centre' relates to the student's intersectional positionality in the training and performance. I utilise Kimberlé Crenshaw's concept of intersectionality, which emphasises the need to consider the interconnected nature of social identities and systems of power when addressing issues of social justice (2017, p. 1) towards more inclusive breath pedagogies within actor training. This research advocates Crenshaw's position of recognising that individuals can experience multiple forms of discrimination and oppression simultaneously due to the intersections of their various social identities concerning race, gender, class, sexuality, and ability.

I hope to challenge breath pedagogies within dominant British-centric voice training of the twentieth and twenty-first centuries. I develop more inclusive practices by inviting students of various social identities to explore a breath pedagogy for speaking Shakespeare. Much of my voice training is in the lineage of who Sarah Werner describes as the 'holy trinity' of voice training (Werner, 1996, p. 249): Cicely Berry, Kristin Linklater, and Patsy Rodenburg. Taking heed of Werner's sentiment, it is a fair characterisation to say that these practitioners, through their training, teaching, and writing, represent large factions of dominant British-centric voice training ideas of the twentieth and twenty-first centuries. All three of these practitioners advocate a process of unlearning 'habits' to achieve a 'natural' voice, and much of this work begins with breath training. This chapter explores an alternative proposition, inviting students to embrace their habits when they engage their breath when speaking Shakespeare.

When liberatory pedagogic principles are applied to breath training, whereby students can critique what they are being asked to explore through an awareness and exploration of their breath, the training can be more inclusive of students. Instead of trying to 'free' the student's breath and voice from the patterns they come with, this chapter proposes that we embrace this embodied experience as part of their individuality and markers of their multiple and intersecting identities. This, in turn, makes space for breath that is, for example, interrupted or extended, shallow or deep, fast or slow – not in tandem with traditional notions of 'proper' breathing (Martin, 1991, p. 37) and therefore inclusive of the bodies that house a diverse range of breath dynamics. This can enrich performance-making by having a breath filtered through students' embodied experience rather than stripping away 'learned habits'.

DOI: 10.4324/9781003393672-6

My contention with 'unlearning habits' is that there is a risk of stripping the student of their embodied experience, working towards a blank canvas or empty vessel, and losing the student's sense of self and uniqueness. Instead, I argue for a more inclusive approach that puts the student at the centre of the process, thereby ensuring that all aspects of training and performance are filtered through the students' wants, needs, and desires, as well as their embodied experience.

The principles set out within theories of critical pedagogy (Paulo Freire) resonate with student-centred actor training, which prioritises the needs, interests, and goals of the student. This chapter explores how the adaptation of dominant voice pedagogies can prompt *conscientização*, which involves critical awareness and critical praxis (Freire, 2021, p. 15) and invites self-awareness, self-determination, and self-direction. This echoes hooks's idea of self-actualisation through self-reflection (2017, p. 1).

Reminding ourselves of Freire's *conscientização* as 'refer[ring] to learning to perceive social, political, and economic contradictions, and to take action against the oppressive elements of reality' (Freire, 1972, p. 15), an important step to make this experience of *conscientização* complete is through self-awareness of personal experiences (Lake & Dagostino, 2013, p. 105). That is, it does not limit the idea of 'habit' to automatic bodily functions, such as breathing, but embraces a holistic assessment of how such patterns have been part of the culture and personal history of the student, which they can bring to training and performance.

For example, I found word association and linking the student's breath to denote characters' thinking increased students' access to and understanding of their self-awareness of their knowledge and experience and their breathing and understanding of Shakespeare.

Starting from this context as a pedagogue and researcher, this chapter centres its interrogation primarily on activity carried out within a workshop series I led entitled 'A Breath Pedagogy for Speaking Shakespeare' with theatre and drama students at the University of South Wales from October 2018 to February 2019. There were one postgraduate and nine undergraduate drama students in the group, with seven attending every session voluntarily. While not in the original design of the research, the workshop resembled participatory action research (PAR), which conceptually aligns with Freire's *conscientização* in its requirement to foster heightened awareness among its participants by encouraging reflection and to actively contribute to the development of new political, social, and economic frameworks. I also use PAR to denote the collaborative nature of the workshops in generating data and perspectives on pedagogical practice. In PAR, the students are engaged as co-researchers, and their voices are instrumental in shaping the research outcomes (Savin-Baden & Major, 2013, p. 245). Observations were collected via video recording, researcher field notes and reflective diary, and a semi-structured focus group reflecting on the series.

The pedagogy proposed here uses a series of moments, referred to as 'critical moments'. These 'moments' take on some characteristics of the similarly named 'critical incidents' used in education research, where they signify events or situations that can shape or transform educational practices, policies, or theories (Tripp, 2012, p. 68). The move from incidents to moments here emphasises the transient nature of breath and training awareness – an exploration of breath and the constant renewal of the context in which it sits.

Here, I detail the formulation of three moments: *Critical Moment #1: self-awareness; Critical Moment #2: self-determination and self-direction; Critical Moment #3: pedagogical intervention.* Each of these is grounded in critical pedagogy and explored in the context of the workshop series.

Breath, Politics, and Performance

The language used about breath is often political. The metaphorical language used within breath work, usually in the context of voice training, reinforces textual signifiers of 'power' or 'force'. Furthermore, 'breathlessness' and 'catching one's breath' seem to sit in a hierarchy regarding physiological efficiency at first glance. When we relate physiology to health, we sometimes tread overtly political terrain (Harrison & McDonald, 2008; Davies, 2012).

References and inferences to how breath might be political can be found in voice manuals. In *The Right to Speak*, Patsy Rodenburg starts her discussion of the politics of speaking and voice about breath, noting that 'we all breathe, and the majority of us speak' (2015, p. 1). Here, breath takes on an egalitarian quality, as echoed in many books/chapters on breath, that cannot always be afforded to voice. Yet tensions within the body can also trap the breath – tensions fostered over a lifetime of interacting in a demanding, fast-paced world. The 'freeing' of the breath is a common theme within voice practice and is most notably accounted for in Linklater's *Freeing the Natural Voice* (2006). She writes:

> To enter and live the life of a different character, one must be able to let go of deeply ingrained breathing patterns and temporarily allow new behaviour from the psyche of the character one is playing to govern the breathing musculature.
>
> (Linklater, 2006, p. 43)

The language here of 'govern' and allowing new behaviours to be controlled by character politicises breath in its relationship to the body and voice. There are implied power dynamics to tension being held in the body and in breath being used as a catalyst to free the body of tension. Sarah Werner addresses the power dynamics created by a 'freeing' of the voice, arguing that 'the naturalisation in voice training of the dramaturgical strategies of the playwright (by insisting that an actor finds the character by breathing like him or her) determines what sorts of performances actors can create' (Werner, 1997, p. 183).

Jane Boston and Rena Cook's collection of essays about the practice of breath training as it relates to live performance, *Breath in Action* (2009), is an instrumental source in locating the politics of breath. Written from various perspectives of vocal and holistic practice, the edition gives a foundation of theory and practice relating to breath as it pertains to training the voice and the idea of breathing 'better' in everyday life.

Alongside Sreenath Nair (2007), Boston identified breath as an under-researched area in the context of actor training. Subsequent research has strengthened that foundation. Examples include philosophical perspectives on air (from the body) and our communal environment (Sloterdijk et al., 2009), control of air (Connor, 2010), and air as it relates to nature and culture (Adey, 2014). Breath is also examined concerning various media, such as cinema (Quinlivan, 2014) and literature (Heine, 2021). Work has also been done to analyse breath within critical race studies (Braun, 2021) and feminist studies (Cavarero, 2002; Irigaray, 1999; Górska, 2016). Of relevance to this study is Sarah Weston's work assessing Linklater and Rodenburg from a feminist perspective. In her work with young women across the north of England, Weston 'explore[s] the connection between engaging in voice training and the young women's conception of their political voice', including breath (Weston, 2019, p. 37). In her PhD thesis, Weston locates an intersection where voice, breath, body, text, performance, and individual 'uniqueness' are brought to the fore (2018, p. 30); this precise intersection is a useful departure point for a critical pedagogy to emerge about breath and speaking Shakespeare.

A Conceptual Framework Bringing Freire's Participation and *Conscientização* to Voice Training for Actors

'Unlearning' within voice pedagogy, whereby students or actors are encouraged to strip away 'habits' and 'conditioning' that are said to restrict 'their' voice and physical expression, proposed by Berry, Linklater, and Rodenburg, not only risks laying the ground for the management and manipulation of such voices but also hinders the notion of dialogue with the student.

Freire describes some features of dehumanisation and why it should not be seen as merely historical:

> Dehumanisation, which marks not only those whose humanity has been stolen, but also (though in a different way) those who have stolen it, is a distortion of the vocation of becoming more fully human. This distortion occurs within history, but it is not a historical vocation. Indeed, to accept dehumanisation as a historical vocation would lead to cynicism or total despair.
>
> (Freire, 1972, pp. 20, 21)

Dehumanisation manifests in the context of respect to the British voice training traditions and the veneration of the move from the 'voice beautiful' tradition to focus on individual student actors that occurred in the mid-twentieth century, which leads to a lack of questioning of those traditions. However, as Tara McAllister-Viel argues, further decolonisation is required to help students develop a more inclusive and comprehensive understanding of vocal technique and expression (McAllister-Viel, 2022, pp. 188, 189).

This research contends that 'unlearning' risks the dehumanisation of the student and the objective is to shape the expressive means the student comes to training with and replace with predisposed standards concerning what voice and breath are acceptable for acting. Furthermore, without utilising strategies from liberatory pedagogies, such as realisation and fostering of *conscientização*, within the actor training studio, we run the risk of merely providing bank learning, where students unquestioningly accept what the teacher imparts, reproducing oppressive structures (Freire, 1972, p. 21). In other words, if the student is not aware of the process and consequence of unlearning habits which potentially reduces their embodied attributes and experience, they risk losing agency and autonomy within their training and performance.

As teachers or trainers, we risk not having to explain our positions and arguments in full. This is not to suggest students are sole judges of 'good' training and teaching practices; instead, through *conscientização* within the training studio, the teacher can begin to gauge whether the student understands the theories or practices as open for discussion. This should also extend to the material in an actor training studio, including Shakespeare's text. The teacher should explain why students are asked to engage in this material and how it can benefit, and this decision should be open to scrutiny of those being asked to engage with it.

To test the hypothesis that participation and *conscientização* can move towards a more liberatory and democratic pedagogic space within actor training, I designed a workshop series where methods within dominant voice pedagogies were tested, enabling students to explore their breath more freely. For this, we critically examined and explored Shakespeare's text.

I took a cue from the editors of the *Handbook of Metacognition in Education* (2009) when they reflected on their earlier book, *Metacognition in Education Theory and Practice*

(1998). Throughout the text, the concept of agency highlights that successful students can take control of their learning. Taking control requires students to be conscious of their learning process, assess their learning needs, strategise to meet those needs, and implement those strategies.

Both my and the students' observations were collected using video recording, a reflective diary by the researcher, and focus groups reflecting on the workshop series to assess successes and failures and shape new pedagogy or pedagogical principles.

Workshop Design: Introducing Participation and *Conscientização* to 'A Breath Pedagogy for Speaking Shakespeare'

In this section, I reflect on my analysis of workshop material through Freire's notions of participation and *conscientização*, working on the basis that the successful fostering of the latter can move towards the former. The problem being addressed is the lack of agency and autonomy, and therefore not full participation, for the student within traditions of breath training that favour 'unlearning habits' as a process towards vocal expression.

Here, I first focus on the initial workshop, where I introduced the principles of my pedagogy to the participants, including the primacy of criticality. To aid a dialogic mode, I made it clear to the participants at this early stage that their thoughts, feelings, and impressions were legitimate and important to the pedagogy, the research project, and their learning. Having received their consent for the workshop to be video-recorded and their experiences to be documented, we discussed the nature of research as a process of investigation and the place of documentation within this process, which I made clear they could review at any time upon request.

I first asked the participants to introduce themselves, asking if they would like to share their career goals with the cohort and why they decided to participate in the workshop series. As well as being resonant with bell hooks' writing on self-actualisation (2017, p. 1), this is in line with the principles of pedagogy, outlined in the introductory chapter of my doctoral thesis, where I advocate a pedagogy where the student is at the centre (Cryer-Lennon, 2022). This is useful for making connections between the work we do within workshops and the student's aspirations and goals.

A similar rationale lay behind incorporating a word association exercise for 'Breath/ing' and 'Shakespeare'. What follows is an analysis of this exercise and reflection on how this led to a *conscientização* for the student relating to their existing knowledge and experience, as well as being exposed to others' knowledge and experience.

Analysis of Workshop – Word Association of 'Breath/ing' and 'Shakespeare': Critical Moment #1 Self-awareness

The workshop was designed around a key exercise that explored the critical possibilities of word association. The working hypothesis of the exercise was to utilise word association with keywords of breathing and Shakespeare. Within a group dynamic, the exercise was expected to lead to an awareness and understanding of the student's own knowledge of these subjects and to establish connections with other participants' knowledge and experience relating to breathing and Shakespeare.

It was only when I started teaching voice through the practice of 'unlearning' habits, as advocated in my training, that I found there could be an issue with suppressing something of the 'inner' self of the actor or student. In one class, when we were using Shakespeare's sonnets to explore central tenets of Kristin Linklater's voice practice, a student, originally from Poland but living in Britain since childhood, said that the process of 'unlearning' made her feel as though she was abandoning a part of herself and her Polish heritage. She explained that the closer she got to how she thought she was supposed to be speaking Shakespeare, the further she got from her voice. She was particularly surprised how the breath work challenged her sense of self. She said: 'The rhythm is not *my* rhythm' (Student A, 2014). This led me to consider how to adapt my voice teaching practice to ensure students did not feel they were losing or compromising their sense of self, culture, or heritage.

The learning aims and objectives of this exercise included the students gaining an awareness of what the concepts of 'breathing' and 'Shakespeare' meant to them, encouraging the development of their initial thoughts into more fully formed expressions through discussion. In addition, an aim was for the students to start making connections between their observations and that of others and explore any contradictions that surfaced.

The participants were asked to write or draw their associations with the words 'Breathing' and 'Shakespeare' on post-it notes and then stick them to the corresponding 'Breathing Board' or 'Bard Board'. After the participants had written or drawn their responses, they posted them on the board. Discussion was then facilitated, asking the students to speak to each other's observations alongside my responses, as pedagogue/facilitator, to the contributions via post-its.

The language used by participants in relation to breath was a mix of technical, symbolic, figurative, and philosophical and some responses leaned towards the physiological breathing apparatus. There were also connections made between breath and voice. Second language students' observations included thinking about the 'universality' of breath and how it transcends language. Terms used included the following: 'lungs', 'mouth', 'nose'; 'diaphragm', 'centre'; 'voice'; 'pace'; 'rhythm'; 'life flow', 'panic attack'; 'expression'; 'singing'; 'deep breath'; 'movement'; 'frustration and exhaustion'; 'essence'; 'projection'; 'windpipe'; 'air'; 'calm'; 'control'; 'soul'; 'sunshine and rainbows'; and 'universality' (Various Participants, 2019).

In relation to Shakespeare, words and phrases posted by students included 'Overrated'; 'Uncomparable' (sic); 'Important'; 'poet'; 'genius'; 'classics'; 'cannot be compromised'; 'The Globe'; 'misunderstood (today)'; 'hierarchical – exclusive'; 'immortal'; 'written to be performed'; 'not taught correctly in schools'; 'done badly quite often'; and 'confusing' (Various Participants, 2019).

There was also a lot of commentary about how Shakespeare is understood and taught in schools today. Among the students who felt confused by the language within Shakespeare's text at times, the majority spoke English as a second language. One student expressed that they felt that the Shakespeare canon was important in the context of world literature.

From the language utilised within a reflective discussion at the end of the session, there was a sense that most of the cohort was more proficient in their terminology around breath/ing than Shakespeare. When speaking about breath/ing, they readily spoke of it about voice, especially in technical and physiological terms. Some participants spoke in metaphorical language about breath and breathing. For example, one participant referenced Cicely Berry's idea of taking the breath down to the centre for stability. Others described their experience of taking part in a voice class. When discussing their experience of Shakespeare, the group generally reflected on their work through the lens of popular culture and intertextuality. Examples included an episode of the time-travelled themed sci-fi TV show *Doctor Who* (Davies, 2007), in which William Shakespeare appears as a character, and the teen romantic comedy *10 Things I Hate About You* (Junger, 1999).

There was a consensus that the work held importance in a literature context. The words and phrases often reflected commentary on the status of Shakespeare as if the work was very far removed from their experience in education or life in general. In contrast, when discussing breath and breathing, there was an easier route to their responses, which was to do with embodied experience.

The word association exercises yielded significant information on the participants' intellectual relationship with breath/ing and Shakespeare. It revealed access points used by cohort members for both concepts in a relaxed setting, which led to fruitful discussions of both topics. At the end of the workshop series, I asked the students to reflect on the word association exercises and what effect they felt that exercise had on the proceeding work. One participant commented:

> I felt after that session that my breath was mine, it might sound silly, but sometimes, when I have performed, I felt as though my breath wasn't mine. It's like it belonged to the text or author or something like that. Like I had to abide by rules that I didn't make up.
>
> (Participant A, 2019)

Similarly, another participant testified:

> I didn't know how much I knew about my body, and I felt like with the word association, and the reflective [discussion], but at the end especially, I was able to get to that . . . knowledge I suppose, through breath. Or at least talking about breath – if that makes sense.
>
> (Participant B, 2019)

The above testimonies indicate an awareness of breath post-exercise, and a perceived power shift from a participant's reclamation of their breath in training and performance. Such increased awareness of their breath echoes Freire's *conscientização* as learning 'to perceive social [and] political . . . contradictions, and to take action against the oppressive elements of reality' (Freire, 1972, p. 15). The contradictions and consequential tension lay in the perceived control the text had over the breath of the participant. Post-exercise, the participant is armed with a strategy to explore and mitigate against this control should they wish to.

In using the word association exercises, I have found it beneficial as a pedagogical device on several counts. These include generating personal reference points to the students, which brought repetition of words, phrases, and themes. This, in turn, led to connections from one individual's experience to another within the discussion section of the exercise. It gave the sense of the cohort being a melting pot of ideas, fostering a collaborative mode and legitimising students' thinking in relation to what 'breathing' and 'Shakespeare' means. It often led to students having more confidence in their ideas within the context of the class. It also worked as a self-generating pedagogy. By offering a sense of the student's knowledge base around the key concepts, the students were engaged cognitively and displayed an active mode of pedagogy. Most importantly, the use of free word association invited the students to indicate anxieties and prejudices about breathing and Shakespeare and have these addressed during actor training. Such raising of their self-awareness about their knowledge and experience facilitated confidence in what each student had to offer, fostering an individualised place from which to start work.

Analysis of Workshop – 'My Thought, My Breath': Critical Moment #2
Self-determination and Self-direction

Using Kate's monologue in Shakespeare's *The Taming of the Shrew* (Act 5, Scene 2 in First Folio, 2004a/1623), this workshop was centred around the 'one thought/one breath' exercise. The working hypothesis for the exercise was to facilitate an awareness that there is no right or wrong rhythm in Shakespeare, inviting individuals to take account of their embodied experience and make variant decisions that resonate with their acting choices through the exploration of their breath. This strengthens the level of participation, as Freire advocates, for the students, allowing their embodied histories to be part of the training and performance of Shakespeare's text. This challenges the notion of 'a proper way' to deliver a line often prescribed within voice training traditions used in British conservatoires (Stamatiou, 2023, p. 70).

During my voice training, I got interested in Cicely Berry's work on text. I trained in Dublin with Helena Walsh, who is a certified Roy Hart-Certified voice teacher and an associate teacher of Fitzmaurice Voicework at The Royal Central School of Speech and Drama. I enjoyed using punctuation in Shakespeare's text to signpost my breath rhythm and it helped me understand the character I was playing. However, when I started teaching voice, students challenged the punctuation within the text because it impacted the breath rhythm and speech patterns. It was only when I suggested doing away with the punctuation altogether, thinking the experiment would fail, that I started to understand how a student/actor coming to a text with their own breath rhythm could lead to a varied performance of the text. In other words, the predetermined and uninterfered-with breath rhythm as applied to speaking Shakespeare took on new possibilities in performance. Here, I explore how this works in practice.

While I reference the experience and responses of a few participants, the focus here is on a specific participant, referred to as 'Participant C'.

Simon Reeves, an acting teacher and former Head of Voice at the Royal Welsh College of Music and Drama, has suggested that a 'loose' rule of thumb when speaking classical or heightened text is that 'notionally . . . a breath equals a thought' (Cryer-Lennon, 2022, p. 307), which alludes to the actioning technique of the actor creating a subtext for the text (Moseley, 2016). This idea was presented to the participants primarily as an experiment that may lead to a discovery about the text they are working on, their potential performance of a text, and their thinking about breathing and speaking Shakespeare. I hoped that such an exercise would initiate a process of exploration and discovery instead of merely focusing on the final performance.

The participants were asked to read Kate's monologue at the end of *The Taming of the Shrew* (Act 5, Scene 2 in First Folio, 1623/2004) to themselves before pairing up to examine a section of the monologue. Each pairing had a different third of the monologue to explore. I asked the participants to identify and discuss where they felt the thoughts began and ended in the text. They did not have to agree with their partner, but only to discuss and make notes on their printouts, indicating where they felt the thoughts lay.

We then came back into a circle, and each pair performed their respective monologue sections together. Two pairs matched each other in pace and rhythm, but one did not. Evident from this reading was that most participants broke the thoughts down, either by using the sentence structure or following the punctuation. However, this changed when one participant, whom I call Participant C for anonymity purposes, exclaimed within the discussion after the performance that she felt the whole speech was a single thought. After I encouraged her to explore how this might manifest in terms of performance, the other participants began to re-evaluate how they approached the text. They were then asked to return to their pairs to apply the one thought/one breath rule using the thought structure they had just developed. Within their pairings, one participant would perform the text followed by discussion and feedback from their partner.

We then returned to the circle to see if any of the performances changed when performing independently, rather than in pairs, and applying the one thought/one breath rule. The individual performances manifested speech patterns of variant styles, such as stream of consciousness, testimony, and recital. Participant C struggled initially to apply the one thought/ one breath rule and feared that she would run out of breath mid-thought. I encouraged her to focus on what effect it would have on the meaning and intention of the text. In the resultant performance, Participant C ran out of breath as she feared but then took an audible inhale and continued to 'run through the thought', a comment she made after the performance (Participant C, 2019). Once she had performed the text, the feedback from the group was that they now heard the speech as a resistance to the literal meaning of the content and as such, a resistance to the character's imprisoned situation. In contrast, when her partner performed the same section applying a different thought structure and using the same rule of one thought/one breath, the group agreed that the meaning sounded like a much more emotional cry for help.

In the discussion afterwards, one of the participants expressed that they felt liberated in the shift from obeying a rhythm. Instead of feeling dictated by the punctuation and structure of the text, they could develop their individual performance rhythm by tapping into individual breath patterns. Another observation was that they were surprised by how the 'consideration of thought and breath in approaching Shakespeare's text could have such an effect on the meaning' (Participant D, 2019), particularly when they did not change the words. This also highlighted for one of the participants 'how the punctuation in a text controlled the thought structure and breath rhythm within a performance' (Participant D, 2019). I took this opportunity to ask the participants how comfortable they felt with challenging punctuation within a text. Some found this an easy process, and others noted that they initially found it jarring to go against the rhythm they felt was already set out in the text. However, they found it helpful to examine how it might be explored through the breath–thought correlation and that they found connections that they had not before.

From the beginning of the workshop series, Participant C expressed that she was 'not a fan of Shakespeare', although it was evident that her knowledge of his plays and text was more significant than most of the rest of the cohort. Her testimony after the workshop that the application of '*my* thought, *my* breath' rule made her feel more 'on board with the performance' (Participant C, 2019) and she felt it was a positive experience in choosing where the thoughts lay and giving voice to those thoughts. As the pedagogical framework shifted from text or author-based to a student-centred approach via prioritising individualised patterns of breath and thought, the student's experience of Shakespeare training improved.

The exciting thing here is not just that she began to engage more with the work via breath. Rather, it was the appetite for self-determination and self-direction in approaching Shakespeare's text, accessed by considering breath and thought. This was highlighted in the discussion at the end of the session by Participant C and the rest of the cohort. They agreed that by accessing their breath with their interpretation of the thought processes of the character, their performance became grounded. In the words of one participant, 'the performance felt as though it was theirs' (Participant E, 2019).

The notion of one thought/one breath brought up various challenges for the participants, not least in making decisions about where the thoughts were, and therefore where a breath may be taken, in reading/reciting/speaking of the text. The journey of identifying where the thought and breath were within the text, to the description of feeling as though the performance was theirs, was an essential critical moment within the pedagogy. It indicated that self-determination and self-direction occurred within this specific pedagogical space. By making decisions about whether to subscribe to established authorities or traditional approaches around punctuation, such as Berry's, Linklater's and Rodenburg's, or to take a more liberatory approach, the students felt like they started 'owning the performance'.

Themes such as 'liberation', 'freedom', and 'choice' were the main topics of discussion at the end of this session. One participant stated that 'having the freedom of choice, within this space, in relation to breath, which is already my own – not that it has always felt that way – meant that I could play the part on my terms' (Cryer-Lennon, 2019, p. 76). Another added 'yeah, I feel as though I was in control rather than the text' (ibid). These discoveries made by the participants, and the subsequent group reflection on such, highlighted that the participants were more aware than they had been before about the power dynamics inherent in studio practice and pedagogical spaces. The shift in centrality that followed, from text instructing where to place breath to a student-oriented and directed approach, fulfils, at least in part, the self-determination and self-direction characteristics of Freire's *conscientização*. This is not to imply that students should abandon the idea of technique or of seeking clarity for an audience. Rather it is to negotiate these aspects on their terms without compromising themselves or their embodied experience. For example, if a student's embodied experience means that they struggle to articulate through traditional ideas of vocal production, then within this pedagogy, we would seek another mode of communication that doesn't compromise the positionality of the performer, such as the use of surtitles.

Analysis of Workshop – A Responsive Breath Pedagogy: Critical Moment #3 Pedagogical Intervention

Using the duologue of Helena and Demetrius in Shakespeare's *A Midsummer Night's Dream* (Act 5, Scene 2 First Folio, 2004b/1623), this workshop used participatory action research (PAR) to develop a pedagogical intervention that I call 'A Breath Pedagogy for Speaking Shakespeare'. The working hypothesis of this intervention was that working with the students as co-investigators in the context of a breath pedagogy for speaking Shakespeare shifted established practitioner/trainer-centred practices to a more student-focused model. Similarly to the above section, where Participant C found that freedom from Shakespeare's text, this exercise facilitated freedom from the trainer. Such a pedagogical situation elucidates the role of the trainer in the context of breath training for speaking Shakespeare.

Intervention implies a responsive mode of pedagogy, which requires the trainer to adapt any workshop or lesson plan to react to the events of any given session. This may include dramatic shifts in their plans, moving towards a teaching situation responsive to the contemporaneous context in which they are faced. What follows is a reflection on a critical moment within the workshop series that saw plans needing to change to accommodate the needs of individual students and how the intervention model can help the trainer in an environment where these changes can happen.

In this workshop, the participants were asked to pair up to explore the duologue and each pair were asked to familiarise themselves with the text before performing it for the rest of the group. In one of the pairs, we had a student from Bulgaria and one from Romania, both of whom considered English their second language. Once they had performed for the group, one of the participants reported that she was nervous and, as such felt her breath 'tensed up' in performance. The other expressed that she felt 'breathless' in performing because she did not know the text. While discussing the breath/ing dynamics they had experienced during performing and how the rest of the cohort received the performance, the group examined difficulties in performing. Another participant, also working in her second language, observed that perhaps the challenges they found may be because they were not performing in their first language. We agreed as a cohort that an interesting experiment could be to perform some of the duologue in their respective first languages. They translated and explored the first few stanzas of the duologue in their language to investigate any resultant difference in breathing dynamics.

The participants translated some of the text and performed. While the rest of the cohort, including me, did not speak Bulgarian or Romanian, we used printouts of the English text to subtitle what we were hearing, maintaining approximate sense of what was being said and when. It was immediately apparent a degree of the tension they spoke about in reading the English text had lifted. There was a greater ease, and the breath was carried to the end of the lines. There was a sense of rhythm to the text, which gave shape to each line, making it easier to follow the subtitles, the printed English text we were following. There was also far more colourful and pronounced intonation within the speech. Both participants advised that the translations they were using were structured poetic text in Bulgarian and Romanian, respectively. Asked how it felt to perform in their home language about breath, one participant said there was much more energy in the text and that the breath was more dynamic. Both participants agreed that they felt more confident in their native language, which had a bearing on the 'flow' of breath, with one of the participants stating that 'she felt freer and more grounded with the breath' in her language (Participant E, 2019). Even though initiated by the students, this work aligns with Kristine Landon-Smith's practice of working with one's background to meet the acting challenges a student actor might face (2020).

It was clear that the intervention, by which I mean responding to the contemporaneous pedagogical context, led to a mode of exploration and discovery relating to one's own breath dynamic for speaking Shakespeare and that these discoveries could then be used as a template for achievement in performance. Pedagogical questions can emerge from such an experiment. Similarly to Landon-Smith's explorations, this workshop highlighted the need for more research on how students who train in English as a second language can replicate the desirable aspects of their performance in their native language within an English language performance. In the context of training international students within actor training programmes in British institutions, it is important to explore how the engagement of home languages can facilitate more engaging and fulfiling experiences in Shakespeare training.

Conclusion

This chapter drew on Crenshaw's intersectionality to ground our concept of the centre as the site where the student enters the training environment, to apply Freire-inspired liberatory pedagogic principles to breath training. It argued that, through word association, linking breath to character thinking, and inviting the students to find solutions to their challenges that are beyond what the trainer can contribute or fully understand through a participatory action model of practice, the training can become more inclusive and promote self-awareness, self-determination and self-direction.

In demonstrating alternative methods to 'unlearning habits' for breath training, as promoted by Berry, Linklater, and Rodenburg, this chapter advocates a pedagogic approach that is dialogic at its core. These methods can be used to tackle oppressions within the training studio, such as the fear of Shakespeare, tensions created by adherence to text and punctuation, and anxieties relating to finding breath when speaking in your second language.

The insights from this research support a discussion-based approach where the student is at the centre through an examination of three critical moments denoting characteristics of Freire's *conscientização*. In particular, the word association exercise facilitated self-awareness; the one thought/one breath exploration invited self-determination and self-direction; and the collaboration with the students to address individual student needs put the student at the centre of their learning. Such principles evoked participant testimonies that implied a greater degree of ownership over their breath in training and performance. Furthermore, by utilising the intervention approach within this chapter, the actor trainer can recast themselves as a facilitator who responds to the contemporaneous events within the training studio, extending their role to include responding to the needs, desires, and goals of the individual student. Further research could bring work to investigate more specifically strategies for making the breath training space more inclusive to a diverse scope of abilities.

References

Adey, P. (2014). *Air: Nature and culture*. Reaktion Books.

Boston, J., & Cook, R. (Eds.). (2009). *Breath in Action*. Jessica Kingsley Publishers.

Braun, L. (2021). *Breathing race into the machine*. University of Minnesota Press.

Cavarero, A. (2002). *Stately bodies*. University of Michigan Press.

Connor, S. (2010). *The matter of air*. Reaktion.

Crenshaw, K. (2017). *On intersectionality: Essential writings*. The New Press.

Cryer-Lennon, D. (2019). *Fields notes: Observations on workshop series 'A Breath Pedagogy for Speaking Shakespeare'* [Unpublished manuscript].

Cryer-Lennon, D. (2022). *"Speake, Breathe, Discuss": Towards a critical breath pedagogy for speaking Shakespeare* [Unpublished PhD thesis].

Davies, R. T. (Executive Producer). (2007). *Doctor who: The Shakespeare code*. BBC.

Davies, S. (2012). *Global politics of health*. Polity.

Freire, P. (1972). *Pedagogy of the oppressed*. Penguin Education.

Freire, P. (2021). *Education for critical consciousness*. Bloomsbury Academic.

Górska, M. (2016). *Breathing matters: Feminist intersectional politics of vulnerability*. Linköping University.

Hacker, D., Dunlosky, J., & Graesser, A. (Eds.). (1998). *Metacognition in educational theory and practice*. Routledge.

Hacker, D., Dunlosky, J., & Graesser, A. (Eds.). (2009). *Handbook of metacognition in education*. Routledge.

Harrison, S., & McDonald, R. (2008). *The politics of healthcare in Britain*. SAGE.

Heine, S. (2021). *Poetics of breathing*. State University of New York Press.

Hooks, B. (2017). *Teaching to transgress: Education as the practice of freedom*. Routledge.

Irigaray, L. (1999). *The forgetting of air in Martin Heidegger*. Athlone.

Junger, G. (Director). (1999). *10 things I hate about you* [Film]. Touchstone Pictures.

Lake, R., & Dagostino, V. (2013). Converging self/other awareness. In R. Lake & T. Kress (Eds.), *Paulo Freire's intellectual roots: Toward historicity in praxis*. Bloomsbury Academic.

Landon-Smith, K. (2020). A pedagogy for twenty-first century actor training: Intracultural theatre practice which embraces pluralistic identity and plays with difference. *Theatre, Dance and Performance Training, 11*(3), 343–350.

Linklater, K. (2006). *Freeing the natural voice*. Nick Hern.

Martin, J. (1991). *Voice in modern theatre*. Routledge.

McAllister-Viel, T. (2022). 'Embodied Voice' and inclusivity: Ableism and theatre voice training. In P. Whitfield (Ed.), *Inclusivity and equality in performance training: Teaching and learning for neuro and physical diversity*. Routledge.

Moseley, N. (2016). *Actioning – and how to do it*. Nick Hern Books.

Nair, S. (2007). *Restoration of breath: Consciousness and performance* (Vol. 9). Rodopi.

Participant A. (2019). *Denis Cryer-Lennon's Fields notes: Observations on workshop series 'A Breath Pedagogy for Speaking Shakespeare'* [Unpublished manuscript].

Participant B. (2019). *Denis Cryer-Lennon's Fields notes: Observations on workshop series 'A Breath Pedagogy for Speaking Shakespeare'* [Unpublished manuscript].

Participant C. (2019). *Denis Cryer-Lennon's Fields notes: Observations on workshop series 'A Breath Pedagogy for Speaking Shakespeare'* [Unpublished manuscript].

Participant D. (2019). *Denis Cryer-Lennon's Fields notes: Observations on workshop series 'A Breath Pedagogy for Speaking Shakespeare'* [Unpublished manuscript].

Participant E. (2019). *Denis Cryer-Lennon's Fields notes: Observations on workshop series 'A Breath Pedagogy for Speaking Shakespeare'* [Unpublished manuscript].

Quinlivan, D. (2014). *The place of breath in cinema*. Edinburgh University Press.

Rodenburg, P. (2015). *The right to speak*. Bloomsbury Methuen Drama.

Savin-Baden, M., & Major, C. (2013). *Qualitative research: The essential guide to theory* and practice. Routledge.

Shakespeare, W. (2004a). *The taming of the shrew*. Wordsworth. (Original work published 1623).

Shakespeare, W. (2004b). *A midsummer night's dream*. Wordsworth. (Original work published 1623).

Sloterdijk, P., Patton, A., & Corcoran, S. (2009). *Terror from the air*. Semiotext(e).

Stamatiou, E. (2023). A screen actor prepares: Self-taping by reversing Stanislavsky's Method of Physical Actions. *Stanislavski Studies, 11*(1), 63–79.

Student A. (2014). *Voice + Body class: Rhythm and the word* [Workshop]. Unpublished reflections.

Tripp, D. (2012). *Critical incidents in teaching: Developing professional judgement*. Routledge.

Various Participants. (2019). *Denis Cryer-Lennon's Fields notes: Observations on workshop series 'A Breath Pedagogy for Speaking Shakespeare'* [Unpublished manuscript].

Werner, S. (1996). Performing Shakespeare: Voice training and the feminist actor. *New Theatre Quarterly, 12*, 249–258.

Werner, S. (1997). Voice training, Shakespeare, and feminism. *New Theatre Quarterly, 13*(50), 183–183.

Weston, S. (2018). *Political voice as embodied performance: Young women, politics and engagement* [PhD, University of Leeds].

Weston, S. (2019). Redistributing the means of vocal production: Voice training as a tool of political intervention. *Journal of Interdisciplinary Voice Studies, 4*(1), 37–54.

5 Training Actors' Voices and Decolonising Curriculum

Shifting Epistemologies

Stan Brown and Tara McAllister-Viel

Introduction

In 2021, during the height of the BlackLivesMatter protests in the United Kingdom, an important book on a popular, certificate speech training approach was published: *Experiencing Speech: A Skill-based, Panlingual Approach to Actor Training: A Beginner's Guide to Knight-Thompson Speechwork®* (Caban et al., 2021). Its aim is 'to see this work taken up across languages and cultures, translated and continually reimagined as a panlingual approach' (ibid: xiv). It was marketed on the back cover as 'a method that focuses on universal and inclusive speech training for actors from all language, racial, cultural and gender backgrounds and identities' (ibid). During a moment when UK and US drama students were calling for their actor training to address the intricacies of intersectional identities and the multiplicities of positionalities, can/should one training approach address 'all language, racial, cultural and gender backgrounds and identities'? Why should a voice/speech curriculum be 'a universal approach' (ibid: preface)? Carefully pinpointing this key premise and using it as a *departure point*, we argue here that this value is not unique to this one text, but can be linked to other mainstream, popular training approaches that also value applications of 'universalism' in contemporary voice training practice.[1] The premise of the book is deeply problematic: the idea that universalism invites inclusivity. This is also a key principle rooted in Anglo-American voice and speech training since the 1960s and embedded in some of the most popular voice training approaches in the United Kingdom and the United States, voice training manuals, and voice teacher certification programmes.[2] The premise of this speech training manual emerges out of a larger epistemology that embraces this value.

This training text is also an example of a growing trend towards certification of voice teaching methodologies, some of which are trademarked like Knight-Thompson Speechwork. Other private certifications, such as Linklater and Rodenburg teacher training certifications, also incorporate applications of 'universalism' in their pedagogical and business models. Here, universalism is used as a business model in which values embedded within teaching practice are framed by their monetary value in the context of private practice (McAllister-Viel, 2019, p. 159). This chapter argues ethical concerns surrounding access when such business models are introduced into actor-training institutions.[3] Also, there is a concern that when independent certification programmes create intimate relationships with academic institutions, voice and speech training becomes homogenised at an institutional level. Building on Gurkiran Kaur Wariabharaj's study into voice certification programmes (2021), co-authors argue that training institutions will struggle to 'decolonise curriculum' when a large part of the curriculum build happens off-site of the institution within a certification programme that may have no external oversight, validation requirements, Equality,

DOI: 10.4324/9781003393672-7

Diversity, Inclusivity, and Accessibility+ code of practice in place, or student support services to mediate student voice trainers' complaints.[4]

This chapter aims to unfold how 'universalism' functions as a key principle underpinning many popular voice training practices within UK conservatoires and by extension any programme in universities and drama schools beyond the United Kingdom that also places applications of 'universalism' at the centre of their curriculum. Another aim is to challenge conversations surrounding popular voice training approaches which write into their histories the myth of inclusivity and diversity of methods, in which 'today's actors, singers and performers have a wealth of techniques to choose from' (Gener, 2010, p. 33). Finally, this chapter calls for an investigation into the relationship between voice certification programmes and training institutions, asking 'do institutions really understand what they are asking for when they request a particular certification?' (Burke in Acker & Hampton, 1997, p. 57).

As co-authors who specialise in training actors' voices within conservatoires (both in the United Kingdom and the United States), we locate ourselves within the contexts of our current posts at actor training institutions. We also bring our intersectional identities as a lens through which we critically examine our intimate subject knowledge of voice pedagogy, specific educational practices in voice within institutional settings, and the current call to 'decolonise curriculum' in actor training. In positioning ourselves, we offer these descriptions: Brown identifies as a Black, cisgender, gay, neurodiverse male in his early 60s. McAllister-Viel is a white, cisgender, queer, neurodiverse female in her late 50s that identifies as a feminist. We work professionally as actors in the United States and the United Kingdom. Our teaching language is English within our training studios.

Ultimately, the co-authors hope to add to ongoing transatlantic conversations on 'decolonizing curriculum' through provocations for discussion with targeted questions on the possibility and nature of epistemological shifts within institutional voice training for actors.

Conversations Surrounding Change in Actor Training

During the twentieth century, not only has actor training undergone great change but also the role of voice in actor training has been reimagined (Boston, 2018). Cicely Berry, former Voice Director for the Royal Shakespeare Company for over 30 years, noted 'a changing theatre culture' (Berry, 2001, p. 29) during her career, which shifted voice pedagogy away from the values of the 'voice beautiful' approach to the establishment of a 'natural/free' voice approach in the 60s and 70s (McAllister-Viel, 2019, pp. 43–46; Kimbrough, 2011; Martin, 1991).

Voice pedagogy is posed at another seismic shift in training towards more explicit anti-racist and culturally competent curriculum. For example, Ann Cahill and Christine Hamel's recently published *Sounding Bodies: Identity, Injustice and the Voice* 'call for voice pedagogues to question every aspect of teaching and coaching practices' (2022, p. 1). Their work offers 'a set of theoretical principles and frameworks out of which new practices may be born' allowing trainings to 'increase attunement to various forms of vocal injustice' (ibid). Amy Mihyang Ginther's edited collection *Stages of Reckoning: Antiracist and Decolonial Actor Training* aims to 'provide readers with theoretical contexts of how actors' bodies and voices intersect with existing acting methodologies and texts so they can adapt Eurocentric material in ways that are less harmful' (2023, p. 2). Cynthia Santos DeCure and Micha

Espinosa's recently published *Latinx Actor Training* offers a text that was 'born out of the urgent need to address the inequities of training that we experienced and witnessed in academia and the industry . . . we saw our students perpetually measured by Eurocentric values' (2023, p. 1). The text aims to 'reimagine and restructure the practice of actor training by inviting culturally inclusive forms and deep investigation into heritage and identity practices' specifically addressing explorations of linguistic identity among its offerings (Santos DeCure & Espinosa, 2023, p. 1).

One of the most notable shifts in conversations around contemporary voice training is the foregrounding of the lived experience of race, gender, dis/ability, accent/dialect, and language preference as well as other complex identity markers as fundamental to the ways voice trainers think and talk about voice practice. Acknowledging the positionality of the teacher and the student in the make-up of the teaching/learning model moves away from assumptions that teacher and student share a 'universal' experience of living and interacting in the world.

Voice trainers Espinosa and Antonio Ocampo-Guzman offer their embodied experiences of race and language preference as Latinos in critiquing the ways 'very few actor-training programs are able or willing to understand the complex navigation of identity – an integral part of the Latino experience' (2010, p. 150). Nina Sun Eidsheim's methodological approach to her research interweaves 'insights offered by scholarship on race and gender' with her own voice training and teaching and lived experiences of race and gender (2015, pp. 11, 15). She wrote, 'My thinking has also been informed by the contradictory ways my voice has been read, depending on whether the listener has access to visual (Korean) or sonic (Scandinavian accent) cues' (Eidsheim, 2015, p. 14).

Previously, the application of 'universalism' through a biomedical model was how exercises could transfer from teacher to student. Former Head of Voice at the National Theatre (England, UK), Patsy Rodenburg, wrote:

> [o]ne of the delights of being a voice teacher is that I can teach in any language . . . anywhere in the world. The anatomical principles of the voice are the same in each place, the main body of sound the same.
>
> (Rodenburg, 1992, p. 268)

Her specific application of universalism suggested an inclusive pedagogy, but it did so through an over-reliance on body as a stable site for learning in which anatomy was the 'essential' category effacing cultural relativism (McAllister-Viel, 2007, p. 99). This approach fails to invite students to engage with difference, differently abled bodies, and different cultural influences on bodies/voices.

A (re)consideration of voice practice challenges the impeachability of the techniques themselves, particularly the value of a 'universal' voice training approach as a key principle which underpins practice. Berry wrote in her first training manual (1973) that the exercises 'appearing in this book are foolproof' (17). Three years later, voice trainer Kristin Linklater wrote in her first training manual that '[t]he framework of the exercises is impeccably designed and has an enduring potency' (1976, p. 2). Rodenburg wrote in 2000, 'I and others work this way because we intend to keep a tradition alive, and we know it is the best experience for an actor' (373). Years later, in order to keep that 'tradition' alive, Rodenburg resigned as Head of Voice from acting conservatoire Guildhall School of Music and Drama, a post she had held for 42 years. Rodenburg was quoted as saying,

I said: "I need help from teachers that teach like I do", and they wouldn't support me. So I had to resign. . . . I have to choose to leave and to work with teachers and actors who are like-minded.

(Ibid.)

When UK actor training came under critical examination during #BlackLivesMatter protests, a 2021 *Guardian* article asked 'are centuries of stagecraft about to be sacrificed?' (Thorpe, 2021). The concern about *sacrificing* stagecraft, points to anxiety surrounding curriculum change and joins previous conversations about training that assume this 'tradition' is sound. Conversations that frame voice practices as part of 'the centuries of stagecraft' representing a 'tradition' that is 'the best experience for an actor' comprised of exercises that are 'foolproof' create, over decades, a discourse that seems to suggest this way of working propels itself forward through the strength of exercises that are universally accessible. When those exercises are questioned and/or dropped from the teaching curriculum, the 'threat to "craft"' (Luckhurst, 2024) signals unwanted change.

Voice trainer Ginther's 2015 article 'Disconscious Racism in Mainstream British Voice Pedagogy and its Potential Effects on Students from Pluralistic Backgrounds in UK Drama Conservatoires' was a landmark article calling for 'a more engaged and critical consciousness surrounding mainstream British voice pedagogy and its assumptions given the increasingly diverse populations within the conservatoire classrooms' (41). Conversations critiquing dominant voice training culture have been building for decades, including critiques from co-authors Brown and McAllister-Viel (Brown, 2000, 2001; McAllister-Viel, 2007, 2009, 2016, 2019). What, then, is the beginning point for current 'decolonizing curriculum' efforts? What reasons exist now for decolonising curricula that haven't always existed?

Co-author Stan Brown notes that he attended more diversity and inclusion workshops at his current training institution within the six months following George Floyd's murder than in his entire 27-year career. More specifically, if BIPOC (Black, Indigenous, People of Colour) allies want change now, why didn't they want it before George Floyd's murder? What was it about that one wrongful death among so many others that made it necessary to suddenly act? Along with the global surge in diversity and inclusion workshops, there has been a global surge in the curiosity among BIPOC about the motivations of BIPOC allies who are suddenly seeking change.

One premise of this chapter is that significant change begins with the individuals that make up and run training institutions and contribute to the structural racism that exists on an institutional level. Here, co-author Stan Brown (henceforth SB) offers a series of provocations as part of a reflective exercise. The aim is for the individual trainer to explore one's motivation as the foundation for grassroots change, placing this as the starting point for curriculum change and development. In this way, the 'changing theatre culture' that Berry noted during her time as a voice trainer moves away from mapping historical landmarks of key training developments towards more interpersonal, individual agency.

SB: One provocation I offer for a deeper understanding of why transparency of motivations is desired is this: if you are in an abusive relationship and are fortunate enough to escape, what would you do if the abuser returned and wanted to be in your life again? If your response isn't an unequivocal NO, you would likely be curious about your abuser's motivations. Why now? What has changed? It is important to note that this provocation is not about assigning all white people the role of abuser. Rather, it is about recognising that those who have been abused are likely to have conditions or boundaries in place to protect themselves from the possibility of further abuse.

I believe that to inspire and inform external action, we must prioritise a conscious cultivation of internal awareness. This is not only about undoing centuries of colonial programming and structure but also about validating the experiences of BIPOC students. Before suggesting curriculum decolonisation strategies, I suggest that all educators take a moment to reflect on their own complicity in colonisation – not as an exercise in assigning blame, but as an opportunity to increase personal awareness and, where applicable, meditate on the notion of taking responsibility. I envision this meditation inspiring creative focus and direction for Diversity and Inclusion initiatives, official corporate statements on race, DEI goal accountability checklists, policy templates, and YouTube videos on decolonising your syllabus.

A second provocation: if I come across someone starving, beaten, wounded, and lying in the streets, how might it be perceived if my first instinct was to take a poll or organise a brainstorming session about how to help instead of taking immediate action to provide aid and support? Unfortunately, many diversity and inclusion events can feel performative, as if we are merely being asked to witness a performance of people talking about doing positive things. This can leave BIPOC feeling mocked or lied to by their colleagues especially when there is little or no tangible progress in the workplace environment after the DEI events end. When I detect this perceived lack of authenticity at DEI events, I instinctively distance myself from the seemingly well-intentioned people around me.

A final provocation: What does it mean if I react negatively when a repeatedly mistreated dog, whom I am trying to help, does not trust me? Despite my pure and positive motivations and intentions, could it be that I am more concerned with reinforcing something positive I believe about myself than I am with providing the dog with nourishment? What does this say about my motivations for offering the dog food?

Before embarking on the process of decolonising the curriculum, I believe it is essential to prioritise the conscious cultivation of internal awareness as a means of inspiring and informing external action. It is important to ask ourselves: Is change truly desired? What is the motivation behind this desire? How can we ask ourselves the right questions without passing judgement? How can we differentiate between what we truly want and what we think others want us to want? How can we ensure that our response is not influenced by what others want for us? While compassion for another's emotional state and well-being can be catalysts for positive change and action, I believe one's primary focus should remain on their own internal awareness and experience of – how do I feel? What do I think? What do I believe?

I understand that these provocations require an unprecedented level of self-reflection and transparency from many. That is, in the intimate space of my own awareness, where I don't have to share information with anyone else, what do I truly desire? I believe many would be disconcerted to discover that they don't want change. (White) privilege would not be an issue if many were not thriving within what has always been the norm.

My use of 'privilege' extends beyond 'White' privilege. That one word 'White' coming from me instead of (co-author) Tara makes a *huge* difference. Coming from me, it's an indictment and an accusation that (angry or not) puts me in a position to be labelled as angry (upset, unhappy, frustrated, etc.). While white people may use privilege in ways that are unique to their identity, I prefer to leave 'privilege' open here. This is because I have strong convictions about not writing from a place of anger and outrage. I strive to avoid it. I believe that it can obscure clarity and compromise the kind of language and perspective I want to access when I'm trying to communicate, collaborate, and learn along with others.

If the norm rewards and reinforces behaviours that perpetuate sameness or impede progress towards change, why would I openly admit a preference for sameness? These provocations are intended to enable individuals to explore their personal truth (even if it is a preference for sameness) without judgement, before taking any external action. I believe that the lack of progress in many diversity and inclusion initiatives is due to people acting before understanding, aligning with, and being guided by their core motivations. In addition, evaluation mechanisms must return to these issues to check if change has taken place.

When I started writing this portion of our chapter, my plan of contemplative action was to engage an Affinity Group of Black colleagues in a dialogue about our motivations for change – interrogating each other to gain clarity and developing a template and process along the way. The hope was that by sharing our outcomes with the full faculty and inviting them to join us, we might create a shared focus and direction for curriculum reform that was truly authentic. While some faculty have eagerly embraced the inherent challenges of evolving beyond outdated paradigms, others view and openly characterise the work of positive change as inconvenient and disruptive. What has resulted is a one-step-forward-two-steps-back effect where progress is concerned. While the MFA suite of programmes that I am a part of at Northwestern University has created a DEI community that is being modelled university-wide, all attempts to engage in dialogue about undergraduate admissions' long-standing disparity between white and BIPOC student population numbers have abruptly ceased without explanation. However frustrating or discouraging, it remains essential for us to continue striving for a more equitable and inclusive educational environment.[5]

There is an enormous amount of work ahead. I'm advocating for work that results from inspired rather than forced action. Action aligned with the genuine desire for positive change. Action which acknowledges that those for whom a decolonised curriculum is intended and who will be most helped by it need healing before they can join in partnership with those, however well-meaning, who seek to decolonise.

Homogeneity in Popular Voice Training Approaches

Building on Stan's provocations, we aim in this section to expose how many popular voice training approaches, despite claims of diversity and inclusivity, actually homogenise training, creating harmful learning environments. We investigate two specific issues we feel need unfolding before 'decolonizing curriculum' efforts move forward: applications of 'universalism' in mainstream, contemporary voice pedagogy, and the problematic relationship between private voice teacher certification programmes and their implementation into actor training institutions.

Anglo-American voice training writes into its history a particular characterisation of diversity of training approaches. This characterisation suggests that there are training techniques to address difference in the classroom. One example of such popular discussions is the *American Theatre* special issue on vocal training for the actor, which writes that '[t]hanks to these voice visionaries [Berry, Catherine Fitzmaurice, Arthur Lessac, Linklater, Rodenburg], today's actors, singers and performers have a wealth of techniques to choose from' (Gener, 2010, p. 33). The implication is that each trainer represents a different approach and so there are many ways to train an actor's voice.

However, of the five leading trainers cited in the *American Theatre* special issue, four received their foundational training at two London-based acting conservatoires between 1946 and 1970: Berry, Fitzmaurice, and Rodenburg graduated from the Central School of Speech and Drama and Linklater graduated from London Academy of Dramatic Art. This situates contemporary voice training for actors in a particular sociocultural and historical place.

Berry, Fitzmaurice, and Linklater all returned to their alma maters to teach voice and all four cite the former Head of Voice at their institutions as having a major influence on their teaching. Later, when developing their approaches, the four pedagogues would interact, for instance, Berry and Rodenburg would work together for nine years at the Royal Shakespeare Company. They all wrote book chapters for the same seminal voice studies collections (Saklad, 2011; Acker & Hampton, 1997; Armstrong & Pearson, 2000). They delivered workshops and lectures together at international conferences (2007 Performance Breath Conference, Royal Academy of Dramatic Art, London, England, UK; 2009 Voice and Speech Trainers' Association Conference, NYC, USA; 2009 Theatre Noise Conference, Royal Central School of Speech and Drama, London, England, UK).

It is not a coincidence that these master trainers share the same or similar key principles, practices, and values, particularly the idea that 'the human voice' is the 'same everywhere' (Rodenburg, 1992, pp. 107, 268); 'I've worked in all sorts of languages – I've worked in China in Mandarin and with Aboriginal people in Australia . . . You work in the same way you work with an English-speaking person. The voice is the voice' (Berry in Ellis, 2010, p. 122); 'I want to highlight the fact that voice is universal and speech is cultural, – all humans have lungs, diaphragm, resonators, vocal folds' (Linklater, 2019). Through its emphasis on universal, 'human' anatomy and physiology, 'the' body becomes the common denominator for the transference of skills between bodies/voices (Aiken, 1900, pp. 2, 3; Berry, 1973, p. 14; Martin, 1991, p. 37). As such, they suggest that the commonality of bodily structures, muscle function, and other materials of voice help their practices cross-cultures and discipline-specific contexts.

Shifting from the Value of 'Universalism' towards Valuing a 'Cultural Voice' and a 'Cultural Ear'

Liz Mills, who teaches in the Commonwealth nation of South Africa, addressed the impact of Empire on voice pedagogy at the University of Cape Town, where she taught. She wrote of her experiences applying Berry's approach to Shakespearian text to 'the South African English speaking student actor' (Mills, 1999, p. 102). She wrote, '[f]or [Berry] all the foundational properties of voice become circumscribed predominately by Shakespeare's texts and by the ethos of the RSC [Royal Shakespeare Company]' (Mills, 1999, p. 102). Mills noted that when Berry discussed the energy of the line, meaning Shakespearian verse (iambic pentameter), this is 'described as close to the rhythm of conversational speech', which 'will be present as a consciously registered pulse for those [RSC] actors in a way that it would not be for the South African English speaking student actor, for example, whose tendency is towards more emphatic stress patterns' (Mills, 1999, p. 102).[6] Instead, Mills argued the centrality of voice concerning culture. Mill's writing aggravated the binary between 'universal' voice and cultural speech (Linklater, 2019) and noted an 'ethos' or value system underpinning the training. She wrote:

> The voice as sonic image signifies meaning in performance. When the making of vocal meaning and the signifying of vocal meaning are held central to the act of theatre, then the voice can be conceived of as having multiple sonic possibilities. The term 'sonic' used here to suggest that the voice is present as a sound image as well as being present as spoken text or vocal gesture.
>
> (Mills, 1999, p. 3)

Mills' argument first de-centred Berry's use of Shakespearian text as 'universal', in which iambic pentameter is characterised as the 'rhythm of conversational speech' by questioning whose speech pattern would this apply. Then Mills disrupted the idea of the 'universal' voice by suggesting that if 'voice is present as a sound image' that carries meaning apart from the meaning language brings, then de-coding the 'sonic image' becomes another kind of language that needs a *cultural ear* to hear and understand the *cultural voice* it listens to. The listener must be able to adapt within this sonic sign system to understand the nuances of sound just as a speaker is with the nuances of spoken word. Kreiman and Sidtis note:

> Because human voices transmit spoken language from the speaker to listeners, the relationship of voice to language has long been of interest to linguists. Early theorist often distinguished the linguistic from the nonlinguistic aspects of spoken message and did not consider voice quality a part of language
>
> (Kreiman & Sidtis, 2013, p. 260)

However, recently 'substantial evidence indicates that familiarity with the talker's voice facilitates deciphering the spoken message itself' (Kreiman & Sidtis, 2013, p. 261). The oral/aural feedback loop between speaker and listener suggests that a 'cultural ear' is the counterpoint to a 'cultural voice'. Because spoken language is linked to its delivery, vocal characteristics 'operate at all levels of language structure' (Kreiman & Sidtis, 2013, p. 261). In this context, Linklater's assertion that 'voice is universal and speech is cultural' creates a false binary for our purposes here. This further evidences the need for intersectional approaches to voice training which understands the interwoven influences of multiple cultural contexts within voice and speech curriculums.

In 2015, Eidsheim took up a similar idea of listening as an experience by a listener who is encultured in a given way, within a larger system in which sounds and their meanings are shaped by cultural, economic, and political contexts (5–6). Jennifer Lynn Stoever's *The Sonic Color Line: Race and the Cultural Politics of Listening* (2016) offered further investigations into how structural injustices create relational experiences of sounding and listening. By 2021, voice trainers, like Daron Oram, reflected on how they and their students were trained in both offstage spaces and drama school spaces towards a 'sonic norm', a phrase adapted from the work of sociologist Nirmal Puwar (Oram, 2021). Another perspective used feminist and race theory to explicitly unfold the ways voicing and listening are 'policed' and are framed through structural injustices (Cahill & Hamel, 2022).

Within actor training, when/if the student actor learns to first understand their own voice in offstage spaces, then craft from this a voice for a character, one can understand voice training on multiple different levels of singular and plural experiences from offstage, through training, and into onstage settings. The psychophysical act of voicing/listening, such as aural/oral feedback loops which exist between the mouth and ear of the speaker to monitor and guide voicing/speech/singing (a singular model of experience), eventually extends to the aural/oral feedback loop between actor's mouth and audience listeners' ears (a plural model of experience) during performance. Thus, as the actor is speaking, the singular aural/oral experience occurs simultaneously with the plural aural/oral experience between the actor and audience. These interwoven experiences, along with other expectations, such as aesthetic *traditions*, are set within larger performance frameworks and are judged through a set of values, or what voices 'should' do under these conditions.[7] The voice(s) and ear(s) of actors and audience members carry with them particular sociocultural and historical contexts and in this way can be understood as embodiments and re-enactments of cultural values and ideas of what a voice can/should be and what a voice can/should do. Stan Brown's and Liz Mills' work helps shift the binary of universal voice and cultural speech towards an understanding of 'cultural voice'.

Brown's work on 'cultural voice', a term he coined to characterise his work in his first *Voice and Speech Review* article (2000), de-centres universalism while also questioning how difference is understood in speech. He wrote:

> [c]asting a generalized version of reality to portray universal truth is dishonest. . . . Both students and teachers bring a unique bank of vocal experiences to voice and speech work. A simple formulaic solution cannot exist to address the witting or unwitting biases of traditional Eurocentric voice and speech training.
>
> (Brown, 2000, p. 18)

'Universality' as a generalised version of reality is 'dishonest' in part because it tends to place Eurocentric values and ways of working as an assumed assessable point of departure for all learners. A cultural voice, then, as a practical method to displace Eurocentrism in training, attempts to develop a more individualistic approach based on the vocal experiences of students and teachers instead of applying a formulaic solution. This means that *each voice classroom is made up of the plural and intersectional identities of each person and is a uniquely developed composite of cultural knowledge.* Designing curriculum within this context means that *the shifting cultural knowledge of the individuals that make up the learning/teaching strategies is an ongoing, ever-changing, dynamic co-authorship between students and teachers.*

How do the dynamics of such a co-authorship of curriculum emerge within institutional settings that may worry that 'centuries of stagecraft are about to be sacrificed' or rely on importing pre-built exercises from certification programmes?

Co-authorship in the Classroom in Comparison to Adaptations of Private Pre-designed Curriculum Built Off-site and Brought into Institutions

Kate Burke in Hampton and Acker's *Vocal Vision* (1997) wrote in her chapter 'On Training and Pluralism':

> A few years ago ARTSEARCH announced a voice and speech position at a West Coast university, an appealing post in a lush setting. . . . Then, my heart sank as I read on to find a particular kind of training specified in the announcement. Could I apply? Should I apply? Would my application even be considered? . . . I want neither myself nor my work labelled with someone else's name. . . . Labels are seductively spare and one-dimensional. Do administrators and theatre trainers call for Berry, Lessac, or Linklater training without a working knowledge of these approaches?
>
> (57–59)

Twenty-five years after Burke published her questions, they are still relevant today. If a large part of the curriculum built for voice training happens off-site of an institution and within a certification programme, how does the institution know what's on offer and integrate this curriculum into their present curriculum, their mission statement, and their Equality, Diversity, Inclusivity, Accessibility, Plus [EDIA+] code of practices? Within UK training conservatories, curriculum is reviewed each year through external examination, and usually every five years through a validation requirement, such as the Quality Assurance Agency for Higher Education, an independent charity working to benefit students and higher education by working with higher education providers and regulatory bodies to maintain and enhance quality and standards.[8] The National Student Survey, taken each year by graduating actors, can act as a monitoring system for what works and what does not work within a teaching system. Other mechanisms such as 'report and support' offer anonymous reporting of abuse at the school level. Within Student Unions, officers are elected to represent the specific concerns of Black students, female students, LGBTQIA+ students, and differently abled students. Although these mechanisms exist in different forms at the co-authors' institutions, we are not suggesting they represent a gold standard, and we are not advocating that private certification programmes simply adopt institutional mechanisms.

Student protests during 2020–2021 demonstrated that current university and conservatoire institutional structures across the sector do not capture and address racism adequately, and similar movements have exposed persistent sexism. However, for many private certification programmes there is little or no oversight from a monitoring, external body. Historically, the internal structures of certification programmes offer access to training directly with the founding teacher. There is no student union to mediate complaints between students and teachers or an anonymous report and support service. The power relationship is heavily in favour of the founder of the programme and can become more difficult to negotiate when the training is offered at their estate, sometimes located in retreat-style, remote locations.[9]

In Burke's chapter, she began by describing her experience answering a job advert on ARTSEARCH which asked for a specific certification to fill the role. Over the years, we have seen the role of certifications within job adverts move from optional to required. There seems to be a tendency for an institution to use the qualifications of the former post-holder as a template for the job advert. For example, if the former tutor was Linklater certified, even if that tutor did not begin the role as Linklater certified but earned that certification mid-career, the job advert asks to replace the outgoing post-holder with another Linklater certified tutor. This means what was once an additional qualification now becomes mandatory for that teaching post. In this way, an institution creates a 'tradition' of training in a particular way which becomes a gate-keeping mechanism. Within this context, how does an institution's voice training break free from 'tradition' and offer other, perhaps very different, approaches to training? Interviewees in Kaur Wariabharaj's research into certification programmes commented:

> Job applicants 'often see this on job listings, that they want you to have a certification in one of these methods . . . so I did the certification. . . . Certified western voice practices have had a monopoly on who gets to work in actor training.
> (Kaur Wariabharaj, 2021, p. 29)

Interviewees felt that it is widely known in the field that, '[q]uite frankly, you're not going to get the job in the States unless you've got either [Fitzmaurice or Linklater] certification' (ibid). Such testimonies suggest feelings of not having a choice but to certify to get a job in a tough teaching market, in which certification is explicitly or implicitly demanded. This creates a relationship between training institutions and certification programmes in which both profit at the expense of the individual.

Certification could help a post-holder with pay and promotion. But the tendency is for the post-holder to pay out-of-pocket for expensive tuition and find the time to train, sometimes for years, while holding down a full-time voice teaching role, in the hope that the promotion committee will award a promotion based on this extensive professional development. Very few institutions will pay full tuition for further education or grant sabbatical leave to train full-time. On top of workshop fees, transport, per diem expenses, and perhaps hotel or other accommodation expenses, some would also have to afford additional costs, like childcare or carers' expenses. Many institutions will not accept childminding and carers' fees as reimbursable receipts for professional development.

Christine Hamel, a Linklater certified trainer, critiqued her experiences in this certification programme when she wrote:

> Most teachers in my own training background (Linklater voice) are white, middle-class ciswomen, that the senior teachers who mentor trainees are typically 50+ in age. That most certified teachers of this pedagogy have had the economic means to become a designated teacher, either privately or through tuition-based higher degree programs (both paths require a 20,000 USD or more investment) speaks to a general picture of values, standards, tastes, and ideals.
>
> (2022, p. 137)[10]

Inarguably, 'the intersection of money and time equate to . . . white privilege' and 'the authority of white privilege is directly connected to having full access' (Kaur Wariabharaj, 2021, p. 32).[11] Hamel also noted:

> [b]ecause many of the teachers in this group come from privileged demographics, their values are likely to converge as the dominant values of the pedagogical culture. These values have material implications for the ways in which their students will take up embodiment and vocal ways of being in the world.
>
> (2022, p. 137)

Wariabharaj's research and Hamel's reflections speak directly to the measurable outcomes that value systems hold within training models and become crafted into the bodies/voices of student actors through a notion of 'stagecraft'. Building on their work, we argue that private certification-based training integrated into well-established drama programmes becomes part of the 'tradition' of the school. Voice teachers are recruited to teach voice in a particular way, according to their certified training. Certification becomes one of the gatekeepers of the values of dominant cultures and perpetuates dominant ideologies. Because certification programmes and training institutions are also businesses, capital is at stake: certification programmes depend on placing alumni in popular, well-recognised drama schools as evidence of the quality and efficacy of their training. Many actor-training institutions have come to depend on outsourcing the development of their curriculum, moving certification from optional to required. Voice teachers, who can spend thousands of their own income on training, are not guaranteed a teaching post or promotion but are recruited to uphold a training culture. Co-authors call for a serious (re)examination of these relationships.

Conclusion

This chapter calls for a (re)valuation, an epistemological shift, in current mainstream popular voice training approaches and asks trainers and the institutions they work for to (re)consider the dynamic relationship of creating decolonised curriculum together. This chapter challenges voice trainers to critically reflect on their motivation for a decolonised curriculum as the starting point for effective change. It also interrogates the myth of diversity of techniques, specifically the application of 'universalism' as a problematic pedagogical model. Finally, this chapter critiques the relationships between actor-training institutions and private certification programmes. To address the urgent call to decolonise curriculum in UK actor training programmes, this chapter contributes to ongoing conversations that centre lived experiences of intersectional identities in advocating for ways trainers should think about, talk about, and practice voice training.

If cultivating a 'cultural voice' is reliant on the unique cultural knowledge of the student(s) and teacher(s) in each classroom, then culture becomes one of the materials of training, a core consideration that needs time, space, and funding to develop. Voice training exercises have the potential to open important means of cultural inclusion and ground anti-oppressive curricula. Centuries of stagecraft are not about to be sacrificed, but they are changing as part of ongoing, necessary, and perpetual change in a changing actor training culture.

This chapter has argued that this changing actor-training culture can/should begin on an interpersonal level, as individual trainers, who people institutions and implement the training, forging change on a grassroots level. Moving from individual responsibility, we then call on institutions to (re)consider their relationships with certification programmes as fundamental to decolonising curriculum efforts.

SB: In my 1997 opening address to the International Symposium on Voice and Speech (Miami University), I delivered the following:

> I stand before you today a textbook case study in what can result from an unconscious acceptance of a racial hierarchy. However unconscious, through a combination of formal training and a lot of passive, mass media programming, I learned to expect my students to adapt to white cultural standards. More specifically, I was making my students conform in their sounds of speech to what I'd been programmed to unquestioningly embrace as 'correct' or 'standard'.
>
> Then, at some point during my time with Richard Armstrong,[12] I began to question my reasons for not listening deeper than a student's dialect and accent. I began to question my thoughts and habits of using speech sounds from white culture as the standard against which speech sounds of all other cultures were judged. Ultimately my questioning blossomed into rebellion. I had to change. Although it was considered unorthodox in my field, I decided to decentralize standard English in my voice and speech work. What if I no longer led with a fixed template and expectations of what speech should be prior to the utterance of sound? What if 'the standard' and point of departure I employed in my work was a consciously cultivated, fully alive, and in-the-moment presence with the range, volume, depth, energy, and power of the human voice? How might that shift my perspective and my concept of 'improvement' and 'growth'?

My decision to reform my teaching approach was met with harsh criticism from many colleagues and students. I was considered something of a heretic and charlatan in my professional organisation and yet, where doing my work was concerned, I'd never been happier.

I don't believe I will ever be considered or will consider myself 'mainstream' in my field. I also don't believe there's one best or right way for actors to train. I do believe that disagreement should always exist. Having a different opinion from others doesn't mean that others shouldn't have their opinions. Case in point, when I was a graduate acting student, a voice and speech teacher told me that I could never speak Shakespeare because the English language didn't belong to Black people. I assume my teacher knew enough history to know that she'd descended from a culture and ethnicity of people who'd kidnapped and sold another culture and ethnicity of people into slavery. Yet she chose to tell me that the language my ancestors were forced by her ancestors to speak would never be spoken at an acceptable standard by anyone with my skin colour. Many will disagree, but my teacher's opinion wasn't the problem. The real problem, as I saw it, was my teacher suggesting that her opinion become my reality.

I sometimes wish that teachers had an equivalent to the principal precepts of bioethics, which states, 'first, do no harm'. Unfortunately, no such precept exists. Unfortunately, inherent racism still exists in voice and speech training. Unconscious bias pervades the academy, reflected in toxic beliefs and practices that equate competence with ethnicity and culture. Fortunately, students are recognising and calling out racism in their training more frequently than when I was a student. This gives me deep hope and I encourage students to continue paying attention to and questioning the origins of any training which appears to have a goal of achieving homogeneity.

Notes

1 Co-authors are sensitive to the concerns that by critiquing this one premise, it may appear they are critiquing the book as a whole, or critiquing KTS Speech training as a system. Instead, the aim here is to pinpoint this specific premise as a departure point for discussing what they argue is part of a value system that can be linked to other mainstream, popular approaches to training actors' voices which adapt, in their own ways, 'universalism'.
2 Authors will return to evidence this later in the chapter.
3 Co-authors focus here on business *models* in which tuition is charged to students who enrol in certification programmes and not the business registration status. For example, Fitzmaurice Voice Institute, Inc. is a US registered non-profit organisation charging a programme fee for the intensive two-year training at $11,800.00 (including $800.00 deposit). This fee is in addition to the cost of 30 hours of prerequisite training. https://www.fitzmauriceinstitute.org/about-the-certification-program accessed 29 November, 2023.
4 Since 2020, many certification programmes have statements of inclusion on their websites. For instance, The Fitzmaurice Voice Institute's website states 'its commitment to diversity and inclusion' and part of its mission is to make available Fitzmaurice Voicework to 'under-served communities' (https://www.fitzmauriceinstitute.org/fitzmaurice-voicework-1) accessed 27 March, 2024. Kristin Linklater Voice Centre includes in its mission 'to formulate, monitor and represent the Kristin Linklater Voice Foundation's Diversity, Accessibility and Inclusivity strategies, policies and objectives through all our work and endeavours' (https://www.linklatervoice.com/kristin-linklater-voice-centre/mission-statement) accessed 28 March, 2024.
5 Dermot Daly takes up a similar question within a UK context with his article 'Actions speak louder than words. An investigation around the promises and the reality of representation in actor training' (2022). In his article, he asks if the statements of support for #BlackLivesMatter that UK drama schools released in 2020–2021 were followed through with measurable change.
6 This also raises additional questions for international students training in English as a Second or Other Language (ESOL), students who train with differently abled speech, and students who are neurodiverse.
7 Also see Evi Stamatiou's 'A Screen Actor Prepares: Self-Taping by Reversing Stanislavsky's Method of Physical Actions' (2023). She argues that self-taping offers the actor the opportunity to listen back to one's voice and evaluate it as an audience member might, asking what their voice 'should' do, or what would be expected by their voice within a given context.
8 www.qaa.ac.uk/about-us#:~:text=The%20Quality%20Assurance%20Agency%20for,and%20enhance%20quality%20and%20standards.
9 The Patsy Rodenburg Associate Programme (PRA) training takes place 'on Patsy's farm in Portugal', retrieved June 22, 2022, from https://patsyrodenburg.co.uk/teachers/. Training in Linklater Voice takes place at the Linklater Voice Centre built adjacent to Kristin's house in Orkney, Scotland, retrieved June 22, 2022, from www.linklatervoice.com/kristin-linklater-voice-centre/about-the-centre.

10 The Kristin Linklater Voice Centre is a retreat-style, residential centre in the Orkney Islands, built adjacent to Kristin's house in which a residential workshop, taught by certified Linklater teachers, is upwards of £1,175.00 per workshop: retrieved June 22, 2022, from https://shop.linklatervoice.com/shop/. Fees for Linklater certification are competitive, compared with others. Patsy Rodenburg's certification programme, 'The Patsy Rodenburg Associate Programme (PRA)', is a two-year programme priced at 17,000 Euros and takes place at her farm in Portugal: retrieved June 22, 2022, from https://patsyrodenburg.co.uk/teachers/. Fitzmaurice Voicework certified training program fee for the intensive two-year training is $11,800.00 USD (including a $800.00 deposit). This fee is in addition to the cost of 30 hours of prerequisite training, a 'base requirement for consideration for acceptance into certification training' with a 'highly recommended 5-day in-person workshop' (https://www.fitzmauriceinstitute.org/about-the-certification-program) accessed 29 November, 2023. The Lessac Institute offers upcoming intensive workshops located on Hendrix College campus (Arkansas, USA) in which workshop fee includes housing: 1 week intensive $1,250.00, 4 week intensive $3,750–4,500.00 depending on 'early bird special rate or LTRI membership discount. LTRI membership is required for all levels of certification ($35–65 range of annual membership fees) and suggested timeline for achieving certification is 1–5 years. Average candidate completion is 3 years. Knight-Thompson Speechwork offers the Teacher Certification Program each June, July, or August in residence at University of California-Irvine (USA) and on special occasions, abroad. Entrance into the program requires three prerequisite courses costing upwards of $2,150.00: Experiencing speech ($850–$950), experiencing accents ($850–$950) and phonetics intensive ($450). The enrolment fee for the certification is $4,000.00 USD. Participation in the certification programme does not guarantee certification; in some cases additional work is required. https://ktspeechwork.org/event/teacher-certification-10/ accessed 29 November, 2023.

11 Some certification programmes address financial accessibility. For instance, the Kristin Linklater Voice Foundation offers The Fran Bennett Scholarship providing 'support to students primarily of colour to attend Linklater Voice Method residential and online workshops' via donations through their website (https://www.linklatervoice.com/kristin-linklater-voice-centre/mission-statement); Fitzmaurice Voice Institute, Inc. offers some student scholarships raised through private donation through their website (https://www.fitzmauriceinstitute.org/about-the-certification-program) accessed 29 November, 2023. The Lessac Institute hosts the Sue Ann Park Endowment Fund Campaign and offers tuition assistance to a limited number of students and only for the Lessac Intensives and Facilitator Training workshops (https://www.lessacinstitute.org/tuition-assistance) accessed 29 November, 2023.

12 Armstrong. www.richardarmstrong.info/about

References

Acker, B., & Hampton, M. (Eds.). (1997). *Vocal vision: View on voice by 24 leading teachers, coaches and directors*. Applause.

Aiken, W. A. (1900, 1910). *The voice: An introduction to practical phonology*. Longmans, Green & Co.

Alberge, D. (2024, March 3). 'Without craft, an actor is a liability': How row over teaching standards is causing a rift in UK theatre industry. *The Guardian*. https://www.theguardian.com/stage/2024/mar/03/without-craft-an-actor-is-a-liability-how-row-over-teaching-standards-is-causing-a-rift-in-uk-theatre-industry

Armstrong, F., & Pearson, J. (Eds.). (2000). *Well-tuned women: Growing strong through voicework*. The Women's Press Ltd.

Armstrong, R. Retrieved October 1, 2023, from www.richardarmstrong.info/about

Berry, C. (1973). *Voice and the actor*. Wiley Publishing.

Berry, C. (2001). *Text in action*. Virgin.

Boston, J. (2018). *Voice*. Palgrave.

Brown, S. (2000). The cultural voice. In *Voice and speech review* (Vol. 1, Issue 1, pp. 17–18). Taylor & Francis online. https://www.tandfonline.com/doi/abs/10.1080/23268263.2000.10761381

Brown, S. (2001). The cultural voice: An interview with Danny Hoch. In *Voice and speech review* (Vol. 2, pp. 124–128). Taylor & Francis online. https://www.tandfonline.com/doi/abs/10.1080/23268263.2001.10761456

Burke, K. (1997). On training and pluralism. In B. Acker & M. Hampton (Eds.), *Vocal vision: View on voice by 24 leading teachers, coaches and directors* (pp. 57–62). Applause.

Caban, A., Foh, J., & Parker, J. (2021). *Experiencing speech: A skills-based, panlingual approach to actor training: A beginner's guide to Knight-Thompson speechwork*. Routledge.

Cahill, A., & Hamel, C. (2022). *Sounding bodies: Identity, injustice, and the voice*. Methuen Drama.

Daly, D. (2022). Actions speak louder than words. An investigation around the promises and the reality of representation in actor training. *Theatre, Dance and Performance Training*, 13(4), 554–572.

Eidsheim, N. S. (2015). *Sensing sound: Singing and listening as vibrational practice*. Duke University Press.

Ellis, S. (2010). The body in the voice: Interview with Cicely Berry. In *American theatre, special section: Approaches to theatre training: Pillars of voice work*. Retrieved October 1, 2023, from www.americantheatre.org/2010/01/01/the-body-in-the-voice/

Espinosa, M., & Ocampo-Guzman, A. (2010). Identity politics and the training of Latino actors. In E. Margolis & L. Tyler Renaud (Eds.), *The politics of American actor training* (pp. 150–161). Routledge.

Gener, R. (2010). Approaches to Theatre Training: Pillars of voice work. *American theatre special section: Approaches to theatre training* Vol. 27, Issue 1, p. 33.

Ginther, A. M. (2015). Disconscious racism in mainstream British voice pedagogy and its potential effects on students form pluralistic backgrounds in UK Drama Conservatoires. *Voice and speech review* Vol. 9, Issue 1, pp. 41–60.

Ginther, A. M. (Ed.). (2023). *Stages of reckoning: Antiracist and decolonial actor training*. Routledge.

Kaur Wariabharaj, G. (2021). *Do western certified voice practices reflect a modern-day colonization by culturally appropriating ancient eastern practices?* [Unpublished MA thesis. Royal Central School of Speech and Drama].

Kimbrough, A. (2011). *Dramatic theories of voice in the twentieth century*. Cambria Press.

Kreiman, J., & Sidtis, D. (2013). *Foundations of voice studies: An interdisciplinary approach to voice production and perception* (Paperback ed., 1st published). Wiley-Blackwell.

Linklater, K. (1976). *Freeing the natural voice*. Drama Book.

Linklater, K. (2019, August 28). *The embodied voice*. Keynote speech given at the 2019 PEVoC meeting in Copenhagen. Retrieved October 1, 2023, from www.linklatervoice.com/resources/articles-essays/161-the-embodied-voice-pevoc-019

Luckhurst, G. (2024, March 4). Teaching titan Patsy Rodenburg quits Guildhall over threat to 'craft'. *The Stage*. https://www.thestage.co.uk/news/teaching-titan-patsy-rodenburg-quits-guildhall-over-threat-to-craft#:~:text=Teaching%20titan%20Patsy%20Rodenburg%20quits%20Guildhall%20over%20threat%20to%20'craft',-NewsMar%204&text=Leading%20acting%20educator%20Patsy%20Rodenburg,what%20they're%20doing%22

Martin, J. (1991). *Voice in modern theatre*. Routledge.

McAllister-Viel, T. (2007). Speaking with an international voice? *Contemporary Theatre Review*, 17(01), 97–106.

McAllister-Viel, T. (2009). (Re)considering the role of breath in training actors' voices: Insights from Dahnjeon breathing and the phenomenon of breath. *Theatre Topics*, 19(2), 165–180.

McAllister-Viel, T. (2016). The role of "presence" in training actors' voices. *Theatre, Dance and Performance Training*, 7(3), 438–452. https://doi.org/10.1080/19443927.2016.1217265

McAllister-Viel, T. (2019). *Training actors' voices: Towards an intercultural/interdisciplinary approach*. Routledge.

Mills, E. (1999). *Theatre voice as metaphor: The advocacy of a praxis based on the centrality of voice to performance* [Unpublished MA thesis, Rhodes University, Grahamstown].

Oram, D. (2021). Decentering listening: Toward an anti-discriminatory approach to accent and dialect training for the actor. *Voice and speech review* Vol. 15, Issue 1, pp. 6–26.

Quality Assurance Agency for Higher Education. Retrieved October 1, 2023, from www.qaa.ac.uk/about-us#:~:text=The%20Quality%20Assurance%20Agency%20for,and%20enhance%20quality%20and%20standards

Rodenburg, P. (1992). *The right to speak*. Routledge.

Rodenburg, P. (2000). *The actor speaks: Voice and the performer*. St. Martin's Press.

Saklad, N. (2011). *Voice and speech training in the new millennium: Conversations with master teachers*. Applause Theatre and Cinema Books.

Santos DeCure, C., & Espinosa, M. (2023). *Latinx actor training*. Routledge.

Stamatiou, E. (2023). A screen actor prepares: Self-taping by reversing Stanislavsky's method of physical actions. In *Stanislavski studies: Practice, legacy, and contemporary theatre* (Vol. 11, Issue 1, pp. 63–79). Taylor & Francis online. https://doi.org/10.1080/20567790.2023.2196297

Stoever. J. L. (2016). *The sonic color line: Race and the cultural politics of listening*. New York University Press, Routledge.

Thorpe, V. (2021, October 17). Why battles over race and sex now take centre stage at UK drama schools. *The Guardian*. Retrieved October 1, 2023, from www.theguardian.com/education/2021/oct/17/why-battles-over-race-and-sex-now-take-centre-stage-at-uk-drama-schools#:~:text=It%20might%20be%20a%20generational,caused%20a%20string%20of%20crises

Part Two

Approaches to Scene Study
as Cultural Intersectionality

6 Reconsidering the Link between Text, Technique and Teaching in Actor Training

Sherrill Gow

Introduction

> Let's face it: most of us were taught in classrooms where styles of teachings reflected the notion of a single norm of thought and experience, which we were encouraged to believe was universal.
>
> (hooks, 1994, p. 35)

As posited by bell hooks, a critically engaged pedagogy calls for teachers to recognise that their teaching may need to change to create spaces where social realities beyond the dominant norm are reflected. I am committed to feminist pedagogy as a way of intervening in actor-training practices that reinforce restrictively androcentric, ableist, classist, Eurocentric, and heterocentric world views. The roots of feminist pedagogy derive from Paulo Freire's concepts (1993) but have been developed further by intersectional feminist thinkers including hooks, 'whose work, which emerged from critical feminist debates in the late 1970s and early 1980s, has informed generations of scholars as they grapple with questions of power and privilege in education' (Light et al., 2015, p. 6). Focusing on the questions of *what* we teach and *how* we teach it – specifically, through the interrelationship between text, technique, and teaching – this chapter shares some of the strategies we engage on the programme I co-lead at Mountview Academy of Theatre Arts (hereinafter Mountview), a UK conservatoire, to mobilise critical approaches in actor-training.

Creating a more liberatory actor training has been a subject of interest for decades (Blair, 1992), yet progress is slow. Movements protesting anti-Black and gender-based violence in recent years have highlighted discriminatory and abusive behaviours in the UK drama school sector. Critiques of actor training reveal an overdependence on binaries, a disposition towards reproducing oppressively gendered and heteronormative behaviours, and a tacit commitment to whiteness as an ideology (Ginther, 2023a; Peck, 2021; Steiger, 2019; Luckett & Shaffer, 2017; Malague, 2013). Repositioning pedagogy in actor training is a fundamental step towards repairing the curriculum, alongside a commitment to explore new strategies. Intersectional analysis is required to address the vectors of oppression and privilege that play out in actor training. Mari Matsuda conceptualises intersectionality as a methodology made up of 'asking the other question'. She writes:

> [W]hen I see something that looks racist, I ask 'Where is the patriarchy in this?' When I see something that looks sexist, I ask 'Where is the heterosexist in this?' When I see something that looks homophobic, I ask 'Where are the class interests in this?'
>
> (Matsuda, 1991, p. 1189)

DOI: 10.4324/9781003393672-9

Asking the other question offers a starting point for a critically engaged acting pedagogy that examines issues of power in the classroom and challenges oppressive biases and structures that obstruct learning.

As Joint Head of Postgraduate Training at Mountview, I hold institutional power in addition to the privilege and power afforded to me as a white, cisgender, heterosexual, non-disabled woman. I have a responsibility to use this power and the space I occupy to create new spaces, advocate for my students, challenge training practices where they are problematic, and seek out new possibilities. This chapter shares some of the changes we have made to our MA Performance programme. My goal here is to encourage actor-trainers and educators to think about how the teaching–text–technique tripartite might interact in new and better ways. To do this, I return to feminist discourse on actor training and performance from the 1980s through the 2000s. Feminist pedagogy tells us that looking back is requisite for moving forward (Crabtree et al., 2009). However, this chapter is not a how-to-guide, nor does it offer conclusive outcomes. At the time of writing, many of the curriculum changes described here have been put into effect recently and I have not collated data to evaluate findings. I position this work as a complex, non-linear and ongoing process that requires continuous change, with no one stopping point. As Lisa Peck argues, there is no easy or singular solution to repair actor training. Instead, '[i]t is vital that we recognise a practice of difference to be a slow and ongoing process of repair as opposed to a quick-fix solution' (Peck, 2021, p. 58). ˙

Text, technique, and teaching form a matrix that can reinforce and reproduce oppressive ideologies and practices. Examining each aspect independently, as well as their interrelationship, has enabled me to identify numerous ways in which feminist interventions can be actively engaged in each area to disrupt the oppressive tendencies of the text–technique–teaching matrix in actor-training. This matrix can be traced back to feminist performance scholarship of the late 1980s and 1990s, which posited a two-sided critique of realism. Firstly, for its linear and mimetic representation that ensconced women in limiting or punishing domestic spheres and Aristotelian structures. Secondly, for a 'psychological "method" acting style' that calls for 'performer and character identification', associated with Stanislavski-based techniques (Aston, 1999, p. 126). Elin Diamond explains that this process 'laminates' the body of the actor and character (1997, p. 4). In so doing, the actor's social, cultural, and embodied experiences disappear under the rubric of a character's 'truth'. J. Ellen Gainor explains that 'Realism as a theatrical style' became 'inextricably linked to acting technique' and the 'hermetic construct of technique, text and production' brought about a wholesale rejection of 'all its components' (2002, p. 168). Gainor asks if Stanislavskian acting theory and feminist theory are truly at cross-purposes or if application is the issue, which Rosemary Malague takes further, positing that it is the link between theory, technique, and pedagogic practice that requires close examination in actor training (2013, p. 25). Making interventions in actor-training calls for taking account of not only *what* we teach in terms of texts and techniques but also *who* teaches it and *how*. Hence, we might consider a triangle composed of three Ts: text, technique, and teaching, with each corner holding a facet with the potential to oppress or, indeed, the possibility of intervention (Figure 6.1).

Texts

When we think of dramatic texts, we might think of those 'great' or canonical works that repeatedly appear on stages. Lizbeth Goodman explains: 'The term "*the canon*", at a very basic level, refers to the set of authors and texts that has been passed down from age to age,

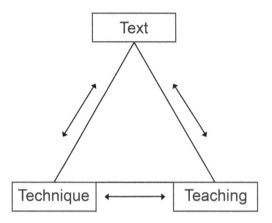

Figure 6.1 Iterative triangle illustrating how text, technique, and teaching interconnect.

generation to generation, with a stamp of approval – with a reputation for being "great"' (1996, p. 6). Thus, a canon has value attached to it, with works being recognised as the most important or best of their kind. The construction of canons and their attendant value systems have long been called into question by gender and race studies. The canon both valorises and marginalises, as 'a project of a class of privileged, powerful, mostly white male subjects whose ideology it represents' (Dolan, 2012, p. 20). A canon asserts value and is established by repetition. Actor training plays a part in this process of repetition, as students practice their craft by working on texts in class, project, and production processes.

Androcentrism – being centred on or dominated by men – is evident in various dramatic canons. Shakespeare wrote 826 male characters versus 155 female characters (Freestone in Peck, 2021, p. 163). Feminist critiques of realism establish that women are regularly positioned as objects rather than subjects and in relation to male characters (wife, mother, daughter). Women are often confined to the domestic and/or narrative structures that drive towards an 'inevitable' or 'inescapable' ending: marriage, incarceration, suicide, or death. The representation of women in musical theatre repertoire is also problematic, with female characters regularly reduced to good or bad, rich or poor, smart or empty-headed, virginal or promiscuous. If women have jobs in musicals, they tend to be gendered: maid, nun, nanny, princess, prostitute, secretary, shopgirl, and waitress, to offer some examples (Lodge, 2020, pp. 143–151). Moreover, the oppression of Asian and Black women in musical theatre brings about specific dynamics of objectification and othering at the intersection of gender, race, class, and sexuality. Heteronormative narratives are the foundation of twentieth-century musical theatre storytelling, which impacts the roles available to women as well as the role of women in those musicals, reinforcing conservative gender ideologies. Heteronormativity privileges heterosexuality, which often shapes the logic of musical theatre storytelling and results in LGBTQIA+ identities being underrepresented or stereotyped (Wolf, 2011, pp. 210–224; Lovelock, 2019, pp. 187–209).

If we consider the canon as a resource – for entertainment, enjoyment, and learning – then we can also understand it as a tool of oppression. Patricia Hill Collins explains: 'Oppression describes any unjust situation where, systematically and over a long period of time, one group denies another group access to the resources of a society' (2000, p. 6). This lack of representation or misrepresentation means that, for women and people from marginalised groups, the didactic function of the canon is skewed away from their material interests.

Texts used in training have implications beyond the rehearsal room, as Rhonda Blair suggests it models ways of seeing and being in the world and functions as a 'training for life':

> [P]erforming a role is a kind of 'training for life', a rehearsal and patterning of a way of being in the world. It guides a young woman in developing a sense of what her choices for living are. Theatrical roles are constructed which make assertions about the way the world is, and more often than not they re-inscribe the dominant culture; hence, they continue to objectify and marginalize women, denying them subjectivity.
>
> (1992, p. 16)

If approached uncritically, engagement with canonical texts reinforces oppressive social orders; the teaching and learning we do in classrooms and rehearsal rooms shape our world views. On a practical level, the texts we engage with have material consequences, including how many and what kinds of roles are available and for whom. The texts that we engage in our training processes have both a qualitative and quantitative impact on students (Stamatiou, 2019, pp. 50–62). In addition to being afforded less time, women are obliged to develop their craft through roles that are often narrow, reductive, and even damaging. Of course, the potential drawbacks of practising skills and technique through canonical texts extend beyond gender.

When my co-head and I came into our positions in 2018, we used texts by Anton Chekhov or Henrik Ibsen in our acting classes for students to learn and practice techniques. Perhaps unsurprisingly, these were texts that we had engaged in within our own undergraduate training. When working through an acting scheme of work using a Chekhov text with a Stanislavski-based process, I became increasingly aware of the additional labour required of students from global majority backgrounds, an imposition articulated by various practitioners (Vasquez, 2023, p. 129; Pettiford-Wates, 2017, p. 107). A supposed 'universal canon' reinforces that the class/rehearsal room is a foundationally white, hetero-cisgender, non-disabled space and asks those from marginalised groups to censor or erase their identities. This was also the first time I had a comprehensive overview of a course, and indeed, responsibility for its content and delivery. This was not the only place in the training whereby global majority students would be coerced to adapt to a white centre. Since that time, we have taken an increasing number of steps to reconfigure and reposition the use of canonical texts as a training tool, and in some places, remove them altogether.

In our recent revalidation, a quality assurance process that occurs on a five-year cycle, we replaced our first-term project, which previously entailed rehearsing a single play or musical, with the Bridging Project, a project designed for students to apply the techniques acquired in the preceding skills weeks and synthesise learning. As part of the Bridging Project, students undertake a contemporary scene study. We ask students to find material that resonates in some way with their experience and identity but to avoid plays that require exploration of a real-life traumatic experience; we want to work from ease and joy, rather than tension and suffering. This strategy builds on Alison Nicole Vasquez's articulation of practice, which asks students to consider: 'Who am I?'; and to 'Look for a play or character that has similarities to your lived experience' (2023, p. 137). Engaging a wider range of playwrights in turn offers access to a wider range and breadth of characters, which helps to create a space where difference is viewed as a strength, where identity is not denied or erased and where people might feel able to participate more fully. This work is impeded if the only texts engaged represent and/or privilege white hetero-cisgender male experience, written by white, predominantly male playwrights. Hence, a plurality of texts is required for a diverse population of students with many, often intersecting, identity positions. The texts we engage have a direct bearing on whether students can bring their whole selves to the training. Rehearsing scenes means that students do not experience the arc of a whole play at this stage in their training, nor do they sustain their interpretation of a role beyond one scene. However, our sense from implementing this strategy is that the gains are greater than the losses. There is greater parity and equitability, and students can choose texts within which they see themselves. We want learning to begin with practices that affirm the identities of students.

Another substantive change made in our revalidation was removing a component called Classical Scene Work, which moved through Greek Theatre, Shakespeare/Jacobean Theatre, Comedy of Manners, Naturalism and Realism. The class involved group discussion, analysis, and scene work. Students explored heightened language and character connection to higher powers or the supernatural; embodiment of the mask, irony and wit, social conventions; and finally, the engagement of objects and architecture from the real world to create an imaginary world. Exploring this range of theatrical styles was a useful exercise for students to develop their practice. However, this structure also reinforced a white, Euro-Western narrative of acting, theatre, and performance. Sharrell D. Luckett and Tia M. Shaffer argue that the received idea that theatre began with the Greeks exiles African thought and practices from a theatre history that 'they rightfully co-constructed' (2017, p. 1). Ultimately, when the word 'classical' is used in training contexts, it refers to Euro-Western art forms, which are implicitly associated with both the foundation and pinnacle of training. Moving towards a more racially just actor-training requires contextualising, repositioning, and accounting for historically excluded theatre, performance, and training traditions.

Our current curriculum includes a series of interactive seminars developed and facilitated by an alumna of the programme, Tania Nwachukwu. These sessions explore Afrocentric paradigms, including the Griot and Hip-Hop performance. They do not focus on extant texts (although students do explore writing themselves), rather they speak to pedagogies and practices and so I will return to them in the subsequent section on teaching. In our revalidation, we replaced Classical Scene Work with a new component called Form and Context. The component does include two pillars of European theatrical convention, Shakespeare and Brecht; however, here they are repositioned to uncover rather than reinforce the hegemonic sensibilities of Euro-Western canons. The emphasis shifts away from playtexts as the primary consideration; rather, this component offers students, as Amy Mihyang Ginther puts it, 'the possibilities of a paradox' where Shakespeare can be critiqued as a colonial power and used to explore tools of poetry: alliteration, assonance, rhyme, iambic, punctuation, imagery, antithesis (2023b, p. 178). Brecht's playtexts are bypassed completely, in favour of exploring the techniques he developed for practical and political purposes, including those identified by feminist theorists and practitioners, who 'have looked to Brecht for ways of confronting and combating sexism in performance by revealing patriarchal structures and dramatising the dialectic of oppression and liberation' (Barnett, 2015, p. 208). Finally, the component explores deconstructing and reimagining canonical texts. This year students engaged with *Three Sisters*, and strategies engaged by the company RashDash and writer Inua Ellams, who have reinvented the play.

To conclude this section, I have shared some of the changes that we have made to how we use texts in our training to create a more inclusive experience for our students. One of the reasons why certain canonical works are taught is their association with certain canons of actor training, a habitual way of thinking that has perpetuated certain lineages. The idea that Stanislavski-based techniques are best practised through Chekhov's texts has been long held in many places. Director Katie Mitchell dispels this notion: 'Many people think that the exercises of a nineteenth-century Russian can only be used when working on a nineteenth-century Russian play. This is not the case' (2009, p. 227). This observation does, however, point to the interrelationship between texts and technique both in actor training and beyond. If we are to trouble the canon, we need to trouble this notion.

Technique

Acting technique is often assumed to be neutral. Yet if engaged uncritically, acting technique often upholds dominant power structures rather than unpicking the biases and oppressive values that play out in the acting classroom and rehearsal room. Elizabeth C. Stroppel advocates for a pedagogy that engages with gender as it applies to individual identity and positionality while challenging the homogeneity of male hegemony. She suggests that actor training regularly marginalises women for its 'inclination toward male adversarial notions' (2000, p. 11) and argues that this form of marginalisation is expressly experienced in training contexts:

> This situation is particularly apparent within the acting training classroom, where students must utilize their whole selves as instruments of enactment in order to participate. In addition, part of the nature of acting techniques implies that such techniques are aesthetic tools, constructed from specific ideological bases. Whether inadvertently or not, acting choices remain by and large with the prevailing power structure.
>
> (ibid)

Stroppel identifies that Stanislavski-based exercises that do not appear explicitly biased often play out in prejudicial ways when gender perspectives are ignored (2000, p. 113).

In this section, I will focus on three fundamental tenets of Stanislavski-based technique: *Objective*, *action*, and *As If*. The most fundamental tenet of a Stanislavski-based approach is the *objective*. Bella Merlin explains the centrality of an *objective* in this acting process:

> You can't really go onstage or in front of the camera unless you know what you are *doing* – and it's hard to do anything if you don't really know *why* it is that you are doing it. What do you want? What's your desire? What do you want to achieve? Who do I want to influence and persuade? Such a desire or drive or impulse is what Stanislavsky called a 'goal' or a 'task' (*zadacha*), a word which then became translated in *An Actor Prepares* as the somewhat more scientific sounding OBJECTIVE.
>
> (2007, p. 73)

I would argue that an *objective*, while clearly related to the text, is open to change. *Objectives* may be established through discussion with a teacher/director, but an effective *objective* is contingent on the actor's capacity not only to articulate but to play it. In my experience, students often choose *objectives* that serve patriarchal and/or heteronormative interests and position women as passive and/or in relation to men. It takes time to identify and play strong objectives. As part of this practice, students may implicitly (or explicitly) reproduce what they have consumed from dominant culture or conform to perceptions of industry expectations. Active attention is required to refocus and to seek out alternative possibilities, not only to resist reinforcing narrow and sexist attitudes but to create more dynamic and nuanced performances.

Another tenet of a Stanislavski-based approach that calls for consideration is *action*. On a basic level, *actions* work to serve the *objective*, that is, action is what a character does to get what they want. Carnicke explains:

> In the System, *action* denotes what the actor does to solve the *problem* set before the character by the *given circumstances* of the play and production. Thus, action seeks to accomplish something: to persuade an opponent, to climb the ladder of success, to revenge one's father's death. Expressed as an active verb, action is both 'mental'/inner and 'physical'/outer; it must be 'apt' in relationship to the circumstances.
>
> (in Hodge, 2010, p. 15)

An oft-used technique to explore actions in UK drama schools is *actioning*, as explained by Marina Caldarone and Maggie Lloyd-Williams (2004). *Actioning* requires finding a transitive verb that works between 'I' and 'you' to describe what the actor is doing to the other person, in pursuit of the objective. Even if students are not taught or directed to choose actions following gender norms, when attention is not given to these dynamics in analysing a scene, song, and/or developing a role, students will often choose actions that have been habitually associated with a particular gender, and in turn replicate narrow ideas about gender and even stereotypes. My experience indicates that women often need encouragement away from playing only actions that would typically be considered sexualised or subservient, to liberate them from stereotypical limitations towards more autonomous and critically engaged representations of women. Opening feminist possibilities in this process begins with finding objectives that do not position women solely in relation to men. Facilitating students' ability to choose actions and choose them critically is key, as Malague emphasises: 'The importance of the action cannot be overstated. For it gives actors something to *do*, something to *accomplish* onstage. And I also believe that it is through action that actors are empowered to make political choices' (2013, p. 97). In addition to teaching *action* and/or *actioning* as a technique, the significance of this choice-making should be signposted in actor-training classes and rehearsal rooms.

Also worth consideration is the Stanislavskian technique, *Magic If* or *As If*. Benedetti's translation of Stanislavski's *An Actor's Work* uses only *If*: 'The actor must ask what he would do "if" the Given Circumstances were really true' (2000, p. 684). Krasner explains *As If*: 'In defining the given circumstances, actors behave *as if* they are living in the situation of the play' (2000, p. 131). Using *If* as part of a process of identification, the actor finds their relationship to the character based on her own experience and perspectives. While seeking out similarities is not necessarily problematic in itself, when women engage with canonical texts, we see how acting technique meets text, which might mean identifying with potentially harmful characteristics and/or deferring to stereotypes. Malague uses Blanche in *A Streetcar Named Desire* as an example; if approached using personal identification uncritically, it requires 'women to stimulate and summon the most fragile, feminine, *vulnerable* aspects of themselves, without any distance between themselves and the characters they portray' (2012, p. 180, original emphasis). Further, there is a risk of defaulting to whiteness by assuming *If* is universally effective. In Lundeana Thomas' *Barbra Ann Teer and the National Black Theatre*, Jessica B. Harris offers:

> As the Black experience in America is quite different from the White one, Black actors are frequently asked to play roles that have nothing to do with the basic reality of their

lives. This may seem to be a contradiction but Stanislavski's 'as if' theory does not always work for Black actors in these times.

(1997, pp. 85, 86)

Often, acting technique is rooted in identifying with a character in some respect, as with Stanislavski's *If*. Recognising cultural difference in actor-training contexts calls for finding multiple pathways into a play-world rather than assuming everyone in a group can connect to or identify with a text in the same way. Vasquez notes how, when working on a Euro-Western text through the prism of Stanislavskian 'truth', tension crept into the otherwise 'relatively free voices and bodies' of the Latinx students undertaking the work (2023, p. 129). Vasquez developed a decolonising strategy for working from a Stanislavskian basis, which recognises cultural differences within the acting classroom (of which I only offer a fragment here). She asks students to

[R]ead the play twice, identity unknown first, and then work from a place of curiosity. Next, they include annotations on their script with a question mark over lines and/or sentences with which they did not connect; an asterisk over the lines and/or sentences that resonated with their lived experience, and finally, a percent sign over a line and/or sentence that was understood easily yet not experienced.

(Vasquez, 2023, p. 137)

Vasquez's approach chimes with Rhonda Blair's 'Not-Not-Me' (1993), which endorses exploring both identification *and* difference as a practicable hybrid approach. As well as recognising differences (not-me), performers use experience and/or imagination to identify with a role (not-not-me). Table 6.1 shows an example of how this exercise was developed by Tania Nwachukwu as a student at Mountview when she played Joan of Arc in *Queen Margaret*.

The concept of 'not-not-me' offers a frame whereby actors can build performance through a palimpsest of (sometimes contradictory) layers that recognise intersectional identities, reposition personal identification, and allow the actor's presence to exist alongside the character.

To conclude this section, it is important to stress that I do not reject Stanislavski-based techniques, I use them in my teaching regularly (emphasising a female genealogy of practice). The pitfalls articulated here can and do extend to other approaches to acting/performance training. The relationship between technique and text is consequential. However, in conversations about inclusivity in actor training, text tends to supersede technique as the driving force of exclusion. Attention must also be given to the technique for its capacity to uphold or perpetuate bias and systems of oppression. Ultimately, I suggest that the efficacy of any training process is predicated on centring pedagogy, which takes us to teaching.

Teaching

As much as the techniques and texts engaged shape actor training, so too does the teaching. In practice, the presence of the teacher and their approach to teaching can (and often does) supersede text and technique. Many problems in traditional actor-training contexts stem from imbalanced power relations between student and teacher, where the relationship between teacher and student operates in a one-way, give-and-receive system. Building on Freire, hooks explains that this is 'the approach to learning that is rooted in the notion that all students need to do is consume information fed to them by a professor', an approach that

Table 6.1 The Not-Not-Me exercise as used by Tania Nwachukwu as Joan of Arc in *Queen Margaret*.

Me	Not-Me	Not-Not-Me
Black British woman of Nigerian heritage	French white woman	Working class and the feeling of being othered
Non-religious	Religious	Being a foreign body in a hostile country
Actor/Poet/Archivist	Heroine/Saint	Patriotism to a land colonised/disrupted by the British
		Feeling of limbo: Joan can't rest until she is avenged; I'm not able to rest until the systems of oppression that affect me daily are dismantled
		The pursuit of peace
		And we both know how to throw shade

reinforces structures of domination through the supposed neutrality of the teacher (1994, p. 14). In actor training, this dynamic is compounded by an anti-critical bias. The directive to 'get out of your head', or as Peck designates, the instruction to 'disembrain' (8–10), is an oft-repeated idiom in actor training. This attitude can obstruct students' ability to think critically and creatively and reinforce power structures that can play out in abuse. While I do not wish to diminish the importance of skills acquisition in an experiential training process, this anti-critical, anti-thinking bias must be challenged to shift some of the oppressive practices that persist in actor training. A critical acting pedagogy embraces moving between the analytic and experiential, immersion, and reflection. Further, critical acting pedagogy emphasises the co-creation of knowledge through a dialogic process, which challenges the traditional hierarchical relationship between teacher and student wherein the teacher holds all the authority. It respects individual learning while relating class and rehearsal rooms to the 'real world' with sociopolitical awareness. In this section, I focus on *how* we teach, with a specific focus on de-centring power in co-creating knowledge. I set out some of the strategies that we have engaged to recalibrate power structures and to centre critical thinking in our training.

A masterclass format is often engaged in actor training. In this arrangement, students perform for the teacher and receive critique while other students observe. As the title suggests, a masterclass emphasises the authority of the teacher. Kathleen Juhl argues that the format of students working on a scene, showing the scene, and then receiving notes from the teacher, 'not only disempowers actors but is a recipe for beginning acting students to develop bad habits because they are struggling to create product-orientated "performances"' (2007, p. 154). The task is to set up a space whereby students can share their work in a way that emphasises an exploratory process where, as Peck advises, an 'atmosphere of trust and relationality is built' and 'choice and action are scaffolded for the actor' (2021, p. 49). To do so, we might think of how we structure tasks, ask questions, and give feedback, not in a give–take, teach–learn, practice–perform dichotomy, but as a non-linear model that involves doing, observing, dialoguing towards a deeper embodied understanding.

At the start of a class, I do a check-in, where students are invited to share reflections and ask questions about the work, or students do some free writing or free drawing and/or a warm-up if required. Moving into scene work, students fill the space in their pairs in such a way that there is no actor/audience spatial separation. A task or exercise is set, which all students explore simultaneously. I move around the space, observing, asking questions, and offering prompts. Once the group has had sufficient time to explore that exercise or execute the task, I pause the work and we watch one pair work for a short time, potentially with some coaching and with the opportunity for those students to articulate their discoveries and for other students to feedback on their work in respect of the task at hand. Then we move to the next task or exercise, watch another pair undertake some of the work, and so on. In respect of scaffolding choice for the actor, I suggest that in current training contexts, developing students' ability to identify and play actions autonomously is typical. As expressed in the previous section on technique, less typical is interrogating this task in the context of gender difference and gendered experience. Feminist acting teachers, including Julh and Malague, recognise that the efficacy of a feminist approach stems from a method of working that emphasises students making choices, de-emphasises the authority of the teacher, and does not reproduce damaging gender stereotypes – this thinking can, of course, be extended beyond gender to race, ethnicity, class, and disability. I have set out how I have reconfigured my 'master' acting classroom. Next, I move onto the flipped classroom, posited by some educational scholarship as a pathway towards a more inclusive learning environment (Lage et al., 2000).

A flipped classroom asks students to do preparatory work in advance of a class. Kim Solga explains:

> What's a flipped classroom? It's a classroom in which students come having done pre-prep, reading or listening to content in advance. It's a classroom where various kinds of group discussions and problem-solving activities take place, *live, between us*. It's a classroom in which students are invited actively to engage in knowledge *production*, to use their embodied minds to test ideas on their feet, and to work collaboratively to challenge status-quo assumptions.
>
> (2016, np)

Anna McNamara posits that flipped classrooms improve understanding of learning as a cyclical process and strengthen independent student activity (2021, p. 528). She notes that some Stanislavski-based acting/rehearsal processes involve independent research in the preparation of a role, which if made use of in actor training, can function as a flipped rehearsal room and facilitate a student-centred approach. We engage in flipped classrooms in various places on the MA Performance programme at Mountview to cultivate critical thinking, make the most of class time, and enable students to process information at their own pace. Giving students information in advance helps to address some of the biases and inequities in learning. Having a 'good' education, economic, and geographic access to live arts/theatre and using English as a first language are all facets that privilege some learners. A flipped classroom enables students from a variety of backgrounds to prepare for class to engage critically with the material presented and process information at their own pace. To do so, we provide students with scholarly articles, reviews, blogs, podcasts, etc., which students engage with ahead of class. To offer some examples from our Form and Context classes, students are provided with material, including 'Interrogating the Shakespeare System' (Sayet, 2020); 'Dismantling Anti-Black Language in Theatre' (Derr & Jadhwani, 2020); Kim Solga's blog post on the Donmar Warehouse's Shakespeare Trilogy (2017); David Barnett's *Brecht in Practice* website (2023); an excerpt from *Disability Theatre and Modern Drama* (Johnston, 2016) on 'Critical Embodiment and Casting', which draws on Brecht's *Messingkauf Dialogues*; National Theatre's production of Ellams' *Three Sisters* (2020, available on Drama Online); and reviews of Rash Dash's interpretation of *Three Sisters*. Ultimately, the flipped classroom enables us to bring a range of critical sources to the curriculum, intervene in actor training's anti-critical bias, and cultivate classrooms where the teacher is not the singular authority.

Form and Context also flips the assessment process. Students mark themselves, making the assessment part of the learning process and further minimising the authority of the teacher. The marking rubric offers descriptors for each band: Sophisticated (80 plus); Developed (70–79); Established (60–69); Emerging (50–59); and Insufficient (Below 50). Students write evidence of their learning based on contribution, subject knowledge, class and group work, and engagement with reading/additional sources. When it was explained that students would self-assess for this component, some seemed resistant or wary of the task. As the process developed, students reflected on their work with balance and care and very few people over-marked themselves. Further, there was a sense of students taking an increased responsibility for their learning. As an exercise, self-assessment illuminates the assessment processes and makes it more transparent for students, demonstrating how teachers too must align progress and qualify attainment using learning outcomes, marking criteria and descriptors. The National Union of Students benchmarking for assessment and feedback calls for assessments to be diverse and collaborative. Further, contemporary assessment strategies require both efficiency and inclusivity. Engaging with wider educational practices and scholarship will enable actor training to expand its approaches concerning assessment and feedback to enhance student learning.

To conclude this section, I return to our seminars on Afrocentric paradigms. In these sessions, students engage with storytelling techniques such as call-and-response, as well as write and perform a rap. In addition to exploring practice, Nwachukwu stresses the paramount importance of pedagogy and summarises the approaches of Freddie Hendricks and Kashi Johnson who both feature in Luckett and Shaffer's *Black Acting Methods*:

Hendricks

- Activism
- Affirming students
- Bringing your whole self and your skills to the rehearsals
- Giving students space
- Meeting students where they are
- No partitions, seeing the artist as a whole
- Ensemble building
- Understanding who students are and what their needs are

Johnson

- A cyclical exchange between teacher and participants
- Creating a safe space
- Centring social justice issues
- Speaking truth to power

Nwachukwu expertly guides students through a seminar whereby these principles are not only signposted but experienced. Both Hendricks and Johnson recognise the political dynamics and potential of a theatre/performance teaching space. Art and activism are put beside each other. Recognising identity is paramount. Learning is positioned as an exchange. These approaches resonate with feminist pedagogies in their assertion that *how* we teach is as important as *what* we teach and emphasise de-centring power in the co-creation of knowledge. These principles, allied with educational scholarship, which asks teachers to scaffold and signpost development and make tasks more practicable (McNamara, 2021, p. 532), can unite in a collaborative teaching-learning process.

Conclusion

I have outlined some of the actions that we have taken at Mountview to expand our provision to teach a variety of texts that go beyond androcentric, hetero-cisgender, and white canons and how we have repositioned actor-training techniques through critical pedagogy. In terms of texts, it is important to consider how simply adding texts does not shift the fundamental problem of whiteness as a default position. Susan Sánchez-Casal and Aimie A. Macdonald warn that an 'additive approach', where material 'related to recognizable minority racial groups' is simply added to an extant curriculum, will fail to shift the hegemonic values of the curriculum (2009, pp. 15, 16). Moreover, the failure to undertake meaningful curricular reform (beyond making additions) upholds 'tacit racist presumptions of the superiority of white and European intellect and ways of reading the world, and thus negatively impacts the learning community for students of all racial identities' (ibid, p. 14). Centring of identities in the classroom increases *all* students' abilities to evaluate social interactions with the wider world and assess ableism, classism, colonialism, homophobia, and racism (ibid, p. 17). Hence, I posit that it is time for those of us who do actor training to think about how we might reposition those 'canonical' texts as a training tool.

Next, we need to see technique as inherently political, that is, there are always dynamics of power at play when we are practising a technique. Amy Steiger points to training's narrow industry focus as a problem. Steiger offers that '[a] market-driven context often reinforces the illusion that, for actors, dissent and critical thinking are inherently political, and training for professional work should take place outside of politics' (2019: np). The 'industry' is often used as a mandate to maintain the status quo in actor training. The industry should not be used as a paradigm for best practice when often it is not. Nor should it be positioned monolithically when there is more than one way to cultivate a career in the creative industry. Finally, we must shift actor training's anti-critical bias, which is reinforced by a narrow industry focus that replicates – quite literally – an educative model that serves those in power, as theorised by Freire.

Repositioning identity and critical thinking in our curriculum have been the two driving forces in moving our curriculum towards an engaged acting pedagogy. Identity puts students at the centre of the process and begins with practices that affirm their experience and knowledge. It calls for students to cultivate an awareness of their own involvement in a hegemonic agenda and an embodied practice that challenges binary thinking and embraces plurality. Validating identity is linked to culturally responsive pedagogies and enabling agency, the ability to act or take action. Emphasising identity begins with practices that affirm students' experience and knowledge. Identity is inextricably linked with acting, casting, and performance processes: 'It is not strictly the labour of acting but is an unavoidable part of the work of being an actor' (Smith, 2020, p. 38). Our students come to training with their experience of the world, through class, disability, gender, race, sexuality, and other markers of identity. I have encountered some teachers who resist the idea of bringing identity into the acting classroom, positioning it as antithetical to imagination and transformation. Acting teachers do not need to 'bring' identity into the classroom; they need to recognise that they are already there. Further, imagination does not supersede the materiality of ideology, as Dorinne Kondo offers: 'While the arts are important sites for imaginative play, the imagination never transcends the social or political' (2018, p. 34). Moreover, she argues that 'The dismissal of "identity politics" arises from a power-evasive notion of identity occluding the racialized, gendered, colonialist power through which identity comes into being' (12). Criticality asserts that performance has greater efficacy when it is created with an understanding of the sociopolitical/sociocultural structures within which it is created and received. Criticality involves questioning received knowledge and investigating how patriarchal, Eurocentric, and heteronormative structures can be dismantled.

In this chapter, I have offered examples of how texts, techniques, and teaching converge. Thinking through the three Ts independently and relationally has the potential to drive innovation of curriculum, pedagogy, and delivery of actor training. There is no single way of fixing or doing things: rather, we need a plurality of approaches and practices, and to employ a variety of texts and actor-training techniques that go beyond an androcentric, heterocentric, Euro-Western canon as well as contextualising those canons within a critical framework. This work needs to be undertaken alongside an engaged pedagogy that critically assesses teaching methods, learning activities and assessment strategies. I desire to share this work in the spirit of exchanging ideas to move beyond a singular norm of thought and experience towards pluralistic and more inclusive actor-training practices.

References

Aston, E. (1999). *Feminist theatre practice: A handbook*. Routledge.
Barnett, D. (2015). *Brecht in practice: Theatre, theory and performance*. Bloomsbury Methuen Drama.
Barnett, D. (2023). *Brecht in practice*. www.brechtinpractice.net/home
Benedetti, J. (2000). *Stanislavski: An introduction*. Methuen Publishing Ltd.
Blair, R. (1992). Liberating the young actor: Feminist pedagogy and performance. *Theatre Topics*, 2(1), 13–23.
Blair, R. (1993). "Not. . . but"/"Not-Not-Me": Musings on cross-gender performance. In E. Donkin & S. Clement (Eds.), *Upstaging big daddy: Directing theater as if gender and race matter* (pp. 291–307). University of Michigan Press.
Caldarone, M., & Lloyd-Williams, M. (2004). *Actions: The actors' thesaurus*. Nick Hern Books.
Carnicke, S. (2010). The Knebel technique: Active analysis in practice. In A. Hodge (Ed.), *Actor training* (pp. 1–23). Routledge.
Collins, P. H. (2000). *Black feminist thought*. Routledge.
Crabtree, R. D., Sapp, D. A., & Licona, A. C. (Eds.). (2009). *Feminist pedagogy: Looking back to move forward*. The John Hopkins University Press.
Derr, H. L., & Jadhwani, L. (2020). Dismantling anti-Black language. *Howlround*. https://howlround.com/dismantling-anti-black-language
Diamond, E. (1997). *Unmaking mimesis: Essays on feminism and theater*. Routledge.
Dolan, J. (2012). *The feminist spectator as critic*. University of Michigan Press.
Ellams, I. (2020). *Three sisters*. National Theatre. Drama Online. Bloomsbury Publishing Plc.
Freire, P. (1993). *Pedagogy of the oppressed* [Originally published The Continuum Publishing Company, 1970]. Penguin.
Gainor, J. E. (2002). Rethinking feminism, Stanislavsky, and performance. *Theatre Topics*, 12(2), 163–175.
Ginther, A. M. (Ed.). (2023a). *Stages of reckoning: Antiracist and decolonial actor training*. Routledge.
Ginther, A. M. (2023b). The possibilities of paradox. In A. M. Ginter (Ed.), *Stages of reckoning: Antiracist and decolonial actor training* (pp. 164–195). Routledge.
Goodman, L., & Owens, W. R. (1996). *Shakespeare, Aphra Behn and the canon*. Routledge.
Hooks, b. (1994). *Teaching to transgress: Education as the practice of freedom*. Routledge.
Johnston, K. (2016). *Disability theatre and modern drama: Recasting modernism*. Bloomsbury Methuen Drama.

Juhl, K. (2007). Feminism in the acting classroom: Playful practice as process. In A. E. Armstrong & K. Juhl (Eds.), *Radical acts: Theatre and feminist pedagogies of change* (pp. 153–169). Aunt Lute Books.

Kondo, D. (2018). *Worldmaking.* Duke University Press.

Krasner, D. (Ed.). (2000). *Method acting reconsidered: Theory, practice, future.* Palgrave Macmillan.

Lage, M. J., Platt, G. J., & Treglia, M. (2000). Inverting the classroom: A gateway to creating an inclusive learning environment. *The Journal of Economic Education, 31*(6), 30–43.

Light, T. P., Nicholas, J., & Bondy, R. (Eds.). (2015). *Feminist pedagogy in higher education: Critical theory and practice.* Wilfrid Laurier University Press.

Lodge, M. J. (2020). Do-Re-#MeToo: Women, work, and representation in the broadway musical. In J. Sternfeld & E. L. Wollman (Eds.), *The Routledge companion to the contemporary musical* (pp. 143–151). Routledge.

Lovelock, J. (2019). 'What about love?': Claiming and reclaiming LGBTQ spaces in twenty-first century musical theatre. In S. Whitfield (Ed.), *Reframing the Musical: Race, Culture and Identity* (pp. 187–209). Red Globe Press.

Luckett, S. D., & Shaffer, T. M. (Eds.). (2017). *Black acting methods: Critical approaches.* Routledge.

Malague, R. (2013). *An actress prepares: Women and "the Method".* Routledge.

Matsuda, M. J. (1991). Beside my sister, facing the enemy: Legal theory out of coalition. *Stanford Law Review, 43*(6), 1183–1192.

McNamara, A. (2021). Flipping the creative conservatoire classroom. *Theatre, Dance and Performance* Training, *12*(4) 528–539.

Merlin, B. (2007). *The complete Stanislavsky toolkit.* Nick Hern Books.

Mitchell, K. (2009). *The director's craft: A handbook for the theatre.* Routledge.

Peck, L. (2021). *Act as a feminist: Towards a critical acting pedagogy.* Routledge.

Pettiford-Wates, T. (2017). Ritual poetic drama within the African continuum: The journey from Shakespeare to Shange. In S. D. Luckett & T. M. Shaffer (Eds.), *Black acting methods: Critical approaches* (pp. 106–122). Routledge.

Sánchez-Casal, S. (2009). *Identity in education.* Palgrave Macmillan.

Sayet, M. (2020). Interrogating the Shakespeare system. *Howlround.* https://howlround.com/interrogating-shakespeare-system

Smith, K. (2020). On being cast: Identity work. *Platform, Theatres of Labour, 14*(1 & 2), 36–51.

Solga, K. (2016). On flipping the theatre studies classroom. . .back again (part 1). *The Activist Classroom.* https://theactivistclassroom.wordpress.com/2016/06/20/on-flipping-the-theatre-studies-classroom-back-again-part-1/

Solga, K. (2017). On the freedom to move, and the freedom to be, part 3. *The Activist Classroom.* https://theactivistclassroom.wordpress.com/2017/01/02/on-the-freedom-to-move-and-the-freedom-to-be-part-3/

Stamatiou, E. (2019). A materialist feminist perspective on time in actor-training: The commodity of illusion. In M Evans, K. Thomaidis, & L. Worth (Eds.), *Time and performer training* (pp. 50–61). Routledge.

Steiger, A. (2019). Whiteness, patriarchy, and resistance in actor training text: Reframing acting students as embodied critical thinkers. *Howlround.* https://howlround.com/whiteness-patriarchy-and-resistance-actor-training-texts

Stroppel, E. C. (2000). Reconciling the past and the present. In D. Krasner (Ed.), *Method acting reconsidered* (pp. 111–123). Palgrave Macmillan.

Thomas, L. M. (1997). *Barbara Ann Teer and the National Black Theatre: Transformational forces in Harlem.* Routledge.

Vasquez, A. N. (2023). Representation matters: The why and how of decolonizing Stanislavski actor training. In A. M. Ginther (Ed.), *Stages of reckoning: Antiracist and decolonial actor training* (pp. 129–142). Routledge.

Wolf, S. (2011). Gender and sexuality. In R. Knapp, M. Morris, & S. Wolf (Eds.), *The Oxford handbook of the American musical* (pp. 210–224). Oxford University Press.

7 Liberating Casting and Training Practices for Mixed-Asian Students

Amy Rebecca King and Robert Torigoe

Introduction: What Are You? Where Are You From? No, but Like, Where Are You *From* From?

'Biracial'. 'Mixed'. 'Multiracial'. 'Half [ethnicity]'. 'A quarter [ethnicity]'. 'Well, I was born in [place], but I was raised in [place] until we moved to [place]. But really my parents are from [place] and [place]'. These are just a few of the terms and phrases that people of more than one race use to identify themselves, including the authors of this chapter.[1] This racial and ethnic identification is necessitated by society's basic need to identify and understand, not necessarily by a person's desire to identify and/or categorise themselves.[2]

'What are you?' 'I'm a human'. But that's not the question being asked. Sociologist Paul Sites theorises that eight basic human needs drive human behaviour: (1) consistency in response, (2) stimulation, (3) security, (4) recognition, (5) distributive justice, (6) rationality and the appearance of rationality, (7) meaning, and (8) control (as cited in Burton, 1987).[3] The need for recognition is rooted in the needs for safety and understanding. Humans must recognise how the varying elements of society coexist and function together to survive. One must be able to label and identify the differences between safe and dangerous. When people recognise something new as identifiable, or similar, they experience a base feeling of security. Fear of the unknown is far more threatening than anything identifiable. If you can label it, you can manage it.

This same theory applies to our consumption of art and media. People engage with art and media that they can relate to. Commonly, audiences try their best to see themselves in the story, and one of the more common ways of seeking connection is through ethnic representation. Media capitalises on this and sells stories directed towards specific audiences. For example, a study from 2009 to 2021 surveyed Americans 15 years and older, and found that among white, Black/African American, Asian, and Hispanic/Latino Americans, Asian Americans had the lowest daily TV consumption rates, ranging from 1.71 to 1.97 hours per day (Stoll, 2022). This is just one of the reasons that fewer Asian stories are being created, leaving fewer casting opportunities for Asian actors.

Regarding Asian representation, one must consider the intersectionality between monoracial Asian Americans and multiracial Asian Americans.[4] It's common for both monoracial and multiracial Black, Indigenous, and people of colour (henceforth BIPOC) in America to experience separation from the white American identity while still having to assimilate into the culture. For example, the pressure to fit in at school when your parents pack you a traditional Asian lunch. Or, the differences in the approach to education and growth/development. However, several experiences are unique to the multiracial BIPOC identity in America. For example, the 'what are you' question is most often experienced by multiracial

DOI: 10.4324/9781003393672-10

people. There might be a disidentification with your own body, as your experience is separate from the experience of both of your parents.

There are even fewer opportunities for mixed-Asian people, who belong to more than one ethnic group. The media is slowly progressing towards more appropriately representational ethnic casting. Names of monoracial Asian-American actors like Sandra Oh, Michelle Yeoh, Daniel Dae Kim, and Randall Park are recognised in more and more households. They play characters that are written specifically for Asian actors. Yet, we see very few stories about mixed-Asian people, and therefore, very few roles being created specifically for mixed-Asian actors. This also means a lack of representation of the unique mixed-Asian experience. Mixed-Asian actors are left with the responsibility of determining their own appropriateness for roles. Where does this leave representation for mixed-Asian students, and the multiracial experience itself?

Our hope with this chapter is to admonish the 'othering' of the mixed-race student in the study of acting on a university campus. This will also expose practices that can marginalise intersecting peoples and identities, including students of the global majority, with disabilities or varying gender identities. Through the lens of two multiracial Asian theatre educators, this chapter offers methods for amplifying the voices of multiracial Asian students in the classroom. Firstly, the chapter presents the unique positionality of the individual authors and their experiences. Through themes of identity, perception, and categorisation, it then responds to questions such as: What are the issues for mixed-Asian actors in the casting industry? How do tokenising and ambiguity affect the representation of the Asian diaspora? What are the varying assumptions associated with mixed-Asian people in America? Why are most stories that follow multiracial characters about struggles with identity? In response to these questions, the chapter unpacks methods for educators to best serve multiracial students, who are already at the peak of vulnerability when they first enter the acting classroom. The outcome of the work shares opportunities for mixed-Asian actors to examine characters that may be adjacent to themselves but also to create pathways for them, and other underrepresented peoples, to tell their own stories in a university setting.

Our Experiences: A Conversation

Amy: My whole life I've gotten the 'what are you' question. My mom is white, and my dad is Japanese, but I was mostly raised by my white family. People constantly asking, 'Why don't you look like your mom?' or 'Are you adopted?' left me questioning who I really was. Where was my place in the world – especially in theatre? In addition to being a mixed-Asian woman, I'm also a fairly average-sized American, larger than the standard ingenue, but too small, and too young, for the larger, older woman. And while the standards and stereotypes of these roles are very problematic, these roles exist. I limited myself by looking for any role where the character's race 'didn't matter', or who didn't have to be considered 'beautiful', because I could get those roles. Growing up in a predominantly white neighbourhood, I even looked for any BIPOC roles, no matter the race. It felt like my ambiguity was an advantage in areas where everyone else around me looked the same and fit the same mould of the leading characters.

Robert: Early on, I had a false perception of the industry. My own identity as a Puerto Rican-Japanese gay cis male was not going to be an issue. I believed I would have to hone my talents to be successful and dreamed of playing many roles that are traditionally played by cis white males. I had little contemplation about race until the casting of Jonathan Pryce in Miss Saigon on Broadway sparked protests from

Asian American actors in New York City. As my career developed, I tried to align with Asian and Latino roles. I quickly came to realise that my mixed ethnicity complicated the process. If I audition for a Japanese role, for example, I may not visually represent Japanese to the casting team. Coming to this realization was harsh but not a deal-breaker for me because I could also find opportunity in ambiguity.

Amy: By the time I got to the real world, I realised that you can't squeeze yourself into moulds. Casting directors want a representative (or token) for that identity to visually match the character exactly. With no opportunities for mixed-Asian women, I found myself in choruses, or in experimental roles that entirely erased race – I wore white face seven times during college.

I had a really difficult time identifying with much of the Stanislavsky-based training, as most of it subscribes to the 'inside-out' acting practice, which was hard for me when I didn't feel like my inner identity showed up anywhere in our studies.

Robert: I received my BA in theatre after a long acting career. Before then, my training came from a variety of sources: private studios, workshops, professional classes, and sometimes higher education settings. I received 'traditional' training and realised I had been trying to conform to the model of a white straight male actor. I don't remember deeply exploring my own identity in these classes. I want to also speak to being gay and effeminate. I recently heard someone referring to playing a cis male role as 'drag'. I think this realistically describes the expectations the industry has for gay actors. I realise that I would need to shift my own qualities to fit these moulds instead of celebrating my identities and working with them in more productive ways to achieve character work, this drag. But, in the process, I left my multiracial identity behind.

Our experiences as mixed actors inform our desire to change this for the students we see today. While there are more BIPOC roles available, the pedagogical practice of engaging students in identity connection with characters remains the same, heavily coloured through a monoracial lens, stemming from the white patriarchy. When your only option is fitting yourself into existing moulds (white and/or monoracial), it's difficult to connect your mixed identity to a character. We want all our students to have the practice of bringing their whole selves to the role, encompassing the intersectionality of all their unique identities: race, ethnicity, gender, sexuality, ability, etc. We want to nurture a path for multiracial students to practice embodying their own identities, hoping that mainstream media will reflect the experiences of these artists by providing more opportunities for representation.

Identity

How do casting practices problematise identity in our classrooms? From the perspective of mixed Asian actors, we will illuminate the identity biases that are inherently present in the classroom. As students who don't even fall on the lines of these biases, we argue that mixed students have a complex relationship with their identity, hindering their ability to create an authentic performance.

Whiteness is central to racial classifications and race relations in the United States and is accepted as the racial norm (Haney-López, 2006). Both media and acting classrooms often borrow such practices uncritically. Casting calls and character descriptions typically list the ethnicity of any character that is not white and leave out the label 'white' for other characters, standardising the normativity of whiteness. American media was once dominated solely by white stories and white casts and production teams. Due to financial inaccessibility, it was also dominated by white audiences. While audiences slowly grew more and more diverse, the progression rate of the emergence of diverse stories has been much slower. Whiteness is not just the racial norm, but the 'cultural, political, economic, physical and scientific norm as well' (Morris, 2016, p. 950). White stories also became the lens through which all audiences could recognise themselves and relate, both by the normalising of whiteness and the availability of this content. Furthermore, since America continues to dominate the global media landscape (Katerji, 2014), white stories continue to be standardised as normal across the world.

In 1986, the First National Symposium on Non-Traditional Casting took place at the Shubert Theater in New York City. AEA hosted this event to address a growing protest among the actors regarding a lack of BIPOC representation on professional stages. In the published transcript of this event, they defined 'non-traditional casting' as [t]he casting of ethnic, female or disabled actors in roles where race, ethnicity, gender or physical capability are not necessary to the characters' or play's development' (Davis & Newman, 1988, p. 4). Often referred to as 'color-blind casting', this model promotes actors are meant to be cast solely on their talent without regard to their race, ethnicity, gender, or physical ability (ibid, p. 3).[5] Currently, the theatre industry boasts 'color-conscious casting' as its answer to diversity on national stages. This model casts people specifically based on race, often creating tokenised characters of colour in the theatrical diaspora.

In Teresa Eyring's article 'Standing Up for Playwrights and Against "Colorblind" Casting', the casting of an all-white cast in Lloyd Suh's *Jesus in India* and a white actor as Martin Luther King Jr. in Katori Hall's *The Mountaintop*, sparked a petition to move towards colour-conscious casting. More than 1,300 theatre industry professionals added their names to this petition, stating

> While theatre has always been a place for transformation, we must also acknowledge the past oppressions and ongoing inequities facing people of color, including an uneven playing field where the vast majority of opportunities . . . are held by whites.
>
> (2017)

University theatre departments need to recognise that we cannot call this history just yet. In November 2020, a study on diversity released by the Actors' Equity Association (henceforth AEA), the American union for stage actors and stage managers, revealed that between 2016 and 2019, only 2.03% of 93,957 professional contracts went to actors who identified as Asian or Asian American and 5.13% to actors identifying as multiracial.[6] In the report released in 2023, we see some growth in diversity in 2021 with 3.17% of principal contracts in a play going to Asian or Asian American identifying actors and 6.74% going to multiracial/ethnic identifying actors (AEA, 2017–2023). This shows some growth in opportunity, but not enough to make any impact on dismantling the normality of whiteness.

The efforts of both colour-blind and colour-conscious casting practices have proven ineffective in creating significant opportunities for BIPOC actors, resulting in less work for professional actors. This also silos the opportunity of work for multiracial Asian acting students to the standard white American canon. The work in this canon is primarily learned through Stanislavsky-based techniques, which invite relation to your identity through a cis-white lens, asking you to call upon identity-based behaviours that are considered natural and universal. However, this begs the question of 'how and to what extent actors (and writers and trainers) have internalised white supremacy as "natural"' (Stamatiou, 2023, p. 62). Unknowingly, these behaviours may be more likely to bring up trauma for marginalised students.

Many of the current inclusivity protocols in institutional casting follow colour-blind casting. In 2017, students at Northwestern University spoke out against the callback list for *The 25th Annual Putnam County Spelling Bee* when no Asian students received a callback for the role of Marcy Park, a traditionally Asian character (Burakoff, 2017). Though the original Broadway production cast a Korean woman as Marcy, the racial requirements for the role were removed once the show was licensed for other productions. The director argued that 'My interpretation of the character . . . is about the toxicity of competition. . . . That is a story and a narrative that is inherently relatable to any . . . regardless of race or background' (Burakoff, 2017). However, senior Shea Lee, who is mixed Chinese, argued that '[i]t's hard enough to convince directors to give us a chance on roles that aren't indicated as for Asian women' (Burakoff, 2017). After Lee advocated for a woman or nonbinary person of Asian descent to be cast because of the severe lack of diversity, one Asian woman was called back. In 2019, Lee also explained that the burden to expand representation is placed on people of colour when it should be the priority for all student theatre (Thanikachalam, 2019). Joy Lanceta Coronel writes that

[t]he casting pool is limited to whomever auditions for the production within the theatre or school community. If the community itself is not diverse and there is no attempt to reach beyond it, then colour-blind casting is ineffective at diversifying the stage

exemplifying the lack of intentionality in expanding opportunities for students of colour (2023, p. 47).

In June 2020, more than 300 theatre artists supported a Black Lives Matter–inspired letter to the theatre industry entitled 'We See You, White American Theatre' (Clement, 2020). They demanded greater visibility for BIPOC across all theatre industry sectors, across cast, crew, creatives and tech, emphasising a 50% representation in these organisations. By looking at some of the most underrepresented groups in the theatre, we can explore the obstacles against a more comprehensive practice of colour-conscious casting and the need to challenge some of the thought processes that accompany this practice.

Most actors will experience typecasting and stereotyping in the theatre, film, and TV industry when auditioning for or landing a role. In *Reel Inequality: Hollywood Actors and Racism*, Nancy Wang Yuen writes:

Typecasting is a common practice in Hollywood. . . . If any actor has starred in a successful film, Hollywood will try to cast that actor in the same kind of role to minimize risk and maximize profits. . . . The actor may become typecast or be cast in a limited repertoire of roles based on qualities such as race, gender, physical traits, and previous roles.

(2017, p. 69)

University students will enter an industry that casts their shows not solely based on talent, factoring in phenotype, race, ethnicity, gender, nepotism, celebrity, and fluency with any required language(s). Casting teams rely on their own knowledge and are privy to their own biases of race, gender, etc. In *Breaking It Down: Audition Techniques for Actors of the Global Majority*, Nicole Hodges Persley and Monica White Ndounou observe that '[c]alls for people of color in the industry breakdowns, even for predominantly Black, Asian, or Latinx shows, are usually very specific and often use racial stereotypes in the descriptions of the characters' (2021, p. 108). These writers empower the reader to address these oppressive practices in a way that is suitable for their own self-care, refusing to audition for the project. Alternatively, if they accept the role, they can work to humanise the character.

By following Hodge's and Ndounou's lead of rejecting conformity and standing up against these biased practices, mixed actors can resoundingly announce their presence and claim space for their mixed identities.

In the acting studio, teachers may introduce a critical action approach to casting by openly discussing different approaches to stereotypical monoracial BIPOC roles. Without immediately erasing stereotypical roles, and ultimately the majority of opportunities for BIPOC students, teachers can help students humanise the roles they might become more immediately available to them within the professional casting world. This approach will bring more visibility to mixed-race actors, and their unique examination of stereotypes will allow for the development of more mixed characters and opportunities.

When Gene Roddenberry created *Star Trek*, he was adamant about including and celebrating a diverse cast to represent his futuristic world with male, female, Black, white, Asian, and Vulcan characters (Krishna, 2020). But would the future have such 'phenotypical' representations of race? Can we imagine a starship crew of mixed-race people that represents this future population? According to the 2020 US Census Bureau,

> [t]he percentage of people who reported multiple races changed more than [the percentage of] all of the race alone groups, increasing from 2.9% of the population (9 million people) in 2010 to 10.2% of the population (33.8 million people) in 2020.
>
> (Jones, 2022)

If interracial marriages are on the rise, and more individuals are identifying as multiracial, there should be consideration towards the representation of mixed-race actors, rising with each generation of university students.

The changing status quo of the theatre industry, pre- and post-pandemic, has been forced to reckon with the systemic racism and biases existing in our industry, a reflection of our society. Rachel Blackburn writes:

> In the midst of a pandemic and in the wake of Breonna Taylor's, George Floyd's, and Ahmaud Arbery's unjust deaths, students and faculty of color began to more fully and publicly release the collective truth of their experience: that their actor training programs have failed and continue to fail them because they systemically perpetuate white supremacy and coloniality. Students from dozens, likely hundreds, of schools across the United States and the United Kingdom created online statements, petitions, social media accounts, and hashtags to speak out about their traumatic experiences as a call to action.
>
> (2023, p. 16)

We can no longer ignore this international outcry. Instead of ignoring how systemic biases undermine the experience of our BIPOC students, we must not only recognise this inequity but tackle it too.

Perception

When non-traditional or colour-blind casting is utilised on the professional stage, film, or TV, a BIPOC actor is likely tokenised. Tokenism is 'the practice of placing or promoting individuals from disadvantaged groups (e.g. women, ethnic minorities, disabled people) into high-profile roles in the organization to give the impression that the organization practices equal opportunity' (Heery & Noon, 2008). When actors of colour are cast to represent diverse communities, they are likely one of a few characters of colour and are most commonly representing monoracial Black, Asian, and/or Latiné[7] supporting or minor characters. Mixed-Japanese actress Amy Hill, for example, is tokenised as monoracially Asian, playing Asian grandmas of different ethnicities in many shows, such as Korean in *All American Girl* and Filipina in *Crazy-Ex Girlfriend*.[8]

What are the current issues with tokenising/ambiguity within the representation of the Asian diaspora? In *Race and Role: The Mixed-race Asian Experience in American Drama*, Rena M. Heinrich explores several of the issues with tokenism. As Heinrich writes, '[m] ixed-race bodies are co-opted by the dominant ideology to fill quotas and act as racial salves without regard for the multiracial's unique positionality', creating an illusion of racial diversity (2018, p. 3). They also play secondary two-dimensional characters with no history, to support the primary white characters. Heinrich continues:

> Persons of color are relegated to the second, subjugated position in an oppositional pair or binary while white subjects occupy the primary position. This process denies these secondary individuals access to the same privileges, agency, or personhood available to white Americans.
>
> (2018, p. 23)

And finally, mixed-race actors must pass as monoracial. Referencing the character Anna Leonowens as Anglo-Indian, erasing her ethnicity in *King and I*, Heinrich observed that '[t]hroughout the 1940s–1960s in America, it is not so much that there was a lack of mixed-race characters, but rather that these characters were hidden under a veil of monoraciality and erased from popular discourse' (2018, p. 34).

These are just a few of the problems with limiting mixed-race actors to monoracial roles. This need to identify people by monoracial groups relates to the basic human need for categorisation. These issues permeate via the construct of race that has existed to 'other' people of colour and maintain the superiority of whiteness. Psychologists Audrey Smedley and Brian Smedley write:

> The fabrication of a new type of categorization for humanity was needed because the leaders of the American colonies at the turn of the 18th century had deliberately selected Africans to be permanent slaves. In an era when the dominant political philosophy was equality, civil rights, democracy, justice, and freedom for all human beings, the only way Christians could justify slavery was to demote Africans to nonhuman status.
>
> (2005, p. 19)

When a multiracial person is cast in a monoracial role, their mixed identity is erased. The mixed-race person confuses the monoracial-minded society that we have maintained. When a person's race or ethnicity cannot be immediately confirmed by an observer, due to an interpreted ambiguity of appearance, the observer demands that the person being viewed identifies as a specific race. This structure of racialisation implies a 'monoracial cultural logic' that dictates monoracial designations to the body politic (Alsultany in Heinrich, 2018: vii). If the mixed-race person is mixed with a Caucasian identity, they must identify with their BIPOC identity first, unless they pass as white. This is not to say that the mixed-race person identifies as white. Many theorists believe that monoracial identity theories are insufficient for understanding multiracial students because they are more than just a combination of two identities (Root, 1992).

For our students, this inequity in how they are perceived can have a major impact on the personal development of the actor, which can affect their entire career trajectory. Educators need to recognise their students via how they identify themselves through critical discussions, empowering their students. Having confidence in this identity will give the actor more autonomy with how they maintain their own authenticity with characters or material that could be challenging. With this confidence, they can develop individualised ways of managing their career and well-being within an industry that doesn't support their individuality.

Categorisation

Pen15. To All the Boys I've Loved Before. Ginny and Georgia. Never Have I Ever. The Summer I Turned Pretty. Shadow and Bone. The Fosters. Even *Wizards of Waverly Place.* All of these stories feature multiracial characters as leads: *Mixed-ish, The Main Event, The Babysitter's Club, In-Between Girl, Dash and Lily . . . .* While they all follow multiracial characters as leads, the common driving force of these shows and movies is not their specific ethnicity, but the themes of 'coming of age' and 'identity crisis'.

Pen15 follows the story of Maya Ishii-Peters, played by Maya Erskine, whose mother is Japanese and father is white, through the stages of early puberty. *To All the Boys I've Loved Before* explores Lara Jean Covey's first experiences with love. Her Korean mother has passed away, so her white father raises her and her two sisters. In *Never Have I Ever,* the hottest guy in high school, Paxton Hall-Yoshida, is Japanese and white. These characters' narratives hinge on their struggle with their identity and stages of development.[9]

In theatre, plays like *BFE* by Julia Cho and *King of the Yees* by Lauren Yee follow monoracial characters struggling with their 'Asianness' in America. The recurring theme of identity crisis for young Asian Americans, specifically mixed-Asian Americans, shapes how mixed-Asian students see themselves in a role. In a world that is trying to move away from the notion of colour-blind casting, and writing more content specifically for different ethnic groups, genders, sexualities and abilities, the work currently being created primarily focuses on the assumed struggles of mixedness, ignoring the complexities of the intersectionality of all other plausible identities.[10]

In 'Seeing Me in the Story: Representation of Multiracial Characters in Multimedia', Harvey M. Vincent reflects on how he identifies with three different multiracial characters in American media: 'Lincoln Clay from the videogame *Mafia III,* Lara Jean Covey from *To All the Boys I've Loved Before,* and Miles Morales from *Ultimate Comics: Spider-Man*' (2019, p. 24). These three characters differ in ethnic make-up, yet Vincent feels represented by all of them as a multiracial person. He elaborates on how multiracial students face microaggressions specifically aimed at disassociating them from their identity on the assumption that they have no history. This creates the multiracial identity crisis, which lends itself to the media's focus on creating stories about multiracial people in their late teens and early 20s struggling to accept their culture, which is portrayed as being vastly different from the culture of anyone else around them.

Our society assumes that mixed-race people are a new category of people who represent a future racial utopia where racism cannot exist, '[a]s emblems of an imagined color-blind world, multiracial people are often used to bolster claims to a post – civil rights era' (Nishime, 2013, p. 7). Despite this discourse, multiracial people have been around for centuries. They've always existed. It's their lack of representation that has limited their presence in the public eye. The common understanding of these microaggressions often brings multiracial people of different ethnic make-up together. Much like Vincent's case, there is a common understanding of being misunderstood, and a culture of shared multiculturalism is emerging. Now that multicultural communities are growing and diversifying, the ways they are represented must grow too. While acting students are typically in the process of self-identification during the learning process, this does not mean that all the content that they work on or see themselves in should be focused on identification. In practice, students should be given opportunities to portray, search for, and create characters that encompass the other greater aspects and challenges of a multiracial person's life.

Other assumptions placed on mixed-Asian acting students include that they have no history; they represent the future and have no past; they will end racism and represent harmony in racial struggles or colour-blindness; they have no identity when it comes to race; they must choose a dominant race but cannot claim white racial identity unless they can 'pass'; they must assume a monoracial role while carrying a multiracial body.

Acting students expect their teachers to have concrete answers about their perception of casting because teachers critically observe them in action. The teacher must navigate all of these assumptions while working with them in class, which may become problematic. Blackburn writes:

> Microaggressions can also occur in casting when we racialize culture, which is to read race over an individual's culture as the leading signification of particular abilities or attributes. . . . Casting then functions as an assumption based on the perception of a student's ethnicity, as opposed to their natural talents as an individual.
>
> (2023, p. 69)[11]

The mixed-race actor must manoeuvre a category-less body on a categorised stage. Among university students who explore acting, most will have to choose roles and material from a canon that does not represent them. They may be overlooked for roles or materials that have rich identities and three-dimensional experiences. Multiracial actors have been in a unique position, shapeshifting and identifying with multiple racial or ethnic identities performed for the expectations of their audience onstage and off.

In *Undercover Asian: Multiracial Asian Americans in Visual Culture*, Leilani Nishime writes that 'Race becomes elastic and visually dynamic. Instead of seeing race as an unchangeable essence within each individual, we can see how the visual boundaries defining racial groups are shifting and unstable, forming one way and then another' (2013, p. 157). Multiracialism provides more racial and ethnic identities within society's constructs. So, the argument is not that multiracial actors will diminish all ideas of race or ethnicity as represented onstage, but rather that they bring unique, individual perspectives that align with the racial, cultural, and ethnic experiences of BIPOC people, in addition to intersecting with gender-, sexuality, and ability-based identities. This empowers students to bring themselves to actor training, rather than falling into the trap of aiming to be like the Hollywood elite that they admire.

Stepping Forward, Not in Place: Practical Applications for the Classroom

These grander issues of identity, perception, and categorisation for multiracial acting students carry a lot of weight. For educators, undoing these biases for themselves, the student, and the practice itself can seem daunting for a class that is constantly varying in cultural experience. As mixed-Asian actors and educators, we propose a series of pillars that aid teachers to push against the status quo and establish a foundation for equitable opportunities and agency in the classroom.

1. Claim Monoraciality

As students, we have experienced classes where our racial make-up is attached to our identity. As multiracial students, we have always had to claim more than one identity, which is not the accepted standard in the room. This normalises the idea that being of one race is considered *normal*. To undo this, as a teacher, it's important to start claiming your monoracial identity. By claiming yourself as monoracial, you standardise the labelling of the complexities of racial identities, including the spectrum of monoracial to multiracial. The act of labelling monoraciality in a room helps multiracial students appreciate their value as a student of multiple experiences.

2. Stop Saying 'You Can Play Anything!'

A common misconception about multiracial, and more specifically, multiracial Asian actors and students is the assumption that they can 'play anything'. This idea exists because of the desire to label multiracial people based on their phenotype. This assumes that multiracial actors can fit any identity when in reality, ambiguity is not valued in the current casting industry. When directed at multiracial people, the phrase, 'You can play anything!' affirms two notions: the appearance of multiracial people is ambiguous, and that ambiguity is equated with adaptability and fluidity, implying that it expands the possibility of roles. For multiracial people, the phrase also affirms that they are recognised as ambiguous. However, the experience of ambiguity and fluidity does not increase their professional opportunities. It's their ambiguous identity that is actively working against them. Because they are not token enough for their race, they are often cast in colour-blind roles, rendering their multiracial identity moot. While the original intention behind the phrase 'you can play anything' may have been an attempt to bring mixed-raced actors into the conversation, as it stands now, it perpetuates the idea that they are not enough of any one race.

Rather than praising the malleability of multiracial students' phenotypes, we should strive to undo this concept by amplifying the uniqueness of the ambiguous experience. The erasure of racial identity that ambiguity imposes is an experience in and of itself, that yearns for attention and exploration. Removing this language also helps avoid pressuring mixed students to play what white teachers deem as acceptable for them when our experience of ambiguity is a unique identity of its own.

3. Learn How Your Students Identify Themselves First

How mixed people see themselves represented right now is almost exclusively through coming-of-age stories. To establish a space where mixed students get to work on roles beyond colour-blind characters or characters who struggle to piece together their identities in their late teens and early 20s, we need to acknowledge the existing identities in the room and the biases associated with them. Referring to Pierre Bourdieu's concepts of *habitus*, *capital*, and *field* applied to text-based actor training, Evi Stamatiou writes:

> [A]ll actor training interactions, including processes of acting, involve a struggle between a dominant ideology and its oppositional ideology. . . . The hidden mechanisms that perpetuate inequalities in actor training should be addressed not in isolation, but holistically and in the context of identity struggles.
>
> (Stamatiou, 2022, p. 103)

Though identity is fluid and always has the potential to shift, learning how our students identify themselves centres them in our focus. Below we offer some exercises that contribute to the mixed actor's need to be included in the classroom; not just in pieces of racial identity that they may share, but as the multiracial identity, its own wholly lived experience. To undo some of the traditional monoracial biases, these exercises can help teachers make better casting decisions with the work that takes place in a classroom or rehearsal space.

Actors hear the question 'Who am I?' as a regular part of our training. Identifying yourself is a key element for developing how your character identifies themselves. Actors also must speculate how they feel that others will identify them. When it comes to casting, actors make very specific choices for each audition to become what they *believe* the casting director wants to see. Your choice of text, voice, movement, clothes, hair, shoes, and even what audition you take, all are based on how you think others perceive you. Ignorance of the balance between how you identify yourself and how you believe others identify you can lead to inauthentic versions of yourself and choices based on insecurities.

In identity exploration, journal exercises can encourage a deeper examination of identity. Ask your students to write down the answers to the following questions: 'How do I identify myself?' and 'How do I believe people in my environment identify me?' After recording their thoughts privately, bring the group together and ask them: 'After answering those questions, how are you feeling right now?'

As mixed actors, at times we were hesitant to explore our identities in our training. We both found ourselves distanced from the group when we shared our experiences. At the time, we both identified ourselves by our parts: 'I'm half (blank), and half (blank)' 'I was raised by (blank), and I feel more (blank), even though I look (blank)'. 'I love (blank) food, but I don't speak (blank)'. We never even knew we had the option to identify as multiracial. We tried desperately to communicate who we are through a monoracial lens, because that's all we knew. It wasn't that we didn't know what our identities were, we only knew how to identify ourselves in segments of a whole person. We were also aware that casting directors tend to select people who present a very strong, monoracial phenotype, and we struggled to figure out where we fit best.

If we did this exercise during our training, our answer to the last question would sound something like, 'We feel horrible'. As mixed people, we've felt that we don't actually resemble anyone else enough to represent a community. We've empathised with other mixed people, but we've never actually met or seen anyone who 'looks like us'. And when it comes to how others perceive us, we assume they try to put us into more than one box or throw us into one giant box labelled 'exotic'.

Potentially, your mixed students could also have this unique reaction. That's okay. This exercise is not for them to have a more concrete way of identifying themselves, discovering how others perceive them, or deepening their connection with their identity. Instead, it invites conversation about phenotypical perception in performance, which brings more direct attention to mixed-acting students. To invite more comfort and ease in the room, the teacher may want to share their experience doing the exercise as well, to show how the intersectionality of their identities might also have a distancing effect.

Journaling also connects actors to their work on a deeper level of creativity. See your students as the creative artists that they are and allow them to write their own roles. Writing can engage acting students further in theatre artistry. Roles that are written specifically for mixed-race actors are essential but hard to come by. This identity-based writing exercise highlights the individuality of multiracial stories and encourages them to articulate their internal experiences through narrative. When students write for themselves, they open doors for marginalised people who don't have that voice in the industry at this moment.

Another way to celebrate students' identities is by focusing on the actors as people first. Sanford Meisner, a successor of Stanislavsky, was fascinated with human behaviour and said that '[a]n Ounce of BEHAVIOR is Worth a Pound of WORDS' (Meisner & Longwell, 1987, p. 4). Unlike Stanislavsky, his primary focus was on the actors' behaviour, rather than the text. One of his principles that connects students to their bodies is the idea that you begin the work as yourself. *You* count the lightbulbs. *You* solve the math problem. *You* practice doing by doing as yourself. This practice of really doing actions as yourself deepens your understanding of your own behaviour, allowing you to investigate why your behaviour physicalises the way it does.

While Meisner's foundational principles of identity are practical, some of them also call upon you to use your personal experience to feed your imagination. Lee Strasberg's method goes even further and teaches emotional memory (Cohen, 2010, pp. 26–33). These methods can expose multiracial students to the possibility of trauma or culture clash within their upbringing. For example, exploring parental relationships may be very different for someone with multiple familial generations in this country, versus someone whose parents come from differing racial backgrounds.

Instead of revisiting past experiences, teachers can perform exercises that allow past experiences to come up but do not directly ask for them, nor privilege emotional response. Through physical practice, the body informs the brain of what it's feeling. The James–Lange theory of emotions states that emotions are felt after our bodies react. We experience stimuli first without an awareness of their effect, then the brain interprets the bodily response and produces a feeling of emotion (Critchley, 2009, p. 88). We can adapt Meisner's element of emotional preparation by physicalising the preparation, and recreating sensorial experiences in the body. If a student has articulated that they need to enter the room angrily, ask them how anger *feels* physically in their body. They may say something like 'heavy breathing, tightness in my chest, all muscles tensed, etc'. To achieve this, they can physically recreate those sensations by running in place, rubbing their chest with the heel of their hand, screaming silently, etc. They could say 'My chest feels empty, or I feel numb, etc'. You cannot assume what their physicalisation of anger looks like, but you can help them find ways of physically recreating it. Rather than asking them to revisit something, they activate their muscle memory, which informs their acting presently. This avoids privileging deep expression of trauma.

The functionality between you and your body already exists. But we may never be aware of it without focused attention. Race certainly comes into play in terms of bodywork because of posturing, impulse, and response, for example, waiting to speak when spoken to, eye contact, and so on. It is essential to start by acknowledging racial differences. It can help a mixed person further understand themselves in society and become a better actor. Even if they are going to play a 'colour-blind, casted role', they now know how to identify that person based on their experiences. More physicalisation keeps the work in the individual student's body sensations, making each of their characters more directly informed by our students' identities.

4. *Slowdown*

A key principle to embody while considering all bias in the room is slowing down. The industry has the habit of producing new work as quickly as possible to increase the numbers for BIPOC representation. Yet, this work can be rushed and made only for inclusivity's sake. It often appears as performative activism, lacking any depth of story or character. In the studio, we want to offer our BIPOC students opportunities to explore their identity through the material, so we seek out new works. This can be very beneficial to multiracial students. However, the stakes are high when the risk is possibly othering or traumatising our students by not taking time to explore the cultural relativism of new works. We don't want to eliminate challenging concepts and texts to avoid all possible trauma by only selecting newer works that aim to represent numbers but are free from any cultural depth. We must take time to slow down, reflect, and encourage critical thinking with all of our material, be it classic or contemporary. bell hooks states: 'I am more willing to read work from the past that includes stereotypically racist, sexist, and/or homophobic thinking when there is a larger context where the vision expressed is more expansive' (2009, p. 110). If we take time to contextualise its presence in the world and in our space, we don't have to eliminate all of our dated and biased depth of knowledge, be it pedagogical principles or a breadth of acting material. On using texts from celebrated author, William Faulkner, hooks continues: 'I would take more time than I did twenty years ago to discuss the political context . . . to enable students to place in proper perspective his allegiance to dominator culture and his use of fiction to both perpetuate and interrogate those values' (2009, p. 110). Including important canonical works that are not currently considered politically correct invites conversation surrounding how these issues function today in our acting classes.

We must acknowledge that while slowing down is necessary, it's almost impossible to slow down when our career is valued based on quantitative and qualitative terms. We can move slowly, but we cannot go an entire class period discussing identity every day. We have learning objectives to meet and lessons to teach, but we cannot fully change how we take care of our students until the system changes to better serve them. Knowing this, it's important to forgive yourself, but also acknowledge the faults of education as they appear.

5.   *It Is Okay to Be Wrong*

Possibly the most important educational principle to embody is the acknowledgement of your own fallibility. No matter how you racially identify in the room, remember how important it is to be okay with being wrong. We all have biases. One of the ways we fall into these traps and cause trauma by enforcing things upon our students is by assuming, with good intent, that what you're doing is best for them. But the truth is, no one knows, not even the student. As we ask of our students, be willing to fail, and rebuild from there.

Conclusion

Acting practices have evolved greatly from the time that we were students to how we as teachers establish our playing spaces today. While the work to undo bias with racial, gender-based, sexual, sexuality-based, and ability-based identities has begun, the mixed identity is just beginning to be recognised as its own unique community. Having introduced the current issues for mixed-Asian actors regarding representation, tokenization and ambiguity, assumptions and identity crises, we hope that you as educators will have a greater awareness of the identity of your multiracial students, and feel encouraged to recognise and centre their identity by upholding these pillars.

This type of work doesn't only benefit mixed students in the room. Monoracial students have also not been widely exposed to the mixed identity. When monoracial students engage with mixed stories, they recognise that they can also empathise with those experiences, even if they haven't been exactly the same. Reiko Aylesworth, multiracial actress and Professor of Practice in Theatre at Meadows School of the Arts, comments:

> All students can expand their capacity to hold multiple realities, resist reductive labels, and see humanity with a more complex and empathetic lens. How could this help but benefit a room full of acting students, or fellow humans for that matter? Mixed-race students offer a growing but mostly untapped resource. As arts educators, we can enrich our classroom by opening ourselves to and cultivating this valuable resource.
>
> (Personal communication 2023)

The goal is awareness, and the awareness of the dominant monoracial voice is what will help continue the creation of mixed stories. By highlighting common human experiences between multiracial and monoracial people, we develop a mutual empathy between multiracial and monoracial identities.

This work isn't easy. We can't simply amplify multiracial identities just by choosing more multiracial material and sharing more multiracial stories. It's not as if we have a giant mixed-Asian canon of plays to pull from. The work may not show immediate measurable progress. Much like how sharing pronouns and establishing language for articulating boundaries do not solve the systemic issues facing the LGBTQIA community or survivors of assault, these pillars will not make the biases against multiracial people disappear. However, it's imperative to take steps towards undoing these biases. By changing our behaviour, we can expose the needs of multiracial people to the monoracial hierarchy, as well as the overwhelming power of the monoracial hierarchy itself. By recognising multiracialism in our classes, we take one step closer to creating an equitable learning environment for all our students. Not in the future, but now.

Notes

1 For this chapter, we will use multiracial Asian because we specifically speak about Asian Americans who belong to more than one race. We consider this different from multiethnic, which could describe someone who has two different Asian ethnicities – they may still identify as mixed, but are monoracial.

2 We have chosen to use multiracial and mixed-race with little contrast. We acknowledge the academic deduction of race as a concept. Furthermore, we should delineate race as a power structure wielded by the dominant race to maintain and 'other' individuals or communities that are not labelled as white.

3 There is great debate within Basic Human Needs Theory, in which many other psychologists and sociologists have theorised different versions of this list.

4 Much of the foundation of the practices in this chapter are aimed to create equity in the acting classroom considering all identities. These include but are not limited to race, ethnicity, gender, sexuality, ability, economic standing, and religious and cultural backgrounds. This chapter focuses specifically on the mixed-Asian identity in America, which both authors claim.

5 Inclusive casting is not a two-way street. In other words, authentic casting was not created to allow white people too play BIPOC characters, which has been described as 'a misuse of inclusive casting' (Stamatiou, 2020, p. 16). We cannot proclaim the support of opportunities for actors of every race while casting white actors in roles that are specifically written for people of colour or traditionally played by actors of colour.

6 These numbers are hard to gauge with only 6,116 contracts issued for that pandemic year. We acknowledge that most of our data is very skewed. This is due to many factors, one being that there are varied global definitions as to what is considered Asian. Some sources include Lebanese, Armenian, and other Western-Asian and Middle Eastern countries as Asian, while other sources don't include South Asian ethnicities such as Pakistani and Indian in the Asian category.

7 'Latiné' is one non-gendered term for the Latino community. 'Latinx' is a similar term, but some individuals in the community argue that this does not fit into the mechanics of the Spanish language. Others in the community also argue that Latiné and Latinx are terms that are both disrespectful to the Spanish language and privileged to academics. We do not claim this term Latiné as the correct term. However, we both believe in the importance of de-gendering academia, and therefore chose this term for this chapter.

8 Hill claims this on her own website which writes that 'Amy Hill is an American character actress and comedian known for often playing Grandmother or motherly type roles in both live action and voice roles'.

9 It should also be noted that in many of these coming of age stories, the main parental figure is typically the white parent. The parent of colour is often killed off, or less central in the story (Radulovic, 2021).

10 These 'coming of age' roles also happen to be in the age range between 13 and 25, which is what most of our students can play. While the roles are age appropriate, they still limit the scope of themes that mixed-Asian actors can identify with.

11 Additionally, Coronel writes that '[t]heatre programs perpetuate problematic industry norms by justifying their choices as a way to prepare them for said industry' (2023, p. 53).

References

Actors' Equity Association. (2017–2023). *Diversity & inclusion reports*. www.actorsequity.org/resources/diversity/diversity-inclusion-reports/

Blackburn, R. E. (2023). Embodying racial consciousness. In A. M. Ginther (Ed.), *Stages of reckoning: Antiracist and decolonial actor training* (pp. 60–75). Routledge.

Burakoff, M. (2017, September 29). Students challenge arts alliance callbacks, demand 'Racially Respectful' casting. *The Daily Northwestern*. https://dailynorthwestern.com/2017/09/29/campus/students-challenge-arts-alliance-callbacks-demand-racially-respectful-casting/

Burton, J. W. (1987). *Resolving deep rooted conflict: A handbook*. University Press of America.

Clement, O. (2020, June 9). 300 BIPOC theatre artists call for reckoning in the White American theatre. *Playbill*. www.playbill.com/article/300-bipoctheatre-artists-call-for-reckoning-in-the-white-american-theatre

Cohen, L. (Ed.). (2010). *The Lee Strasberg notes*. Taylor & Francis Group. https://ebookcentral.proquest.com/lib/uhm/detail.action?docID=481031

Coronel, J. L. (2023). Societal othering of Asian Americans and its perpetuation through casting. In A. M. Ginther (Ed.), *Stages of reckoning: Antiracist and decolonial actor training* (pp. 42–59). Routledge.

Critchley, H. D. (2009). Psychophysiology of neural, cognitive and affective integration: fMRI and autonomic indicants. *International Journal of Psychophysiology, 73*, 88–94 https://doi.org/10.1016/j.ijpsycho.2009.01.012

Davis, C. T., & Newman, H. (1988). *Beyond tradition: Transcripts of the first national symposium on non-traditional casting* (1st ed.). Non-Traditional Casting Project.

Eyring, T. (2017, January 6). Standing up for playwrights and against "Colorblind" casting. *American Theatre*. www.americantheatre.org/2016/01/07/standing-up-for-playwrights-and-against-colorblind-casting/

Haney-López, I. (2006). *White by law: The legal construction of race (Critical America)*. New York University Press.

Heery, E., & Noon, M. (2008). Tokenism. In *A dictionary of human resource management*. Oxford University Press. Retrieved July 17, 2023, from www.oxfordreference.com/view/10.1093/acref/9780199298761.001.0001/acref-9780199298761-e-1298

Heinrich, R. M. (2018). *Race and role: The mixed-race Asian experience in American drama*. University of California, Santa Barbara, United States – California. *ProQuest*. http://eres.library.manoa.hawaii.edu/login?url=www.proquest.com/dissertations-theses/race-role-mixed-asian-experience-american-drama/docview/2122316122/se-2

Hill, A. (Unknown). *Amy Hill*. Retrieved June 13, 2023, from amyhillactor.com/

hooks, b. (2009). *Teaching critical thinking: Practical wisdom*. Taylor & Francis Group. ProQuest Ebook Central. http://ebookcentral.proquest.com/lib/uhm/detail.action?docID=452100

Jones, N. (2022 June 10). *2020 census illuminates racial and ethnic composition of the country*. www.census.gov/library/stories/2021/08/improved-race-ethnicity-measures-reveal-united-states-population-much-more-multiracial.html

Katerji, O. (2014). Why US media conglomerates will continue to dominate the global media land-scape in the 21st century, but only so at a diminishing rate. *ResearchGate.net*. www.researchgate. net/publication/261991965_Why_US_Media_Conglomerates_Will_Continue_To_Dominate_the_ Global_Media_Landscape_in_the_21_st_Century_But_Only_So_At_a_Diminishing_Rate

Krishna, S. (2020, February 11). Star trek's most significant legacy: Diversity. *Supercluster*. www. supercluster.com/editorial/star-treks-most-significant-legacy-is-inclusiveness

Meisner, S., & Longwell, D. (1987). *On acting*. Random House.

Morris, M. (2016). Standard White: Dismantling White normativity. *California Law Review, 104*(4), 949–978. www.jstor.org/stable/24758741

Nishime, L. (2013). *Undercover Asian: Multiracial Asian Americans in visual culture*. University of Illinois Press. ProQuest Ebook Central.

Persley, N. H., & Ndounou, M. W. (2021). *Breaking it down: Audition techniques for actors of the global majority*. Rowman & Littlefield Publishers.

Radulovic, P. (2021, March 9). Netflix has a troubling problem with its biracial characters. *Polygon*. www.polygon.com/2021/3/9/22321700/netflix-biracial-characters-essay-trope

Root, M. (1992). *Racially mixed people in America*. Sage Publications. https://us.sagepub.com/en-us/ nam/racially-mixed-people-in-america/book3595#description

Smedley, A., & Smedley, B. D. (2005, January 1). Race as biology is fiction, racism as a social problem is real: Anthropological and historical perspectives on the social construction of race. *American Psychologist, 60*(1), 16–26. https://doi.org/10.1037/0003-066x.60.1.16.

Stamatiou, E. (2020). Inclusive casting debunked: Towards holistic interventions in staged perfor-mance. *Interdisciplinary Perspectives on Equality and Diversity, 6*(2).

Stamatiou, E. (2022). Pierre Bourdieu and actor training: Towards decolonising and decentering actor training pedagogies. *Theatre, Dance and Performance Training, 13*(1), 96–114. https://doi.org/10. 1080/19443927.2021.1943509.

Stamatiou, E. (2023). Emotion memory versus physical action: Towards anti-racist pedagogies that make way for critical praxis. In *Stanislavsky and race: Questioning the "System" in the 21st century* (pp. 62–79). Routledge, S.l.

Stoll, J. (2022, September 2). U.S. daily TV consumption by ethnicity 2021. *Statista*. www.statista. com/statistics/411806/average-daily-time-watching-tv-us-ethnicity/

Thanikachalam, N. (2019, May 27). Overlooked: Students in theatre emphasize need for minor-ity representation. *The Daily Northwestern*. https://dailynorthwestern.com/2019/05/27/campus/ overlooked-students-in-theatre-emphasize-need-for-minority-representation/

Vincent, H. M. (2019). Seeing me in the story: Representation of multiracial characters in multimedia. *The Vermont Connection, 40*(1). https://scholarworks.uvm.edu/tvc/vol40/iss1/5

Wang Yuen. N. (2017). *Reel inequality: Hollywood actors and racism*. Rutgers University Press. https://doi.org/10.36019/9780813586328

8 Liminal Casting

Self-Inquisitive Scene Study in Actor Training

Evi Stamatiou

1. Introduction

Following the resurgence of the Me Too and Black Lives Matter movements, actor training practitioners and scholars address how current curricula problematise social equality concerning race, gender, ability, class, and sexual orientation. Rachel Blackburn calls for a 'continuance for acting teachers to question the practices of whiteness within scenework pedagogy' (2023, p. 72), including casting. Casting, which is assigning students roles from written texts, is among the prominent issues that problematise typical actor training methods (Coronel, 2023). I have previously argued that the classical canon roles for women limit their opportunities to develop their acting skills because they are usually stereotypical and less substantial than their male counterparts (Stamatiou, 2020). Inarguably, through casting decisions, acting tutors affect how students from marginalised communities experience the acting classroom and develop their acting skills in said environment.

Higher Education Institutions (henceforth HEIs) in the United Kingdom are held accountable for how they 'promote equity of access and embed inclusive policy and practice' (Morgan & Houghton, 2011, p. 8). Tackling inequitable casting processes in actor training is crucial because besides limiting career prospects and the experience of students from marginalised communities, it can also undermine their wellbeing. Traditional casting practices 'can lead to increased racialized suffering' (Coronel, 2023, p. 46), because of 'problematic characterizations that often perpetuate stereotyping and lead to harm' (ibid, p. 47). When cast in roles that require 'vulnerability', which is considered a key attribute for the development of acting skills, students from Black and Global Majority backgrounds 'may be confronting anxiety, self-hatred, and/or depression in relation to their journey to embody said vulnerability, particularly in a predominantly white space' (ibid, p. 46). Casting is a particular problem for the actor training curriculum that involves produced plays or workshop productions of the practical study of extracted scenes and monologues, all of which are established methods for facilitating the development of characterisation skills. The problem becomes more perplexing if we respond to recent research calling for intersectional approaches to text-based actor training (Ginther, 2023, p. 249; Stamatiou, 2022a).

This chapter is inspired by Freire's and hooks's critical pedagogy. It brings the concept of liminality to actor training and focuses on an action research cycle (Elliott, 1991, p. 85), which is part of an ongoing participatory action research process (Kemmis et al., 2013) that improves the inclusivity in my text-based acting class. I argue that text-based acting classes that linger in the preparation of multiple roles, instead of culminating in the performance of a single role, involve more equitable and inclusive casting practices. The first part of the chapter contextualises, theorises, and presents the scheme of work of an acting class that

DOI: 10.4324/9781003393672-11

I designed in early 2022 to promote maximum student agency concerning the selection of roles, narratives, and processes. The second part of the chapter evaluates the effectiveness of the scheme of work using analysis of student contributions during an end-of-module reflective discussion and subsequent anonymous feedback within standardised evaluations. The conclusion summarises the insights from the two sections and foregrounds the opportunity for HEI module evaluations to improve inclusivity in the curricula.

2.   Developing the Scheme of Work

The first part of this section illustrates how current efforts to develop inclusive casting practices in actor training resonate with recent educational frameworks of inclusive curriculum design (Morgan & Houghton, 2011) and co-creating curricula with the students (Bovill et al., 2011) that promote student agency in HEIs. The second part of this section brings the concept of liminality to casting to create a hypothesis concerning how casting practices in actor training can maximise student agency. The third part of the section offers an account of the process of co-creating a scheme of work for a scene study class that was applied with 30 first-year students on the BA (Hons) Acting in the United Kingdom at the University of Chichester in 2022.

Context and Rationale

Scene study is a traditional actor training method that involves extracting a scene from a play to rehearse 'just to exercise the actor's instrument' (Loney, 1989, p. 317) instead of preparing for a public production. It supports the actor to develop characterisation skills, with a focus on embodying scripted characters. Konstantin Stanislavsky primarily discussed the actor's process in scene study while directing plays (1973, pp. 4–12), as he had little time to train actors outside of rehearsal (Nikolai Demidov in Vahtangov & Malaev-Babel, 2011, p. 8). My understanding of scene study resonates with Uta Hagen's. She watched trainees perform a duologue in front of their peers and tutor (HB Studio, 2018, 3:00–6:50) and then invited the performers' reflections on 'what worked well and what didn't and why didn't this work' (ibid, 7:12–7:15). She then responded to the reflections with feedback for improvement, using vocabularies from the actor's process, such as 'substitution' (ibid, 9:00–9:30) and even herself performed an imaginary scenario to illustrate how human behaviour manifests in the actor's physical score (ibid, 11:30–12:13). Finally, she extrapolated learning for the whole class (ibid, 13:07–13:56). My approach resembles 'scene study that encompasses multiple playwrights and/or genres', accompanied by acting exercises that invite more general imagination skills' (Hess, 2016, p. 200), which is common for beginning actors.

While developing 'an inclusive canon as classroom foundation' is a priority (Blackburn, 2023, p. 65), different casting problems can arise. In roles available for their ethnicity, students felt alienated (Coronel, 2023, p. 51), stereotyped (ibid, p. 52), and 'pigeon-holed' (Blackburn, 2023, p. 24), and tutors experienced pressure to 'simply exchange one racialized assumption for another' (ibid, p. 64). Such casting interventions distract scene study from focusing on 'an individual student's educational needs' (ibid) with realistic representation being a priority (ibid, p. 65). Helpful casting strategies include assigning students open scenes, which do not give information about the characters' identities, to gain an 'insight into the characters they are comfortable portraying' or inviting students 'to write their own scenes' or 'research and choose their own scenes' for scene study (ibid); providing 'diversified performance opportunities to students' (Coronel, 2023, p. 53); and inviting '[c]ritical dialogue on casting practices' as part of the curriculum (ibid, p. 54), while prioritising the students' well-being (ibid, p. 57). Such strategies approach casting as a work in progress and invite students to cast themselves.

The move from 'assigning roles' to collaborating with the students on their casting resonates with the co-created curriculum as a collaboration between students and staff. A recent review of working with students as partners for curriculum creation identifies strategies such as students taking 'more active roles in shared decision-making', fostering collaboration 'based on respect, reciprocity, and shared responsibility', 'negotiating issues of power', drawing 'on critical pedagogy to provide alternative possibilities for partnership-based learning and teaching' and 'knowledge socialism' that promotes 'shared decision-making and the co-creation of knowledge' (Lubicz-Nawrocka & Owen, 2022, p. 794). Curriculum co-creation seems to 'benefit the student experience', 'develop co-creators' resilience when negotiating the curriculum and navigating challenges collaboratively', facilitates 'strong working relationships between students' and 'between students and staff', and leads to 'positive outcomes for both students and staff reflecting on meaningful and rewarding learning and teaching experiences' (ibid, pp. 794, 795). Actor training curricula can, in the process of teaching and learning acting skills, integrate student–staff collaborations that design and test inclusive practices. In scene study, mentoring and coaching methods that support the students to select their scenes or write original scenes reflect what has been described by education scholars as a co-created learning environment, or 'a relational and dialogic site' (Barnett & Coate, 2011, p. 141). Such collaborative processes introduce a critical approach to casting as part of the student's embodied knowledge of acting.

Blackburn and Coronel focus on the casting challenges for Black and Global Majority students. The key principle of inclusive curriculum design, to 'recognise that effective practice for one group can and should be an effective practice for all' (Morgan & Houghton, 2011, p. 12), invites an expansion of their equitable casting practices beyond the focus on race to embrace multiple and intersecting identities. To embed inclusivity at the design stage of a module, or an acting class, the scheme of work should be 'anticipatory', meaning it should encompass all students with multiple and intersecting identities, dominant and dominated, visible and invisible; it should be 'flexible' to accommodate all learners and learning environments; 'accountable' with clear 'equality objectives and actions agreed'; 'collaborative', aiming to recruit students and stakeholders in ongoing feedback processes (ibid); 'transparent' in all relevant decisions, and; 'equitable' for all students (ibid, p. 13). The challenge for the acting tutor is to take the above principles and enact them in their classroom in a way that can be clearly communicated to students and interested stakeholders and manifested through the schemes of work.

Bringing Liminality to Casting Processes to Promote Inclusivity

I apply case study research methodology because it tackles questions that 'require an extensive and 'in-depth' description of some social phenomenon' (Yin, 2018, p. 4) such as how social power can be tackled through casting in a scene study class. Case study research is 'an empirical method that investigates a contemporary phenomenon (the 'case') in depth and within its real-world context, especially when the boundaries between phenomenon and context may not be clearly evident' (ibid, p. 15). To achieve such depth, it is crucial to establish from the start 'theoretical propositions to guide the design, data collection, and analysis' (ibid). I developed the following hypothesis for my case study in 2022: an unfinished casting process that, instead of preparing a role for a final performance that is assessed and graded, maximises student agency to sustain the question 'which one of these roles feels better in preparation for me?'

The concept of liminality foregrounds the above hypothesis. Coined by the anthropologist Arnold Van Gennep in 1909, liminality describes the phase during which a person passes from one identity state to another during a 'rites of passage' process (Kertzer in Van Gennep, 2019: vii). Even from its conception, liminality did not refer only to 'life course stages' but any transition of the individual from an initial state to a final state (ibid: xix). In the context of scene study, the initial state involves the student getting a role that will support their development during the acting class, and the final state involves the student embodying such role. Van Gennep observed three 'rites of passage' phases: separation, which involves the departure from the initial state; liminality, which is an ambiguous or processual phase during which the individual gradually transitions from the 'before' to the 'after' state; and incorporation, which finalises the adoption of the new identities that manifest the final state (2019 [1909], pp. 11–14). With casting, the separation phase involves the actor's decision to initiate the characterisation process for a specific role; the liminal phase involves the actor's exploration of how their body, voice, and imagination can serve the role in preparation and rehearsal, including the juxtaposition of the actor's and the role's identities; and the incorporation phase involves embodying the role in performance.

The use of liminality in identity construction in organisations illuminates how the agency of the actor can be maximised during casting processes. Such research approaches identity as 'being constructed and reconstructed through a dynamic interaction in which a person is 'cast' in an identity by others (Karreman & Alvesson, 2001); seeking to project an identity to the outside world (Brown, 2001); and taking on (or enacting) behaviours, symbols, and stories of an identity (Sims, 2003)' (Beech, 2011, p. 286). This resembles how the student explores their castability in the acting studio. The tutor and peers suggest suitable roles for them, the student suggests, or secretly desires, the kind of roles they want to perform, and they employ their body, voice, and imagination in manifesting the assigned or chosen role in their performance, which involves the performance of identity markers. Because the typical industry practice is to ascribe roles based on looks and expects the actor to accept the role unquestioningly, students rarely question what is imposed on them as suitable casting. And very often the students themselves are unsure of what roles might be suitable or how to resist castability practices. So, the acting classroom becomes a site of exploring casting possibilities in search of the 'right' role for them.

The problem with what is assumed as the 'right' character for a student is the associations with typecasting, which limits casting opportunities to roles with the same social identities as the actor, such as age and gender (Zuckerman et al., 2003, p. 1021). Typecasting is broadly accepted because 'it at least carries the recognition necessary for securing future work' (ibid), reflecting similar categorisations in other work sectors which 'label' individuals with certain skillsets and use screening processes to select one individual among job applicants with the same 'label' (ibid, p. 1032). However, in the acting industry, typecasting 'delivers an oversupply of leading roles for white, male, middle-class actors while ensuring that those who deviate somatically are restricted to largely socially caricatured roles' which can be 'experienced as offensive and discriminatory' (Friedman & O'Brien, 2017, p. 359). So, in the acting classroom, typecasting harms students from marginalised communities because it restricts the actor's body, voice, and imagination to stereotypical representations.

Also, the reduction of the student to a 'simple, focused identity' (Zuckerman et al., 2003, p. 1021) problematises intersectionality, missing the opportunities associated with the complexity of the student's multiple identities. For example, certain roles with different somatic characteristics than the student's might resonate more with some of their other identities, such as their religious and political beliefs or life experiences, prompting motivation for exploration, and authentic acting decisions. If we consider the three stages of the characterisation process rite of passage (the initiation, when the student agrees to take on a role, the rehearsal, and the performance), then the abandonment of the final performance of the character minimises the embodiment of stereotypical representations, and therefore harm. It shifts the focus to the exploration of the character during the liminal state, enabling critical realisations concerning stereotypical representations.

Approaching casting as a liminal phase, as opposed to a final phase, promotes student agency in the acting studio. The liminal phase entails dialogue between an individual's 'social identity', which is determined by external discourses, and their 'self-identity', which keeps 'a particular narrative [of the self] going' (Watson, 2009, p. 431). In the acting studio, the student's social identity associates them with roles with similar identities/bodily characteristics, which might be far from the roles that they desire to perform. The liminal phase's dialogue allows for 'experimentation, reflection and recognition' (Beech, 2011, p. 286), allowing for 'partial and incomplete identity changes' (ibid, p. 287) that may cause the student to resist the final state of the rites of passage. Working at the intersection of structure and agency, liminal practices expand understanding of self-identity/social-identity as mutual construction. Consequently, in preparation for the role, the student critically reflects on how dominant ideologies influence their casting opportunities and how their choices and decisions concerning casting can resist such ideologies. Because the inherent criticality leaves the student in an ambiguous state in relation to the role they prepared, rather than focusing on an assessed final performance, we prioritise self-inquiry to enable a liminal casting practice.

In my 2022 project that I will discuss in the next section, the tutor and students tackle power structures in scene study through ongoing self-inquiry. The acting tutor facilitates students to develop critical reflection as part of their acting skills and, by doing so, they learn from the students how to be teacher-collaborators and co-develop inclusive teaching content. Because qualitative research requires 'multiple sources of evidence, with data needing to converge in a triangulating fashion' (Yin, 2018, p. 15), this case study analyses the scheme of work that was developed to tackle multiple and intersecting axes of oppression, the final reflective discussion between teacher and students, and the standardised student evaluations. The data is examined against the hypothesis that the recruitment of students as partners in a liminal casting process in scene study promotes the principles of the inclusive curriculum: the consideration of intersectionality, clear equality aims, collaboration, transparent decision-making, and responsiveness to the individual needs of students.

To weave and sustain such a critical and reparative thread into the scheme of work, class activities alternated with reflective discussions about student showings. The students' role as co-investigators of how the class could be developed to a more inclusive version climaxed during a 30-minute reflective discussion at the end of the module, which invited student reflections on inclusivity.

What Happened in Class

Between January and May 2022, I taught 30 first-year students on the BA (Hons) Acting at the University of Chichester in two groups of 16 and 14 people, keeping the numbers even to facilitate the use of duologues for scene study. The class focused on techniques which encouraged the actor to explore a psychophysical approach to their work through ongoing reflection on 'what works' and 'what doesn't work' concerning acting choices that manifested their acting strengths. The module spanned ten 4-hour weekly sessions.

Throughout the ten weeks, the students were mentored to make choices concerning the texts and techniques used and to select collaborators. Collaboration was embedded in different ways: in class during tutor-led group workshops, with peers during independent rehearsals, and during work-in-progress showings in class. Critical perspectives were encouraged through reflexivity during warm-ups that explored aspects of culture and identity, seminars on readings and viewings, group reflections on practice, peer-led feedback on showings, and ongoing feedback on digital logbooks. Three key teaching strategies from the scheme of work enabled inclusivity: warm-ups that invited individual expression and different aspects of identity; an understanding and application of casting as liminal, which means that the roles explored were in search of a student's ideal casting – what makes them feel most comfortable and illustrates their best acting; and the peer feedback concerning what choices manifested best acting. Below I expand more on these three strategies.

The two-part warm-up was inspired by the Black acting methods techniques of circle formation and check-ins (Dunn, 2019, p. 77). It developed an icebreaker exercise that was introduced to me in 2010 by Complicité's Lilo Baur during my participation in a weekly workshop on Lecoq's physical theatre, and the capoeira circle that was introduced to me in 2011 during a Zekora Ura Theatre residency in Brazil. Complicité's icebreaker exercise gets the group into a circle and invites each participant to say their name with a matching gesture, followed by the whole group to mimic their performance. The facilitator offers the first gesture which is repeated by the whole group. This is continued around the circle until all participants have performed their names with a matching gesture. The same sequence is repeated at double tempo and triple tempo.

I found this name/gesture exercise an ideal vehicle for checking in. It acknowledges multiple and intersecting identities in the room because a person's name is central to their identity. When each participant selects a gesture to accompany their name, their movement patterns start emerging, offering a glimpse of their individualised social experience. The mimicking by the rest of the group involves an embodied engagement with each other's experience. This exercise opened all ten sessions, but in every consecutive session, I invited different aspects of identity such as pronouns, feelings, likes/dislikes, including vocalisation and more abstract matching gestures. Each time I invited suggestions from the group concerning which aspect of identity to explore.

The second part of the warm-up involved 6 minutes of freestyle dancing around the circle, instead of capoeira, while two students every time choosing one song each for the group to dance to. Inspired by the capoeira circle, individuals got in the centre of the circle to show off dance moves, as themselves during the first song, and as a character that they were exploring or wanted to explore during the second song. This activity encouraged individuality and the choice to dance alone within the group. It encouraged an appreciation for each other's music choices while alternating the centring of each student's music taste and dance moves. It was also a joyful experience in ways unfamiliar for a class, inviting one's full self into acting, which created intimacy among the group.

After the warm-up, each class included individual or group improvisations that explored a particular concept/technique from Hagen's studio, such as 'Representational' versus 'Presentational' acting (2010, p. 12) or 'Substitution' (ibid, p. 34). After each student presented the improvisation, they reflected on their experience applying the concept or technique on stage. Focusing on the performer's physical score, their peers offered feedback on which acting choices worked or seemed logical, which the performer used to corroborate their experience.

After the improvisations, each class involved practical scene study that tried to avoid casting the student in roles that might stereotype them or lead them concerning castability but, lingering on the liminal phase of characterisation, used the texts as vehicles for the further exploration of concepts and techniques. For example, after the improvisations of the first class, students practically explored scenes from Caryl Churchill's play *Love and Information* (2012), which involves short open scenes that offer little information about character identities. The students were invited to aim for Presentational acting, drawing on themselves to discover character actions and working 'on stage for a moment-to-moment subjective experience' (Hagen, 2010, p. 12). Then individual reflection focused on how the student attempted to use the concept in practice, followed by peer reflection on how certain acting choices manifested as Presentational or Representational acting. The focus on the individualised application of the concept rather than interpreting the writer's dramaturgical choices centred the liminal phase of characterisation.

In the third session, the students explored the concept of 'Substitution', which means imagining something from the actor's life in the place of the character's life, so they might better relate to the character's experience (Hagen, 2010, p. 35). Working with a range of suggested monologues, from a variety of genres, and including their own self-selected materials, enabled choice to explore roles that represented their experience and values, as opposed to how they sounded or looked.

The fourth session invited an experience of alienation from a character, where most students would feel distant from the rehearsed characters but should resist stereotypical representations and, instead, look for ways to associate their experience with the character's. I offered scenes from Peter Morgan's screenplay *The Crown* (2020) to explore the 'Magic If' (Hagen, 2010, p. 154). The scenes were presented as rehearsed readings, following improvisations that invited the students to consider themselves as members of a family with high status and social power.

From the fifth session, the students chose a partner. They selected a scene that would be used for the rest of the classes to familiarise them with acting techniques further, but in a way that their casting in a role would remain unfinished business as if the right role for each student hadn't been written yet.

To corroborate whether the casting choices in the class were inclusive, I invited a 30-minute reflective discussion at the end of the module, which considered intersectionality, clear equality aims, collaboration, transparent decision-making, and responsiveness to the individual needs of students. At the end of the discussion, I reminded students to use the end-of-module standardised evaluation to note any further relevant concerns that they did not disclose during the face-to-face discussion. The next section presents the analysis of the student contributions during our reflective discussion and the standardised evaluation. Casting is among the practices that the students brought up.

3.   Analysis of Reflective Discussion and Standardised Evaluation

The reflective discussion (Stamatiou, 2022b) was set up through an invite to the whole group at the end of their final scene showings to voluntarily participate in an end-of-module conversation which would be recorded for research purposes. The discussion would investigate the extent to which inclusivity has been effectively experienced concerning casting processes through maximum student agency concerning the selection of roles, narratives, and processes. I noted that, because my position as a teacher inevitably would affect the conversation, anonymous end-of-module standardised evaluations would be also used as data. All students voluntarily joined the discussion.

The students identified as positive practice the development of an acting-specific vocabulary that focused on how the actor's choices manifested through the character's physical behaviours. Used during group reflections on scene showings, it facilitated a breaking down of the acting process to body, voice, and imagination, liberating the scene study from text analysis. In the words of Maria (anonymised):

> I really appreciate it that during the first lesson you gave us the language for talking about the body, the voice and the imagination so then for all the sessions we had this language in our head and we could use it for all the work.
>
> (in Stamatiou, 2022b, 00:10:03)

The development of such language was inspired by Phillip Zarrilli's phenomenological approach to acting in *(Toward) a Phenomenology of Acting* (2019), which embraces that the description of any phenomenon, including acting, can vary depending on the individual that provides it and is valuable in that it opens a conversation on the matters described. This new language promoted equality because it did not assume any previous learning. It also prompted an understanding that each student would interpret acting choices in different ways depending on their multiple identities, but the mere description of their peers' physical scores centred on each performer and their learning.

To ensure multiple perspectives, the students in the audience were invited to identify what worked or not on stage, by which we meant combining truthful representation with keeping the audience interested. When students started their observations with something like 'You would expect the character to. . .', which shifted the focus from the manifestations of acting to the text analysis, or 'This reminds me of what I do in life', which shifted the focus from the manifestations of acting to audience reception, I invited the speakers to rephrase their reflections with a focus on how the acting process and imagination of their peers manifested in physical behaviours. I contributed with my observations on scene showings last to avoid leading the conversation. Usually, I had little to add to the students' observations apart from extrapolating learning concerning the preparation process that could be applied in all scenes. For example, in a scene that started with a character entering a room, the student chose to leave the studio and use the studio door as the imaginary room's door. When their peer observed that 'it worked how you started the scene, entering from outside the space', I highlighted the effectiveness of the 'Five Senses' technique by saying:

> This observation suggests that using the space with its surroundings, instead of miming doors or walking from what would be the 'wings' of the stage, helps with being in the moment. The actor believed more in the character's reality because they saw the door closed from outside the studio; touched the door handle and felt the cold metal; heard the 'click' of the lock opening; saw the room and their scene partner, and then closed the door behind them and stayed in that private space with the other character. This simple choice to use the studio door invited the use of 'Five Senses' in ways that might not have been pre-planned.

Hagen's writing on 'Five Senses' (2010, pp. 60–64) was suggested reading, which illustrates how all the readings enriched the class with new language about acting. My description above illustrates how the students and I were learning together.

Our collective observations in the above example helped improve the actor on stage and their acting process by validating a choice that they will hopefully repeat. We also invited all other actors to consider using the actual space and real props in their scenes. At the same time, the focus on the physical score acknowledged the multiple perspectives in the room and how each one of us has different experiences and ways to manifest, describe, and interpret human behaviour. In this manner, the studio was de-centred from the texts and the interpretations of such texts, and therefore from casting. We supported each other in validating an acting-specific language liberating our discipline from texts, directors, and production processes. Instead, we focused on how each student's body, voice, and imagination manifested acting choices that worked while embracing the tacit, unique, and individualised physiological, psychological, and social experiences in the room. This resonates with the inclusive curriculum's aim to consider the individualised experience of the student, embracing the multiple and intersecting identities in the room.

The students identified as a second positive practice that class methods and materials were aspirational in orientation. Stella (anonymised) testified that the linking of class content about 'what's to come after uni', such as 'opportunities and what we need to do in terms of auditions and direction and stuff' made her 'excited about performing' (in Stamatiou, 2022b, 16:20–16:45). For example, an observation that using real props, instead of performing empty-handed or miming props, helps with being in the moment led to a note of how an actor can use the script that is often given at auditions and castings as something the character could use in the scene rather than pretending that it is not in the actor's hand and pulling their attention after every other line. In a scene set in a restaurant or bar, the script can become a menu; in a scene in a room or public space, it can become a newspaper or book, and; so on. Such linking of class content to the student's future contributes to transparent decision-making concerning the selected class content, instead of generalised learning outcomes and expecting the students to extrapolate 'transferrable' skills from classes.

Peter (anonymised) reinforced the importance of an industry-focused class, with a specific reference to casting. Peter's testimony that the class helped students to 'think about casting and future opportunities' and '[e]verything we are doing in this class seems that we are doing this for a reason. It gives meaning' (in Stamatiou, 2022b, 15:38–16:14) indicates a successful actor training thread that combined critical and employability skills.

As discussed through examples from the scheme of work, almost every week the students were offered scenes from different plays and even screenplays to work on, and eventually chose a scene that moved them or involved a dramatic situation that they would enjoy exploring with their body, voice, and imagination. This invited them to develop an individualised understanding of how casting works for them, driven by the aim to identify potential acting strengths and select the most appropriate scenes for self-promotion and development. Sophia (anonymised) appreciated being asked 'what kind of actors we want to be and what we want to do' (in Stamatiou, 2022b, 21:01). Matching the students' aspirations with the aims of the class motivated them, maximising learning opportunities. In exploring characterisation tools, such as 'Substitution', 'Visualisation', 'Spontaneity', and the 'Magic If', through embodying a variety of roles the students processed how different dramatic scenarios might inspire them, work for them, and resonate with the roles they want to perform.

The students' appreciation for constructive feedback with a focus on individuals' self-actualisation indicated transparency in decision-making, which is a key principle of the inclusive curriculum. Dominic (anonymised) noted that 'it's good that we don't get a false perception' through me (the tutor) being 'very honest with all of us in so many capacities as actors' by which he meant that my feedback aimed to 'always give ways to improve and discover extra layers we can add, rather than saying good job' (Stamatiou, 2022b, 20:13). This invites a reconceptualisation of transparency in decision-making in actor training. Many acting teachers give general and always encouraging comments after student showings, instead of facilitating detailed discussions about specific acting choices. Even though their practice is well-meaning and praises student effort, it can limit the improvement of the student-performer and confuse the rest of the students.

Georgia (anonymised) also praised me for my advice 'always for improvement' (in Stamatiou, 2022b, 22:00). These testimonies illustrate appreciation for the acting class as a work in progress, fostering a liminal process primarily of self-inquiry and then as technique training. This indicates that characterisation technique can be taught as a liminal process, shifting teaching aims from the learning and manifestation of acting skills to experimenting with and reflecting on acting concepts, ultimately developing individualised strategies towards self-inquiry concerning characterisation. Scene study can linger on the liminal phase of casting, during which students experiment with and reflect on how characterisation tools support their body, voice, and imagination to create physical scores that resonate with their ideal roles. These liminal explorations with any character, and ideally, characters chosen by the student promote the resistance to final casting states that feel discriminatory, offensive, or unfulfilling. The testing, questioning, and reflecting on what would be the ideal casting for each student shifts the acting process in scene study towards more student-centred models and invites an approach to casting as a transitional space or liminal process.

The appreciation of casting as a liminal process can be illuminated by the observation of one of the two Global Majority students in the class. Mo (anonymised) referred to the scenes from *The Crown* which were distributed following the 'Magic If' workshop that invited everyone to imagine that they were members of a royal family, perhaps born in it or affiliated with it in other ways. Students were invited to avoid mimicking the real people portrayed but manifest a royal version of their own means of expression, visualising themselves as having the highest social power possible. Assuming that no royals were among my students, the scenes were expected to invite everyone's awareness of their means of expression such as ways of moving and talking. Even though the juxtaposition of their means of expression to the British Royal family might have been an inevitable starting point to characterisation, my instruction to visualise themselves as royal without changing their ways of moving and talking validated their means of expression and helped them appreciate them instead of masking them. This promoted equality in the room, as no means of expression were considered superior.

Mo observed that 'coming to this class there were a lot of barriers that have been broken, scripts that I wouldn't have touched' (in Stamatiou, 2022b, 23:49), implying that he never imagined himself cast as a royal – casting him as Prince Philip was experienced as a 'barrier' that was broken. Alongside developing his individualised version of a royal, he witnessed multiple other royal characters that utilised the means of expression of his peers. During the showing of the scenes, nobody tried to imitate the real people, which exaggerated the absence of scenes with socially powerful characters that walked and talked like the people in the room. This was the last scene experienced before they selected their scenes independently. I hoped it would inspire the students to find scenes that embraced their means of expression, moved them, and reflected their career aspirations in roles that self-actualised them. The understanding that such roles might not exist yet, prompted an understanding of each student's casting as liminal until the role initiates their move to a final casting state.

Direct questions concerning inclusivity, such as 'Did you feel represented among authors and case studies discussed for the class?'; 'Did you feel comfortable setting your boundaries?'; 'Did you feel these things worked among your group?'; and 'Was there anything that could have been done better?', were mostly affirmed through non-verbal communication. Lyla (anonymised) praised that 'Whenever there was text with trigger warnings everyone was careful to voice it and respectful to our boundaries, so this was helpful' (in Stamatiou,

2022b, 24:30). The student's mentioning of the trigger warnings as a shared practice among the group highlighted the importance of establishing 'community agreements' (King, 2023, p. 34), which are agreed rules relevant to acting that reflect ethical principles.

The group identified good practices to be taken forward in my scheme of work, showing an appreciation for my efforts to create an inclusive environment and tackle casting issues, which was validating. But, perhaps, my presence hindered a critical approach to the class content and materials. So, in closing the reflective discussion with 'If there is anything else that you couldn't say in this environment you can write about it in the end-of-module standardised evaluation', I invited more critical perspectives through anonymity. The next section analyses the students' anonymous responses.

Analysis of Anonymous Evaluations

Standardised module evaluation surveys in UK higher education invite students to answer anonymously a set of questions that examines current teaching practices, fostering a collaborative and comparative process for developing module content and practice (Wiley, 2019). Students' perspectives on standardised evaluations suggested that they helped facilitate comparison between different modules but lacked 'sensitivity to individual module contexts and schedules', which makes them 'only partially effective as a means of teaching evaluation', highlighting a need to 'triangulate its results with data obtained through alternative evaluation mechanisms' (ibid, p. 55).

The questionnaire that my students answered anonymously at the University of Chichester (University of Chichester, 2022) measured responses for all three classes of the Acting Skills 2 module: my acting class, a voice class, and a movement class. It used the 5-point Likert Scale, which is '[a] type of psychometric response scale in which responders specify their level of agreement to a statement typically in five points: (1) Strongly disagree; (2) Disagree; (3) Neither agree nor disagree; (4) Agree; (5) Strongly agree' (Preedy & Watson, 2010). It also offered space for further comments after each question. Most of the responses of the 24 students who participated were between 'Agree' and 'Strongly Agree', resonating with the typical positive overall evaluation of the module that I witnessed during the last five years as module leader. This section analyses the comments offered to those standardised questions that illuminated our reflective discussion at the end of my acting class to extrapolate further feedback for improving my class moving forward. I highlight the words that resonate with our reflective discussion concerning inclusivity and individualised engagement, and I anonymise the tutors and classes for ethical reasons.

Words that imply inclusivity, or the lack of, were found in all comments prompted by the question '[w]ere your ideas listened to and, where possible, acted upon? Did you feel confident asking questions and making suggestions?'. The words are italicised in the comments: '*the teachers worked with us* no matter what we looked like and no matter what level we were currently at. My *ideas were fully understood* and *asking questions* if I was unsure was easy as everyone was understanding and helpful'; '[a]s we performed *we as a class gave feedback as did X TUTOR this allowed everyone's opinions and ideas be heard*'; and '*I felt what I contributed was welcomed* and always had fun in the class and felt we all did great work' (Anonymous Q13). What stands out from these comments is an appreciation of an individualised relationship with the tutor and for encouraging the individual voice of the student to affect the class.

The only criticism for the overall module was given in response to the same question as above. The student wrote: '*I felt very uncomfortable in X CLASS as I didn't feel X TUTOR knew my name and that made me feel forgettable and embarrassed*' (Anonymous Q13), implying that the tutors of the other two classes got this right. This comment highlights the importance of acknowledging the individual in the room, previously discussed as 'check-in' (Dunn, 2019, p. 77). I will bring this comment to the idea of a scene study class as a rite of passage that invites the student to take on a role to explore for the duration of a session or longer. When the student is given a role by X tutor, who does not try to acknowledge and know them, they are invited to enter the liminal phase of the characterisation process feeling 'uncomfortable', 'forgettable', or even 'embarrassed'. This undermines their motivation to experiment with and reflect on the techniques while they are in such an ambiguous phase and problematises their confidence to critically assess how appropriate or desirable any role can be for them. A nameless student feels they lack the agency to reject roles given to them by tutors who do not see them as individuals. A tutor who does not see individuals in the studio but 'casting types' is more likely to ignore the students' desires and complex identities and assign roles uncritically. So, approaching casting practices as liminal processes feels equally crucial learning for the tutors, which my acting students taught me at the University of Chichester in 2022.

Findings

Overall, the triangulation of the scheme of work, the reflective discussion and the standardised evaluations identified good practices that can be taken forward to improve my scene study class. These include establishing a common vocabulary for peer reflection on scene showings; testing multiple scripts during scene study; and approaching casting as a self-led liminal process. Practices that need more development include community agreements; establishing a co-created curriculum culture across classes, courses/modules, and programmes; and finding ways to train all staff in resisting casting as a final state in assessed performance but redirecting their teaching and assessment towards the continuous evaluation of the student within aforementioned self-led liminal processes.

An unexpected finding derived from the comments provided in the standardised survey. The responses indicated that the vocabulary introduced to the students during the in-person conversation was used in the anonymous evaluations. When comparing this year's anonymous evaluations with the equivalent of the past three years, I observed that a focus on transparent decision-making and individualised approaches that embrace intersectionality was sustained, even though the students gave more detailed answers this year. But it was the first year that the students referred to clear equality aims and intersectionality, either positively or negatively, manifesting an awareness and assessment of the scene study practices and content as inclusive or exclusive.

The unexpected observation from this project, that the reflective discussion before the anonymous evaluations invited contributions on inclusivity in the anonymous comments, begs for further research. This question can be carried forward: How can tutors during the first lesson facilitate the creation of a commonly understood language for talking about intersectionality and inclusivity, so that henceforth students can activate this language in practice and reflection of practice for all the work? Such a question invites HE tutors of acting and beyond to devise ways in which the schemes of work for their classes function as ongoing vehicles for developing more inclusive actor training materials through student contributions.

Conclusion: Liminal Casting in Actor Training

Prior efforts to decolonise casting practices in actor training stressed the importance of student agency concerning teaching practices and materials used, empowering the students to make choices for themselves and liberating them from assumptions that the roles on offer, with the same ethnicity or gender as them, resonate with their social experience or their acting ambitions (Blackburn, 2023; Coronel, 2023). The merging of such efforts with current developments in inclusive curriculum design inspired a scheme of work for a scene study class that sidelined text analysis as the core process for characterisation in favour of analysing what kind of physical behaviours in physical scores manifest the acting strengths of individual student-actors. Alongside a journey of discovering what kind of dramatic situations move each student and reflect their desired career, the class recruited students through a co-created curriculum model to collaborate with the tutor in developing inclusive teaching practices and materials. The participatory action research cycle was analysed through the scheme of work and the students' observations concerning the inclusivity of class content, all of which were corroborated with anonymous comments at the end-of-module standardised evaluation.

What all good practices identified had in common was putting the student at the centre of the learning process, by prioritising their expressive means instead of what texts ascribe to characters; by focusing on how their acting choices worked for them in manifesting as being in the moment, in the full glory of their own acting strengths that might even contradict the text; by embracing in class their identity characteristics such as their name, well-being needs, and boundaries; and by depending on their contributions, during reflective discussions on showings, to extrapolate learning for the whole class. Another interesting finding was that the phenomenology-inspired language that invited a focus on the actor's body, voice, and imagination, and was encouraged to be used during reflections, had an impact beyond sidelining text analysis, in that it promoted transparent communications and ultimately a co-created learning environment of trust. An unexpected finding was that such reflective discussions at the end of the module, which introduce questions and vocabularies about inclusive teaching materials and practices, can work as alternative or parallel evaluation mechanisms, making standardised student surveys more useful for developing inclusive practices for actor training and beyond.

Considering the ongoing debates surrounding inclusive casting practices in actor training, this chapter invites the development of scene study in ways that tackle assumptions about assigning students with 'the role that suits them' to showcase their best, or 'the role that challenges them' to learn outside their comfort zone. Instead, actor training practices and materials can approach casting as a liminal process of self-inquiry in search of the final casting state, or role, that hasn't been written yet, as the student tests what moves them and what works for them during their transition between multiple roles.

References

Barnett, R., & Coate, K. (2011). *Engaging the curriculum in higher education*. Open University Press.

Beech, N. (2011). Liminality and the practices of identity reconstruction. *Human Relations*, 64(2), 285–302. https://doi.org/10.1177/0018726710371235

Blackburn, R. E. (2023). Embodying racial consciousness. In A. M. Ginther (Ed.), *Stages of reckoning: Antiracist and decolonial actor training* (pp. 60–75). Routledge.

Bovill, C., Cook-Sather, A., & Felten, P. (2011). Students as co-creators of teaching approaches, course design, and curricula: Implications for academic developers. *International Journal for Academic Development*, 16(2), 133–145. https://doi.org/10.1080/1360144X.2011.568690

Brown, A. D. (2001). Organization studies and identity: Towards a research agenda. *Human Relations*, 54(1), 113–121. https://doi.org/10.1177/0018726701541014

Churchill, C. (2012). *Love and information* (First TCG ed.). Theatre Communications Group.

Coronel, J. L. (2023). Societal othering of Asian Americans and its perpetuation through casting. In A. M. Ginther (Ed.), *Stages of reckoning: Antiracist and decolonial actor training* (pp. 42–59). Routledge.

Dunn, K. A. (2019). Hidden damage: When uninformed casting and actor training disregard the effect of character embodiment on students of color. *Theatre Symposium*, 27(1), 68–79. https://doi.org/10.1353/tsy.2019.0005

Elliott, J. (1991). *Action research for educational change*. Open University Press.

Friedman, S., & O'Brien, D. (2017). Resistance and resignation: Responses to typecasting in British acting. *Cultural Sociology*, 11(3), 359–376. https://doi.org/10.1177/1749975517710156

Ginther, A. M. (Ed.). (2023). *Stages of reckoning: Antiracist and decolonial actor training*. Routledge.

Hagen, U. (2010). *Respect for acting* (2nd ed.). John Wiley & Sons.

HB Studio. (2018, November 27). Uta Hagen's acting class – YouTube. *YouTube*. www.youtube.com/watch?v=RLSkEL3T6JI

Hess, E. (2016). *Acting and being: Explorations in embodied performance*. Palgrave Macmillan.

Hobbs, J. (Director). (2020). *The crown* (S4. E10). Netflix; Netflix.

Karreman, D., & Alvesson, M. (2001). Making newsmakers: Conversational identity at work. *Organization Studies*, 22(1), 59–89. https://doi.org/10.1177/017084060102200103

Kemmis, S., McTaggart, R., & Nixon, R. (2013). *The action research planner*. Springer.

King, G. (2023). Black queer autoethnographies. In A. M. Ginther (Ed.), *Stages of reckoning: Antiracist and decolonial actor training* (pp. 23–41). Routledge.

Loney, G. (1989). The American actor prepares: Scene-study for oblivion? *New Theatre Quarterly*, 5(20), 315–320. https://doi.org/10.1017/S0266464X00003638

Lubicz-Nawrocka, T., & Owen, J. (2022). Curriculum co-creation in a postdigital world: Advancing networked learning and engagement. *Postdigital Science and Education*, 4(3), 793–813. https://doi.org/10.1007/s42438-022-00304-5

Morgan, H., & Houghton, A.-M. (2011). *Inclusive curriculum design in higher education considerations for effective practice across and within subject areas* (p. 20). The Higher Education Academy. http://s3.eu-west-2.amazonaws.com/assets.creode.advancehe-document-manager/documents/hea/private/resources/introduction_and_overview_1568037036.pdf

Preedy, V. R., & Watson, R. R. (Eds.). (2010). 5-point Likert scale. In *Handbook of disease burdens and quality of life measures* (pp. 4288–4288). Springer. https://doi.org/10.1007/978-0-387-78665-0_6363

Sims, D. (2003). Between the millstones: A narrative account of the vulnerability of middle managers' storying. *Human Relations*, 56(10), 1195–1211. https://doi.org/10.1177/00187267035610002

Stamatiou, E. (2020). A materialist feminist perspective on time in actor training: The commodity of illusion. In M. Evans, K. Thomaidis, & L. Worth (Eds.), *Time and performer training* (pp. 50–61). Routledge.

Stamatiou, E. (2022a). Pierre Bourdieu and actor training: Towards decolonising and decentering actor training pedagogies. *Theatre, Dance and Performance Training*, 13(1), 96–114. https://doi.org/10.1080/19443927.2021.1943509

Stamatiou, E. (Director). (2022b, May 13). *End of class reflective discussion*. MS Teams; Evi Stamatiou Research Archive.

Stanislavsky, K. S. (1973). *An actor prepares* (26. pr). Theatre Art Books.

University of Chichester. (2022). *Acting skills 2 evaluation survey* [End of module evaluation survey]. University of Chichester.

Vahtangov, E. B., & Malaev-Babel, A. (2011). *The Vakhtangov sourcebook*. Routledge.

Van Gennep, A. (2019). *The rites of passage* (2nd ed.) (M. B. Vizedom & G. L. Caffee, Trans.). The University of Chicago Press.

Watson, T. J. (2009). Narrative, life story and manager identity: A case study in autobiographical identity work. *Human Relations*, 62(3), 425–452. https://doi.org/10.1177/0018726708101044

Wiley, C. (2019). Standardised module evaluation surveys in UK higher education: Establishing students' perspectives. *Studies in Educational Evaluation*, 61, 55–65. https://doi.org/10.1016/j.stueduc.2019.02.004

Yin, R. K. (2018). *Case study research and applications: Design and methods* (6th ed.). SAGE.

Zarrilli, P. B. (2019). *(Toward) a phenomenology of acting*. Routledge, Taylor and Francis Group.

Zuckerman, E. W., Kim, T., Ukanwa, K., & Von Rittmann, J. (2003). Robust identities or nonentities? Typecasting in the feature-film labor market. *American Journal of Sociology*, 108(5), 1018–1073. https://doi.org/10.1086/377518

Part Three

Structural Intersectionality in Values and Assessment

9 We Can Imagine You Here

Acknowledging the Need and Setting the Stage for Multi-Layered Institutional Adaptation at Yale University's School of Drama

Jennifer Smolos Steele

Introduction

> Imagination is the beginning of creation. You imagine what you desire, you will what you imagine, and at last, you create what you will.
>
> –George Bernard Shaw

Higher Education research and practice illuminate the need for systemic, structural change to create more equitable and inclusive learning environments. As a proud alumna of some of the most esteemed post-secondary programmes for training actors and musicians, and in my current role serving as Dean, School of Visual & Performing Arts/Artistic Director, Santa Clarita Performing Arts Center at College of the Canyons in Los Angeles, California, I am immersed in critical conversations and collaborations as my colleagues and I strive to meet rapidly evolving expectations in our institutions and within the world of professional practice. I also recognise and acknowledge my privileged perspective as a white female scholar and administrator in Higher Education. I am grateful to be included in this collection of chapters as we embark upon timely conversations informing future research in our field. Arts education is an ongoing transformative process composed of committed learners, professors, and administrators who desire to deepen their understanding of and engagement with the world around them. However, many institutions and programmes struggle with adapting to rapidly evolving educational, social, and political landscapes. Their central mission is often neither reflected nor enacted in the policies, programmes, and pedagogies of the place.

Many schools are grappling with how to implement substantive, meaningful change, especially as they seek more inclusive, equitable practices. Change is never easy, and for many of us working in Higher Education, it can often feel painfully slow, impossible, and/ or devoid of significant impact. An optimistic slogan on our school's promotional materials invites wondering how, or perhaps *if*, we are actively engaged in the pursuit of that mission, vision, and values as part of our daily work. We may invite guest artists to campus to explore anti-racist and anti-oppressive pedagogies. However, when the one-week residency concludes, how often do we find ourselves drifting back into our habits – to that which is known to us – especially in predominantly white institutions? We may engage in curricular revision endeavours, spending several months discussing that which must be taught, and ultimately recycling problematic practices and material. We may find ourselves unable to figure out exactly how, where, or when to begin, wondering how resources of time, personnel, budget, and bandwidth are allocated in support of such initiatives. While studies of

DOI: 10.4324/9781003393672-13

organisational change abound in the literature, absent are studies focused on *how* organisational change occurs in post-secondary actor-training programmes. To meaningfully understand institutional adaptation, we must investigate *how* change is approached, designed, and enacted.

The David Geffen School of Drama at Yale University engages in ongoing institutional transformation while simultaneously embracing valued traditions in training and artistic practice. This chapter critically analyses their multi-layered approach to adapting physical structures, curricular choices, and pedagogical delivery. The language used in their latest institutional mission and values statements aims to *reflect* and *shape* the organisational cultures and structures within the place. A singular, strategic mission and ongoing institutional self-reflection shape pedagogies, practices, and people within Yale Drama. With a focus on who is brought in to teach, to learn, and providing resources for success, ongoing adaptation occurs within an organisational culture of constant questioning as faculty and administrators strive to cultivate a safe space to learn/brave space to create for students immersed in all theatrical disciplines. Through the conceptual frameworks of Organisational Saga and Self-Designing Systems theories, this research highlights the identified need for ongoing reflection-in-action and continuous acknowledgement that adaptation is necessary. This, combined with a multi-layered approach for designing, developing, and implementing adaptive processes, promotes conscious, strategic design in an ongoing effort to manifest substantive change.

This chapter focuses on organisational dynamics and adaptation within one highly elite, educational environment with a long, complex history, and predominately white male leadership. In acknowledging the present and looking *towards* the future, this research is intended to initiate long overdue, critical conversations regarding *how* change may be approached, designed, and enacted in post-secondary performing arts programmes. Change initiatives are often neither possible nor sustainable without recognisable structural change, often requiring support from administration. The analysis of Yale Drama's efforts to enact a multi-layered approach to acknowledging and implementing institutional change contributes to future conversations and ongoing critical analysis by scholars and practitioners in our field.

Background

From 2018 to 2021, I conducted a multi-site research study investigating how faculty and administrators in three post-secondary institutions balance traditional techniques and innovative practice as they prepare actors for the profession (Smolos, 2021). I wanted to understand how faculty and administrators in post-secondary actor-training programmes determine their institutional direction, respond to the evolving demands of the professions, and develop practices that promote further innovation in training. The purpose of that study was to better understand how they approach, design, and implement training programmes that influence and respond to changes in their internal and external environments. Given the specific focus of the research, students and alumni were not included as participants in the study. Future studies will include the voices of the students to assess the impact of these adaptations.

Evidence from that study indicated that while faculty and administrators were grappling with very similar dilemmas, how they approached these challenges were distinctive. Participants shared difficulties regarding how to implement meaningful change in support of equity, diversity, and inclusion (EDI). The unique organisational culture, structure, and different response patterns within each institution served to facilitate or impede change. Faculty and administrators at Yale Drama shared extensive insight detailing how they acknowledge the need for, develop, and enact EDI efforts. Given the depth and breadth of their contributions, this multi-layered approach serves as the singular institutional example for this chapter.

Methodology and Conceptual Framework

Faculty and administrators in actor training programmes are working with the next generation of storytellers and are often creative professionals in the field. As such, they are consistently engaged in work on the self, the search for truth, and reflect upon how to better themselves, their students, and their programmes. Narrative inquiry was selected as the methodology for capturing the lived experience of such individuals. Narrative inquiry is defined as follows:

> [A] way of understanding experience. It is collaboration between researchers and participants, over time, in a place or series of places, and in social interaction with milieus. An inquirer enters this matrix in the midst and progresses in the same spirit, concluding the inquiry still in the midst of living and telling, reliving and retelling, the stories of the experiences that made up people's lives, both individual and social.
>
> (Clandinin & Connelly, 2000, p. 20)

This definition of narrative inquiry makes an important distinction between thinking *about* stories and thinking *with* stories. Instead of conceiving narrative as an object, 'thinking with stories is a process in which we as thinkers do not so much work on narrative as of allowing narrative to work on us' (Morris, 2002, p. 196). While John Dewey's theory of experience (1938) is most often cited as the philosophical underpinning of narrative inquiry, Jean Clandinin elaborates:

> Framed within this view of experience, the focus of narrative inquiry is not only on individuals' experience but also on the social, cultural and institutional narratives within which individuals' experiences are constituted, shaped, expressed and enacted. Narrative inquirers study the individuals' experience in the world, an experience that is storied both in the living and telling and that can be studied by listening, observing, living alongside another, and writing, and interpreting texts.
>
> (2007, pp. 42–43)

The narrative inquirer is compressing and selecting the materials of lifetimes into an essentialised form to aid in understanding. Within this study, data sources for analysis included transcripts from multiple interviews with each participant, comprehensive field notes, and other resources available from each institution.

To understand the forces at play regarding institutional adaptation and stasis, and the deeply woven, embedded fabrics of organisational practices within each place, I incorporated Organisational Theory. The conceptual framework of Organisational Saga and Self-Designing Systems theories (Clark, 1972; Cook & Yanow, 1993; Morgan, 1997; Purser & Passmore, 1992; Weick & Westley, 1996) revealed a critically important relationship between the mission of the institution and the development of organisational practices that will ultimately either promote or inhibit change. These theories, when used in tandem, illuminate new ways of understanding how post-secondary acting programmes adapt and change.

Institutional saga highlights the importance of history, the claim of a unique accomplishment, and a sentiment held by a particular group. Burton Clark (1972) defined organisational saga as follows:

> An organizational saga is a collective understanding of a unique accomplishment, offering strong normative bonds within and outside the organization. Believers give loyalty to the organization and take pride and identity from it. A saga begins as strong purpose, introduced by a man [sic] (or small group) with a mission, and is fulfilled as it is embodied in organizational practices and the values of dominant organizational cadres, usually taking decades to develop.
>
> (178)

A saga is more than a story, and although the conditions for initiation of the saga often vary widely, there are many ways in which a unified sense of a special history may be expressed within an organisation, through personnel, the program, the external social base, the student subculture, and the image of the saga. As we will discover in this chapter, the saga at Yale Drama to raise the standards of practice internally and externally continues to evolve within a multi-layered approach for transformation.

Theories of organisations as self-designing systems reveal how institutional learning occurs:

> Self-designing knowledge work systems are thinking and learning organizations that have well-developed self-diagnostic capabilities, allowing them to question their governing assumptions and reassess their relationship to changing environmental demands. . . . Knowledge work organizations 'learn how to learn' by maintaining processes that critically examine key assumptions, beliefs, tasks, decisions and structural issues.
>
> (Purser & Passmore, 1992, p. 55)

Self-designing systems have well-developed self-diagnostic capabilities allowing individuals within the organisation to question assumptions and reassess actions in relationship to changing demands in the external environment. Routine interaction with the task environment generates information about ways to improve performance, allowing for small, continuous change to occur. Self-designing organisations gain much of their identity from their ability to restructure and adapt. People working in the organisation sense and perceive environmental, external influences while evaluating internal conditions to make decisions regarding behaviour and action. This theoretical perspective aids in analysing Yale Drama's self-diagnostic capabilities and responsivity to changes within its internal and external environments. As suggested by the participants' own words, ongoing reflection/questioning is a quintessential aspect of the organisational culture, leading to continuous reassessment of practices, pedagogies, and policies.

This conceptual foundation aligns well with the methodological approach of narrative inquiry because it is particularly sensitive to the experiences of people at work in organisations and their attention to institutional history/cultures and organisational learning. We tell stories about our own lives and the institutions in which we work. And we also live within these stories. The institutional mission has a profound impact on shaping decision-making, storytelling, and beliefs, and ultimately revealing the values that underpin the organisational culture of the place. How those beliefs and values become institutionalised throughout the organisation is revealed through the stories we tell ourselves and others, the pedagogies we select, the practices we engage in, and the people with whom we collaborate.

Yale University's School of Drama

Yale University founded a Department of Drama in 1924 through a gift from Edward S. Harkness, B.A. 1891. Almost a century later, a transformative gift from David Geffen would further shape an evolving saga and significantly enhance self-designing capabilities within this wealthy, elite institution. As indicated in *YaleNews* on 30 June 2021, 'students at Yale's drama school will no longer pay tuition, thanks to a $150 million gift from entertainment executive and philanthropist David Geffen' (Peart, 2021). As the largest on record in the history of American theatre, this donation has made Yale Drama the only institution of its kind to eliminate tuition for all degree and certificate students, removing financial barriers in perpetuity.

In early 2019, I met the Dean of the School of Drama and Artistic Director of the Yale Repertory Theatre, James Bundy. Bundy acknowledged 'the onerous and punitive costs of attendance' and discussed that 'If we wanted to have a diverse community, we needed to lower the financial barriers to participation' (2019, personal communication). Allocating the gift from Geffen towards greater accessibility for students to attend the Drama School indicates how Yale's saga and self-designing capabilities are enacted through the decisions of its leadership.

The central mission states that the 'David Geffen School of Drama and Yale Repertory Theatre train and advance leaders in the practice of every theatrical discipline, making art to inspire joy, empathy, and understanding in the world' (Goff-Crews, 2022, p. 19), which promotes a combination of artistic, social, and critical skills. The statement invites faculty, staff, and students to pursue such goals collectively, impacting the narratives, folklore, and rituals within institutional practices while also influencing processes for decision-making.

Such desire is also traced in the institution's Values statement, which combine 'artistry', 'belonging', 'collaboration', and 'discovery' (Goff-Crews, 2022, p. 19). Artistry implies an expansion of 'knowledge to nurture creativity and imaginative expression embracing the complexity of the human spirit'; belonging promotes putting people first, centring well-being, inclusion, and equity for theater makers and audiences though anti-racist and anti-oppressive practices; collaboration suggests developing 'collective work on a foundation of mutual respect, prise the contributions and accomplishments of the individual and of the team', and; discovery includes wrestling with 'compelling issues of our time. Energised by curiosity, invention, bravery, and humor, we challenge ourselves to risk and learn from failure and vulnerability' (Goff-Crews, 2022, p. 19).

The language selected to define each value outlined above aims to shape the organisational culture of the place. In discussing the power of words, Pierre Bourdieu (1991, p. 41) writes that language is not only a means of communication but also a medium of power through which individuals pursue their own interests. When individuals use language, they implicitly adapt their words to the demands of the social field that is their audience (Bourdieu, 1991, pp. 41–42). Every linguistic interaction, including those deemed to be personal or insignificant, bears the traces of the social structure that it both expresses and helps to reproduce (Bourdieu, 1991, p. 43). The stories we tell ourselves (saga) and the language we use to shape our organisational structures/cultures initiate and sustain the development of our ability to transform, to adapt, and ultimately to change. Future research is needed to assess the impact of this evolving mission and to investigate the power dynamics embedded within the language selected for the mission and values at Yale Drama.

We Can Imagine You Here

The message 'We Can Imagine You Here' welcomes prospective students, faculty, and staff, serving as a powerful shaping mechanism for the selection of faculty and students. These words acknowledge historical recruitment processes and communicate a developing commitment to equitable and inclusive practice. It is a primary responsibility to reassess

> who comes here to teach, who comes here to learn, and who comes here to work. In every case, we inclusively recruit those who are leading practitioners and those who show potential for leadership and provide them with the resources to energise their bravest and most responsible choices in the classroom, studio rehearsal hall, onstage, in the field, and in the wider world.
>
> (Bundy in Goff-Crews, 2022, p. 17)

Bundy's words promise ongoing transformation in thought and action as he welcomes the interrogation of artistic and managerial practice while inclusively recruiting practitioners from the field. As a new initiative at Yale Drama, time is needed to assess this active reimagining of what inclusive recruitment can, and perhaps should, look like.

'We Can Imagine You Here' is also reflected in the School's publications, such as the Bulletin of Yale University. The publication dated 30 August 2022 writes:

> Never before in the School's history have we been so challenged to reflect on and rebuild our practices, in the context of a global pandemic, financial upheaval, and our keenly felt moral obligation both to acknowledge our history and to take steps to dismantle racism and anti-blackness in our pedagogy and theatre making. Our ongoing production work at the School and Yale Rep must center the development of anti-racist policy and practice for years to come. We strive to build an increasingly inclusive art form joyfully recognize our shared humanity, celebrating differences, and honoring the intersectionalities of identities and cultures.
>
> (Goff-Crews, 2022, p. 17)

These statements actively acknowledge past, present, and future challenges within an organisational culture striving for increased inclusivity. These words in concert with the message 'We Can Imagine You Here', serve as powerful statements in shaping the future values of and direction for the institution.

It becomes more complex when we analyse how such values are enacted by the leadership team. While many schools talk about increasing inclusivity and minimising financial barriers, far fewer make tangible and strategic strides in that direction. As the only programme in the United States that trains in all disciplines of the Theatre, Yale Drama is a complex ecosystem of coordination within an environment of constant questioning: 'What are we doing, how are we doing it, what should we be doing differently?' (Bundy, 2019; Rodriguez, 2019, personal communications). Ongoing self-reflection in action fosters new pathways for evolving practice and encourages new voices into the conversation. Within the ongoing development of critical humility in the leadership team, the 'We' and the 'You' in *We Can Imagine You Here* continue to evolve for students, faculty, and staff moving towards anti-racist practice.

Towards Anti-racist Theatre Practice

As may be expected from a wealthy, elite, Ivy-League, predominantly white institution with historically white male leadership, Yale Drama includes a complicated history of institutionalised oppression. Marginalisation and subjugation are often entrenched within the organisational cultures and structures of an institution, requiring commitment from multiple constituent groups to acknowledge the past and adapt towards a more inclusive, equitable future within the place.

Yale Drama maintains a deeply rooted text-based approach to acting. Bundy explains:

> Text was fundamental for the founding of this institution because it began with a playwriting program run by George Pierce Baker, who was Eugene O'Neill's playwriting teacher. So, to the extent that you base your work on text – which is not a culturally neutral choice – you then have a responsibility, I think, to break the components of acting down to techniques, and subjects of attention that are not inherently oppressive. And so, the question becomes, what are those? What are those techniques and experiences? And what is the relationship of the particularity of identity to expression through those techniques?
>
> (2019, personal communication)

A text-based approach for training actors contains a multitude of embedded challenges and problematic historical inequities, especially for students of colour – making it difficult for Yale to claim to be moving towards anti-racist practices in Theater. However, Bundy's acknowledgement that text-based work is 'not a culturally neutral choice' illustrates a self-reflective attitude and constant interrogation of *how* to address inherent problems embedded within a text-based, primarily Western approach.

In an effort to address some of these questions, and reflect upon its self-designing capabilities, the School has implemented a series of evolving workshops and curricular requirements as current faculty and administrators work to enact anti-racist desires, as outlined in the *Yale Bulletin*:

> [A] core component of the curriculum for all students is an introductory workshop . . . entitled *Everyday Justice: Anti-Racism as Daily Practice* and is required for all students and full-time benefitted faculty and staff. The workshop serves as an introduction to key frameworks and strategies for the development of anti-racist practice and is offered annually at orientation. *Everyday Justice* is also a prerequisite for anti-racist practice coursework required in all academic programs at the School.
>
> (Goff-Crews, 2022, p. 141)

Anti-racist theatre practice as a core curricular component demonstrates how the saga of the place evolves in relationship to changes in the world of professional practice. All First Year Acting Students enrol in *Anti-Racist Rehearsal Coordinator Fundamentals*. Taught by Nicole Brewer, 'this course incorporates social and restorative justice, cultural competency, and self-care to create an embodied experience where actors learn to utilise their sphere of power to disrupt white-supremacy culture in processes of creation' (Goff-Crews, 2022, pp. 29, 36). As a passionate advocate for anti-racist theatre and artist of colour, Brewer brings an important perspective to the School. Such new voices have been instrumental in promoting ongoing adaptations of anti-racist strategies across various disciplines.

In Theater Management, students enrol in *Toward Anti-Racist Theatre Practice in Theater Management and Responsive Arts*, which involves

> collective cultural production designed to research and generate artistic programming that expands an institution's capacity to respond to stakeholders, new frontiers of audience participation, and new and hybrid skills, practices, and aesthetics that support meaningful and consequential public communication.
>
> (Goff-Crews, 2022, p. 123)

Such modules invite students and faculty to engage in important dialogues regarding future art practices, environments, and new frontiers for exploration.

This work extends beyond the classroom through the David Geffen School of Drama Equity, Diversity, and Inclusion (EDI) Symposium Series. Community members are invited to

> [e]xplore topics related to anti-racism, equity, diversity, and inclusion in pedagogy and professional practice, providing opportunities for cross-pollination of ideas and discourse between the School, Yale Rep, and the greater theater community. The symposia are an opportunity to amplify the identities and perspectives of those who have historically been underrepresented, so that we can center their and others' experiences.
>
> (Bundy in Goff-Crews, 2022, pp. 153–154)

Creating spaces and forums for these important dialogues across all disciplines within the School demonstrates that the people at Yale Drama acknowledge the past/present while working towards a more inclusive, equitable future. Because identities relating to race, gender, class, ability, and sexual orientation are a critical part of the discourse surrounding the actor's study of the human condition, the students selected for these MFA programmes are given tools to look introspectively while developing their craft.

These learning opportunities are in service of preparing graduates to raise the standards of practice in the field. By no means have they exhausted or completed these efforts, but implementing such interventions serves as an important starting point for ongoing adaptation and transformation towards anti-racist practice. Additional research is needed to assess the impact of these efforts.

A Safe Space to Learn/A Brave Space to Create

As a result of the 2015 Association of American Universities (AAU) climate survey on sexual assault and sexual misconduct, Yale increased the visibility of its Title IX resources and expanded its prevention programming. Title IX prohibits sex-based discrimination in any school or educational programme/activity receiving money from the federal government in the United States. Chantal Rodriguez, Associate Dean & Title IX coordinator, noted that the MeToo Movement established by Tarana Burke in 2017, 'had already reached a fever pitch and we saw instances of Title IX reporting skyrocket at the University' (2019, personal communication). People felt they could report, and that there was a mindfulness surrounding the importance of reporting instances of discrimination, sexual harassment, or sexual violence. Rodriguez explains:

> Sometimes Title IX matters are not so clear-cut. There might be racial discrimination. For example, if people live intersectional lives and have intersectional identities, so sometimes

it's parsing that out, and I do a lot of guiding people through those concerns. A Title IX coordinator doesn't actually determine fact or truth, we just guide the process.

(2019, personal communication)

While most institutions have a Title IX Coordinator/Director within Human Resources, it is rare for a school within a larger university to have its own. At Yale Drama, this position is designed to support the specific needs of graduate students in Theater, including those who are living intersectional lives and have intersectional identities, and mitigates potential dangers for students working on material with heightened emotional and/or violent content. Allocating institutional support to foster safer spaces for artistic growth illustrates Yale Drama's self-diagnostic and self-designing systems capabilities.

In addition to increasing the visibility of Title IX resources, a rehearsal protocol was developed for scenes with sexual content and sexual violence. This rehearsal protocol, for classroom work and productions at Yale Rep, was the first of its kind at Yale and, through annual reassessment, continues to influence ongoing practice internally and externally. As evolving research and guidance for practitioners indicates (see Mackie-Stephenson, 2023), the use of a rehearsal protocol, in conjunction with inviting Intimacy Directors and Choreographers to campus helps student actors, directors, playwrights, designers, and stage managers understand the importance of safety within the creative process. It is also an integral part of the school's mission to prepare students for the profession.

Cultivating this safe/brave space environment at Yale includes a collective understanding that actors must use themselves – including both lived and imaginative experiences – to replicate this work numerous times throughout a rehearsal and performance schedule. Deep, raw, sensitive emotions and thoughts converge in bringing complex characters to life onstage and when the curtain descends, the actor is often left to grapple with those inner complexities on their own. At the request of students and in addition to a large variety of wellness resources, the school now has a non-clinical, licensed professional counsellor who 'supports students at the School with short-term mental health and wellness needs including, but not limited to time and stress management, conflict resolution, social and cultural belonging, and self-care' (Goff-Crews, 2022, p. 136).

Establishing a Title IX Coordinator specifically for the School of Drama, developing a rehearsal protocol, collaborating with experts in the field of Intimacy, and hiring mental health professionals foster a safer learning environment. In addressing the immediate needs of a changing student landscape and really listening to their requests, Yale Drama demonstrates a willingness to adapt policies and pedagogies to meet evolving demands. This, coupled with an investment in promoting their graduates' longevity in the industry and a continued quest to raise the standards of practice, demonstrates an ongoing commitment to multi-layered institutional adaptation in response to changes in its internal and external environments.

Towards Greater Equity and Inclusivity

Given the competitive industry and requirement for actors to be versatile artists capable of working in multiple forms of media, Yale has very specific criteria for Drama students. Actors selected for this programme are not only diverse, skilled storytellers, but must also demonstrate collaborative skills for working with other creatives, such as designers, directors, playwrights, and stage managers. A demonstrated commitment to diversifying the student population while striving for increased equity continues to evolve as the programme works to become more inclusive and accessible for all.

The student population has diversified significantly in a surprisingly short period of time. In the words of Bundy:

> In the acting program right now, I would say the really noticeable thing about the program is that 68% of students in the acting program identify as people of color. That's over-representation compared to the general population, but it's not surprising to me because I think – especially in the current moment – the observations of the dominant culture, broadly speaking, are less interesting and less pressing right now. So, it's unsurprising to me that it feels like the actors who have the most to say are actors of color. A higher percentage of actors of color have something original and pressing to contribute to the dialogue about what it is to be human than do people from the dominant culture. And if an actor's education is really a human education, it's understandable that that would be playing out in the student body.
>
> (2019, personal communication)

In 2014, the student population identifying as actors of colour was 45–50% and only three years later, the programme began to admit equal numbers of men and women, ending historically repertoire-based decisions determining the typical ratio of men to women as 10:6 or 9:7. Students questioned why the repertoire would determine who has the opportunity to train as an actor – especially in a programme that also trains playwrights – and structural changes were implemented. As a result of this move towards greater gender equity, the following year's class resulted in 8 women, 7 men, and 1 non-binary actor.

A progressive shift in one programme creates a ripple effect for the other theatrical disciplines within the school. For example, when Yale Drama shifts 'to a more equitable acting program with respect to gender, that means the directing program must rethink how it casts. Or even what plays it chooses' (Bundy, 2019, personal communication). The decision to bring more women, non-binary, and people of colour into the acting programme has served as a significant force for reshaping the other disciplines. Directors, playwrights, and designers must all adapt to the changing internal landscapes within the school, further contributing to the preparation of future leaders to change the field.

When a historically white institution in New England has 68% of its student population in the Acting Programme identifying as people of colour, an ongoing commitment to practices that value active listening, constant questioning, celebrating differences, responsiveness to changing student landscapes, and understanding evolving needs in the profession must also be prioritised within the organisational structure and culture. In the words of Rodriguez, 'deep listening and deep analysis of the structures we have to adjust in order to respond to these real concerns from students' (2019, personal communication). This is facilitated in part by the work with artEquity, which guides students through a process of identifying their social location through intersections of their identity. Students in all disciplines are provided tools and a shared vocabulary for the work being asked of them in the classrooms and on stage. Faculty and staff go through these workshops separately, with further opportunities to participate in an optional workshop series throughout the year. Given the safe/brave space learning environment and the personal nature of this work, specific examples were not shared by the participants.

Additionally, an EDI working group and multiple Affinity Groups work on specific initiatives each year. In the hustle and bustle of university life, it is often very challenging to assemble all key constituents to be in the same room at the same time. Semester calendars coupled with production deadlines and the intensely demanding culture prompted decisive action in order to prioritise and integrate EDI as a fundamental part of the programme for all MFA candidates in the Drama division. As explained by Rodriguez:

> One of the first challenges we faced in creating that group was when everybody could meet because our schedules were so ridiculous. So, we made a change into the actual production calendar of the school. We built in a two-hour window every month during which rehearsals were not held and we keep clearing more things to make people's attendance possible. It doesn't mean that the whole school comes, but you have to at least create the space where people could go.
>
> (2019, personal communication)

Creating the space and time for these important conversations to occur had to be prioritised for this work to be possible. Structural changes – particularly regarding the schedule – were introduced to foster these important dialogues and periods for reflection. Rodriguez continues:

> We're constantly identifying barriers to participation in the organization on multiple fronts. We ask, what are the barriers for people? It could be that they didn't have a protocol for which to follow to ensure their safety. One of the big things is to analyze if someone brings a problem to us, is it a barrier that we actually have the power to adjust?
>
> (ibid)

Taking the time to acknowledge and analyse a problem, identifying the embedded barrier(s) within it, and working to determine how to adjust or sustain ongoing self-reflection in action. 'Taking the time' and 'making the time' both are important within this organisational culture. Since 2021–2022, the academic calendar at Yale Drama includes five days each term known as 'Community Days' in which classes are suspended to allow for cross-programme and/or all-school activities. The Yale Bulletin offers more information:

> Each term, classes are suspended to create time and space for joyful community connection and more opportunities for interdisciplinary learning. Historically, Community Day activities range from all-school meetings, EDI Symposium Series events, workshops and lectures, community-wide meals, and/or social gatherings.
>
> (Goff-Crews, 2022, p. 142)

In valuing such EDI initiatives and making the time for these efforts to be feasible, structural changes are prioritised across the School.

In addition to increased efforts surrounding racial and gender inclusivity, the commitment to EDI has expanded to include issues of disability and accessibility. Only a few years ago, the Acting Programme admitted a student in a wheelchair for the first time. In many universities, facilities are not up to American Disabilities Act (ADA) standards until renovations occur. While the seating for audiences at Yale Rep had to be accessible, it was not until this student was admitted to the Acting Programme that the stage was also made accessible. Physical structures, including a lift to the stage, had to be modified to ensure full access to necessary facilities. Consultants from the disabled artist community also helped students better understand the identity of disability and how to support accessible working conditions.

Yale's commitment to EDI is also reflected in the approach to naming spaces, with recent efforts to celebrate successful individuals from marginalised communities. Rodriguez explains:

> There are many spaces in universities like this where you go into a really fancy room, and you're sitting around really old portraits of white men, and you don't see yourself reflected. Our students were like: 'Look, this institution of the Drama School, actually there have been contributions by people of color and women and disabled folks, a wide variety of people, historically, so we want to honor them and name them'. And in naming a room like the August Wilson Lounge, that's a way to help be a more inclusive space, 'cause people walk in, and you're honoring that legacy. But it's also like: 'Oh, I can see myself here'.
>
> (2019, personal communication)

Valuing Yale's saga and rich history is balanced with an understanding that current and future students, faculty, and staff must be able to imagine and see themselves in the place. As the School continues to evolve, the spaces themselves will adapt amidst ongoing efforts to become more inclusive for faculty, students, and staff.

One of the inherent challenges at Yale, and shared by many of us in Higher Education, involves efforts to diversify the faculty and staff. Students' ability to 'see themselves' at a particular school can no longer only be reflected by diverse groups of peers or institutional installations celebrating diverse alumni. Students are asking for faculty and staff who reflect an institutional commitment to EDI. Yale Drama faces ongoing challenges because 'these are predominantly white institutions, and their diversity of the student body is not matched the diversity of the acting faculty' (Bundy, 2019, personal communication). Rodriguez explains:

> [w]e can diversify the student body faster because we lose a third of it every year when they leave, and the Acting department has been able to diversify really quickly. You don't just throw out valued faculty or staff. It's a longer-term process.
>
> (2019, personal communication)

Inviting new voices to the institution as faculty, guest artists, workshop practitioners, and consultants is a mechanism for actively addressing some aspects of this challenge. However, it will take many years to substantively diversify the faculty in meaningful ways and more research is needed to understand the impact of these adaptations.

Despite numerous examples of institutional adaptation presented in this chapter, the work at Yale Drama has only just begun. Rodriguez describes this ongoing work with her colleagues:

> We are continuing to look at questions of disability and accessibility. We're working with a foundation that is trying to specifically talk about accessibility. We gathered the Dean and our Assistant Dean and went to a conference meeting with heads of other programs. Oftentimes in these kinds of meetings, people go like: 'Oh, my gosh, Yale University is so advanced'. And we might be advanced, but we really try not to sit on those laurels, 'cause outside people will tell you: 'You're doing amazing work'. And then the students will remind us not to get comfortable because there's so much work to be done. And we continue to brainstorm: 'Okay, so what's next? What are the next steps of this?'
>
> (2019, personal communication)

For Yale Drama, the next steps should involve robust evaluation mechanisms as a guiding principle within the program's training and as an approach for meeting the challenges of the moment while developing new pedagogies and practices for the future. As indicated within this multi-layered approach to institutional transformation, faculty and administrators must not attempt to address these issues and challenges in a vacuum. Instead, they bring in experts and consultants, confer with peers at other institutions, listen to students, and reflect upon the implications of their decisions.

Conclusions and Implications for Future Research

As I reflect upon this chapter, I recognise that important scholars in the field have expressed concern that EDI work can be performative and has become a marketable commodity within a neoliberal economy. Having witnessed this first-hand, I concur that such performativity exists. To apply meaningful changes, faculty and administrators at Yale have designed, developed, and implemented structural changes, allocated resources, and stated an ongoing commitment towards greater inclusivity. Yale is a predominantly white, historically very privileged institution with a complicated history and significant fiscal resources. It is important to acknowledge that these tremendous monetary gifts have prompted and sustained many EDI efforts at Yale Drama and that many challenges have not yet been resolved. I also recognise that this research focusing on organisational dynamics and institutional change in post-secondary actor training programmes is both necessary for engaging in future critical conversations and glaringly absent from the literature.

This research is intended to inspire critical conversations regarding *how* change may be approached, designed, and enacted in post-secondary performing arts programmes. Through these examples of multi-layered, ongoing efforts at Yale Drama, we witness organisational saga and self-designing desires in concert with pedagogies and practices that invite people to adapt in response to changes within internal and external environments – setting the stage for transformation not only within the School of Drama but also within the world of professional practice. Future research is needed to assess the impact of these efforts, to further investigate power dynamics in relation to organisational dynamics, and to include many voices absent from the current narrative. We need to study the reimagining of hiring practices at Yale Drama and to assess the impact of these adaptations. We also need to include the lived experiences of students and alumni in future research. With the continued expansion of programmes across the globe, and an increasingly competitive professional landscape, it behooves us as faculty and administrators working in post-secondary performing arts programmes to better understand the impact of our decisions on the pedagogies, processes, policies, and populations within the places we serve.

References

Bourdieu, P. (1991). *Language and symbolic power*. Polity Press.

Bundy, J. (2019). Interviewed by Jennifer Smolos. 13 February, New Haven.

Clandinin, D. J. (2007). *Handbook of narrative inquiry: Mapping a methodology*. Sage Publications.

Clandinin, D. J., & Connelly, F. M. (2000). *Narrative inquiry: Experience and story in qualitative research*. Jossey-Bass.

Clark, B. R. (1972). The organizational saga in higher education. *Administrative Science Quarterly*, 17(2), 178–184.

Cook, S. D. N., & Yanow, D. (1993). Culture and organizational learning. *Journal of Management Inquiry*, 2, 373–390.

Dewey, J. (1938). *Experience and education.* Collier Books.

Goff-Crews, K. (2022, August 30). David Geffen school of drama 2022–2023. *Bulletin of Yale University, 118*(14). https://bulletin.yale.edu

Mackie-Stephenson, A. (2023). *Intimacy directing for theatre: Creating a culture of consent in the classroom and beyond.* Routledge.

Morgan, G. (1997). *Images of organization* (2nd ed.). Sage.

Morris, D. B. (2002). Narrative, ethics, and pain: Thinking with stories. In R. Charon & M. Montello (Eds.), *Stories matter: The role of narratives in medical* ethics (pp. 196–218). Routledge.

Peart, K. N. (2021, June 30). With gift from David Geffen, Yale's drama school goes tuition-free. *Yale News.* https://news.yale.edu/2021/06/30/

Purser, R. E., & Passmore, W. A. (1992). Organizing for learning. *Research in Organizational Change and Development, 6,* 37–114.

Rodriguez, C. (2019). Interviewed by Jennifer Smolos. 13 February, New Haven.

Smolos, J. (2021). *The art of balancing traditional technique and innovative practice: Toward a framework for understanding stasis and change in post-secondary acting programs* (Publication No. steinhardt.nyu10787) [Doctoral dissertation, New York University]. Proquest Dissertations and Theses Publishing.

Weick, K., & Westley, F. (1996). Organizational learning: Affirming an oxymoron. In *Managing organizations: Current issues* (pp. 190–209). Sage Publications.

10 Complex Movements for Change
A Case Study

Niamh Dowling

Introduction

If we are to better understand how to enable the optimal conditions for systemic and sustainable change across an institution, it seems vital to interrogate our processes. Systemic change refers to the need to confront the root causes of issues rather than solely dealing with the symptoms, so recognising a need for transformation in every aspect of an organisation's processes, policies, and structures: tackling hard-wired habits of working, mindsets, power dynamics, and history. The collective power is strengthened through the active collaboration of people and departments in this work.

I write as a movement practitioner and as Principal of the Royal Academy of Dramatic Art (henceforth RADA) having joined in 2022. I draw on somatic knowledge to enable embodied change and reflect here on the intersecting praxis that shaped this first stage towards institutional change, its material components, and its mobilising practices. I see the institution as the body, a complex organism, made up of multiple and distinct components moving together, starting with the individual parts, and harnessing their collective momentum.

This process can be considered as a complex movement: merging somatic practices with a business model to orientate towards social justice and a more equitable organisation. This is viewed through the lens of the Alexander Technique and the therapeutic Systemic Constellations, which bring awareness and potential transformation to the relational body and structural frameworks for change, in this case, the leadership model of Theory U (Scharmer, 2009). The structure here maps the context and the timeline for the project and then reflects on the foreseeable process of structural change through the three stages of Theory U – letting go, presencing and letting come – to situate this process as intersectional praxis.

Context

Founded in 1904, RADA has trained some of the world's most established actors, writers, directors, and technical specialists. Recently awarded world-leading status (Office for Students, 2022), RADA is a small, specialist institution offering Higher Education level vocational training for theatre and performance, providing one Foundation Degree, two BA degrees, and one MA degree. With 180 students, RADA is one of the smallest Office-for-Student-funded providers of vocational degrees in the United Kingdom in theatre, design, and technical stagecraft.

RADA's training aims to foster the artistic, intellectual, and personal growth of students and to create an environment within which graduates can emerge as leaders in their field, creative artists, highly skilled, culturally aware, and positioned to have foremost careers

DOI: 10.4324/9781003393672-14

within the profession. With 4,500 applicants each year for 28 acting places and 30 technical and stage management places, RADA has a great choice in the selection of its students. For the past ten years, the development team at RADA have generated £400,000–£500,000 for bursaries each year to support talented young people from low-income backgrounds to train regardless of any past inequalities of opportunity (HE Student Data, n.d.). Of the current Acting Students, 50% are Black and Global majority and since 2020, 50–58% of all students receive some sort of financial support from RADA.

The past few years have been challenging for the drama school sector in the United Kingdom, both physically and emotionally, with the impact of COVID-19, Black Lives Matter and MeToo movements, and the cost-of-living crisis for staff and students. Since then, policies, processes, and procedures have been updated, reflecting sector-wide changes: funding bodies have changed their emphasis, arts council, trusts, and foundations have recognised the need to review their priorities beginning the process of building access, inclusivity, belonging, representation, equality, equity, and social change into their organisations to varying degrees (Arts Council England, n.d.). COVID-19 demanded new operational practices, such as running the Academy online and subsequently back in the studios with the necessary regulations requiring smaller groups due to social distancing, twice the space and twice the number of staff. The impact of these financial costs continues to affect UK drama schools.

The Senior Leadership Team at RADA set out initially to consider the most relevant training for the twenty-first century, with the ambition of reframing/decolonising the curriculum and underpinning it with a more integrated approach to embedding anti-racist approaches. This part of the process was led by the Director of Equity, the Registrar, and Directors of Training. It became apparent very quickly that to attempt to address the question of what needed to be reviewed within courses, we had to review the bigger context in which the courses were operating and the bigger system of which they were a part. There were so many factors that both contextualised the practice and that would be impacted by the change. This meant undertaking and leading systemic change across the whole Academy led by author, Niamh Dowling, and Vice Principal, Helen Slater.

Intersections and Complex Movements

How do you scaffold and facilitate systemic redirection in an institution? What frameworks and practices help shape this movement? When you think of the institution as a type of organism, intersecting and in a constant state of becoming, then looking to forms of movement knowledge, somatic and from nature, can guide us in this process. In thinking through this praxis, I acknowledge the impact of my intersectional identity: as a woman, as Principal of RADA, as a movement and performer training practitioner working with the intersecting methodologies of Alexander Technique and Systemic Constellations. Working with a somatic practice that creates the conditions for personal change, alongside an experiential practice that explores complex societal and multi-stakeholder issues, in relation to the change management model (Theory U), has enabled and underpinned the first stage of complex movement at RADA.[1]

Understanding individual human movement helps us when steering group movement. The Alexander Technique, developed by Frederick Alexander, is a body system for discovering inefficient movement patterns and accumulated stress that get in the way of our natural capacity to move effortlessly and in accordance with how we are designed (alexandertechnique.com). It is a useful technique for enhancing balance, support, coordination, ease, and freedom of movement. A desire for change may arise from injury, and self-awareness, and as awareness develops over time, we become more tuned into what might otherwise remain 'under the radar' (Ascham, 2022).

Putting these principles into practice in a managerial setting was a breakthrough for me and the Alexander principles expanded and opened in front of my eyes. Recognising habit, inhibition of habitual responses, understanding faulty sensory perception, giving directions and primary control applied to more than the body allows managers to become more mindful of the way we go about our daily activities which is necessary to make changes and benefit. In understanding the metaphorical transferability of my work as a movement and Alexander teacher and how an understanding of the nuance of the micro in the body applied to the macro of an organisation, I incorporated my prolonged training in Systemic Constellations.

Systemic Constellations, created by Bert Hellenger, are a solution-focused healing approach that considers the whole picture of a family or an organisation as a component of a larger collection of systems, including its social, cultural, political, and historical contexts (Rowland, 2017). It has the power to reveal unseen forces, often including past generations or excluded elements, that may be actively entangling us in the present moment. It allows an organisation to perceive 'what is' rather than our normal incomplete pictures.

In leading the process of redirection, I am informed by my embodied and embedded knowledge of these two practices, allowing us to work from the uniqueness of the individual in relation to the network of the institution. The link between the organisation of the somatic and developmental knowledge of the body in Alexander Technique and the wider systemic understanding of Constellations offers an embodied understanding of movement systems designed for institutional change. The somatic systems intersected with the main framework shaping the movement for institutional change at RADA which is Theory U.

Originally developed by American academic Otto Scharmer, Theory U is illustrated in Figure 10.1. It provides a transformative direction for movement methodology based on listening/sensing ('letting go') and emerging/presencing ('letting come'), described as moving

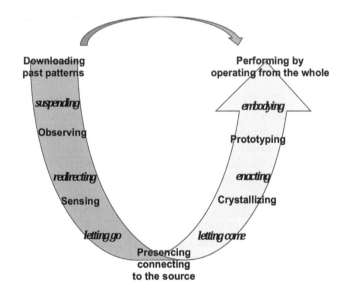

Figure 10.1 The journey in Scharmer's Theory U.

'from an ego-system awareness that cares about the well-being of oneself to an eco-system awareness that cares about the well- being of all, including oneself' (Scharmer & Kaufer, 2013, p. 2).

Theory U is not a prescribed process of what to do or how to do it but rather an order of stages to concentrate on. Firstly, it identifies the need to become aware of how things are in the organisation and not arrive at workshops and discussions with predetermined results or a desire to resist change. The workshop leader plans a workshop that will establish the right environment that will allow participants to let go of rigid thinking, connect with their intuition and imagination, and allow new ideas and a new future to emerge. It begins by leaders listening for a period without judgement to the voices and relational mechanisms within the organisation, one early outcome of the methodology is to clear a space for the organisation, as a community, to emerge its qualities and strengths, conflicts, and obstacles to change. In our case, we did this by offering the space for this engagement and involvement in a number of workshops across all members of the organisation as described as essential for change. Scharmer advocates:

> Decision-makers across the institutions of a system have to go on a joint journey from seeing only their own viewpoint (ego-awareness) to experiencing the system from the perspective of the other players, particularly those who are most marginalized. The goal must be to co-sense, co-inspire, and co-create an emerging future for their system that values the well-being of all rather than just a few.
>
> (2013, p. 13)

Enabling an inclusive conversation that works with the positivity of difference underpins this work. RADA's movement for systemic change is underpinned by the understanding and embodiment of these intersecting frameworks and methodologies. Starting with the individual body, Alexander Technique offers a very detailed approach to a reorganisation of the system and design. Systemic Constellations is a phenomenological method for resolving conflicts in organisations, businesses, and personal lives. It provides a mechanism to map the current reality, address the underlying forces at play, and find a solution. Theory U gives the direction of travel. These three approaches intersect with, beside and through each other, and underpin the process.

Timeline

Setting up the circumstances for systemic change was relatively straightforward to launch at RADA. There were many areas the staff wanted to unpack as we began to look at developing the next strategic plan: workloads, relevance, habits of operating, embedding Equality Diversity and Inclusion, and specifically anti-racism, relationship to the industry, space to keep updated, research, and above all, the purpose of the work we do.

The process towards institutional change began in June 2022. We started with several workshops (20 hours) with the Senior Leadership Team (henceforth SLT). It seemed that despite significant improvements in inclusion over the past five to ten years, the external image was still one of white, middle-class students, which was very different from reality.

To create the conditions for regeneration and institutional change to happen, the U-Theory process outlines three phases. Each of these phases, sensing, presencing, and realising, involves the creation of a specific environment to support a particular type of understanding and learning.

Stage 1: Sensing or Letting Go

The first exploratory workshops with SLT ran from July to September 2022 and focused on in-depth discussions about the past, embedded beliefs, the organisation, perceptions, issues, challenges, values, and purpose. In considering how RADA is perceived externally, we identified several key questions: Do we perceive ourselves to be trainers or educators? Do we serve or inform the industry? Are we world-leading? Are we a community of practice? Do we champion and innovate? How do we reflect our heritage? Are we held back by our history? Is actor training a craft? Is it art? How do we prepare for the emergent future? We established initial areas that may eventually become strategic aims, such as representation, pioneering practice, world-leading training, industry-leading, equity and diversity, financial stability, estates, and others. This information was gathered using a questionnaire which went to all students, staff, and council and a planned series of workshops run for staff, students, and trustees.

Stage 2: Presencing

In the second stage, a series of workshops were held over seven months, with the SLT, staff, student groups, and trustees. The workshops were designed to initiate discussion on participants' experience of the organisation, positive and negative, and where it could move. In advance of the workshops, all staff, students, and trustees were surveyed for their view of the way they and the institution were valued. The Senior Leadership Team worked for an initial period to uncover the core tenets of the institution's purpose (transformational actualisation and empowering change makers) and then drafted a proposed mission, values, and goal statements that were shared for reworking at the workshops. Staff, student, and council participants in the subsequent workshops were invited to discuss and feedback on the mission and offer alternatives to the draft values and goals.

Stage 3: Realising or Letting Come

Throughout each of the earlier workshops with staff and students, suggestions and proposals emerged which were fed into later workshops with other staff, students, and council. As a result, the articulation of a new strategic direction began to accumulate and emerge through workshops, creating the foundation of a new strategic plan. Alongside this, all of the senior leaders at RADA and the chair of the council took part in a one-day Systemic Constellation workshop.

In the next part of this chapter, I consider these stages in relation to the knowledge of somatic practices.

Sensing (Stage 1): Coming to Awareness, Letting Go, and Alexander Technique

The Coming to Awareness and Letting Go stage within Theory U intersects with the first stages of the somatic knowledge of the Alexander Technique where 'noticing' and 'letting go' offer an immediate alignment. The starting point of both processes focuses on becoming aware of what is going on and noticing how it is impacting the fuller system. Becoming aware that to decolonise any element of the organisation, we will look at the whole organisation, our values, mission, and our bigger purpose.

A person with postural habits that have caused great pain in their shoulders may go to visit a teacher of the Alexander Technique wanting their shoulder to be 'sorted'. As you become aware of the habit that produces the pain, you start noticing the knock-on effect on yourself and the rest of your body. Tension in the shoulders, for example, may cause a tightening in the neck, a compression in the spine, and lifting of the shoulders. All this results in pain which can affect emotions and cause anxiety, anger, fatigue and, in some cases, immobility. Many of the physical problems we experience are the direct result of the way we use our bodies. How we do what we do consciously or unconsciously affects the way we move physically, which has been described as 'use affects function' (Soar, 2023).

Within the principles of the Alexander Technique, a teacher does not try to solve the problem of the shoulder or narrow the student's focus on the painful part of the body. They don't address difficulties or destructive habits directly to 'correct' them. The teacher begins the lesson by setting up the conditions whereby the student is open to learning, experimenting, and trying something new. Alexander work encourages the student to let gravity influence and organise the body which allows things to emerge. Through the Alexander lesson, we learn more about our body so that we can cooperate with our design and not try to micromanage our system at any level, posture, movement, health, or creativity. This creates the conditions for not end gaining, being curious, allowing things to emerge, becoming aware and conscious of how things are, and recognising there are other options available to us and that we have choices. Change happens indirectly, which offers a productive model for someone desiring change. This reflects Paulo Freire's practice of conscientisation, enabling a critical pedagogy (Freire Institute, n.d.).

The same practice aligns with Theory U's becoming aware and letting go of what you know, not short cutting the process so that new possibilities and knowledge can emerge. In Theory U, there is a shift from a personal, individual-centred approach to a collective, group-centred one to move towards a more sustainable, healthy organisation (TRIGGER). This process of letting go of the old ways of doing things and letting come to source our best future possibility establishes a subtle connection to a deeper source of knowing and understanding as a group.

The purpose of the SLT's initial workshops in June 2022 was to have a deeper understanding that RADA was at a point, after the challenges of previous years, to spend reflective time together as a team, away from day-to-day business and operational decisions. This gave us time to explore individual and shared values and to begin work on a new mission, or statement of purpose, as we moved into business planning for 2023 onwards. It became apparent in the first workshop that we needed to clarify the bigger purpose and values of RADA beyond producing actors, technicians, and managers for mainstream theatres, TV, and the film industry.

As part of the introductory tasks, SLT colleagues were asked to use a single word, symbol, or diagram to describe how they saw RADA in the present and what they would like for the future. Their responses are illustrated in Table 10.1.

The images and metaphors in Table 10.1 identify awareness of a present that feels hidden, undernourished, stuck, and confined, whereas the aspirations for the future are for flow, light, expansiveness, abundance, and nourishment. Discussions ensued about potential areas that could derail that journey, such as fear, not listening, external factors, hierarchical power structures, finances, lack of trust, lack of clarity about the destination, and many others. We concluded that we needed to design and share in a transformative journey with the entire organisation; to work with clear, consistent, and compelling communications; to foster a dynamic process with engagement of staff, students, the industry, and the council; to agree on values and ethos, with agility, clear direction, and trust; to seek financial stability, holistic thinking, and care of the RADA community and beyond.

Table 10.1 Description of RADA using word, symbol, or diagram.

RADA *now*	RADA *future*
Light and energy contained within a box/ restricted by a frame	Light freed and moving outwards with direction and energy
Sleepy – a broken bed	Unlimited flow and direction
Chaotic	Confident
Obscured – hidden under a cloud	In full sunlight
A single flower not yet in bud	A meadow of flowers
A plant in need of water	A thriving plant
Chaotic and tangled branches and roots	A strong and healthy tree with branches growing upwards and outwards

SLT began to identify ethos and values and eventually agreed on an initial list of 30 values that became the basis of a questionnaire with eight questions which was sent to all staff, students, and council members. All groups had questions on motivation, communications, and values, and staff also had questions on feeling valued and working as a team. The questionnaire was designed to get a sense of levels of engagement and feelings of visibility among the RADA community and to give us starting points for discussion around personal and organisational values in order to design a workshop. When filling out the questionnaire, we invited each participant to choose eight values from a list or to propose alternative values. The listed values included collaboration, creativity, treating everyone equally, respect, rigour, inclusivity, safety, developing my practice, integrity, quality, risk-taking, authenticity, empathy, growth, attention to detail, welcoming, transformative, experiential learning, community, industry impact, fairness, valuing difference, representation, innovation, ethical, enabling, progressive, valuing heritage, social impact, sustainability, pioneering, exemplary, exclusive, global and UK economic impact, and equitable.

The only additional value that was added by those completing the questionnaire was a commitment to climate change. There was a total of 150 responses to the questionnaire (90 staff and 60 students) and the results were illuminating. They indicated that motivation, feeling valued, opportunities for professional development, effective collaboration, and an improvement in internal communications were key. This last point, not uncommon to see in organisations encountering instability, challenges, or unplanned change, requires a well-designed, interactive communications strategy to enrol individuals and teams in transformation and future ambition. As a result of the combined responses to the questionnaire from the three groups, the final eight values were a shared commitment to innovation, ethics, progression, transformation, empathy, equity, fairness, and sustainability. These values were then carried forward as a basis for designing the workshop with staff and students. The deeply encouraging aspect of the responses to the questionnaire was the similar responses across both staff and students which clearly indicated a shared motivation for engagement with RADA. Although this is a very general indication of values, it is also limited in its scope by those who chose to fill in the questionnaire and we don't know the viewpoints of those who did not complete it. The very process of staff and students choosing values includes everyone in the dialogue, enabling all identities to be represented, and reflects Freire's model of conscientisation as an example of intersectional praxis.

Alexander Technique and Theory U both begin by recognising obstacles and blocks, gaining clarity on the challenges ahead, and providing a framework for structuring or reorganising thought. They both provide the circumstances for a quality of presence and a way of being, whether they are guiding fundamental transformation in the physical body or inside an organisation. Both encourage you to listen openly and deeply to physical responses and engage the self. Although one process is felt through the body, and one communicated through language, the degree of presence, awareness, focus, and consciousness that each person or participant operates from affects the outcomes of the workshops we ran.

In both these practices, imagery and imagination play a crucial role, whether they are used to create release and direction in the body or to work with the imagination linked to discovery, invention, and originality because they involve the idea of a possibility rather than the reality of what might, or could, be. Imagery and imagination partially share the same underlying neural structures, although they refer to different mental processes (Vecchi, 2019). The capacity to build an internal representation, such as an image or a movie that is displayed in our minds, underlies both practices and offers the potential for envisioning the future. Offering possible words that could be chosen, rejected, or replaced helps participants to see possibilities.

Presencing (Stage 2) and Systemic Constellations

The Sensing stage of Theory U asks for a commitment to openness in heart, mind, and will (Scharmer & Kaufer, 2013, p. 21). This position comes from seeing the system from the outside, having a picture of the whole, an important factor in building an organisational view, recognising that it takes in all voices, including those at the margins, to build a more diverse, resilient, and agile organisation. This process sets up the conditions for presencing, the half-way point of the U-curve, where the transition from 'letting go' to 'letting come' takes place.

There is a common understanding in several fields of the value of being *in the present*, or *in the moment*, both of which imply a heightened sense of awareness and mindfulness. It is a core requirement for actors, athletes, and others to be in the present of the imagined conditions of the play or the actual circumstances of the game. Leadership training promotes it.

The highly tuned physical awareness that is developed in the Alexander Technique is akin to the 'felt sense' which is the somatic awareness called upon in Constellations. This state of being in the present is a desired outcome of both the Alexander Technique and Constellation work. It allows new possibilities to emerge and to be in a balanced and poised state of readiness for making different choices. My experience and training in both of these somatic practices have informed my understanding of the transferability of this knowledge to the management of change within RADA. Both practices require a state of physical and emotional presence, where a participant is not blocked and limited by habitual responses, so that they can allow past and present, gravity and direction to come together, setting up the conditions to restore balance and order in the body or the wider system.

Similarly, in Theory U, presencing describes a balance between the presence of the past and the emerging future to enable the authentic self. According to Helio Borges, 'Presencing happens when our perception begins to happen from the source of our emerging future' (2020). There is a collapsing of the boundaries between the three types of presence, which are the presence of the past or the current field, the presence of the future or the emerging of the future, and the presence of one's 'authentic self'. When this co-presence, or merging of the three types of presence, begins to resonate, we experience a profound shift, a change in the place from which we operate. The stage between past and future is a threshold or gap which, to cross it, voices of judgement, cynicism, and fear must be resisted. We need to ask two fundamental questions: 'Who is my Self? What is my work?' Presencing is the gap that separates the descending and the ascending arrows of the U process. It is a place of profound reflection and insights, where the emerging future comes to light and the participants see with new eyes.

Systemic Constellations is a system-sensing practice which aligns beautifully with the Sensing stage of Theory U and scaffolds and builds on the development of personal presence in the Alexander Technique. Systemic Constellations is a somatic approach to understanding and bringing to awareness what is happening in an organisation as a system and serves as a powerful tool for navigating complexity and helping individuals and teams move through challenging dynamics with greater ease, efficiency, and alignment (Collective Transitions, 2023). To uncover patterns of interaction and interdependent relationships within a specific system, such as an organisation, a community, or a project, this facilitated collective practice employs a 'felt-sense' methodology that mainly relies on somatic response. Through this procedure, participants build a dynamic model or map of a specific system to see how it interacts and gain a better knowledge of it as a whole. It can illuminate the deeper and more subtle dynamics that inform our behaviours, decisions, and unfolding experiences. A facilitated collective practice relies heavily on somatic responses to surface patterns of interaction and interdependent relationships within a particular system, such as an organisation, a community, a project, or a movement. Through this process, participants jointly, through their bodies in space, create a dynamic model or map of a particular system to visualise the patterns of interaction and widen the shared understanding of a given situation.

The staff at RADA are working within embodied performance practices. The similarities between the somatic practices of the Alexander Technique, Systemic Constellation work, and the developmental stages of Theory U as articulated above were very clear to me. Offering a professional development day for senior staff in Systemic Constellations offered the opportunity to bring senior leaders into an embodied understanding of what we were letting go of and the changes the organisation was going through in this process. Thirteen senior members of staff, including the full SLT, Head of Student Well-being and HR Director, and Chair of the Trustees took part in a full-day workshop with Systemic Constellator, Judith Hemming, to look at what blocks, history, and experience were slowing RADA down and holding us back. We set out to identify issues which go below the radar and create stresses, challenges, and a loss of energy to see if we could identify these and heal something of the past. Judith brought a team of 17 experienced and trained constellators who worked with constellations as part of their work as coaches, consultants, and counsellors to be representatives in the system. All persons in the group introduced themselves at the start of the workshop and identified their hearts' desire for the day. Several staff spoke about the weight of RADA's history and the impact of Black Lives Matter on the Academy. After everyone had spoken, Hemming commented:

> Well, it feels good that there's harmony here and I really can hear that this is an organisation that you love and want to make work and its energy isn't quite right.
>
> It's coping with indigestion from the past. And it's coping with going so fast that it doesn't know quite how to bed itself down and be ready for the future. So, I think this might be a really helpful day and I can feel, given what a spectacularly significant organisation you are, that you are not presenting yourself very confidently, and that is very striking to me. Something has dented you. And what you have gone through is way over and above what you've individually deserved. So, something's happened collectively to the spirit of RADA which we might be able to attend to.

(2023)

This set the agenda for the day. To ascertain what has so impacted the spirit of RADA, Judith asked us to name what we would like represented in the mapping of the constellation and she proceeded to set up representatives for several areas. The task of a representative is to use their own sense of perception and sensing to notice what is emerging in their experience regarding the person, persons, object, or aspect they are representing and then when prompted by the facilitator, to share the truth of this experience.

Based on what we now agreed, the facilitator chose representatives for the following areas for the first constellation:

• Spirit and Reach of RADA
• Accumulated strength
• Events that have knocked RADA
• Beneficiaries of RADA – not specified what they are

The representatives created a 'living map' of RADA on the floor. This is not dramatherapy or psychodrama, although the analogy might be helpful to understanding some of the process. Through discussions, we established several elements, and a representative was chosen as a stand-in for each element, moving in the space to map the organisation. The facilitator guides the representatives to notice any feelings or sensations. They move them around and use their position and feedback to work through and ease tensions, seeking a resolution to the area being explored.

We could see the wider forces that were affecting RADA and how these factors might line up in a way that freed us from entanglement with our past. By allowing the entire system to unwind and regain its strength and vitality, a potential resolution unfolded. The constellation addressed the underlying issues and provided fresh perspectives, a deeper comprehension, and a healing experience. A range of issues were explored – from the highly strategic to an operational difficulty. In the first constellation, we stayed with untangling the present from the past and freeing ourselves from constraints so that we could look for future possibilities to emerge.

In the second constellation, we looked at the history and messiness of the past, the challenges felt by the staff, and how we felt immobilised by the overwhelming number of external and internal factors of recent times. We looked more deeply at some of these events and the dramatic impact they had had on RADA, including racism, power structures, history, MeToo, Brexit, BLM, the cost-of-living crisis, and COVID-19. It was a complex, moving, often challenging workshop and by the end of the day, many areas had been untangled from each other and lines drawn under past challenges. By the end of the workshop, there was the sense that the process of clearing things up had begun. The final constellation of the day was an embodied and shared understanding of solutions lying in transparency, communication, and connection as essential to moving forward.

Alongside this work with SLT, we initiated workshops with staff and students to work towards defining mission statement, values, and goals as a way to be present together. These strands were interrelated, interdependent, and informed by each other. Over the seven months, a total of 250 staff, students, and council took part in voluntary workshops and fed back, commented on, and edited statements, added ideas, made proposals, and focused discussions.

We chose to use a World Café structure (Holman, 2012) because we wanted a dialogic approach to engaging staff and students in discussions. The World Café is a simple and powerful methodology that can evoke and make visible the collective intelligence of a group, increasing the capacity for effective participation in discussion and pursuit of common aims.

It ensures that the voices of all stakeholders are heard and respected, especially those that have been marginalised in the past. The structure was used as a means of gathering suggestions, feedback, and proposals. In this model, small groups worked in a cluster to explore or discuss a topic or question. Other groups nearby discussed other topics and, as they talked, noted ideas, responses, and suggestions. The conversation in each small group was linked to the unfolding collective conversation of the whole group. It created a lived experience of participating in a dynamic network of conversations that continually evolved and co-evolved within the series of workshops over the months.

Through a combination of discussions, editing, colour coding using post-it and flip charts, we accumulated proposals from the previous workshop groups. Every aspect of our mission and purpose was discussed at length, mindful of how we could manifest our mission statement in practice. There was a strong desire from all participants to include social impact and social justice as part of the discussions. After every three workshops, the mother sheet was updated so that the work accumulated, as captured in the examples below. For the purposes of this writing, the colours have been shown through three different typefaces.

Staff were given written versions of statements in the workshops and in small groups they discussed the text adding comments and phrases on the paper. For example, one version of the statement wrote:

> The Academy is a world-leading/radical conservatoire centre for making and producing live work. It is a community of practice/practitioners/practices with the purpose of training, upholding and championing the craft of dramatic art. By harnessing tradition and innovation, and through collaboration and empathy, we aim to effect transformations in humanity, society and the global creative economy.
>
> (personal communications, 2023)

Critical responses by a small staff group about the above statement indicated dislike about descriptions as 'word-leading', 'making and producing live work', and 'effect transformations in humanity, society and the global creative economy'; enthusiasm about the terms 'radical conservatoire', 'community of practice/practitioners/practices', 'championing' and 'empathy', and; suggestions to add the words 'students' and 'reimagining' (ibid).

The accumulated discussions were consistent in wanting to ensure that the final statement recognised RADA as a leader in practice, that it included both acting and technical areas, and that it highlighted positive change both internally in RADA as well as within the industry and beyond. There was a delicate balance between wanting to claim RADA as world-leading and fear of being overconfident and arrogant. This work continued until January 2023, by which time the statements had accumulated into the following agreed version of our aspirations:

> RADA strives to be a progressive and inclusive community of practice that inspires innovation and bold action. Through our world-leading training in the dramatic and production arts we nurture creative expression, empower individuals, and seek to influence positive change in the theatre sector and wider community.
>
> (ibid)

Alongside this mission statement and through the responses to the questionnaires, we arrived at several areas for discussion that could and did, eventually, become goals or strategic aims. The seven previously cited values (innovation, ethics, progression, transformation, empathy, equity/fairness, and sustainability) were edited through the workshops into four: empowerment, progression, inclusivity, and creativity.

The dialogic approach in the workshops, which reflects a critical pedagogy, has ensured equitable access and participation for all participants and provided a problem-posing conversation structure, designed to centre on a diversity of opinions and multiplicity of viewpoints. A commitment to equity, inclusion, representation, and belonging underpins our approach to this process. Finding just the right word can be a challenge and we wanted to set up the circumstances for workshop participants to take part in a dialogue about words. Words not only convey information, but they also reflect values, beliefs, and aspirations. The words we choose convey respect for differences in people's gender, race and ethnicity, age, abilities, and sexual orientation. If language and the words we choose to represent ourselves are to be genuine, they need to own and become embodied and reflected in all decisions and behaviours. This is where we can work with the knowledge of somatic practices as a model for systemic transformation and a tool for social justice work.

Letting Come (Stage 3) and Realising the Emergent Future

Letting come means capturing the actions. This is the stage in the Theory U model where we begin to articulate actions. Our task was to capture and develop the new ideas that were emerging from the workshops and to begin to make them explicit and fully formed in an overall plan and emerging strategy. The final agreed priority areas were a direct result of the priorities, proposals, and decisions made by staff, students, industry, council, and graduates in the workshops. For an emergent strategy to work well, everyone needs to constantly look at the periphery – not just in the direction of the end goal. This aligns with the principle within the Alexander Technique of not end-gaining. End-gaining means trying to reach our goal without any thought as to how we get there. The process must take priority over the result so that we know that the result has arrived at a deeply embedded and consultative process for all those involved in forming the priorities and direction for the organisation.

As a starting point for goals and recognising the emergent future, SLT identified what categories would most exemplify the emerging agreed values in practice and how might they subsequently become actualised. This resulted in seven different strands of action for discussion in the workshops with staff and students. In this section of the workshop, participants populated a chart with ideas, proposals, and options for activities that could come under the following headings:

1. *Representation:* how to ensure more diverse representation in our students, staff, pedagogy, and curriculum content.
2. *Relevance:* progressive training, industry connectivity, internationalism.
3. *Sustainable organisation:* need for growth at many levels, stabilising finances, developing people, embedding behaviours.
4. *Business integration:* a shared purpose of the commercial and the charity through working with RADA Business.
5. *Pioneering practice:* investment in professional development, self-directed work, developing postgraduate study, and research.
6. *Facilities:* capital investment, rationalising the estate.
7. *Sector leadership:* a generous community of practice.

Suggestions under these headings included the development of postgraduate provision, research, activities with industry, partnerships, and national and international collaborations.

Several new potential postgraduate courses began to emerge: Technical Theatre courses, Writing, Leadership and Acting courses which are an exciting first step towards a radical reappraisal of ethical and equitable training. Prioritising anti-racist and anti-oppressive practices and pedagogies, we aim to graduate inquisitive, questioning, open-minded, collaborative creatives. The programmes will include and prioritise diverse thinking and innovative approaches to familiar subjects/issues and aim to reframe the status quo of training across the board. It is a reassessment of historical and recent changes in the industry, both in live and recorded media, and will aim to build on the best existing practices and look at new ways to sustain, support, develop, and express the shifting realities of modern industry.

We identified the key building blocks of a strategy for an innovative and sustainable academy that is a leader in the creative industries. The vision and goals for RADA for the next five years are built on growth and innovation from excellence, equitable and sustainable practice, a renewed relevance to industry, and impact beyond the academy, locally, nationally, and internationally. Each of these strands is underpinned by four guiding principles: people strategy; equity, inclusion, and social justice; organisational sustainability; and innovation.

These all accumulated into a coherent summary which forms the structure and framework for the new strategic plan, as represented in Figure 10.2.

The collaborative and creative workshopping that culminated in the selection of the specific words initiated their action through consistent checking, revisiting, and monitoring in the next stage of our development plan.

Conclusion

There have been intersecting methodologies working beside each other throughout this process that have enabled an embodied movement for change. Figure 10.3 shows how the knowledge of the Alexander Technique and Systemic Constellations, presented in boxes, have worked in parallel with Theory U.

My own intersecting identities have deeply informed leading this process and the weaving of the overlapping relationship of the three areas as processes and frameworks, aligned

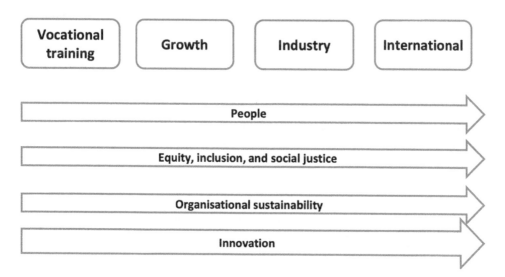

Figure 10.2 Strategic priorities and underlining guiding principles.

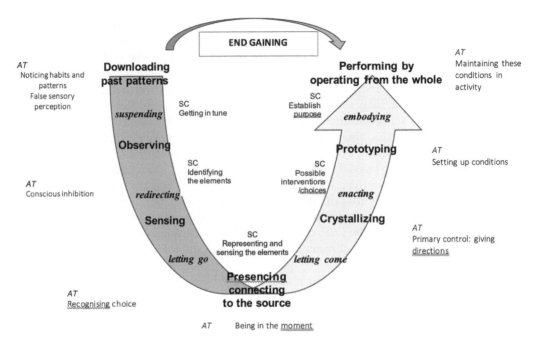

Figure 10.3 Alexander Technique, Systemic Constellations, and Theory U.

to an experiential understanding of the practices. They act as a cogent mycelium, underpinning the process of change RADA is undergoing.

We are now in the process of agreeing on the strategic plan for the next five years with all stakeholders. This is happening in the context of reviewing all internal processes, the curriculum, and the most effective use of current resources before any additional layers of development are added. Our financial recovery plan is a critical part of the strategic plan to restore the financial stability and sustainability of the organisation. This runs parallel to investing in new emerging developments identified this year, which will enable future growth in several areas.

The original task of decolonising the curriculum at RADA provoked the work discussed in this chapter. The circumstances are now much better to undertake this piece of work on existing courses because there are clearer priorities and direction. Frameworks have been agreed and there is an articulated context of shared ambitions and activities from both staff and students. The work of this process can only be maintained through the actions that it has manifested, the courses, philosophies, behaviours, partnerships, and collaborations that are embedded within the agreed mission, values, and goals. And so, the work continues!

Note

1 It is important to acknowledge that all three of these approaches have originated through the work of white men and that there are alternative somatic and change management practices that might facilitate this embodied approach, including the work of Black and indigenous scholars. Adrienne Maree Brown's is a great example, bringing together somatics, eco-politics, and social justice work (2017).

References

alexandertechnique.com. (2020, January 20). *What is the Alexander technique and what are its benefits? The complete guide to the Alexander technique.* https://alexandertechnique.com/at/

Arts Council England. (n.d.). *How the arts council will change.* Retrieved October 22, 2023, from www.artscouncil.org.uk/lets-create/delivery-plan-2021-2024/themes-actions/how-arts-council-will-change

Ascham, L. (2022, March 15). What exactly is the Alexander technique? *Lucy Ascham.* https://lucyascham.com/what-exactly-is-the-alexander-technique/

Borges, H. (2020). *Published in field of the future blog.* https://medium.com/presencing-institute-blog/theory-u-presencing-crossing-the-threshold-into-the-field-of-the-future-26acf37c44e8

Brown, A. M. (2017). *Shaping change, changing worlds.* AK Press.

Collective Transitions. (2023). *Intro training: Systemic constellations for societal change.* www.collectivetransitions.com/sc1

Freeman, J. (Ed.). (2019). *Approaches to actor training: International perspectives.* Macmillan International.

Freire Institute. (n.d.). *Concepts used by Paulo Freire.* Retrieved October 22, 2023, from https://freire.org/concepts-used-by-paulo-freire

Ginther, A. M. (Ed.). (2023). *Stages of reckoning: Antiracist and decolonial actor training.* Routledge.

HE Student Data | HESA. (n.d.). Retrieved October 22, 2023, from www.hesa.ac.uk/data-and-analysis/students

Hemming, J. (2023). *Systemic constellations workshop [professional development for social change].* http://www.movingconstellations.com/

Holman, P. (2012). *The change handbook: The definitive resource on today's best methods for engaging whole systems.* Readhowyouwant.

Office for Students. (2022). *World-leading specialist provider funding – outcome.* www.officeforstudents.org.uk/media/7bd645bb-079e-42a8-b061-5710b96ecc11/world-leading-specialist-provider-funding-outcome.pdf

Rowland, E. (2017, July 31). *A hidden architecture – the orders of systemic change.* www.wholepartnership.com/hidden-architecture-systemic-orders-change/

Scharmer, O. (2009). *Theory U: Learning from the future as it emerges.* Berrett-Koehler Publishers.

Scharmer, O., & Kaufer, K. (2013). *Leading from the emerging future from ego-system to eco-system economies.* Berrett-Koehler Publishers.

Soar, T. (2023, October 13). *Use affects function.* Alexander Technique. www.alexander-technique.london/articles/defining-the-alexander-technique/use-affects-function/

Vecchi, T. (2019). Imagery and imagination in psychological science. *IMG Journal, 1*(1), 312–317. https://doi.org/10.6092/issn.2724-2463/11078

Whitfield, P. (2021). *Inclusivity and equality in performance training: Teaching and learning for neuro and physical diversity.* Routledge.

11 Developing a Social Justice PWI Acting Studio through Equitable Assessments

Elizabeth M. Cizmar

Introduction

I am a white, cishet assistant professor of acting and directing with ten years of teaching experience. I currently work at Vanderbilt University, a four-year Predominantly White Institution (PWI). Prior to teaching at Vanderbilt, I taught at Franklin & Marshall College, Bucknell University, Tufts University, and the American Academy of Dramatic Arts (AADA). Except for AADA, which is a professional conservatory, these are liberal arts institutions where students enrol in foundational acting courses for various reasons and with varying degrees of acting experience. Assessing a student's aptitude in the performing arts is a challenge because evaluating artistic expression can be subjective. But perhaps the challenge is not the notion of grading itself, but rather how PWIs have created inequitable classroom environments and upheld antiquated assessment criteria. This challenge is further amplified by the neoliberal consumerist culture shifting education away from process. I identify antiquated assessment criteria as grading mechanisms that privilege white cis men. This includes, for example, assessing participation based on who speaks in class. In the United States, there is increasing awareness of inequity in practical-based college-level acting courses regarding the historical prioritisation of white cishet male playwrights and bias towards Eurocentric training.[1] Yet, acting teachers who are interested in incorporating intersectional frameworks need to go further by reevaluating their studio environments, syllabi, and assessment models.

Rethinking assessments to integrate alternative grading structures starts with reframing the classroom to consider how intersectional identities shift from semester to semester. The fundamental problem with traditional assessment perpetuates a 'universal' approach, which assumes all students have the same level of experience and knowledge. Significantly, research at PWIs in the United States reveals that students from historically marginalised groups tend to participate less, while cis white men dominate conversations and exercises in group work (Tatum et al., 2013, p. 746). Arguably, this reflects society at large, but as educators, we can evaluate each semester as its entity and make pedagogical decisions based on the individuals enroled in the course. Drawing upon research in higher education, my primary scholarship on Ernie McClintock, and over a decade of teaching experience, I am in the process of restructuring my fundamental acting course to reflect what I am calling a social justice acting studio. Upending previous modes of evaluating student actors to foster this type of exchange takes courage, commitment, and practice. The concept of a social justice acting studio dovetails off scholars Robin DiAngelo and Özlem Sensoy's idea of a 'social justice classroom' (DiAngelo & Sensoy, 2019, p. 2), which bases course content on developing strategies for constructively interrupting patterns of social injustice. The scope

DOI: 10.4324/9781003393672-15

of this chapter focuses on classroom dynamics, participation, and the teacher's positionality as entry points for performance-based instructors to rethink modes of evaluating students to promote equity and inclusivity.

My revitalised assessment model employs McClintock's Jazz Acting aesthetic framework, which is steeped in African American cultural traditions and is centred on community and self-determination. McClintock was a founding figure of the 1960s Black Theatre Movement who established the Afro-American Studio for Acting and Speech (established 1966), the 127th Street Repertory Ensemble (established 1973), and the Jazz Actors Theatre (established 1991). In McClintock's technique, the Afrocentric notion of community is reflected in the ensemble dynamic and the actor–audience relationship, and self-determination is realised through self-expression (Cizmar, 2023, pp. 12–13). In Jazz Acting, there is a continual play between the collective identity of the ensemble and the individual actors. I apply ensemble and self-expression to reevaluate assessments to consider both the collective make-up of a class and the individual identities of each student. I offer my Fundamentals of Acting grading criteria as an invitation to consider alternative grading structures. This chapter encourages acting teachers to self-reflect, consider the intersectional dynamics in the rehearsal hall, and provide a pathway for equitable assessment through the model of a social justice acting studio.

Methodology and Theoretical Framework

This research began through Vanderbilt's Junior Faculty Teaching Fellowship (2021–2022) and developed into a conference paper at the 2022 Association for Theatre in Higher Education conference. In spring 2023, as a scholar-artist in residence at the Santa Clarita Performing Arts Center, I conducted student and faculty workshops. As of now, I am in the planning stage of an action research project and will implement changes in my fall 2023 Fundamentals of Acting class at Vanderbilt.[2] I have identified a series of anti-racist interventions to restructure my acting syllabus according to McClintock's framework of ensemble (community) and self-expression (self-determination).

Anti-racist education is a proactive strategy which argues that the sociopolitical landscape permeates classroom environments where those socialised in the West are conditioned to uphold white privilege (DiAngelo, 2012, p. 4). Therefore, anti-racist educators seek 'to interrupt these relations of inequality by educating people to identify, name, and challenge the norms, patterns, traditions, structures, and institutions that keep racism and white supremacy in place' (ibid). By committing to anti-racist education, the acting classroom is necessarily understood as a microcosm of society in which no one, including the instructor, is a neutral party.

I am extending the concept of anti-racist education to consider how grading assessments can be instruments of social justice because every aspect of the course is part of the microcosm. Participation is a hot-button issue, and many instructors have eliminated it as an assessment category because it can fuel an inequitable environment. In a 2023 *Inside Higher Ed* article, technology reporter Susan D'Agostino noted that especially in a post-pandemic world, 'many faculty members have begun to question long-accepted notions of whether participation . . . should count in a grade at all' (2023). Yet understanding participation as students simply speaking in class discussions discriminates against neurodiverse students and can favour white cishet male students. In an acting class, student engagement is paramount, and participation as a category provides an entry point for instructors to revamp the classroom environment. We can turn to research from DiAngelo, who identifies internalised dominance versus internalised oppression, which requires strategic and thoughtful consideration:

> Two key concepts are relevant to understanding common challenges to the courage, commitment, and practice required for social justice action: *internalized dominance* and *internalized oppression*. Internalized dominance occurs when members of dominant groups internalize and act out (often unconsciously) the constant messages circulating culture that they and their group are superior and thus entitled to their higher position. Conversely, internalized oppression occurs when members of minoritized groups believe and act out (often unconsciously) the constant messages circulating in the culture that they and their group are inferior and thus deserving of their lower position.
>
> (DiAngelo & Sensoy, 2019, p. 3)

Given this construct, an instructor may have the instinct to eliminate participation. However, studies also show that 'classroom participation has been linked to student learning and achievement' (Tatum et al., 2013, p. 746). Hence, the solution is not to eliminate participation but to redefine what participation looks like and how it is quantified.

My research on the life and legacy of McClintock informs the content of my course. Beyond introducing Jazz Acting, I apply his principles and extend his philosophy to upend traditional assessment structures. Advanced Jazz Actors invite a play between the collective ensemble and the individual artist. The ensemble correlates with the Afrocentric notion of community in which actors riff off one another in performance yet have a strong sense of a collective identity. Self-expression, tied to Malcolm X's notion of self-determination, is 'a demand that African Americans actively assert themselves in daily social and political life' (Cizmar, 2023, p. 13). Self-expression establishes the actor as a critical contributor in the production process, as opposed to a director's symbolic marionette.[3] Through these concepts, I am aiming to establish a social justice acting studio by envisioning grading criteria to strike a balance between the collective make-up of the ensemble and individual contributions. Because Jazz Acting is also about riffing in the moment, I have intentionally created flexibility within my assessment model to continually respond to the intersectional identities in the playing space.

Intersectional Classroom Dynamics and Assessments

To establish equitable assessment and contend with internalised dominance and internalised oppression, an acting instructor must acknowledge their classroom as an intersectional space. In 1989, Kimberlé Crenshaw coined the term intersectionality as a framework to understand the multiple identities a person holds and how those characteristics intersect.[4] While we are all at the intersection of difference, it is important to recognise that the origins of this framework emanated from addressing violence and discrimination against Black women. Significantly, intersectionality addresses missteps in conversations about inequality:

> We tend to talk about race inequality as separate from inequality based on gender, class, sexuality or immigrant status. What's often missing is how some people are subject to all of these, and the experience is not just the sum of its parts.
>
> (Steinmetz, 2020)

In performance, intersectionality is further complicated by the very act of representing a character with a separate identity from the actor. I propose that intersectionality provides acting instructors with a porthole to see how internalised dominance and internalised oppression can shift, based on the content of class discussions, monologues, scene work, and assessment mechanisms.

When it comes to class discussions, Robin DiAngelo and Özlem Sensoy's research in higher education reveals how the dynamics of internalised dominance and internalised oppression negatively impact both the dominant groups and the minoritised groups, risking inequitable assessments. In an acting studio, internalised oppression can result in historically marginalised groups identifying the studio as an unsafe space. In acting, the students must be fully present, engage in exercises, and establish trust within the group. Minoritised students may include non-cis-folx, people of colour, people with disabilities, and neurodiverse communities. The cost of internalised oppression manifests itself in silence. This silence can be a result of responding to resistance or hostility by the dominant group, feeling lack of trust in the classroom, being penalised for a nondominant opinion, risking invalidation, being outnumbered by the dominant group, and not seeing any allies in the room (DiAngelo & Sensoy, 2019, p. 3). Assessment-wise, if an acting instructor solely assesses participation based on speaking in class, then minoritised groups are unfairly penalised, affecting their final grade in the course.

When there are discussions in the classroom about race or gender, the dominant group (commonly identified as white, cis, and male) is often silent. The silence from the dominant group can be due to being hesitant to say the wrong thing, not wanting to dominate the conversation, seeing themselves as 'innocent', and expecting minoritised groups to speak about their position (DiAngelo & Sensoy, 2019, p. 3). Additionally, white-identifying students and teachers often turn to the minoritised groups to represent the whole of their minoritised identity. Not only does this dynamic impact participation assessments, but it perpetuates, for example, the dominant group's assumption that there is one monolithic Black experience. As far as engagement with the material, this imbalance of silence and vocality from minoritised and dominant populations in the classroom inevitably affects assessments when instructors use antiquated assessment models.

To establish equitable assessments in the acting studio, personalisation is critical – especially for those who hold multiple marginalised identities. Part of this personalisation for the students is the acting instructor acknowledging their own positionality. As Crenshaw suggests, '[s]elf-interrogation is a good place to start. . . . We've got to be open to looking at all the ways our systems reproduce these inequalities, and that includes the privileges as well as the harms' (Steinmetz). The acting instructor's identity as an authoritative figure holds immense power. We are part of the university system and have to work within these parameters and, yet find pockets of resistance to promote social justice.

Assessment and the Acting Instructor's Positionality

Interrogating one's positionality and how we may have contributed to an inequitable classroom environment can be an uncomfortable but necessary process to yield more equitable assessment models. As DiAngelo and Sensoy remark: '[a]nti-racist action requires us to challenge our patterns and respond differently than we normally would' (2019, p. 4). Yet by engaging in this anti-racist action of self-interrogation, acting instructors will lay the foundation of creating a safe, generous environment for students to express themselves. Self-interrogation is aligned with anti-racism pedagogy because anti-racism is about actively identifying and opposing racism to change policies, behaviours, and beliefs that perpetuate racist ideas and actions.[5] Thus, for me as a white, cishet woman, self-interrogation is necessary anti-racist action. Through this, instructors can critically evaluate their past assessment models and ascertain where bias may have impacted grading structures. By talking about our positionality in the classroom, students will further understand how in the Western world and the university context, we are socialised to uphold the status quo. Concepts known as critical humility, established by the European-American Collaborative Challenging Whiteness, and critical generosity, theorised by Jill Dolan (2013), are productive tools of self-interrogation.

I turn to the members of the European-American Collaborative Challenging Whiteness, who have identified critical humility as an anti-racist practice. The collaborative is a group of scholars – Carole Barlas, Elizabeth Kasl, Alec MacLeod, Doug Paxton, Penny Rosenwasser, and Linda Sartor – who created a coalition based on their work at the California Institute of Integral Studies to foster research about 'white supremacist consciousness' (European-American Collaborative, 2007). They define critical humility as 'the practice of remaining open to discovering that our knowledge is partial and evolving while at the same time being committed and confident about our knowledge and action in the world, however imperfect' (ibid). Within the acting classroom, assessments can be co-created with students to yield a meaningful experience and avoid evaluating a student based on talent. This framework fosters confidence and foregrounds growth and development in assessment.

To start, consider critical humility in the context of a PWI and acknowledge that these institutions are grounded in white supremacist values. Oftentimes, white folx in both academic and non-academic environments become defensive when they are associated with white supremacy. However, there is a distinction between a white supremacist and a white supremacist consciousness. A white supremacist refers to a person who believes that white people are the superior race. White supremacist consciousness 'refers not to a person, but to the system of thought that grows out of the values and norms associated with the nation's white founders' (European-American Collaborative, 2007). Just as all human beings in the Western world are socialised to participate in inequality, PWIs are historically invested in upholding white supremacist ideals. Thus, acting instructors need to be more self-reflective in terms of the language they employ, the universal truths they subscribe to, and how they assess and critique their students.

One of the most important ways instructors facilitate their students' development is by providing feedback, very often through assessment of performances, scene work, and exercises. Because identities, training, and experience are tethered to teaching methods, it is crucial to consider how an instructor critiques their students. I propose adapting Dolan's notion of critical generosity as a mode of listening, critiquing, and engaging with students' creative process.[6]

Dolan identifies critical generosity as 'an ethical rubric through which to think and write about performance' (Dolan, 2013). It was created as a way for critics and artists to engage in a dramaturgical process to clarify for readers' knowledge of each other's work and, thus, write with a deeper, more contextual understanding. Significantly, critical generosity is not an act of promotion:

> I don't consider critical generosity boosterism. Critical generosity can be useful for those of us committed to the arts as social engagement, with deep beliefs in its ability to reach people, change minds, affirm alternate visions of how we live in the world, and deliver hope in the potential of a different, more universally equitable future. Our critical

engagement in such cases needs to be precise, productive, and generative, rather than blandly cheerleading for anything that seems to fit a progressive political agenda.

(Dolan, 2013)

Many of the questions grounded in critical generosity start with 'how' and 'why' to engage in thoughtful analysis and unpack the particulars of a performance, rather than a general impression of whether something was 'good or bad'. In the acting classroom, akin to Dolan's framework, there is ample opportunity to pose questions about how a scene is developing. After two actors present a scene, the instructor can ask the following questions: Why does this scene work? How has the actor's performance reached the audience? How can we identify that these scene partners are 'in the moment'? How did you see a specific technique manifest and propel the actor's character forward? Critical generosity should not be laden with 'That was good' statements but to 'try to parse out how and why a performance worked' (Dolan, 2013). Applying Dolan's notion of critical generosity, then, falls under the framework of critical pedagogy to empower students through dialogue.

In the acting studio, pointing out what doesn't work on stage can also be a critically generous act, yet can be tricky to navigate. Students can be tempted to direct their peers in an unproductive manner. If a student directs their scene partner, this could be an expression of internalised dominance as they take over the shape of the scene, potentially initiating self-consciousness in their scene partner. So, in the acting classroom, critiques can be framed as a conversation between instructor and performer where 'critical engagement becomes a strategy for dialogue' (Dolan, 2013). Dialogue between student and instructor is particularly important in a social justice acting studio because the individual growth of the actor is carefully considered and assessed.

Putting It into Practice: Fundamentals of Acting

Conferring with higher education scholars like D'Angelo and Sensory and implementing McClintock's self-expression and ensemble framework has propelled me to reconsider assessment structures that will go into effect for Vanderbilt University's fall 2023 Fundamentals of Acting course. Fundamentals of Acting is offered to all undergraduate students, where we meet for approximately 2 hours twice a week. The fall semester starts in the last week of August and concludes in the first week of December. For this case study, I break down the assessment structure I am reworking for this course as follows: Ensemble Engagement (25%), Individual Growth (25%), Reflective Spectatorship (10%), Actor's Notebook (10%), Midterm Monologue (15%), and Final Scene (15%). Each category focuses on collaboration, self-expression, spectatorship, reflection, and technique in performance. In terms of acting techniques offered to a foundational class, students are introduced to a variety of methods, including Method Acting, Practical Aesthetics, and Jazz Acting, where they learn and support one another as an ensemble. By the time they work on scripted material, actors exercise artistic autonomy in choosing what technique will serve them best. Ultimately, I aim to strike a balance between McClintock's notion of ensemble building and self-expression (Cizmar, 2023, p. 11).

Participation as Ensemble Engagement (25%)

Research in higher education reports that classroom participation has been linked to student learning and achievement. In particular, 'critical thinking behaviors increase in classes with a higher degree of participation, peer interaction, and instructor praise' (Tatum et al., 2013, p. 746). In performance-based classes, I assert that the questions asked by students and the quality of personalised feedback from the instructor engender artistic growth. Additionally, rehearsal time both during class and outside class yields a higher level of achievement and increased confidence. However, students who rarely participate in the traditional mode (speaking in class) can interpret the classroom as 'a threatening environment and are worried about how they are perceived by classmates and instructors' (747). Therefore, there is a core conflict between the educational value of participation and students, who for various reasons do not feel safe or comfortable commenting during a class period.

I propose replacing the term 'participation' with 'Ensemble Engagement' to reframe the ways instructors and students think about participation and interact with their ensemble. Integrating a collaborative assessment practice will yield more equal power between the teacher and the students. At the beginning of the semester, instructors can provide time for the class to discuss and determine Ensemble Engagement criteria because from semester to semester, the demographic of classes shifts. We must

> allow students to . . . set guidelines as a group, soliciting and then formalizing boundaries for discussion. By helping create ground rules, students become invested in the course and begin to trust it as a safe environment to try out ideas and ask questions.
>
> (Alvarez, 2016)

An invitation for students to collectively decide on the assessment criteria for Ensemble Engagement requires the teacher's guidance. This collaboration establishes the ensemble dynamic early on as they come to a consensus, with my guidance, on how the ensemble should try to interact throughout the semester. Before the discussion, providing a handout with a list of questions can stimulate thought about how an unconventional participation model could serve all students.

I will pose general questions and then invite the students to consider the assessment criteria. Some questions include: How can we evaluate effective collaboration? What does the word engagement mean to you? What does it mean to be an ensemble? I will provide these questions the day before this discussion, so students can come prepared with suggestions. This approach may alleviate anxiety for those who are typically quiet during class discussions. Preparation also includes submitting answers in a shared document hosted on the university's web-based course-management system.

Ensemble Engagement could include prevalent categories, such as speaking during the class period, but there are other productive ways for engagement to yield more inclusivity. Criteria to consider could include active listening. For example, when two students are working on a scene, those observing could write down and identify areas of growth for their peer actors. At the end of class I collate the comments and distribute them to the actors who worked that day, engendering a supportive environment. I leverage online forums where I ask questions about the day's class and students provide commentary. Providing multiple modes of feedback mechanisms, both during and after class, can foster an inclusive and participatory acting studio.[7]

Individual Growth as Self-expression (25%)

The Individual Growth category supplies ample opportunity for the instructor to tailor and personalise an educational experience for each student. In this personalisation process, a useful question is, how can students of different backgrounds find meaning? I apply the concept of McClintock's self-expression in establishing Individual Growth criteria for each student. Similar to Ensemble Engagement, students may not have the language or know where to start when thinking about what growth means to them, especially if this is their first experience acting. Thus, I schedule individual meetings with each student and provide a self-assessment tool for actors to identify areas of growth. At the end of the semester, actors will determine their success. The collaboration between student and professor situating the actor as self-assessor therefore shifts the power dynamic where the student has more agency in their educational goals and evaluation.

At a liberal arts institution, students have various reasons for enroling in a foundational acting class and have a range of experience. In my classes, some students aim to have a career in the theatre, while others are trying to improve their public speaking skills and build confidence. Some students enrol in the course to fulfil an arts requirement as a hopeful way to lighten their load or take a break from STEM (science, technology, engineering, and mathematics) classes. Students also have many obligations such as sports practices and jobs as well as extracurricular activities. With students of varying backgrounds, experiences, and responsibilities, personalisation in the acting studio is essential for growth and accountability.

At the beginning of the semester, in one-on-one meetings, the instructor can ask each student about their reasons for enroling in the course and their artistic aspirations. Echoing Ensemble Engagement, a handout can signpost potential areas of growth, including developing engagement during class discussions, developing expression in physicality, developing range in vocal expression, improvisation, concentration, and developing collaboration skills. Students will choose three areas of growth to work on throughout the semester. At the end of the term, they will assess and rate themselves on a scale of 0–100. They will have to justify why they are giving themselves that score and self-reflect (Sambel et al., 2012, p. 128). Through thinking reflexively about who they are as individuals and co-creating criteria with the instructor, there is full transparency in how they are being assessed, while alleviating any fear that assessments are based on talent.

Reflective Spectatorship (10%)

As part of the course, students are tasked with attending two performances to think about spectatorship from the actor's perspective. The two-performance model invites them to focus on the foundation of the course: self-expression and ensemble dynamics. They can choose which performance will correlate to the critical lens of self-expression and ensemble dynamics, respectively. This reflection can take the form of a post on our online course-management programme where students comment on each other's reflections. Dolan's article on critical generosity can be distributed to provide a framework for students to think about performance to avoid assessing whether a performer or performance was 'good or bad'. These reflections encourage students to bridge the gap between what they are learning in the rehearsal studio and how they are thinking about performance and spectatorship. In other words, the aim is not to replicate that of a professional theatre reviewer which, in a producer's best-case scenario, recommends the show to the reader resulting in higher ticket sales; rather, the assessment will be based on how the students apply the language of the course to spectatorship and their successful application of critical generosity.

For one of the reflections, they focus on self-expression by analysing and writing about one actor's performance, using the vocabulary and language of the class in their response paper. Some prompts include: What were some character choices made and why did they work? How did the actor connect to the language of the playwright? Why was this a stand-out performance for you? If you were playing this role, which technique would you apply (sense memory, Jazz Acting, practical aesthetics) to realise the full potential of the character? By thinking about approaches to character and acknowledging the strengths they see on stage, they will develop the skills to engage in analysing performance from the actor's vantage point.

For the ensemble dynamics reflection, aligned with jazz aesthetics, students are asked to think about the company of actors on stage and how they created a collective voice. Jazz aesthetics in this context focuses on evaluating the effectiveness of the ensemble working together as one cohesive unit and responding truthfully in the moment, just as jazz musicians riff off of one another, but stay true to the melody. I note in this assignment that the focus of this response should not be about the student's opinion of the play or the directorial approach, but rather the actors' interactions with one another to establish a unified ensemble. Some questions include: What were the most memorable moments achieved by the ensemble? And why were these so successful? In group scenes, how did non-speaking actors in each scene, support the play and other characters on stage? How would you describe the collective voice of the ensemble? By applying jazz aesthetics to ensemble analysis, students will pay attention to actors who aren't speaking and, how, in those moments, the ensemble must be present and provide support throughout the play.

These reflections can be posted on an online learning forum and the students are asked to respond to at least three posts from others. My acting class regularly consists of 14 students. If a student elects to respond to 14 posts, then they will receive extra credit. Extra credit requires more work in which the students will be able to read and assess different perspectives. By having the students respond to the online forum, they engage with their ensemble through technology, building a sense of community outside the classroom.

Actor's Notebook (10%)

The Actor's Notebook requirement is something I've included in my syllabus since my first acting class in 2013. At Vanderbilt, students are quite consumed with grades and high achievement. Therefore, providing a low-stakes assessment category gives them more freedom to relax and reflect. Low stakes in this context means that so long as the students submit the assignment on time and with the minimum word count, they receive full credit. It provides space for the actor to communicate directly with me and pose questions, concerns, or comments that they otherwise may not feel comfortable expressing in a group setting. Students submit written reflections on their progress six times throughout the semester. With the implementation of the Self-Growth assessment strand, they will be able to use these categories as a jumping-off point. Additionally, they will be scaffolding their self-assessment so that by the end of the semester, they can leverage what they've been thinking and writing for over 14 weeks.

Notes that students take in class are also a valuable source for the Actor's Notebook. Previously, I've required students to have a writing utensil and physical notebook, unless they require accommodations. However, in applying critical humility, I realise that with this stipulation, students can be 'outed' as neurodiverse. In my efforts to create a social justice acting studio, I no longer have this requirement. Rather, students are permitted to use a tablet, laptop, or notebook. However, on electronic devices, I request that they turn off Wi-Fi. This decision came from discussions with colleagues and my Junior Faculty Teaching Fellowship at Vanderbilt. By providing more flexibility and options for students to take notes during class, they can more easily fulfil the assignment and have real-time reactions to reflect on after class.

Midterm Monologue (15%)

The Midterm Monologue assignment affords an opportunity for the students to self-determine acting material, technique, and how they will be assessed. By mid-terms, students will have explored exercises from techniques including animal work, sense memory, and physicality inspired by music. Even for professional actors, finding monologues can be challenging, especially when trying to strike the balance of finding compelling content while avoiding pieces that are overdone. To support the students in choosing monologues, my syllabus includes an addendum of plays with pertinent information such as themes and character breakdown. In a foundational acting class, the requirements for the monologue include choosing a character whose lived experience the actor can relate to. In considering intersectional identities, it is imperative that, as instructors, we don't assume identities based on face value. Another requirement is that the student can envision being reasonably cast in this role in a full-scale production. Actors upload their monologue selections and provide a written justification for why they chose this character. So long as it is well-argued, they are approved to move forward with the selection. By considering their identities and experiences in monologue selection, the students will be more fully invested in the character development process.

Another strategy in exercising McClintock's self-expression in assessment is charging the students with choosing the technique they apply to their monologue. Notably, based on my MFA training and knowledge of the current pedagogical approach, affective memory is not a practical approach taught at the Actor's Studio and should not be employed in the acting classroom.[8] I often tell my student actors that having a plethora of tools will supply even more options when approaching a range of characters. For example, sometimes a physical approach provides a strong kinaesthetic connection, whereas other times, tapping into a sensory world will offer a smooth entryway to the character. They rehearse their monologues at home and then in smaller groups during class time, eventually performing one by one. About half of the class works at a time, while the other half observes. Those working start with breathing work and relaxation exercises. Then, in their own time, they begin to work on their chosen technique without language. Once they feel they have 'earned' their lines, they begin to organically integrate line by line without a specific timetable to encourage being in the moment. By integrating rehearsal time in class, they can switch approaches – this flexibility allows for artistic autonomy where students decide which technique resonates with them most for a given piece. Assessment-wise, I have five categories on the rubric. Two of these categories are consistent for all students: memorisation and application of technique. For the remaining three categories, each student individually chooses how they want to be assessed. Therefore, the assessment model for the monologue will establish consistency in the fundamentals of acting (memorisation and application) yet provide space for the individual to be assessed according to how they want to artistically develop.

Final Scene (15%)

By the time actors are ready for their Final Scene, they are also familiar with repetition[9] and practical aesthetics, along with methods learned for the monologue. The students are assigned scenes with scene partners approximately the week after their Midterm Monologues. I choose the characters, plays, and scene partners because, at this juncture in the semester, I will be better acquainted with the students and can gauge how personalities mesh in the collaborative process. I carefully consider the roles they are drawn to that also challenge them. I am thoughtful in my selection and consider their actor's reflections as part of the selection process. There also seems to be some excitement at being 'cast' in a role chosen specifically for them. In typical casting situations, actors are not given the choice of what role they want to play in a professional production. Unless an actor self-produces or establishes their own company, the power of casting lies in the hands of a director or casting director. Of course, an actor can choose to take part or not. Therefore, for the Final Scene, choosing scenes and characters provides a bit of insight into the fact that as actors, there are certain things, like casting, that are outside our control. However, even within restricted circumstances, actors can exercise agency.

Just as with the Midterm Monologue, each actor chooses what technique they'd like to apply to their character creation and scene development. This often raises questions about two actors using divergent techniques in the same scene. Yet this provides an additional opportunity to bridge the gap between the rehearsal hall and the professional world. Certainly, if scene partners want to use the same technique for rehearsal purposes, they have the freedom to do so. However, if one actor wants to try their hand at practical aesthetics while another student employs animal work, they are also welcome to do so.

Similar to the Midterm Monologue assessment model, there are two fixed categories: memorisation and application of technique. Based on their Midterm Monologue, they can apply my feedback and identify areas of growth. For the final three categories of the rubric, each pair of scene partners will determine how they would like to grow as an ensemble of two. For example, potential categories could be fully interacting with the physical space (props, set pieces, etc.), increased improvement in breaking line readings, etc. Because each scene is unique, the area of growth can emanate from the specific challenges of that scene. By deciding these three categories at the beginning of their rehearsal process, they will be able to remain focused on learning outcomes that they decided together. It gives them measurable goals and sets the standard that they are working together. Therefore, each pair will be assessed according to their individual growth as actors and invested in collective criteria.

Conclusion

Establishing a social justice acting studio to create more equitable assessments requires time, energy, and flexibility throughout the course of the semester. Understanding limitations of traditional assessments and recognising the nuances of intersectional dynamics necessitates adjustments throughout the semester. Yet reconsidering a syllabus and creating a nimble class structure that prioritises Self-Growth and Ensemble Engagement will inevitably increase the instructor's labour demands; more discussion during class time may mean some of the content could be compromised. The act of self-interrogation is also time-consuming, but critical when creating a more equitable creative learning environment.

This leads me to ask: What is the purpose of acting assessments? I have concluded that given the course is situated in a liberal arts environment, assessment is less about manifesting perfect technique. Rather, the equitable assessment provides a distinct opportunity for individualised learning and growth, putting the student at the centre. The implementation of McClintock's conception of artistic self-determination and community-building will serve the students beyond their college careers and across professions. Acting assessments provide the opportunity to upend Eurocentric methods of assessing to address the collective identity of an ensemble and honour the individual needs and growth of individuals.

Willingness for students to engage in a collaborative process such as crafting Ensemble Engagement and determining Individual Growth is a foreseeable challenge, especially for students who have never taken an acting class. Therefore, it will be imperative to provide guidelines and key terms so that the students have the language for crafting assessment criteria. The next stage of this research is applying these changes in my Fundamentals of Acting course and evaluating how to continue to develop a more equitable classroom and learning environment. Although students fill out course evaluations issued by the university, I will also provide my own evaluation for students on these very changes. Student feedback will be paramount. Restructuring assessment models under the framework of a social justice acting studio at institutions grounded in Eurocentric education models increases faculty labour. However, taking actionable steps to upend previous modes of evaluation will improve the educational experience for the students where all voices and perspectives are valued and included.

Notes

1 Refer to the *Black Acting Methods* (Luckett & Shaffer, 2017), *Ernie McClintock and the Jazz Actors Family* (Cizmar, 2023), and *Method Acting and Its Discontents* (Enelow, 2015) for further research debunking the commonly held belief that Stanislavski-based training is universal.

2 The action research model is a result of framing teachers as researchers. The teachers-as-researchers movement emerged in the 1960s in England. Following this model, I think of my classroom as another place of research in which I can apply anti-racist pedagogy to create a more equitable studio environment. For more information on the teachers-as-researchers movement, refer to *Action Research for Educational Change* (Elliott, 1992).

3 Notably, McClintock's iteration of self-expression echoes the theories of Harlem Renaissance thinker Alain Locke. In 1927, Locke advocated for the actor and argued that 'a race of actors can revolutionise the drama quite as definitely and perhaps more vitally than a coterie of dramatists' (Locke, 2001, p. 263). For more information on McClintock's acting theory and how it is historically situated, refer to *Ernie McClintock and the Jazz Actors Family* (Cizmar, 2023).

4 Kimberlé Crenshaw is a Columbia law professor and civil rights advocate, and critical race theory scholar. While this term intersectional has been extended beyond the scope of women of colour, it is critical to understand and acknowledge the origins of the term. Refer to an interview with Crenshaw where she discusses 'intersectional erasure' in the Trump era: 'What's most problematic about the contemporary conversation is the complete irrelevance of women of color' (2017).

5 Boston University provides an excellent online resource breaking down anti-racism with additional resources, including articles, key terms, and book suggestions. Refer to www.bu.edu/csc/edref-2/antiracism for more information.

6 Jill Dolan 'riffs' off David Román's 1998 book *Acts of Intervention: Performance, Gay Culture, and AIDS*, which he explores critical generosity in spectatorship: His work charts HIV-positive gay men watching *Angels in America*. 'He described with love and concern how they took care of themselves while watching a marathon showing of the two-part, epic play. The way David detailed their viewing context made manifest and material how our bodies sit in front of performance, with friends, lovers, and strangers, and the attention they require to be sustained' (Dolan, 2013).

7 Scholars Kay Sambell, Liz McDowell, and Catherine Montgomery research the various ways the UK-based Assessment for Learning (AfL) can offer instructors opportunities to establish effective learning spaces through collaboration and dialogue, authentic assessment, formative assessment, peer and self-assessment, student development for the long term, and innovative approaches to effective feedback. For more information, refer to *Assessment for Learning in Higher Education*.

8 Contrary to popular belief, the Actors Studio Drama School does not teach 'becoming the character' and one losing their sense of identity on the stage. Furthermore, affective memory (or drumming up emotional traumas) as a means of accessing character is not typical, nor is it encouraged.

9 Note that the repetition taught in my foundational acting class is from Atlantic Acting School's practical aesthetics, as opposed to Sanford Meisner's repetition.

References

Alvarez, E. H. (2016, September 25). Fostering open communication in a culturally diverse classroom. *The Chronicle of Higher Education*. www.chronicle.com/article/fostering-open-communication-in-a-culturally-diverse-classroom

Cizmar, E. M. (2023). *Ernie McClintock and the Jazz actors family: Reviving the legacy*. Routledge.

Crenshaw, K. (2017, June 8). *Kimberlé Crenshaw on intersectionality, more than two decades later*. Columbia Law School. www.law.columbia.edu/news/archive/kimberle-crenshaw-intersectionality-more-two-decades-later

D'Agostino, S. (2023, January). Should class participation be graded? *Inside Higher Ed*. www.insidehighered.com/news/2023/01/04/should-class-participation-be-graded-college

DiAngelo, R. (2012). Nothing to add: A challenge to white silence in racial discussions. *Understanding and Dismantling Privilege*, 2(1), 1–17.

DiAngelo, R., & Sensoy, O. (2019). "Yeah, but I'm shy!": Classroom participation as social justice issue. *Multicultural Learning and Teaching*, 14(1), 1–9. https://doi.org/10.1515/mlt-2018-0002

Dolan, J. (2013). Critical generosity. *Public: A Journal of Imagining America*, 1(1–2). https://public.imaginingamerica.org/blog/article/critical-generosity-2/

Elliott, J. (1992). *Action research for educational change*. Open University Press.

Enelow, S. (2015). *Method acting and its discontents: On American psycho-drama*. Northwestern University Press.

European-American Collaborative Challenging Whiteness. (2007). Developing capacity for critical self-reflection when race is salient. *Transformative Learning: Issues of Difference and Diversity* [Proceedings of the Seventh International Conference on Transformative Learning]. University of New Mexico College of Education, Albuquerque.

Locke, A. (2001). The Negro and the American theatre. In H. L. Gates & J. Burton (Eds.), *Call and response: Key debates in African American studies*. W. W. Norton.

Luckett, S. D., & Shaffer, T. M. (2017). *Black acting methods: Critical approaches*. Routledge.

Sambel, K., McDowell, L., & Montgomery, C. (2012). *Assessment for learning in higher education*. Routledge.

Stamatiou, E. (2022a). Pierre Bourdieu and actor training: Towards decolonising and decentering actor training pedagogies. *Theatre, Dance and Performance Training*, 13(1), 96–114. https://doi.org/10.1080/19443927.2021.1943509

Steinmetz, K. (2020, February). She coined the term "intersectionality" over 30 years ago: Here's what it means to her today. *Time Magazine*. https://time.com/5786710/kimberle-crenshaw-intersectionality/

Tatum, H. E., Schwartz, B. M., Schimmoeller, P. A., & Perry, N. (2013). Classroom participation and student-faculty interactions: Does gender matter? *The Journal of Higher Education*, 84(6), 745–768. https://doi.org/10.1080/00221546.2013.11777309

12 Singing Pedagogy for Actors
Questioning Quality

Electa Behrens and Øystein Elle

Introduction

Music in theatre, as any other subfield of the arts, has histories of colonialism, sexism, and silencing to address and undress as we move towards a more responsible future (Ewell, 2020; Ross, 2020). Singing pedagogy as a subset of actor training still often works within master/apprentice models and operates to a larger degree than, for example, improvisational practices, with notions of 'right' and 'wrong'. This chapter unpacks an artistic research project on music and singing in performance pedagogy which questioned what is quality in music performance. It outlines the project design, context, experiments, outcomes, and evaluation.

The project was a Norwegian 'kunstnerisk utviklingsarbeid' project.[1] It was distinct from other pedagogical art-based research methodologies, in the explicit ways in which students had autonomy to effect results within practical and reflective stages. This method allowed us to research power dynamics in teacher–student relationships. As Lyotard reminds us:

> Knowledge and power are simply two sides of the same question: who decides what knowledge is, and who knows what needs to be decided.
>
> (1979, pp. 8–9)

The project is informed by Robin Nelson's notion of Practitioner Knowledge (2006), and aimed to uncover and articulate via critical reflection, the tacit knowledge of students and teachers, which we premise includes unconscious biases. During the process, we employed strategies from Action Research to account for the spiral nature of knowledge production; we fostered artistic process in dialogue with moments of reflection; and prompted new proposals. On the challenges of Practice as Research (henceforth PaR) methodologies, Trimmingham writes:

> The problem of methodology centres on the fact that the material on which the research conclusions are based depends almost entirely on a creative process, and the process, in fact, has many disorderly features.
>
> (2002, p. 56)

The 'disorderly' features were key to this research, as they expose normative systems and invite unlearning and institutional critique as generative process of worlding.[2]

DOI: 10.4324/9781003393672-16

Intra-acting Multivocality

Katherine Meizel writes that each of us has many, often cultural, voices, which she calls multivocality (2020). Our project created a polyphony of voices, which means sounding many different voices simultaneously. But it is also characterised by multivocality, which means that each individual spoke from and moved between different positionalities, such as artist and pedagogue or student, and, significantly, also disagreed with oneself. Multivocality references a similar complexity as intersectionality. We choose multivocality as lens. Intersectionality is a term that resonates with critical race studies, and to use it as a catch term for diversity seems counterproductive. Secondly, as this project is grounded in voice work, multivocality is evocative of how complex individual positionalities might manifest. Likewise, while intersectionality references social markers which might be considered as fixed, such as race and gender, multivocality offers a sense of fluidity, highlighting that the individual might have some agency in how they voice themselves. In terms of critical pedagogies, it is important to work against notions of any teacher/student holding a fixed position to which another is critical, but rather to acknowledge criticality as a motor for agency. This means that each individual can shift between positionalities and embody the complexity of internal disagreement.

Theoretically, this mode of working is grounded in Karen Barad's notion of *intra-activity*, which Whitney Stark describes as follows:

> Intra-action is a Baradian term used to replace 'interaction', which necessitates pre-established bodies that then participate in action with each other. Intra-action understands agency as not an inherent property of an individual or human to be exercised, but as a dynamism of forces (Barad, 2007, p. 141) in which all designated 'things' are constantly exchanging and diffracting, influencing and working inseparably. Intra-action also acknowledges the impossibility of an absolute separation or classically understood objectivity.
>
> (2016)

We suggest that each of the involved individuals were *intra-acting*, both within themselves, between themselves and other group members, and between themselves, the music, the lyrics, the space, and other objects at play. In 'questioning quality', our aim is not to define different qualities that imply binaries, such as classical versus contemporary, but rather to consider how conscious/unconscious notions of quality are made and unmade as different materials and bodies *intra-act*.

In terms of writing format, although this piece is co-written by involved pedagogues, we attempt to make transparent the places where we spoke from different perspectives. Visually, this takes the form of framing a reflection, from either Øystein or Electa as a quote, separating it from the main body of the text (our collective researcher voice). We also try to centre the student voice, including their reflections not only as three-line quotes, but as larger chunks. The aim is to de-centre the teacher perspective and highlight the student's contribution. We are also very aware of the reader's present, yet silent multivocal voice, and how this will generate further insights. As you read this chapter, we invite you to consider your positionalities and how they affect how you *intra-act* with this material.[3]

Who We Are

The project was conceived by the course leader of the BA Acting at the Norwegian Theatre Academy (henceforth NTA), Electa Behrens, and the singing teachers Øystein Elle and Ruth

Wilhelmine Meyer.[4] NTA is an established, experimental conservatory. We have a curated programme of international workshops and do not work with letter/number grades, but rather a system of continuous oral feedback. Pedagogue specialisms and backgrounds combine baroque music, avant garde, music theatre, punk, world music, extended vocal technique, Shakespeare, and post-dramatic approaches to text/song/sound. We have worked together for seven years, worth mentioning here Elle's and Behrens's research series You and Me, which explores the ethics of aural diversity, critical whiteness, and New Materialist approaches to voice (Behrens & Elle, 2021).

Project Design

Students from across three NTA programmes, BA in Acting, Scenography MA in Performance, and one guest from the BA in Folk Music at the Norwegian Academy of Music (conservatory) collaborated for four weeks in a theatre-making project that resulted in a public showing. The main aim was to disturb the binary of canon versus non-canon and invite an understanding of quality as plurality, in other words, as quali*ties*. This was achieved through an exploration of student agency;[5] the de-centring of the teacher; a notion of collectivity and allyship, by inviting each student to lead/compose one sonic world and everyone was in each other's sonic world;[6] an ambition to create a heterogeneous whole by gathering these diverse worlds into one performative whole, and; an emergent, but not moralistic, dramaturgy that invited the audience to 'stay with the trouble' of the research question (Harraway, 2016, p. 1). We took inspiration from carnival, in its ambulatory and heterogeneous format. It was clearly articulated that carnival was not invoked as an appropriative copy, but rather invited the participants to coexist and represent a multitude of voices, relating to Mikhail Bakhtin´s notion of polyphony and carnivalesque (1984).

The Quality Onion

This project aimed to unpack quality *within* the field of music performance. After project completion, we reflected on the 'quality onion', by which we mean the series of 'institutions' that related to the performance. How these structures affected the work became very clear during the process. These layers included the university, the department, the courses, the teachers, the students, the processes, and the live performance. In the studio, these other outer layers can seem invisible, yet they are always present. This next section briefly explores some of the 'quality' contradictions at these various layers of the event. While reflecting on this horizontal cross section of an onion, it is important to remember that the individuals moving within these different circles bring with them the multivocality and complex positionality which is a kind of vertical layering, creating a complex 3D field of forces at work.

University, Department

Østfold University College, where NTA is based, states:

> The quality system shall contribute to the university achieving the goals for educational quality that have been established through current legislation and through the Strategic Plan. . . . The quality system must provide good conditions for targeted, systematic and continuous quality assurance . . . and for the development of a good culture for quality.
> (Østfold University College, 2023)

NOKUT ('Nasjonalt organ for kvalitet i utdanninga' translated: national organ for quality in education) is a quality assurance organ, which accredits, periodically reviews and eventually revokes accreditation to universities in Norway; NOKUT is the audience for this quote. As a department, NTA offers this narrative about the program: 'Values informing the education rely on listening, collaboration, staying with failure, re-imagining material relations, excavation and play' (Norwegian Theatre Academy, 2023).

The programme is challenged to manifest quantifiable quality while encouraging failure and play. Tony Fisher and Evie Katsouraki in *Beyond Failure* critically reflect on how the British system equates failure with underperformance, rendering it undesirable and justify how market models of 'quality' affect arts pedagogy (2019, p. 12). This illuminates why student and pedagogue attitudes shifted when it was decided that the project should end in a public presentation. There was expressed stress about whether the show would be good enough. This highlighted a paradox: failure as a positive quality of teaching and learning within the programme but not something valued in front of an audience. In this case, it was not the system imposing market models, but rather the involved artists themselves, who evaluated their own work differently when the context changed.

Course, Teachers, Students

Voice teaching at NTA emphasises intersectional vocal expression. We teach an array of techniques to challenge, for example, conventions of 'beauty and ugliness' and gender norms. We alternate between students choosing their own material and pedagogues leading theme-based courses. Students bring in musical genres based on aesthetic taste and cultural background. We do not teach a 'comprehensive decolonized syllabus' but, drawing on critical theories that are taught on other modules, we tutor each student individually towards creating a diverse musical expression grounded in their own intersectionality. Although the course content embraces a decolonial perspective, the pedagogical format, of a single student working with a single teacher behind closed doors, is reminiscent of 'traditional conservatory training', which has embedded in it many hierarchical power structures. When singing training occurs *mostly* within this frame, it is easier for the cultural/aesthetic backgrounds of those individuals to be the quality framework, which includes each individual's unconscious bias. Daron Oram writes that 'it is possible to perceive the presence of an invisible listening ear in every studio . . . to which training and performances are constantly being tuned' (2019, p. 288). At NTA we have both students who come classically trained and those whose pre-BA experience might mirror Madimabe Geoff Mapaya's sentiment:

> An African student wishing to study music at a South African university still has to musically and culturally excommunicate him or herself first from the music of birth in order to gain university entrance.
>
> (Mapaya in Davis and Lynch, 2022, p. 151)

Even if we attempt to offer a safe space for vocal exploration, this will be affected by the complex lived experiences of the individuals in the room. Significantly, this project allowed the three voice pedagogues to co-teach, and allow students also to navigate their teacher–student relations within the context of group collaboration. Having the same people in a different context made all the difference in how we each took responsibility for our own positionality and how it facilitated art making.

Vocal Material

Students were asked to prepare *vocal material* for the project start. To resist cultural assumptions that begin if we said, 'bring a song', we said bring *vocal material*, referencing New Materialist concepts, as a hopefully decolonial and antidiscriminatory departure.[7] This was supported through introductory lectures and conversations.[8] Jerzy Grotowski remarks:

> Being products of different systems of transcription (both in the sense of musical notation and in relation to recording) and not of the oral tradition, Westerners mistake singing with melody. They are pretty much able to sing anything that can be notated in notes. But they are completely unable to notice such things as the vibratory quality of the voice, the resonance of the space, the resonators of the body or the way in which the vibrations are carried through the out-breath.
>
> (Grotowski et al., 1987, p. 36)

Since Grotowski's reflections, the field of music has diversified greatly. His provocation to oust melody as the central spine of a musical work, however, speaks to the invitation we were making by asking students to bring 'vocal material' and not a 'song'. The students came with a wide range of vocal materials, at varying degrees of having been worked into repeatable forms. The first sharing was inspirational, full of common themes, and play. The second sharing a few days later prompted disagreement. Some students practised their material as closed units with a beginning and an end. Others spliced together their material into collective constellations. We understood that we were listening differently. Elements, such as melody, which some pedagogues assumed the students would develop as a repeatable form, turned out to be not the elements the students saw as central. Hence there was a sense of pedagogues saying that something had been 'lost' as the piece developed from the first sharing to the second. At the same time, the students experienced a building of their work by focusing on different elements.

In classical music, there is a notion of a piece developing through a vertical process of refinement of a fixed score, which is implied in Grotowski's quote above. The music *is* what is on the paper, and it defines mostly sounds made by the mouth and instructions of how they should be performed. As Paul Barker writes, 'in score we trust' (2004, p. 79). From other traditions, such as score-based compositions, jazz, and improvisation, not to mention non-Western traditions such as yoik (a Sámpi tradition) which conceptualise music fundamentally differently and include other modalities as key elements of the performance (such as physicality), the model of repetition of melody/dynamic/tempo as method for increasing quality is not appropriate. Focusing on vocal material became not a common ground of neutrality, but rather a site where our differing approaches were exposed.

It became clear that the first step was for students to clearly articulate and dialogue with pedagogues about what their vocal material was and its quality frames. To facilitate this, halfway through the project we discarded the ambulatory dramaturgy and developed a frontal space with seated audience. The interactive framework could potentially reproduce bias or instigate a kind of quality competition, as it allows the audience to choose to spend more time with one music than another. The linear approach, with a priority on collective involvement in all sonic worlds, challenged the audience and students to fully immerse in each world, whether familiar or uncomfortable.

Pedagogue *Intra-action*

Nina Eidsheim, reminds us of the complexity of hearing. She writes:

> [D]oes any music exist . . . independent of that which a culturally structured and informed sensory complex gives rise to . . .? Or . . . is the music we can sense in any given cultural moment merely a reflection (or indeed a confirmation) of our limited ability to perceive that moment?
>
> (Eidsheim, 2015, p. 11)

We brought this quote to the vocal performance studio and asked: As pedagogues, what can we hear? This self-critical reflection was one of our starting points. Despite this intention, we found how unconscious bias would surface instinctually in a moment of teaching. As pedagogues who experience us as having shared perspectives, the diversity of our reactions to this process highlighted our positionality. Upon reflection, Electa testified:

> I thought I knew what this project would bring up for me. Instead, I found myself not as brave as I had hoped to stand for my own perspective. I found myself questioning my own quality in relation to my colleagues, engaging with ghosts of my own past teachers. I felt torn between my institutional responsibilities and artistic sensibilities.

On the same matter, Øystein said:

> As an artist relating to the complexity of musical and theatrical expressions, which requires for the performer/composer to enter fields where one is not an expert, I think of my artistic approach as somehow punk. However, this project . . . was challenging. Although I work within composed theatre, polystylism and noise, my practice is highly connected to my conservatoire training. This is applicable both in how I work, and what I expect from . . . collaborators. That is preparation, rehearsing, repetition, and hard work. This dissonance in parts of the project makes it more interesting. I chose to trust the process and be responsible as a collaborator, rather a leader. An unfamiliar but very useful experience in a teacher-student relationship.

The backgrounds of each teacher became more articulated, as we co-facilitated group reflections. The project thus offered an interesting dissonance of the teacher being both de-centred and at the same time less 'neutral'.

Questioning quality within one's own work is not just about rejecting generic traditions. The process of being educated is a series of personal relationships with individuals. Grotowski writes:

> What can one transmit? How and to whom . . . . These are questions that every person who has inherited from the tradition asks himself because he inherits at the same time a kind of duty: to transmit that which he himself has received.
>
> (1999, p. 12)

Moving away from your own tradition can feel like an act of betrayal against your teachers.

What happens when a student witnesses a pedagogue experiencing this process? Is there a place within an institutional frame for this kind of radical research which implicates institutional critique on a personal level for teachers and students? One student reflected:

> I experienced (in this project) especially people coming from a background rooted in a strong tradition and aesthetic, that they experience a form of battle with the tradition. . . . Both having a tradition, as a foundation . . . but in that process also fighting with the . . . rules. . . . This project offered a space to investigate the messiness . . . and what we perceive as quality. . . . Confronting your own and. . . collaborators' perception to create a space for . . . questions.
>
> (personal communication, 2023)

As another student reflected, the pedagogues became 'beacons of different ideas of quality' and made students aware of when they were gravitating towards one 'quality' instead of another, because one was choosing one pedagogue over another. A third student added:

> [W]hen we summed it up, the question of quality was just as much a question (and a really interesting one) about power structures. . . . [I]s it possible to somehow be in a position as a teacher in an institution. . . . [I]s it possible then to not somehow define quality in the project . . . if you are both setting the frame for how to research quality but at the same time participate artistically.
>
> (ibid)

We found ourselves questioning how to best hold the pedagogical situation. To borrow thinking from Robin DiAngelo's work on white fragility, a process of unpacking own privilege often results in struggling 'to sustain the discomfort of not knowing, the discomfort of being racially unmoored, the discomfort of racial humility' (2018, p. 14). This is a necessary first step towards embracing a greater diversity of perspectives.

Ann Cahill and Christine Hamel write about hesitation as a strategy:

> Developing more just habits of receiving a wide diversity of vocalized sounds . . . will require significant experiences of hesitation, disruption and discomfort. . . . Such hesitation may involve . . . disorientation, but . . . disorientation can be a productive element of moral agency, particularly in the context of sustained structural inequalities.
>
> (2019, p. 81)

For those of us used to having our perspectives confirmed by the world around us, feeling unmoored, can feel potentially negative, hesitation like weakness. Can we embrace these strategies as teaching methods which promote structural change at an institutional level? As Twitchin quotes the poet/potter Mary Caroline Richards in 'the art of learning':

> It is not a matter of doing things right or succeeding. It is a matter of plasticity . . . of pressing on. . . . So-called failure is a form of success. Without it we would never get anywhere. Failure is transformation in the form of our expectations. . . . It deepens our awareness.
>
> (Twitchin, 2018, p. 48)

If viewed as a one-off workshop which should produce a known set of skills, this project 'fails'. If working with a notion of educational quality as Richards argues for, this project develops the skill of unpacking bias, which is perhaps that which must occur first in the creation of new artworks. As the pedagogue Ruth reflects: 'Just asking the question (of quality) is already a changed perspective . . . and that is perhaps the most important thing an art institution can do now?' (Personal communication, 2023).

Performance

The performance was 1 hour long in a black box with a fixed frontal audience (Figure 12.1). The walls were constantly animated with film material and the stage always held all the performers and instruments used. The dramaturgy moved from one student-led etude to the next, with all students performing throughout. To give a sense of audience experience:

> It was a rollercoaster of a performance! . . . Like everybody fighting for something – but at the same time doubting whether they fight on the same team as the others or if their idea is worth fighting for. . . . The fragility that occurs on an overall reading . . . hence opens up questions of relationships between community and quality, the role of subjectivity in performance. . . . It is somehow super fragile and powerful at the same time. . . . As an audience, I felt . . . one is sort of made responsible as well, for one's own judgements. What do I like? Why? . . . [W]hat does that say about me?
>
> (Tormod Carlsen, personal communication, 2021)

Figure 12.1 Last musical scene of Questioning Quality. The song performed: Antiworld, originated by Nina Hagen in 1982, sung here by Madelen Larsen. Also pictured Ester Thunander and Guillermo John Magno. *Photo:* Cecilio Orozco Martínez.

Three of nine student performances are discussed to present a diversity of ways that the task was met, while still privileging each example with ample space to go a bit in depth.

Folk Song (Re)sculpted Hybrid

This piece is a subtle work of microtones and almost imperceptible shifts. Human bodies become one with each other and the viola. Abstract images on the walls offer atmosphere and slow time (Figure 12.2).

The student-performer, Laura Spottag Fog, hybridised folk singing with sculptural elements. She reflected being 'interested in feeling music in an abstract way to challenge [her] understanding of it. Maybe that's where the sculptor's mind kicks in, in the sensing with every part of the body'[9] She continued:

> I found a lot of inspiration from folksongs being music for the people by the people, a time where the songs was made of stealing and patch-working, given, telling, traveling through cities/land and time. It wasn't important to know exactly where it started, but to hear it now and re-tell/sing it to the next. I used a version of the ancient folk song Rosensfole performed by Agnes Buen Garnås. The language she uses is a mixture of different Nordic languages.
>
> My time as a classical musician, haunts and blesses me in my work. My guilt of not using my expensive viola, I bought when I was so focused on getting into the classical conservatory, clouds my love for music sometimes. I couldn't figure out how to take the

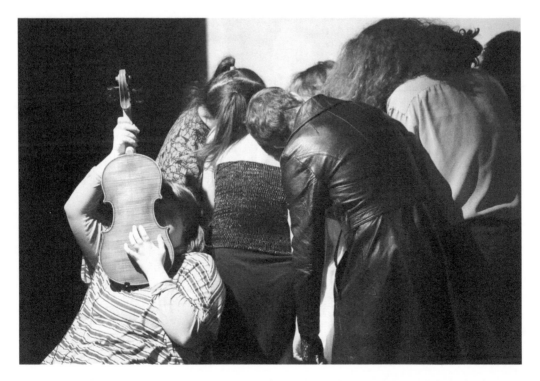

Figure 12.2 The beginning of the student's musical scene. First, there is silence and then, slowly, some microtones appear from the student with the viola, Laura Spottag Fog. *Photo:* Cecilio Orozco Martínez.

music, my instrument back and make it my own. Experimenting with a contact micro-
phone I could peel and touch the layers of my viola, into tiny sounds and textures I could
amp up and enjoy with pleasure. With my own voice, I could sing the song into the box
of my viola, using it as a house for my voice, making my voice travel around hitting the
wood, and getting expanded by the contact mic.

From a tutor's perspective, Electa noted reading 'the student's work as an act of empowerment, of reclamation: it renegotiates quality on a personal level'. Øystein commented:

Perhaps the quality of this performance lies in the transfer of the traditional material
focus of the folk music tradition to a sculptural performance in a contemporary hybrid
performance context. Rather than quality through virtuosity she offers virtuosity through
details. The precision of the old tradition transformed to a new form within the field of
extended composition.

Multiphonic Self

This piece, completely written by the performer, started in the dark in the audience with a
provocative lilting text that morphed into a guitar solo, rap, and then strobe light event with
humorous and feminist undertones (Figure 12.3).
This student's response to the provocation of quality was to work relationally, re-centring
her original artwork outside of existing traditions and developing a dramaturgy in which

Figure 12.3 This moment occurs in the middle of this musical scene, Frederikke Hooge is singing and
playing the guitar. *Photo:* Christian Bermudez Aguilar.

each moment in her piece is 'heard' in relation to that which came before. Reflecting on her journey, Frederikke Hooge wrote:

> I researched the field of extended vocal technique, and the method of multiphonic voice. Inspired by . . . a performance by Alex Nowitz, a vocal artist/composer who sees himself as 'a sound dancer who strives to make sound visual and comprehensible'.[10] I decided to work with the body of the voice, as a percussive instrument . . . in the spoken word meeting a melodic landscape in an almost sound-sculptural manner. Composing my own material to meet a genre.
>
> It felt . . . very 'trial and error' . . . to push the freedom/possibilities within rules. . . . I felt lost in the 'trial' . . . consumed with wanting it to look or sound a certain way. Working with different genres, it became clear . . . I could work with the edge of the form. Playing with the potential possibilities and limitations – creating a total/extended composition.
>
> I faced . . . questions . . . about history, context and my own view upon what quality is, and how it should be materialized. Will it always be connected to the history of the genre/medium and the performer's references? How do you make something that questions the structure itself/that it's built upon?

From the perspective of Western music, Peter Kivy, unpacked by Roland Jackson, gives a definition of authenticity, which could be one of the unconscious quality rubrics with which this piece might be examined. It includes 'composer authenticity' which implies 'respect for a composer's original conception', 'sonic authenticity', which describes the quest to restore the sound materials with which a composer worked, 'personal authenticity', which means 'the esteem accorded the performer's individual expression, which may at times deviate from what a composer indicated', and 'sensible authenticity', which considers 'the meaning attached to a performance by its audience' (Jackson, 1997, p. 1) This breakdown offers an understanding of quality as multiple and factor-based and can be a starting point for how to consider quality in this context. Some of the piece works with rap as an identifiable aesthetic, inviting a consideration of how rubrics of quality within this subfield inform a reading of a genre-crossing piece.

From a rap studies perspective, there are also questions of authenticity. Anthony Kwame Harrison discusses authenticity in rap and hip-hop and points out the unstable nature of the term by saying: 'Authenticity aims to strike an agreement between the presentation of something or someone (as authentic) and the reception or acceptance of that presentation. Thus, authenticity is both constructed and contested and therefore in a perpetual state of flux' (Harrison, 2008, p. 1785). Michael Eric Dyson noted that 'authenticity becomes a node through which flows arguments about who is capable, or not, of legitimately interpreting a culture-and, therefore, participating in its most esoteric goings-on' (Jones & Dyson, 2006, p. 787).

Responding to these provocations and exposures within the process, the student reflects on how a piece might involve different traditions of music and their accompanying quality rubrics yet at the same time find an alternative mode of evaluation, based rather on an approach of intra-action. In the words of the student:

> I wanted to work with something self-composed that could be its own unit . . . by letting different materials and genres merge into '*one*'. Not necessarily meaning 'one' coherent material, but more letting the different genres and 'quality' of a material shape the next *thing/material* and the audience's perception of the material.

I experienced not necessarily becoming the master of a certain discipline by obtaining technical precision, but more sampling from a genre. Combining the expression with personal material in a both humorous and unapologetic way. Insisting on the form and questioning what musicality is. Working with sound both as visual/aesthetic form and as identity. Creating a platform where I as the author/composer could set the tone, change it, introduce another 'tone', letting the audience experience something multifaceted that could make them question their own embedded expectations/understanding of the quality connected to the genre.

What tickles me as a performer/composer – is building a form that you can break in unexpected ways. I compose with my voice, my body, the instruments/objects and the audience on stage, wanting to make the experience tangible.

From my journal: 'I don't want to create floating soundscapes with beautiful effects and sounds. I just want to play around with an amplifier. Attach my fake legs and swing them around. Connecting my body to the instrument. Making my body the instrument'.

By transferring skills from one artistic area to another, the student is creating quality in a 'punk' manner, artistically connected to new amateurism and authentic in the context of the project.

Embodied Deconstruction[11]

This musical scene came about halfway through the piece (Figure 12.4). Originally, it was meant to be the singing of Nisi Dominus RV 608. IV Cum dederit by Antonio Vivaldi

Figure 12.4 The moment of the musical scene where Alba Greve has, stopped the violin accompaniment and taken out the paper to read. Also pictured: Nicolaj Frederik Wamberg. *Photo:* Cecilio Orozco Martínez.

(circa 1713–1717). At the dress rehearsal, the student, Alba Greve, came out and sang a few notes. Then stopped and, unexpectedly, took out a crumpled paper and read:

> This 'speech' was not planned. We were supposed to play this piece. . . . But it was suggested to us yesterday that we did not know it well enough. . . . So, what is quality. . . . In this case, one could get the idea that quality is, whether we are able to perform this piece well enough sonically, clean sounding and with respect to the composer . . . I was meant to wear this trash bag dress and wig. On the back wall, this projection of blood . . . embryos . . . a C-section to make a harsh visualization of the text of the song . . . in the meeting with a . . . light voice and the . . . angelic . . . violas, was meant to create a contrast between the . . . harsh and the fragile. . . . Would the contrast be visible enough even if we were not able to perfectly play . . . sing the song . . . . We will never know if you would have found other, unexpected qualities in the piece. . . . We will never find out because I, as I have done so many times before, fell into the trap of chasing quality, in its most polished and 'perfect' form, instead of looking for it in the places we often forget to look, in the imperfect, unpolished . . . ugly and unpredictable. . . .

This performative action simultaneously broke and made the project. It was a rebellion that crumpled the 'work' done within the process and at the same time, in terms of the final dramaturgy, became a hook in terms of audience interpretation. In a space where it seemed like 'everything was allowed', it found what was forbidden. After the performance, the student reflected:

> I went in . . . with a very limited idea of what the word quality means. . . . I never managed to untie this semantic knot . . . and it, therefore, became the . . . focus, 'How to question what is good/bad?' . . . 'Can something "bad" be good? Who gets to decide?' . . . [T]his piece (the song) represented . . . Western and classical ideas of high quality. From the get-go I wanted to destroy this piece of music . . . to question quality in the most basic way, by working in opposition. How could I make this beautiful piece into something bad and ugly? . . . I ended up trying to recreate a baroque style which wasn't within my singing skills, and which I didn't have the focus to rehearse, and pair it with a visual universe of my own. And instead of questioning what qualities the piece could have and what quality might be, I ended up trying to fit myself and the piece into a preconceived notion of what quality is.

Speaking from his perspective within baroque music, Øystein reflected:

> A quality performance in classical music would be based on the privilege/sacrifice of spending countless hours practicing. In its traditional context, it is difficult to see alternatives to this. In 'questioning quality', I wanted to see what added value could lie in an avant-garde approach to practice and skills, which also may involve rigorous rehearsal, but from another perspective. This means the work lies in using one's artistic core as a starting point, regardless of the tradition the source material belongs. The avant-garde has always involved radical choices. In such a context, a less elaborate and more punk/DIY treatment of the material could lead to other qualities. Initially, this piece appeared not to be done in a radical, experimental manner or with an avant-garde approach, nor did it seem that work was invested in order to align it closely with its original tradition. However, how the piece turned out — involving an abrupt cessation of the performance of the song one third of the way through and let the rest of

the song be replaced by a meta-text offering critical commentary on the project's theme and context — may indeed be regarded as an avant-garde act.

In terms of how this student work challenges structures, Electa asked:

> In what ways can we critically reflect on the musical traditions and rehearsal strategies we suggest? Should the student, who works two jobs and cannot rehearse after school be exempted from working within certain aesthetics or have their work judged as 'lower quality'? Is rehearsal and hard work a universal quality rubric applicable to all genres or can we together articulate more precisely the relationship between rehearsal method and desired output?

Even though the student expressed an intention to deconstruct classical 'quality', the process confronted them with how they reinscribed it. It was only when the deconstruction was embodied, within the high-stakes situation of an unplanned disruption to a public performance, that the dismantling happened as an action, rather than a thought. Although pedagogy today has an increasing focus on facilitation and creating open spaces for learning, in this case, it was the situation of resistance, both within the student and from the pedagogue that prompted learning.

Conclusion

Questioning quality in singing pedagogy is not possible without navigation of the complex entangled histories associated with quality within the university setting, considering the multiple intersecting axes of oppression that reproduce social hierarchies. In terms of critical pedagogies, this project does not reproduce the narrative of the 'freethinking artist stuck within the repressive/decolonial/sexist institution', but rather reflects the entanglement of human agency and responsibility in researching and effecting structural transformation. To critically investigate music, we needed to question the institution which framed it and our own multivocality within it. Pedagogy involves the juxtaposition of institutional, and personal, critique.

Contributing to the conversation of diversifying music education, the project suggests reconsidering quality at three levels: source, rehearsal, and output. Source material, which would have been rejected if we considered quality on the value system of written composition, produced 'quality' results. 'Hard work' is potentially not the only method towards quality outputs. The context in which a piece is listened to and the sonic world it inhabits informs how we understand its 'quality'. The suggestion would be to move away from a linear understanding of 'quality at the start + hard work = quality at the end', but rather to engage with students in unpacking how the methods at each stage inform results.

This research offers an examination of pedagogical strategies that involve de-centring of teachers, student agency, embracing of hesitation, and implication. This project explored a distinctive fluidity of student–teacher leadership. When the teacher transitions from being an authoritative figure (even when embodying a sense of lightness) to becoming a co-collaborator, a crucial question arises: How does this affect teacher–student trust?

This inquiry challenges an unconscious tendency prevalent in performance pedagogy, which assumes that by de-centring yourself as a teacher, personal preference is suspended, and student agency effectively granted. In such logic, we can be at risk of reinscribing modernist ideas of neutrality, as well as risking stepping away from, instead of into our greater ethical responsibility for navigating positionality in the classroom. In this project, our 'power' became clearer as we stepped away from it. By ethically and actively implicating ourselves as artists within the creative process, we teachers could adopt a strategy that acknowledges power dynamics and strives towards generative practice.

This project questioned the unconscious assumption that 'co-teaching = teachers agreeing'. If the field is looking to embrace a diversity of students, aesthetics, and methods, we must celebrate the performative dissonance that manifests as a response to the multiple and intersecting power dynamics in the room. We did not necessarily disagree elegantly, but what future methods can embrace dissonance as a creative working method, hesitation as strategy, making transparent the complexity of the pedagogical role as 'the one who should know', inviting new teaching spaces. It should be noted that our disagreements felt perhaps more uncomfortable because we assumed we held common values: embracing diversity and ethical practice can sometimes be most difficult the more 'alike' we perceive ourselves to be.

The research fundamentally challenges hierarchical frameworks for evaluation. To value one student 'better' than the other on the same criteria would imply the judgement of one culture or aesthetic as more valued. Instead, this project proposes an alternative approach. Can we de-centre Western values by centring the quality rubrics of the culturally and aesthetically specific work of each student? And importantly: Can we involve the student in articulating what 'quality' means within their work, rather than the teacher projecting assumptions? Is this a way of disrupting the pattern of evaluative practices simply reinscribing Western values upon whatever decolonial or process-based practice a working method might suggest?

In terms of time frames, if we are interested in inviting complex artistic research practices into an educational setting, maybe the assessment structure needs to mirror research timelines, in which there is more time between performance and reflection. Does the assessment pattern of evaluating a project directly after completion predetermine what kind of knowledge is produced? Does it also unconsciously affect and limit how pedagogues plan their teaching? Do we only teach something that can be 'quality assured' within the time frame?

On the level of course descriptions, it becomes evident: if a course is opening for a diversity of aesthetic responses, the assessment criteria must be closely examined, to make sure they are not privileging one working mode. Including students in the process of project planning, as one suggested, could be a compelling way to disturb the evaluation pipeline. This project explored quality as relational, culturally specific, and *a process of intra-action*, a complex 'dynamism of forces' in entanglement. It offered strategies for inviting not-knowing, unlearning, hesitation, and mutual respect into practices which assert 'quality' at all levels of pedagogy multivocal positionality.

Notes

1 Kunstnerisk utviklingsarbeid and PaR are similar but not identical. 'Kunstnerisk utviklingsarbeid' (literally translated as 'artistic development work') historically is characterised by a resistance to the academisation of art and prioritised the artwork over the reflective aspects of projects. The common translation is Artistic Research (https://snl.no/kunstnerisk_utviklingsarbeid).

2 Spivak's notion of *worlding* (1985, p. 247), Bourdieu's *habitus* (1977), and Camilleri's *bodyworld* (2019) all are related frameworks which inform this core question of how a practice and person is embedded and finds agency within their material (necessarily cultural) context.

3 Ethically, it is important to stress that this work represents the reflections of 6 out of 13 co-investigators, and is necessarily partial. We extend a great thank you to all involved, for their bravery, questions, and willingness to engage.

4 www.hiof.no/nta/english/people/aca/ewb/index.html, www.hiof.no/lusp/res/personer/und-forsk-ansatte/oysteine/index.html and www.wilhelmine.no/.

5 Evi Stamatiou's discussion of Bourdieu's *habitus* and *acting offer* offers potential tools for decolonial practice to explore related territory (2022, p. 96).
6 We consciously called these 'etudes' 'sonic worlds' to articulate the concept that no music stands alone. Instead, it is always in relation to and actively creating a world which it inhabits. This references Spivak's notion of worlding and Bourdieu's *habitus*.
7 There are many musical practices in the world which would be excluded if we were to begin from a notion of 'a song' as the starting point. In Sámpi culture, for example, a yoik is not a song, it is not sung, includes other aspects that are essential to the expression such as bodily gestures. Likewise, it is considered 'larger' than music, 'The yoik is not just music. [Its] functions are much broader than that. They are routes to social contact' (John Turi in Weinstock, 2019).
8 This included among other things viewing the lecture: You and Me as Vocal Material and a lecture by Øystein on extended composition, new amateurism, etc.
9 All student reflections denoted as quotes have been written by the student in relation to the development of this piece of writing. In that sense, their writing are not statements gathered in one context which we have placed and framed here, but rather their own reflections in relation to this further development of this reflective stage of the research.
10 Quote from programme notes.
11 These etudes which the students made did not have titles, as they were not separate numbers, but rather scenes in a whole. This title is here meant to tune the reader into the discussion which the section unpacks.

References

Bakhtin, M. (1984). *Rabelais and his world* (H. Iswolsky, Trans.). Indiana University Press. (Original work published 1965)

Barad, K. (2007). *Meeting the universe halfway: Quantum physics and the entanglement of matter and meaning.* Duke University Press.

Barker, P. (2004). *Composing for voice.* Routledge.

Behrens, E., & Elle, Ø. (2021). *You and me as vocal material where and when do we meet?* www.critical-stages.org/24/you-and-me-where-and-how-do-we-meet/

Bourdieu, P. (1977). *Outline of a theory of practice.* Cambridge University Press.

Cahill, A. J., & Hamel, C. (2019). Toward intervocality: Linklater, the body, and contemporary feminist theory. *Voice and Speech Review, 13*(2).

Camilleri, F. (2019). *Performer training reconfigured: Post-psychophysical perspectives for the twenty-first century.* Methuen Drama.

DiAngelo, R. (2018). *White fragility, why it's so hard for white people to talk about racism.* Beacon Press.

Eidsheim, N. S. (2015). *Sensing sound: Singing and listening as vibrational practice.* Duke University Press.

Ewell, P. (2020). Music theory and the white racial frame. *Music Theory Online, 26*(2). https://mtosmt.org/issues/mto.20.26.2/mto.20.26.2.ewell.html

Fisher, T., & Katsouraki, E. (2019). *Beyond failure: New essays on the cultural history of failure in theatre and performance.* Routledge.

Grotowski, J. (1999). Untitled text by Jerzy Grotowski. *The Drama Review, 43*(2), 11–12.

Grotowski, J., Chwat, J., & Packham, R. (1987). Tu es le fils de quelqu'un [You are someone's son]. *The Drama Review: TDR, 31*(3), 30–41. https://doi.org/10.2307/1145800

Harraway, D. (2016). *Staying with the trouble: Making Kin in the Chthulucene.* Duke University Press.

Harrison, A. K. (2008). Racial authenticity in rap music and hip hop. *Sociology Compass, 2*(6), 1783–1800. https://doi.org/10.1111/j.1751-9020.2008.00171.x

Jackson, R. (1997). Authenticity or authenticities? – Performance practice and the mainstream. *Performance Practice Review, 10*(1). https://doi.org/10.5642/perfpr.199710.01.02

Jones, M. D., & Dyson, M. E. (2006). An interview with Michael Eric Dyson. *Callaloo, 29*(3), 786–802. www.jstor.org/stable/4488359

Lyotard, J.-F. (1979). *The postmodern condition: A report on knowledge.* Manchester University Press.

Mapaya, M. G. (2022). Misalignment of university-based music education with modern-day South African musical praxis. In J. A. Davis & C. Lynch (Eds.), *Listening across borders: Musicology in the global classroom* (pp. 151–165). Routledge.

Meizel, K. (2020). *Multivocality: Singing on the boarders of identity.* Oxford University Press.

Nelson, R. (2006). Practice-as-research and the problem of knowledge. *Performance Research, 11*(4), 105–116. https://doi.org/10.1080/13528160701363556

Norwegian Theatre Academy. (2023). *Welcome to NTA.* www.hiof.no/nta/english/

Oram, D. (2019). De-colonizing listening: Toward an equitable approach to speech training for the actor. *Voice and Speech Review, 13*(3), 279–297. https://doi.org/10.1080/23268263.2019.1627745

Østfold University College. (2023). *Quality assurance system for education.* www.hiof.no/english/about/educational-quality/

Ross, A. (2020, September 14). Black scholars confront white supremacy in classical music. *The New Yorker.* www.newyorker.com/magazine/2020/09/21/black-scholars-confront-white-supremacy-in-classical-music

Spivak, G. C. (1985). The Rani of Sirmur: An essay in reading the archives. *History and Theory, 24*(3), 247–272. https://doi.org/10.2307/2505169

Stamatiou, E. (2022). Pierre Bourdieu and actor training: Towards decolonising and decentering actor training pedagogies. *Theatre, Dance and Performance Training, 13*(1), 96–114. https://doi.org/10.1080/19443927.2021.1943509

Stark, W. (2016). *Intra-action, Whitney Stark.* https://newmaterialism.eu/almanac/i/intra-action.html

Trimingham, M. (2002). A methodology for practice as research. *Studies in Theatre and Performance, 22*(1), 54–60. https://doi.org/10.1386/stap.22.1.54

Twitchin, M. (2018). What chance failure? In T. Fisher & E. Katsouraki (Eds.), *Beyond failure: New essays on the cultural history of failure in theatre and performance* (pp. 37–54). Routledge.

Vivaldi, A. (circa 1713–1717, 2021). *Nisi Dominus RV 608. IV Cum dederit.* Vocal Space Lines. A. Nowitz, Performance at Sentralen, Oslo, Norway.

Weinstock, J. (2019). *Yoiking, a Sami musical expression.* https://nordics.info/show/artikel/yoiking

Part Four

Interpersonal Intersectionality

Learning Edges

13 Developing the Actor Trainer
Welcome, Trust, and Critical Exchange

Jessica Hartley

Introduction

This chapter reflects upon the knowledge that I have gained when working to support actor trainers on an MA/MFA in Actor Training and Coaching (ATC) at the Royal Central School of Speech and Drama (Central), in the United Kingdom. From my position as a queer, cis-gendered, female, dyslexic, white, course leader, I reflect upon the discourses that impact the well-being of the actor and the teacher. I articulate some ways that these discourses are brought to consciousness, made transparent and framed in my daily teaching. These are then exemplified in reflections on welcoming students and building trust. The critical pedagogies of Paulo Freire, bell hooks, and Jacques Rancière focus on the emancipation of the student through a conscious praxis of dialogue between teacher and student. From different positions, these critical pedagogues articulate a tension between school structures and mechanisms which dehumanise people, and the conventional ways that some schools compel students back to their own oppression. I recognise that because actors and teachers utilise their whole being in their art, and their identity is tied into the work and professionalism of their school, the power dynamics between actors, their trainers, and the school context can be particularly impactful and the complex interrelationships that build between teacher and student warrant consideration. I assert that teaching and training are embodied art forms which bring together academic knowledge, physical practice, and reflexivity. Later in this chapter, I utilise psychoanalytic theory to identify the ways that teachers and students emotionally regulate each other as a form of attachment. In so doing, I hope to draw us into a dialogue a conversation with the embodied practices of teaching and learning in acting.

I work under the following three premises: firstly, acting teachers profoundly shape the artistic practice and well-being of students, as well as shaping acting epistemologies. This has been robustly articulated in the works of Ross Prior (2012), Mark Seton (2010, 2021), Lisa Peck (2021), Amy Mihyang Ginther (2023), and through the practices of Anne Bogart (2023), Sharelle Luckett (2023), and Vanessa Ewan (2023) who I credit as foundational influences on my teaching praxis.

Secondly, this profound impact upon student actors can 'not only re-present hegemonic systems [of oppression] on stage, but . . . supports the ongoing reproduction of inequality by offering normatives under the guise of actor training' (Spatz, 2015, p. 158). Ben Spatz's critique of training argues for a 'reframing of trust' within the field, most particularly to antagonise the power of directors and teachers which limit and stratify actors' perceptions of themselves. Like Lisa Peck (2021), Peter Zazzali (2022), Rosemary Malague (2012), Sharelle Luckett and Tia Shaffer (2016), and Petronilla Whitfield (2021), Spatz's recognition of the breaches of trust committed under the guise of 'training' gives actor trainers pause to

DOI: 10.4324/9781003393672-18

reflect upon 'what [teachers'] bodies can do' in training spaces (2015, p. 1). This chapter, therefore, engages with reframing pedagogical trust as a movement from dependency upon the teacher towards the agency of the actor.

Thirdly, while the exercises and approaches to acting are theorised and categorised very particularly, the impact of the teacher–student relationship is an emergent discourse within conservatoire education. Much is written about *what* is being taught in acting classes, and aspects of *who* is teaching and studying it are now being debated in contemporary literature (Zazzali, 2022; Ginther, 2023), the simple consideration of *how* trainers work in physical relation, through their voice, script, embodiment, and care, is under-theorised. Therefore, I advance considerations upon what it means to work as a 'comrade-explorer navigating new terrains of loving aspects of ourselves within our performance work' (Ginther, 2023, p. 1), who has 'an outsized role in [student actors'] personal development' (Zazzali, 2022, p. 194).

I utilise poetry to reflect upon the ways that I teach. For political theorist Jacques Rancière, within education (as in all sites of political action) there are stratified hierarchical mechanisms which demarcate who is allowed to do what and say what. My poetic intervention is designed to articulate, reflect, model, and alter my perception of moments from my practice, as well as destabilising the conventional model of academic writing. For Rancière, poetry offers emancipatory opportunities for the listener, student, or person with whom you are communicating because it does not explicate; poetry evokes 'a distance between words and things which is not deception' (1999 p. 51). He states that poetry, by attending to personal experience, 'decomposes and recomposes' notions of reality and produces a 'fresh sphere of visibility' for the writer (ibid, p. 42). I write poetry to clarify my embodied practice of facilitating learning, and as a way of 'knowing' the pedagogical techniques that I use. Writing poetry is part of my reflective practice as a teacher, which draws from phenomenology (the description of feeling as knowledge) and queer theory (the destabilisation of hierarchy).

Frame
Invite
Propose
Unbalance
Begin

Welcome

We recruit an inspiring cohort of students onto the MA/MFA. They constitute an intersectional ensemble[1] of 18–20 students and, at the time of publication, the students range in age from 20 to 58 years, are representative of a range of genders and sexualities, and have plural cultural backgrounds. They are diverse in neurotype, in physical (dis)ability, and have differing socio-economic backgrounds and statuses; first languages are multiple, with many students fluent in three or four, with representation from major and minor religions, and a range of spiritual positions. Many of the identity characteristics above are intersectional and many students embody several traits that subvert what Nirmal Puwar would call the 'somatic norm' of a Drama School (2001). The students' backgrounds in acting are equally diverse, with some of the older students having sustained high level careers as professional actors/performers, drama teachers, or having diverted from creative industries. The younger students may be fresh from or close to their undergraduate experiences, having trained in Classical Acting, Musical Theatre, Corporeal Mime, Peking Opera, Applied Theatre, or having different derivations of a 'drama' degree; some have come from the fields of anthropology, archaeology, or film studies. Many are parents, and/or carers, and some commute long distances to London for in-person classes. All the part-time students have jobs at various levels: from highly paid corporate practice, teaching at various levels, to working in supermarkets, in bars, and driving taxis. What brings the cohort together is a shared hunger to interrogate and invigorate their teaching practice, consolidate their appreciation of the field of actor training, and an openness to learn as part of a complex community. Successful applicants demonstrate kindness and reflexivity at audition and are not scared to change their minds.

The first day of any new year is exciting and demanding. I embody a vibrantly visible position. As curator of a journey the students have invested a great deal of time and money to attend, I am host, validator, and model. I am the face of the institution, and of myself: I am both Dr. Jessica Hartley SFHEA, PhD, and *just* Jess; precarious and powerful; critical, inviting criticality and directly critiqued; knowledgeable and ignorant.

I start the programme with the question '*who are we?*' Because while some of the positional categorisations that I listed above are known to me, what this *means* directly for them as trainers is *particular*. One student's experience is different from another despite two people identifying as 'Muslim' or 'Colombian' or 'neurodivergent' or 'AFAB' on their application: and this lived experience of intersectionality will manifest in different levels of knowledge, confidence, and expertise. I invite a dialogue with identity as soon as I ask the question 'who are you?': the way that I manage the conversation can build trust or mistrust, so I must handle it with care.

The simple act of taking time for a name to be said correctly, heard correctly, and articulated as a 'story' allows a potential moment in which people are valued. This year I began the exercise with 'my name is Jess, not Jessica or Jessie, only my mother calls me Jessica. I am not Doctor, or Professor or Ma'am. I am Jess. My pronouns are she/her and they/them.[2] The story of my name is. . .'. Everyone in the circle then practices my name, for some it is simple, for others more complex, the hard J is unfamiliar in some mouths, and easy in others. We go around the group and each student is given the time and space to teach their name and tell a story. The purpose of this exercise is to seed two correlative ideologies: that the course supports students to honour their identity, and the ensemble is responsible for respectfully dignifying each contribution.

There are aspects of culture that are emphasised and discovered by each ensemble group. One year, from a Russian-British student, I learnt the different ways names, nicknames, and pet names come into being, and when I tactfully used one of those names to her later in the day, I saw the power it had to bring joy to her demeanour. She had been heard and by using a specific version of her name, she had been affirmed. Other students are keen to tell us their English names as well as their birth names; or the names that they go by, rather than what is written on their registration documents. These names are validated. We rehearse together the pitches of a Sichuan Chinese or Farsi name, the nuanced dialects of a familiar name through the accent of the named student, and the important aspects of culture that are made visible and invisible when a person is invited to bring aspects of their identity into the space. The students also begin to understand the fragility of hearing their name adapted or adopted by people who can attend to it with care, or carelessly. This exercise establishes a learning environment that strives for cultural competency through affirmation, correction, and celebration.

In this first group session, my position is to lead and to model, being both expert (in my own name) and student (of the other names). As bell hooks reminds us, 'it is often productive if professors take the first risk, linking confessional narratives to academic discussions to show how experience can illuminate and enhance our understanding of academic material' (hooks, 1994, p. 48). Robin Phelps-Ward and Wonjae Phillip-Kim highlight the vital importance of names. They articulate that 'the stories of our names support the critical consciousness raising conversations' which pertain to narratives of supremacy and marginalisation within higher education (Phelps-Ward & Kim, 2022, preface). So, the way that a student's name and pronouns are welcomed, valued and made precious by a group of students establishes a key premise of our community, that if we are to value each other, we must first learn how to listen. Moreover, I must be mindful to model and practice my ability to 'hear' the students and do so transparently. It is important for me to practice seriousness and precision and, significantly, to be at ease[3] when being corrected. hooks states that '[as] a classroom community, our capacity to generate excitement is deeply affected by our interest in one another, in hearing one another's voices, in recognizing one another's presence' (1989, p. 16). As Nichole Margarita Garcia et al. articulate, '[i]t is important for . . . students to know that their social position based on their names is of value and pedagogically contributes to the development of problem-posing learning in the classroom environment' (in Phelps-Ward & Kim, 2022, p. 73). Because the ATC programme focuses on the ways students are taught, it is down to me to make transparent how I am teaching, and the theoretical foundations of my ideology as a choice within the learning space. This mode of critical pedagogy may be a new experience for the students and some have a strong emotional response to this work. The stories of their name can awaken homesickness, grief, and longing; it can also awaken nervousness and tension hidden in jokes or asides. I need to acknowledge and validate the responses free from judgement. I tell them that their emotions are welcome, but not mandatory; the stories don't have to be 'deep'. I invite them to reflect upon the feelings and behaviours that arise, witness where they come from and take time to process if needed.

Psychoanalysts have long argued that teaching in Higher Education can be understood by the student as a '*domain-specific* attachment relationship' because teachers are perceived as stronger and wiser significant others who are available and supportive in times of need (Pistole & Watkins, 1995, p. 8). Containing a student's emotional responses is enmeshed with my pedagogy, and with my identity as a person and teacher. It is to me that they will turn when they are struggling with their learning. The idea of 'stronger and wiser' can draw the student compellingly back to an asymmetric relationship with their teacher, and this asymmetry cannot be changed but must be acknowledged. To set the tone of my pedagogy from the beginning, it is important to welcome and value each of them and notice how they are responding to my presence in their learning journey whilst supporting them to notice it too. Validating their position as different and also equal, I am a teacher and student, learning different things from them, but still learning. I have to place boundaries upon my role, so my story isn't one in which I am made vulnerable. I model playfulness, and at the end of the class, I remind the students to drink water, and maybe go for a walk. I tell them that I am going to take 10 minutes for myself and go outside. If students want to talk, I 'read' their desire and either say 'walk with me', or 'I need to process, can you give me ten minutes please? I'll see you in my office in ten'. In so doing, I ensure that I look after myself, and transparently create my boundaries for the group, while also recognising that the need to talk to me may be urgent.

After this naming exercise, I reflect to the students that we have just engaged in an 'academic' moment which brings together theory, personal understanding, and engaged pedagogy. The choice to frame the time spent learning and teaching names as an academic moment is deeply personal for me as a dyslexic academic. In my years of struggle to understand my own writing, articulating, and thinking processes, I have deconstructed many aspects of the 'academic' landscape, and the way that the performances of 'academia' can be encountered as an 'ongoing narrative of inequality' (Spatz, 2015, p. 158). Students often come to a master's level programme worried about writing essays, worried about reading theory, worried about being 'wrong'. I spent years feeling I had no place in academia myself. Some students believe that they are coming to the MA to learn what to say and how to say it in a way that will open the door to jobs within a university, conservatoire or film set. In revealing the performances of the 'academic' as a part of my 'pedagogic script' and as a technique to be learnt based on skills they already have, I return the student to the centre of a journey that *they* are responsible for. I suggest that being an academic or a pedagogue is about working with and challenging theory, adapting, and researching it in each professional context and teaching it to others; while understanding how, to quote David Takacs, 'your positionality biases your epistemology' (2003, p. 1). A recognition of positionality, and a celebration of it, therefore, becomes an act of consciousness-raising as well as a moment of welcome.

Educational philosopher Tyson Lewis articulates Freire's theories into three clear premises: Firstly, 'teaching [is] a beautiful act'; secondly, 'epistemological curiosity' is a necessary attitude for students (and teachers), and thirdly, 'consciousness raising [is] emancipation' (Lewis, 2012, p. 18). My second invitation to the students resides in the question: How have you been taught?

By focusing on their own teachers, the students take a reflexive position on education and epistemology. How they have been taught will influence the way they feel about education and how they will teach. I invite them to reflect upon who taught them the most, how they taught it, and whether they (as students) knew they were learning it. In thinking through the question 'How were you taught?,' the trainee teacher finds a perspective on pedagogy as a technique that has the potential to impact their students' engagement and love of acting. They will often question me further asking: 'What do you mean by 'most'?' 'Does it have to be a teacher?'; in passing responsibility back to them, answer 'whatever that means for you today', and 'I'll leave that choice to you', I give them the power to identify environments of learning that are pertinent. They begin to define learning directly through naming it and analysing it. Themes emerge from the analysis, and regularly students suggest that love is the pedagogical tool that most impacts learning: a parent's love of literature, a teacher who inspired a love of acting, or the experience of being loved by an audience.

Love is a powerful element with the Black Acting Methods *7 Day Affirmations* by Tia M. Shaffer: 'I do my art for the love of it' (2020). While love is a contentious aspect in teaching theory, in this instance Shaffer's pedagogy centralises the power of the actor to identify where they are emotionally invested in their work (Shaffer, 2020). Shaffer reminds students how they started, and what is at stake in their careers. I do the same. By discussing the experience that the student arrives at the school with, we can reflect upon different epistemological and emotional positions regarding pedagogy and pedagogues. Moreover, through hearing from each other, the students begin to recognise the subjectivity of their relationship to education more deeply, and they begin to reflect upon the educative discourses that either drew them towards further learning or, conversely, sent them away from it; made them feel like actors or made them feel like imposters. Many of the MA students say that they are drawn to teaching in order to change the way that actors are trained *because* of the way that they were asked to homogenise their identity, under the guise of training. They work in loving relation to their younger selves, who they seek to 'heal' through their practice. This homogenisation has, for some, had long-term consequences. In subsequent sessions on intersectionality, imperialism, and disability, the students are invited to gently share the dehumanising practices of the training they received (it is never mandated, and I make it explicit that we need to support them 'carefully' so as not to retraumatise or objectify them). This is precisely what Paulo Freire would call 'conscientisation', becoming cognisant of the subjectifying and objectifying ways that students have been schooled, and the role that their teachers have had in their understanding of art and themselves. As the Course Leader who asks these questions, and values the individual answers given, I am placed in a complex affective relationship with the students: curating a pathway and beginning a process of pedagogical awareness: acknowledging the risk[4] of awakening past experiences. The students naturally begin to build a relationship with me because I am the person responsible for inviting that awareness.

> *The group land on my body*
> *I attend, I listen, I watch, I question, I witness*
> *I reflect, we reflect, I reflect, I brace, I ground*
> *I change the class focus, I attend*
> *I rewrite, I give testimony, I receive testimony, I observe silence*
> *I remain conscious of their need to be supported, and of my need for boundaries*
> *I validate, I validate*

Building Trust

Students form strong attachments to the teachers who work with them, and teachers form attachments to the students that they work with (Riley, 2011). While attachment theory emerges from child development, the consequences of attachment will impact upon a person's ability to formulate relationships through their life, and it is therefore useful for a teacher to notice relationship patterns when working with students. Attachment theory is the hypothesis formed by Mary Ainsworth and John Bowlby (Ainsworth et al., 1978; Bowlby, 1969) which asserts that all significant relationships are formed through attachment, and that those attachment patterns are codified through early childhood experiences of security and insecurity. According to psychotherapist David Wallin, 'co-created relationships of attachment are the key concept for development and confidence to explore the world', and a person's 'stance of the self toward experience' is vital in understanding a person's relationship to others (2007, p. 1). It is important to note that attachment styles are not considered as fixed, but as flexible schemas, which evolve as new relationships are formed. Research has indicated that attachment styles can change in subtle or drastic ways depending on contextual relational experiences (Gillath & Karantzas, 2019). While critical consciousness provides students with a new understanding of themselves, the work of Freire, hooks, and Ranciére largely ignore the emotional and psychological impact of this shift in understanding and therefore the responsibilities of teachers to practice mindfully. This chapter seeks to acknowledge and honour the emotional labour that comes from supporting students in this way and give some theoretical foundations upon which to support a boundaried pedagogy that cultivates the agency of the students.

Theories of attachment in Higher Education, as typified by the psychoanalyst Philip Riley, recognise that 'teacher–student relationships are fundamental to understanding classroom behaviour by teachers as well as students, and directly effects students' outcomes' (2011, p. 1). While it is not my intention to psychoanalyse each student, the framework of attachment theory enables me to become conscious of, and thereby able to acknowledge, the different ways students may seek validation, avoid, or challenge me as their course leader; and, conversely, the ways I may respond to that behaviour. Once I begin to reflect upon it, I can then begin to change my practice, and maybe teach others to do the same.

According to Riley, 'there are multiple attachment dyads in any classroom', between the teacher and each student, between the students themselves, and between the students and the institution that you are working in (2011, p. 30). Ted Fleming suggests that attachment styles manifest as 'strategies that adults employ for dealing with stress, anxiety, change and the challenges of teaching and learning' (2008, p. 9). Seton advances this in relation to actor training as a 'mutual though not necessarily equitable *interdependency*. Students always looked to the teachers for guidance, approval and recognition. . . . Both the teachers and the students [are] located in a continuum of formation and habituation' (2010, pp. 8–9). The students begin to attune to the teacher/trainer and coach to regulate their behaviour and, in doing so, form an attachment that impacts upon the outcome of their learning. It stands to reason, therefore, that the student-teachers on ATC are forming attachments to me as their main support mechanism through their degree. Wearden et al. (2005) suggest that four different types of attachment can be seen within the behaviours of all students and that different behaviours may manifest for different teachers exacerbated during times of stress.

1) Secure students and secure teachers will have a positive view of themselves and others; they are likely to trust others and feel *worthy* of others' attention. Arguably, developing this trust, positivity, and self-worth is the purpose of education. While this presents differently in each student, and will be modified in relation to culture, gender, age, etc., a secure student will confidently ask for support and receive support without too much embarrassment or defensiveness. Trust will come easily after the students and teachers see the reciprocity of behaviour.

2) Students and teachers who are categorised as 'dismissive' are more reluctant to trust others. They will likely want to work autonomously or on their own and may become distant within challenging or new situations because they trust only themselves. These people are likely to mistrust teachers, students, directors, or theorists and may struggle within an ensemble unless given task-specific actions that allow them to be an individual. The challenge for an educator with a dismissing student, or a teacher who has a 'dismissive' attachment style is that the dismissal is perceived to denote value. A student may feel devalued by a dismissive teacher, and a teacher may feel devalued by a dismissive student. Once this dynamic has been ascertained, it is very hard to break, and the student's learning outcome will be impacted by it. Moreover, as articulated by Riley, 'the teachers self esteem, motivation and even attrition are impacted by insecure attachment' (2011, p. 54).

3) 'Preoccupied' students and teachers do the reverse, they are likely to become dependent upon others around them, seeking affirmation, or help. They are likely to have a negative self-view and rely on the opinions of others to provide their self-worth. They are likely to trust authority figures without question. We can see this when a student is entirely focused on seeking affirmation at the end of the class from peers or teachers, or constantly looking to the teacher during a class. Some focused attention paid to the affirmation models of education throughout the learning journey may support teachers and students towards independence.[5]

4) Finally, 'fearful' students combine a negative view of the self and others and avoid forming relationships altogether for fear of getting hurt. Fleming suggests that '[a]n awareness by the tutor or organiser which reach out to potentially isolated students may provide some of the structure required to assist the student to [begin to] experience security'

(2008, p. 41). While a fearful student is rare in actor training, and/or postgraduate teaching, they are present. Noticing that a student is isolated is important and I seek to check-in with a fearful student at regular intervals either through tutorials, or by saying 'hello' on arrival and asking 'did you have a nice weekend?' While attachment may be only one reason for this (others may be neurotype, introversion, distraction due to home factors and more), through noticing when a student is withdrawing or withdrawn from moments of interaction with me, I can begin to identify the strategies that the student is using and whether they support or to derail their learning, and begin to offer different scaffolding approaches to welcome them more fully into the learning.

The ATC students are taught by acting teachers as if they were trainee actors. They reflect and discuss the tasks and the ensemble's different ways of learning. By validating the positional intersections that the group bring, I am also opening the teachers' epistemological curiosity about the way that they can support students directly through adapting their pedagogy, rather than habitually privileging the positionality of the teacher. I celebrate the centrality of the students in all sessions I teach, and the students become increasingly aware of the pedagogical models I employ to support them.

The way that a student may create and form an attachment to me is not only a manifestation of the attachment mechanisms that they inhabited during childhood but becomes consolidated in response to my behaviour moving forward. Students will engage with affect regulation: they repeat behaviours which that elicit desired responses from others. Wallin advises that 'the process of affect regulation here is one in which the [person], through a kind of "social biofeedback", comes to associate the initially involuntary expressions of her emotions with the responses of the caregiver' (2007, p. 101). This process is therefore not conscious, but a learned pattern of response and adaptation to the social information being presented. Students will regulate themselves, their behaviour, emotions, and academic practices in relation to the teacher, particularly one they spend many hours with, and with whom they express emotion, or feel vulnerable. It is important for a teacher to observe the affective patterns a student is manifesting, reflect upon their behaviour in response, and make transparent the strategies they are employing.

If students present the performance(s) of self that led to affirmation from their teachers directly, then in secure partnerships the communication style between two people can be called '*collaborative and contingent*' (Wallin, 2007). One party signals, while the other answers with behaviour that says, in effect, 'I can see how you're feeling and respond to what you need' (ibid, p. 21). Securely attached connection manifests and evolves as the dyad adapt, empathise, correct/reject, praise, and set appropriate boundaries. I have readily available tutorial/pastoral time for any student who wants or needs it and can come from students signing up or me saying 'I see that you are a bit quiet this week, would you like a tutorial to process what is going on?' These sessions are half an hour. I ask what the student wishes to discuss, and ask them specifically 'what do you want to leave with?' At the end of each session, I remind them of their purpose, ask if that has been met and if it hasn't, suggest they book an additional slot with me, or with a counsellor. I also validate and affirm students: 'Thank you for bringing this to me', 'or 'Yes, that really is hard for most people'. I want them to leave the tutorial with clear strategies to use moving forward, and a sense of their own ability to succeed. There are times on the journey when students will cry and apologise for crying. My response is always: 'Your tears are welcome here'.

In these ways I make transparent that students' learning is my prime concern, and how I am purposely framing what I say, and how we practice together to create a significant critical awareness within the pedagogical dyad on ATC. In so doing, I also communicate my own need for boundaries and autonomy.

> *I notice the security*
> *I notice the precarity*
> *I notice entanglement*
> *I work out what to say, to do, to engage, to challenge*
> *I feed back, I feed forward, I nourish, I starve*
> *I listen, I validate, I reflect,*
> *I call out, I call in*[6]
> *We notice, we shape, we support*
> *We converse, we collaborate.*

Critical Exchange

Students on ATC have sessions on intersectionality, privilege, imperialism, gender, and power as part of their training. Themes are unpacked theoretically, and students reflect upon them in relation to their own learning and teaching. The use of the geographical and psychoanalytical term 'third' spaces (sometimes capitalised, sometimes thirdspaces) has become part of the wave of theories that frame practices which ideologically attend to integration, inclusion, and equity for students. Third spaces are a concept coined by sociologist Ray Oldenburg in the 1980s to refer to a physical location in which conversation is the primary goal. It has evolved to consider the ways that people behave to reflect a different hierarchical relationship to others, and the discursive means through which people can challenge or destabilise power dynamics. In actor training, these moments come when teachers ask students 'What would you like to work on today?' but also arise within pastoral work; they arise when 'texts' are chosen to draw specific students or identities to the centre of the art. Sociocultural theorist Homi Bhabha (1994), suggests that the Third Space is an equaliser because it 'challenges our sense of the historical identity of culture as a homogenizing, unifying force' (p. 54). The creation of a Third Space stages the possibility of collapsed traditional hierarchies and the breaking down of binaries (us versus them) to introduce more reflexive and equitable relational system between people (Bhabha, 1994). Edward Soja describes Third Space as a space of 'extraordinary openness, a place of critical exchange . . . a space where issues of race, class and gender can be addressed simultaneously without privileging one over the other' (Soja, 1996, p. 5). This critical exchange is only possible when trust is a transparent discourse in the learning space.

Within actor training, Roanna Mitchell recognises that this understanding of 'being with' involving 'surrender, recognition, and responsible action' is present in certain aspects of performer training, such as improvisation (2022, p. 231). Mitchell recognises that the relationship between performing and teaching 'helps me grasp [teaching] in an embodied manner as well as intellectually, reminds me that performer training contains techniques through which we can practise "being-with"' (ibid., 232). Mitchell articulates that there is knowledge, borne out of being in rehearsal rooms as actors within an ensemble that we may utilise to navigate the pedagogical imbalances within the space and challenge orthodoxies. So, on ATC, I draw the students back to the question of how they were taught, what they already know, how they listen to each other, what they expect of teachers (and therefore of me), what their skills are as performers, and how they might use this knowledge to create a conscious teaching praxis.

Psychoanalyst Jessica Benjamin articulates the possibility that 'thirdspace' connections between people can be creative, mutually differentiating, and relational (2018). She defines the conditions under which a therapist and client may co-create a space in which each is understood as wholly human. According to Benjamin, 'we know of the other's mind as an equal source of intention and agency, affecting and being affected' (2018, p. 3). She continues that this relational state of equal positioning permits people to 'experience the other as a responsive agent who can reciprocate the desire for recognition versus an object of need or drive to be managed within our own mental web' (ibid). Benjamin suggests that this can only be done through the 'attunement' of the parental, pedagogical, or therapeutic figure. While they hold the power (and this is made transparent), the dialogue affirms that *different* position as a mobilising aspect of their dyad within which they *both* play a part. Repeated sign-posting and public reflection upon my own pedagogical script with the ATC students reinforces my position, the power dynamic between us, and the role the students play in their own learning. Central to this is my desire to further a peer-driven critical exchange with students who will become (and often already are) my contemporaries, and my teachers.

I walk into a Royal Central School of Speech and Drama training space and I have tremendous power as a teacher. Students anticipate that I am here to support their learning, their development, and their artistry as teachers, performers, and people. They have invested a great deal in their training: personally, financially, and culturally. The students will be impacted by this; it makes them precarious in their grounding, and particularly susceptible to building an attachment to me. The field of actor training is formed on understanding the power of teachers, directors, and audiences which actors need to regulate, attend, and be visible within. This skill of attention can be developmental, useful, and epistemological for teachers if they are conscious of it, and if they critically engage with their practice. My role in building trust is to create a language of critical exchange that is validatory and non-hierarchical. I was delighted, for example, last year when a group of students pushed me out of the training room, saying: 'We don't need you today, Jess, go for a walk or get a tea, we got this, we will find you if we need you!'.[7] They had begun to trust themselves, and each other, and no longer needed me to 'contain' all their exchanges.

Understanding the different ways that students will enact their attachments to teachers can provide a useful framework from which to view students' and teachers' security. Moreover, by being consistent, open, reflexive, and individuated in their attention – teachers can work with students to develop a practice from which to explore their identity and find its power. In so doing, teachers may also build a space where they too are seen as a whole person, equal in 'agency and intention' to the students (Benjamin, 2018, p. 3). These relationships can be flexible, individuated, specific, and mutually differentiating; teachers must transparently reflect upon their power, the attachment relationship, and how this plays out in their teacher–student interactions, while providing the conditions under which students may learn to do the same. We learn to listen to each other and support each other, to understand ourselves, and, therein, begin to find the power of our unique identities.

My role thereby shifts trainers from teaching an approach to acting, to teaching an approach to actors. I do this through modelling and articulating my role as a teacher of teachers. This practice is a complex embodied act of attention, self-awareness, and strategies to notice and acknowledge identity and agency between teacher and student. This practice *may* support teachers to create secure attachments in their working lives, consolidate existing relationships built upon trust and mutual understanding, and provide a template for their students moving forward. In the hope that teachers and actors may create the foundations for braver pieces of art and mindful resilience for us all.

> *I surrender*
> *I recognise*
> *I pause, I reflect, I take responsibility*
> *I give responsibility*
> *They are responsible*
> *We learn*

Notes

1 I utilise the term ensemble through the entire programme as a collective noun for the group of students. I understand it in relation to the French tradition, and as defined in the Collins Dictionary as 'a group of individuals working together with common purpose' (2023) www.collinsdictionary.com/dictionary/english/ensemble-acting).
2 The introduction of a pronoun check is an important consideration within a diverse cohort. I choose to do it by framing it as an important aspect of my name/naming. I model it as part of the practice but I do not mandate it within the exercise because the group are at different stages in their trust, and have different levels of knowledge about how or why it is important. The act of stating my pronouns is a tactful welcome and invitation to others in the group, like any true invitation, it can be rejected, or accepted. ATC students are fully introduced to pronouns at a later stage, as part of the curriculum discussion on sex, gender, sexuality, and their impact upon teaching, learning, and discourses in acting.
3 For Michael Chekhov 'the actor should burn on the inside with an outer ease' (Rushe, 2019, p. 34). His state of 'ease' is an active and focused engagement of poise and grace, while having a clear and deep connection to feeling. When at 'ease', an actor, performer, and person is listening with their whole being to the performances of others.
4 If a student arrives with pre-existing trauma, this can arise within classes and sessions. I work in a trauma-informed manner as typified by Phyllis Thompson and Janice Carello. Trauma informed teaching is a process that cultivates recognition of the impact of trauma, recognition of the signs and symptoms of trauma, responds by integrating knowledge, and resists retraumatisation (Thompson & Carello, 2022, p. 17).
5 The affirmation models of education may be found within the work of Freddie Hendricks or the writings of Brené Brown. However, for now, I would like to reference my teacher–student Lee Mengo who teaches at Bridgend College in Wales. Mengo uses Paul McGee's three questions in his practice: 'Who has the biggest influence on your life? Who deserves most credit for where you currently find yourself in life? Whose advice and opinions do you tend to always act upon?' (McGee, 2015, p. 38). Mengo's students joyfully shouted 'myself' when asked this in an acting class I observed in 2023. It is clear to me that these students had been securely and deeply supported by Mengo to understand their power as actors.
6 The difference between calling out and calling in is articulated by Prof. Loretta Ross. Calling out is when someone tells someone directly that something they have said or done is wrong. Calling in is an act of conversation: 'Calling out assumes the worst. Calling in involves conversation, compassion and context. It doesn't mean a person should ignore harm, slight or damage, but nor should she, he or they exaggerate it. "Every time somebody disagrees with me it's not 'verbal violence'"'. Professor Ross said. 'Overstatement of harm is not helpful when you're trying to create a culture of compassion' (2020, personal communication).
7 Actually, the way they said it was (much to my delight) much less polite, but I will leave it to your imaginations as to what they actually said.

References

Ainsworth, M. D. S., Blehar, M., Waters, E., & Wall, S. (1978). *Patterns of attachment: A psychological study of the strange situation*. Erlbaum.

Benjamin, J. (2018). *Beyond the doer and the done to: Recognition theory, intersubjectivity and the third*. Routledge.

Bhabha, H. (1994). The third space: Interview with Homi Bhabha. In J. Rutherford (Ed.), *Identity: Community, culture, difference* (pp. 207–221). Lawrence and Wishart.

Bhabha, H. (1994). *The location of culture*. Routledge.

Bogart, A. (2023). *Masterclasses held at RCSSD, 2021*. https://www.gitis.net/en/news/news-140/

Bowlby, J. (1969). Attachment and loss: Vol 1. Attachment (2nd ed.). Basic Books.

Collins English dictionary. (2023). Retrieved March 26, 2023, from http://www.collinsdictionary.com/english/creative

Ewan, V. (2023). Unpublished conversations with the author.

Fleming, T. (2008). A secure base for adult learning: Attachment theory and adult education. *The Adult Learner: The Journal of Adult and Community Education in Ireland, 25*, 33–53.

Gillath, O., & Karantzas, G. (2019). Attachment security priming: A systematic review. *Current Opinion in Psychology, 25*, 86–95.

Ginther, A. (Ed.). (2023). *Stages of reckoning: Antiracist and decolonial actor training*. Routledge.

hooks, b. (1989). Choosing the margin as a space of radical openness. *Framework: The Journal of Cinema and Media, 36*, 15–23.

hooks, b. (1994). *Teaching to transgress: Education as the practice of freedom*. Routledge.

Lewis, T. (2012). *The aesthetics of education theatre, curiosity, and politics in the work of Jacques Rancière and Paulo Freire*. Bloomsbury.

Luckett, S. (2023). *Acting methods for the 21st century black acting methods studio*. https://blackacting-methods.mykajabi.com/products/acting-methods-for-the-21st-century/categories/2150735188/posts/2160884079

Luckett, S., & Shaffer, T. M. (2016). *Black acting methods: Critical approaches*. Routledge.

Malague, R. (2012). *An actress prepares: Women and "the method"*. Routledge.

McGee, P. (2015). *S.U.M.O. (Shut Up, Move On): The straight-talking guide to creating and enjoying a brilliant life*. John Wiley & Sons.

Mitchell, R. (2022). Not not doing therapy: Performer training and the "third" space. In *Theatre dance and performer training*. Taylor Francis.

Peck, L. (2021). *Act as a feminist: Towards a critical acting pedagogy*. Routledge.

Phelps-Ward, R., & Kim, W. (2022). *The power of names in identity and oppression*. Taylor & Francis.

Pistole, M., & Watkins, C., Jr. (1995). Attachment theory, counselling process, and supervision. *Counseling Psychologist, 23*, 457–478.

Prior, R. (2012). *Teaching actors: Knowledge transfer in actor training*. Intellect.

Rancière, J. (1999). *Disagreement: Politics and philosophy*. University of Minnesota Press.

Riley, P. (2011). *Attachment theory and the teacher-student relationship*. Routledge.

Ross, L. R., in Bennett, J. (2021). *What if instead of calling people out, we called them in*. Retrieved from June 2023, www.nytimes.com/2020/11/19/style/loretta-ross-smith-college-cancel-culture.html

Rushe, S. (2019). *Michael Chekhov's acting technique: A practitioner's guide*. Bloomsbury.

Seton, M. C. (2010). The ethics of embodiment: Actor training and habitual vulnerability. *Performing Ethos*, 5–20. https://doi.org/10.1386/peet.1.1.5_1

Seton, M. C. (2021). What we "profess" as professionals and how we behave – are they the same thing? *The Official: International Journal of Contemporary Humanities, 5*(1), 1–18.

Shaffer, T. M. (n.d.). *Black acting methods: 7 day affirmations*. Retrieved October 2020, from www.blackactingmethods.com

Soja, E. W. (1996). *Thirdspace: Journeys to Los Angeles and other real and imagined places*. Blackwell.

Spatz, B. (2015). *What a body can do*. Routledge.

Takacs, D. (2003). How does your positionality bias your epistemology? *Thought & Action, 27*.

Thompson, P. and Carello, J. (Eds.) (2022). *Trauma Informed Pedagogies: A guide for responding to crisis and inequality in Higher Education* Palgrave McMillan.

Wallin, D. (2007). *Attachment in psychotherapy*. Guildford Press.

Wearden, A. J., Lamberton, N., Crook, N., & Walsh, V. (2005). Adult attachment, alexithymia, and symptom reporting: An extension to the four-category model of attachment. *Journal of Psychosomatic Research, 58*(3), 279–288.

Whitfield, P. (2021). *Inclusivity and equality in performance training teaching and learning for neuro and physical diversity*. Taylor and Francis.

Zazzali, P. (2022). *Actor training in anglophone countries*. Routledge.

14 Scaffolding Consent and Intimacy in the Acting Classroom

Bridging the Gap between Learning and Doing

Joelle Ré Arp-Dunham

Introduction and Positioning

Although my artistic philosophy had always been concerned with what educational theorist bell hooks defines as 'education as the practice of freedom' (1994, p. 6), my PhD programme opened doors to converge scholarship, artistic practice, and the necessary tools to realign my teaching based in anti-racist and more equitable consent-based practices. Extrapolating from Pierre Bourdieu's concept of *habitus*, which can be loosely defined as one's manifested temperament and outlook shaped by social conditioning, as a manifestation of social power, Evi Stamatiou asserts the need for acting training to address the multiple and intersecting identities of actors (2022, p. 23). As authors of a performance, not just conduits for a playwright or director, actors' bodies holistically shape that performance. hooks contends that the liberatory practice of the classroom must include teaching students that 'we all bring to the classroom experiential knowledge' (1994, p. 84). Exposing that experiential knowledge, or lack of it in some cases, can be frightening. So, the acting classroom needs to be a space where the community is built to allow for trust and support for students to step out of their comfort zones and make bold choices in their work while honouring their identities. Like children, adult learners still need to feel valued and safe (Fordham Institute, 2021). Recent debates and practices advocate for a holistic approach to mental, emotional, and artistic consent in the acting studio (Sigman-Marx, 2022; Rikard & Villarreal, 2023). This trust can't happen unless everyone in the class feels they have control over what they consent to do and not do, feel and not feel, and touch and not touch. hooks asserts that '[p]rogressive, holistic education, "engaged pedagogy" . . . emphasizes well-being. That means that teachers must be actively committed to a process of self-actualization that promotes their own well-being if they are to teach in a manner that empowers students' (1994, p. 15). Well-being is essential for students and educators alike.

While I always try to create nurturing spaces for exploration both in my classrooms and rehearsal spaces, many dramatic situations lend themselves to actor discomfort. The nature of creating life experiences of characters often requires physical intimacy between actors, both pleasurable and painful. Actors tell the characters' stories through *their* bodies. Fight choreographers have been employed to promote the safety of scenes with combat, but there have not traditionally been people who can help stage other types of physical intimacy. When I discovered an emerging body of professionals who specialise in this, I jumped at the chance to learn from them.

I began taking workshops with Tonia Sina from Intimacy Directors International and continued more extensive study with Chelsea Pace and Laura Rikard from Theatrical Intimacy Education (TIE). I immediately brought in concepts from each to the professional

DOI: 10.4324/9781003393672-19

production of *A Midsummer Night's Dream* I was working on. TIE's Boundary Practice was especially transformational. This three-step process allows actors to show where their partner can touch them, experience that touch, and then verbalise where the touch was (Pace, 2020, pp. 24–39). In addition to introductory consent discussions and exercises, the Boundary Practice helped create an emotional intimacy between actors, allowing the actors to follow their impulses more freely to physically touch their scene partners and explore various character actions at an earlier stage than I found typical in the rehearsal process. In addition, the actors were incredibly enthusiastic about the techniques expressing their relief at 'getting that part over with'. It felt as if we had jumped ahead two weeks into rehearsal, ultimately saving time.

Intimacy protocols can serve as methods to fulfil some of hooks's philosophies on the liberation of students as well. Inspired by the emancipatory and transformative education theories of Paulo Freire, hooks believed that education should be 'the practice of freedom' (1994, p. 4), with a goal of 'critical consciousness' (1994, pp. 36, 196). She stressed that education's aim 'is to prepare students to live and act more fully in the world' (2015, p. 103) and challenge the 'dominant oppressive systems' therein (1997, p. 7). Part of these transformations must include the well-being of students, also central to consent and intimacy protocols (1994, p. 15). A consent-based classroom provides tools towards these goals.

The exercises and structure outlined in this chapter reflects the incorporation of concepts and practices from my trauma-informed and consent-based trainings[1] filtered through my own lens, and current understandings of the way the actor's body/brain works (cognitive science), along with my 25 years of theatrical practice.[2] Using a Participatory Action Research methodology (henceforth PAR), I developed scaffolded exercises to successfully infuse consent and intimacy principles into my acting classes. PAR is an approach reflective of hooks's ideologies, designed for emancipatory exploration 'to inform grassroots collective action' (Cornish et al., 2023, p. 2). The authority of personal experience, gaining knowledge through action, recognition that the process of conducting research is as important as the outcomes, and the 'critical dialogue' of the participants are its key principles (Cornish et al., 2023, p. 2). Each of these tenets are explored in the scaffolded intimacy protocols.

Three levels of acting classes at Kansas State University – 'Fundamentals', 'Intermediate', and 'Advanced: Consent and Intimacy' – offered the critical practice research for the investigations. Each of these classes features primarily undergraduate students in a Bachelor of Arts program. Most of the Fundamental students are non-theatre majors, while theatre majors comprise the majority of the other two classes.

Scaffolding Need and Development

As I introduced the practices I learned from TIE and Intimacy Directors and Coordinators (henceforth IDC) into my undergraduate classes, however, I saw a distinct discomfort for many students with quickly jumping into physical touch between scene partners before social and non-touch physical intimacies were created. Students understood the processes and wanted to do them, but they couldn't help feeling discomfort and even anxiety with the large step going immediately from an introduction to skin-on-skin touch. Even students who knew each other often felt uncomfortable. I could see the hesitation, hear the nervous giggling, and experience the lack of communication between partners. Whereas the professional actors I worked with made the jump easily, the less experienced, and in this case younger, actors did not. In addition, my experience with the professional actors was pre-COVID, and with students was after the worst of the COVID closures, likely causing additional anxiety around touch.

I started experimenting with exercises to scaffold intermediate activities to bridge the leap from *learning about* consent to *giving consent* for touch. Scaffolding is an educational concept stemming from the sociocultural theory of cognitive development of Lev Vygotsky in the 1930s (van de Pol et al., 2010, p. 1). He stressed that children learn best from interaction with others who know more than they do (Shah & Rashid, 2017, pp. 5–7). At the beginning, the teacher provides the information and guidance, becoming less and less instructive as the child masters the concepts or tasks. Vygotsky also encourages peer-to-peer learning as part of this collaborative approach (Hausfather, 1996, p. 3). This idea of co-production of meaning rather than a master teacher imposing ideas upon a student is reflected in the educational philosophies of hooks, another inspiration for my investigation.

This idea of reaching a complex task by an advanced learner (or teacher) providing step-by-step tasks that can build a student's skills to reach a level of mastery soon became known as scaffolding. Much like the scaffolding in constructing a building, each platform becomes a support for reaching the next level. Importantly, managing students' frustration with the tasks is essential (Hausfather, 1996, p. 7).

Over the years, a consensus developed that three aspects are necessary for educational scaffolding: contingency, fading, and transfer of responsibility (Cornish et al., 2023, pp. 2–3). Contingency means that the tasks must be based on student response, and fading indicates that teacher guidance must fade over time until the transfer of responsibility lies in the student's hands. The following intimacy protocol scaffolds reflect each of these growth steps.

Although predominantly focused on cognitive learning, the idea of scaffolding does include the element of emotional salience. It is difficult to learn when anxieties are high just as it is difficult to act in a scene when fear-filled or anxious. Neuroscientist Antonio Damasio asserts that there is a loop between emotion and memory – each inseparable from and affecting the other (1994). Learning, which can be considered a form of memory, can be promoted by positive emotions and hindered by what we perceive as negative emotions. While the specific act of touching another human does likely not need to be learned, the specific places that one is giving consent to be touched and receiving consent from another to touch them do have to be learned. Personal physical boundaries are situationally dependent and can be nebulous. It can be difficult to judge where stretching of limits on our acting, which implies growth, crosses into transgressing boundaries, which involve negative emotions associated with stress. These negative emotions may indicate to an actor that they are transgressing a social norm in some way, such as causing embarrassment, or that they are experiencing a threat to themselves inducing a fear response (Arp-Dunham, 2023, pp. 42–44). More extreme fear responses manifest as Fight, such as arguing over the validity of an exercise, Flight, such as needing to leave space, and Freeze, such as stopping with complete inaction. Perhaps the most common indication of fear in the acting classroom is the Fawn response, wherein an actor just does as they are asked, completely repressing what their own body is telling them (Zingela et al., 2022, pp. 2–3).

Fear is even more complicated, however. 'Fear of the unknown may be a, or possibly the fundamental fear' and it underlies all anxiety (Carleton, 2016, p. 39). Fear that is focused on the future and often takes place over a period of time is anxiety (Lieberman & Shankman, 2016). Actors usually don't know what to expect when they have a physically intimate scene that needs to be staged at some indefinite point in the future. By introducing early in the class or rehearsal process touch after some emotional intimacy has been established, which can be also described as trust between partners that lowers embarrassment risks, the anticipatory anxiety can be lessened. Since anxiety and fear interfere with learning in the body–mind loop, reducing anxiety and fear helps learning (Joëls et al., 2006, p. 156). Actors have more cognitive space available for other acting concerns when they aren't worried about transgressing or being transgressed (Arp-Dunham, 2023, p. 39). Educational experts also believe that scaffolding may work so well as it decreases cognitive load in learners (Kirschner et al., 2006, pp. 80–81; van Merriënboer et al., 2003, pp. 5–8).

Cognitive load describes the mental effort it requires to do an action. It comes from the cognitive science understanding that working memory – the part of memory in which we can manipulate input and repeat items for longer-term memorisation – can only deal with a finite amount of data at a time (Baddeley, 2007, pp. 557–559; Cowan, 2015, pp. 536–538; Skulmowski & Rey, 2017, p. 2). When too much information needs processing, we can feel overwhelmed. Because of this, strategies that create less cognitive load are often preferred – like saying, 'yes' to a director even if the act lies outside the actor's boundaries. Actors need to practice creating solutions that fit within their boundaries in a lower-stakes classroom environment, so they don't default to the easy 'yes' when in the rehearsal room.[3]

Expanding Student Consent: Frameworks for Choice in the Acting Classroom

Student Survey: While there is a clear outline and learning outcomes for each class well before we begin, I cannot know what individual goals each student has. In the past, since many acting classes centred the Colonialist idea of the all-knowledgeable instructor, handing wisdom down to ignorant students, it was often expected that roles would be assigned to students strictly based on what the instructor felt best suited them. But a liberatory practice suggests that I cannot assume what an actor may wish to work on as I have no lived experience of their life. To address the needs of each student holistically, and trust the experiential knowledge they bring with them, which is key to PAR, students fill out an initial survey asking about what they need from our class community to enhance their learning. Questions include preferred names, pronouns used, learning differences they may have, and theatrical experiences and tastes. It also includes open-ended questions on what types of roles they'd like to play, including identification with social identities such as gender, race, sexuality, and more, their concerns and fears for the class, and a space for anything else they'd like to tell me to help them get the most out of their experience. I also encourage them to let me know if any of these change over the semester including specific needs. This first step in consent allows students to guide not only how they exist in the classroom but also what scenes they may later be assigned, and other adjustments to put their needs central to the class. They know I am interested in who they are as a person in the room, opening communication and a space for the self-actualisation hooks inspires (1994, p. 15). The survey is slightly adjusted for each level of class as part of the PAR research. For instance, for Intermediate students I add 'What are three of your greatest strengths as an actor?' and 'What are at least three acting skills you'd like to improve in this class?' as they may need to have acquired sufficient experience in the Fundamentals class to effectively analyse their own acting skills.

Community Agreements: To reduce the hierarchical practice of instructor-led rules for the classroom, Community Agreements allow students to decide what they need from the tutor and each other, both as individuals and as a group. In addition to serving as a necessary second step in PAR research, this practice also exemplifies hooks's ideas of classrooms as communities. hooks writes:

> We must build 'community' in order to create a climate of openness and intellectual rigor. Rather than focusing on the issues of safety, I think that a feeling of community creates a sense that there is a shared commitment and a common good that binds us. . . . It has

been my experience that one way to build community in the classroom is to recognize the value of each individual voice

(1994, p. 40).

I divide students into smaller groups with one person acting as scribe and instruct that everyone in the group needs a chance to voice their needs for a space in which they can feel supported or as multidisciplinary artist and advocate Noelle Diane Johnson says, '[b]y establishing limits for ourselves and others we give everyone involved the space to explore, play, and discover in ways that reduce harm and increase joy' (2022, p. 1). I offer an example of one of my needs for the space, such as listening to each voice in the room with openness, so they have a starting point. After each small group feels satisfied with what they've created, they come together and then we craft language to incorporate each need into a class document. The Community Agreement usually ends up consisting of about ten guidelines. Students come back to these agreements from time to time over the course as needed. I rarely need to mention them as students are quick to remind each other. This second layer of consent builds trust in the room to create a stronger sense of freedom that allows for braver choices, and with less fear of embarrassment, in addition to a better sense of well-being. While I did not develop the use of Community Agreements, I mention it here as an important early building block of a consent-based classroom.

Consent Basics Discussion: The third step I use in creating a consent-based classroom is a deliberate discussion of what consent is and how it affects actors. Students are usually familiar with the concepts of consent in inter-personal relationships, as it is emphasised in many of Kansas State's orientations. For those who've been in plays before, however, the old theatre practices of obedience to a director and answering 'yes, and' to what they are given by another actor, can already be habitual. Even for those less theatrically experienced, the power dynamics of saying 'no' to a professor or director can be quite uncomfortable. So, applying the first step in scaffolding, contingency, which includes basing tasks around student responses, calls for an adaptation of broad ideas of consent into the theatrical sphere. For our purposes, I emphasise that it is about the autonomy of the individual so they can fully support and become a part of the group. I think this framing is important to reinforce the community aspect of the class. We discuss the power dynamics of consent; how it must be 'fully informed'; that it is conditional, by which I mean with this person now, in this situation, and revocable at any time. We talk about various kinds of intimacy, including within family and friend relationships, sexual situations, and staged violence.

Communication Pathway: Students also have the department Communication Pathway that offers steps for further discussions with a faculty or staff member as well as an online form if they'd like various kinds of additional support or just to inform someone of a harm that was caused, with an option for anonymity. This Communication Pathway builds on pre-established institutional processes, providing additional and alternative means to foster dialogue and promote safety.

Self-care Cue: Self-care cues are cues that an actor can give to indicate that they need some space for self-care. They can serve to interrupt the Fight, Flight, Freeze, or Fawn fear responses as well as confusion from overwhelming sensory inputs or mental processes. Theatrical Intimacy Education teaches that any word not common in a script can be chosen for actors to say when they need to take a break from whatever is happening. They often use the word 'button' and suggest pairing this word with a physical action such as a double tap on the actor's upper chest (Pace, 2020, pp. 17–19). Actors may use just the word, just the physical gesture or both to indicate they need a pause, then verbally describe what it is they need. There are many variations on this. In classes, I usually use the words 'time-out' accompanied by the hands in the traditional 'T-shape' that many of us learned in sports programmes so students use familiar gestures while experiencing a stressor. The self-care cue gives actors a tool to disrupt the stress response, so they don't default to 'yes' but instead take their time to bring their pre-frontal cortexes back 'online' and make a choice with full consent. Of course, just 'knowing' this will not necessarily lead to its use, so we must practice it throughout the course.

Consent Practice: Once we have the Consent Basics Discussion and have a self-care cue in place, we can practice asserting consent in a safe environment. I usually start with Pace's 'Simon Says with a Twist' (2020, pp. 19–20). After playing a few rounds of traditional Simon Says students are instructed to simply reply 'no' as Pace suggests, and not do the action if they don't want to. Of course, after a few simple instructions, a difficult suggestion such as 'Simon says do a cartwheel' is offered. Most students will giggle and say, 'no'. After a few more easy tasks I add an outrageous one like 'Simon says go outside and run ten laps around the building'. Everyone says 'no' to this. Then we discuss the exercise, pointing out the power dynamics of the 'professor–student' relationship and how it makes saying 'no' difficult for some people, even when they've been instructed to do so. Of course, some people really enjoy saying 'no' and we discuss the liberation that can come with that act.

While Pace's Simon Says adaptation worked well as an experiential exploration of actors' reactions to challenges in consent practices, I found that jumping from this step directly into partnering touch exercises such as Pace's Boundary Practice (Pace, 2020, pp. 24–30) was usually too big a leap for my students.[4] Unless the students were already good friends, they tended to avoid eye contact, laugh and blush in embarrassment, rush through the process as fast as possible, and hold their breath throughout. When I discussed this with them, they invariably said it was the dreaded, 'awkward!' I also got the sense that some of the students went along with whatever their partner did and/or what they thought they were 'supposed' to do. Many students have not had experiences that helped them find their physically intimate boundaries in performance environments; many have never even thought about them. Others know that eye contact makes them uncomfortable as it also feels like an intimate act. I saw the need for intermediate steps that allowed more flexible options than the yes–no dichotomy we practised, and exercises to bridge the gap between an introduction to a partner and touching/being touched and holding eye contact with a partner. Each of the following exercises serves as a scaffold to bridge this chasm. These reflect the second PAR principle of gaining knowledge through action as they promote hooks's call for ways to increase student's self-actualisation. This also begins to challenge the 'dominant oppressive system' (hooks, 1997, p. 7), including the traditional theatrical and screen industries.

First Scaffolded Exercise: How about Instead. . .?

The first step I add to Pace's Simon Says exercise allows students a third option to 'yes' or 'no': 'how about instead. . .?' followed by an alternative suggestion. For instance, when I offer 'Simon says to drop and give me twenty push-ups', they may say 'yes' and start the push-ups or say 'no' and stand where they are or say 'how about instead I tap my knees 20 times' and then do that. I encourage them to state an alternative that is a negotiation, not something completely random and something they are willing to do. After several varieties of this exercise, we discuss it again giving students the opportunity to reflect with others on their own inclinations if they wish, as part of the PAR process of collaboration through dialogue. Students who found saying, 'no' to a professor difficult, even when encouraged to do so by the game rules, found great relief in having an option that protects their boundaries without the uncomfortable feeling of confrontation a 'no' can bring. This adjustment leads to creative and fun responses and since all actors are doing it at once there is little social pressure to cross their own boundaries. By this I mean go along with the ask even though they feel significant discomfort.

Second Scaffolded Exercise: Partner May I?

The next step is to allow some peer-to-peer social pressure for a more difficult consent exercise. While Twisted Simon Says deals primarily with the hierarchy of professor–student, 'Partner May I?' provides consent practice with their fellow classmates. It also works well to help students get to know each other, both in a classroom environment or in a workshop/ rehearsal. Firstly, I remind students that they can always opt out of an exercise or part of an exercise and that they also have the self-care cue (time-out) if needed. Then I instruct students to walk through the room, just noticing it. After a few minutes, I ask them to change awareness to themselves, focusing on various areas of their bodies. Next, I ask them to shift focus to the others in the room, just noticing them. I add in making eye contact with the others as they walk past each other. Then I instruct them to hold, turn to a nearby person, and take turns saying 'Hi, I'm (name) ', and wave at them. After they've exchanged only names, they immediately go on to another person until they've met three or four people.

Then I prompt them to stop in front of another classmate and whoever has on a lighter coloured shirt will say 'Hi I'm (name). May I shake your hand?' The other will say 'No' and walk away. After a bit I switch to the darker coloured shirt asking the same question. After a bit, I add the option of 'how about instead we _____'. I suggest they may wish to give a high-five, do a little dance, tap elbows, or some other creative greeting. I point out that they may need to have additional dialogue to find a solution that they are both comfortable with – no one has to say yes! They continue until they have greeted everyone in the room. They then come to a circle and I ask how it felt to say 'no' to a peer and then how it felt to receive the 'no'. While there's always a few students who enjoy the acted defiance, most admit to feeling uncomfortable saying 'no' to a peer even though it is part of the game. Most also say a part of them felt a little hurt by receiving the 'no' as well. 'No' is often perceived as confrontational in Western society, especially in theatre where we have been taught the improvisational rule 'yes, and . . .' suggesting we must always accept an offer by another actor (Second City, 2023). Most students prefer the option to give a compromise suggestion, although when I press them on it, they admit that it wasn't always easy. It took more time and they found they had to put in effort to think of creative solutions. I point out that coming up with a creative solution takes more cognitive load than blindly answering 'yes'. And although a 'no', often has more social ramifications, it, too, requires less cognitive work as there is little 'thinking' to be done.

Third Scaffolded Exercise: Space Shapes

I adapted the next theatre exercise, what I call 'Space Shapes', to allow students a chance to interact with their scene partner in a physically intimate way without touch in a lower-stress situation. This next scaffold allows students to experientially learn what bodies can do in space in relation to one another in a non-threatening way. It takes students from a minor level of embarrassment at bodily proximity and unnatural physical positions to a place of comfort as they learn to stretch their social norms. It also promotes hooks's idea of self-actualisation as students experientially discover how their body and ideas change in relation to their partner.

With a class, I will often introduce the concept by having students interact physically with a chair first. They are instructed to find all the ways they can discover to interact with the chair, including sitting on it, it is sitting on them, turning it to various angle, etc. Once they have exhausted the possibilities, I ask them to do a similar experiment with their scene partner but without touching them. Actor A moves into a random physical position. Actor B looks at them for a moment and then assumes a different physical position in relation to Actor A. They both feel this for a moment, then Actor A steps out, looks at Actor B and makes a new physical relationship with their body. This continues until they can all move seamlessly and quickly from one shape to the next without stopping to think about it. If I have had some resistance, extra nervousness, or giggles, I will often let them continue until they have worked that out of their system and a sense of comfort sets in. I also mention to them that story lines will likely develop as humans love to make things into narratives, but just to let them appear and then dismiss them without moving them forward (Zak, 2014). When actors watch each other for more than about 15 seconds and seem like their ideas for additional physical relationships have run out, I encourage them to go 'over or under' the other actor in some way. Space Shapes can be done regularly in a classroom with different partners to help actors build trust and get used to physical proximity. Afterwards, I once again encourage actors to reflect on the exercise as to when they were comfortable and when they weren't and what made them feel each of those things. This scaffolding step helps actors to better understand their own physical reactions and begin to isolate the nebulous space between discomfort and boundaries.

Fourth Scaffolded Exercise: Mirror Variations

Variations on traditional Mirroring exercises are the basis for the next step in the intimacy scaffolding. These series of increasingly intimate actions help partners be more comfortable both with touch and eye contact. Actors stand about 3 feet apart (1 meter) and place their hands palm to palm with about 4 inches (10 cm) between them. Actor 1 slowly moves their hands as Actor 2 'mirrors' them with the same movement (the right hand is mirrored by the left hand). Actors need to move very slowly so the movement can be exacting, and I cannot tell who the leader is. After they settle into the exercise, I encourage them to add in eye contact – one of the primary goals of the exercise. For many actors eye contact is more intimate than touch and this may cause some discomfort. If it is more than discomfort and is a boundary, actors can look into the '3rd' eye (centre of forehead) instead so they still can use peripheral vision for the hand movement. I have found that this emotionally neutral eye contact is an important rung on the scaffolding for most actors as they develop acting partner intimacy (screen acting in particular relies so heavily on eye contact!).

Variations fend off boredom, challenge their physicality and encourage teamwork while building intimacies. Variations include switching leaders, negotiating movement with no leader, adding full-body physicality to the mirroring, and adding in vocal mirroring. After all of this, they are usually becoming comfortable with each other and having fun.

At this point, I add in palm-to-palm touch as they continue mirroring. This is much easier, and students usually report afterwards that the energy of the touch is fascinating when the primary sense goes from visual to touch. I always give them the option of simply closing the distance between their palms to 1 cm if touch is not comfortable. This is more difficult but the added concentration along with the heat from the others' hand is also worth exploring. If a heavy touch scene will be involved, I sometimes add in the option of touching from palm to elbow as they continue to mirror. Regular reminders to encourage eye contact are usually needed throughout the exercise, and a suggestion to rest and shake out their arms if needed can be helpful.

Fifth Scaffolded Exercise: Touch Visualisation

After all these partnering exercises, I find students are usually ready to enter the most intense part of the process: when they express their touch boundaries to each other. I have found that Pace's and Rikard's Boundary Practice as outlined in *Staging Sex* to be a wonderful tool (2020, pp. 24–39). They frame it as defining 'fences' around parts of the body that are off limits for their scene partner to touch. I explain that in the following exercise, their scene partner will be touching them in the places they give consent.

Inspired by Advanced Consent and Intimacy students' observations that they hadn't had a chance to think about where their boundaries with their acting partner may be before the exercise begins, I added a scaffold just before the Boundary Practice begins. This step allows students to visualise what their partner's touch may be like for them. In addition to preparing themselves for the touch, this pause allows the breathing to slow down. Slow, deep, diaphragmatic breathing has been shown to have calming effects that can help alter emotional states. The diaphragm's phrenic nerve (which allows breathing) connects to the vagus nerve, which connects the heart, lungs, upper digestive tract, and other organs of the chest and abdomen. It can suppress the sympathetic nervous system (which secretes chemicals that can activate the Fight, Flight, Freeze, and Fawn responses) and activate the parasympathetic nervous system creating a calmer, more positive state (Hamasaki, 2020).

I ask students to close their eyes or create a soft focus, as they listen to their breathing for a moment, switching to an introspective attention. After a few moments, they are instructed to use their mind's eye to travel to the top of their head and imagine their scene partner's hand touching them there. Then I talk them through all the non-bathing suit areas slowly giving them time to imagine what the touch will feel like (in my classes and workshops I stipulate that everyone has a fence around all bathing suit areas). I lead them down to the bottom of their feet. Once they've had a chance to visualise the touch it is then time to communicate it.

When time permits, students can also represent the boundaries they visualised graphically, as suggested by a student when we were discussing additional tools to explore boundaries. She felt having a contemplative time to colour a chart that corresponded and communicated her boundaries to her scene partner would be helpful. I agreed to try it as additional sensory modalities are often helpful for communication.

We started with a free body outline found online, added instructions, and then printed one for each student. Markers, crayons, and coloured pencils are provided along with class time to fill in the chart after they've visualised their boundaries with their scene partner. Red indicates an area that is off limits (so at a minimum they all have pelvic areas in red), yellow marks an area that may be available to touch in certain circumstances with specific permission, and green suggests places a partner can touch while working the scene without having to check every time. If time is a concern, students can take the chart home and do it for homework. They then keep the chart with them so they can double-check themselves if their boundaries have shifted and they can remind each other with a visual tool.

TIE's Boundary Practice

Then it is time for Pace's and Rikard's Boundary exercise which works in a three-part process. First, Actor A will use their own hand to touch themselves in all the places on their body Actor B is given permission to touch while working on the scene (not outside of class or in different scenes). Once Actor A has shown where touch can occur on their body, they ask Actor B for their hand and proceed to move Actor B's hands over all the same areas where they just gave permission to be touched (Pace, 2020, pp. 26–27). After this second step is complete Actor B tells Actor A where they saw their fences. Actor A can confirm or correct them as needed. Then they go through the same process with Actor B.

I theorise that this show, touch, tell model works so well because it gives actors multiple steps to test what they think are their own boundaries as well as varying sensory modalities to experience their partner's boundaries. By working on vision, touch, and then verbal reframing, multiple areas of the brain are involved increasing understanding and improving memory (Abiola & Dhindsa, 2012). The repetition also helps actors remember their partner's boundaries in the long term.

While simply discussing boundaries and areas of touch can work of course, these extra steps help students test their own boundaries and remember their partner's boundaries, so they are less likely to accidentally cross them. This process also pre-empts the actors who just say, 'you can touch me anywhere' subtly pressuring their partner to do the same. As the responsibility for learning and remembering their partner's boundaries are transferred to the student by this point, it fulfils the final condition of scaffolding. Check-ins, wherein actors just quickly review their boundaries and communicate any adjustments, are a further extenuation of this transference.

Conclusion

The scaffolded exercises outlined in this chapter build upon the consent and boundary exercises that TIE offers, helping students grow towards the liberatory, student-centred, and engaged pedagogy of hooks. PAR, the methodology reflective of her emancipatory philosophies, is well illustrated throughout. The authority of personal experience, gaining knowledge through action, recognition that the process of conducting research is as important as the outcomes, and the 'critical dialogue' of the participants are all central (Cornish et al., 2023, p. 2). Contingency, fading, and transfer of responsibility, the aspects necessary for educational scaffolding, are also baked into the way these intimacy protocols are structured (Cornish et al., 2023).

I began scaffolding consent and intimacy practices to create a space for authentic and self-actualising work to flourish. When student actors understand their boundaries, have communicated them to others, and have agreements and other tools in place to support them if conflict or harm occurs, actors can be freer to explore material and grow in their craft. Students have given extensive positive feedback and I see their ease with each other when working on a scene with physical intimacy. While there is some anticipatory anxiety before we go through the scaffolded exercises, students relax more, have better eye contact, and make more choices to touch their scene partners than when I haven't used these scaffolded techniques. Students experience less anxiety and save their cognitive load for other acting processes. A student sums it up nicely: 'These exercises just made everything more comfortable and less awkward. Surprisingly, it ended up actually being fun as we got to know each other so much more easily. What a relief!'

Notes

1 While the majority of my consent and staged intimacy training is with Theatrical Intimacy Education, I have also taken relevant classes with Intimacy Directors & Coordinators, Intimacy Coordinators of Color, Intimacy Directors International, Thumbprint Studios, Johns Hopkins University, and Kansas State University.

2 See Ré Arp-Dunham, J. (2019). Page – body – performance: A journey into active analysis and how it helps the actor's body learn. *Stanislavski Studies*, 7(1), 43–56. https://doi.org/10.1080/20567790. 2019.1576107 for how I incorporate cognitive science and active analysis into my work.

3 For a more detailed explanation of the cognitive science, see Arp-Dunham, J. (2024). Stanislavsky and intimacy: The brain-body responds. In *Stanislavsky and intimacy*. Routledge.

4 Pace also outlines a modification to a traditional theatre Circle Game (2020, pp. 20–21) as an additional consent exercise, but I have never been able to make this work, quite possibly due to user error.

References

Abiola, O., & Dhindsa, H. (2012). Improving classroom practices using our knowledge of how the brain works. *International Journal of Environmental & Science Education*, 7(1), 71–81.

Arp-Dunham, J. (2023). Stanislavsky and Intimacy: The brain-body responds. In J. Arp-Dunham (Ed.), *Stanislavsky and Intimacy* (pp. 29–52). Routledge.

Baddeley, A. D. (2007). Working memory, thought, and action. In *Oxford psychology series* (Vol. 45, pp. 556–559). Oxford University Press.

Carleton, R. (2016). Fear of the unknown: One fear to rule them all? *Journal of Anxiety Disorders*, 41, 5–21.

Cornish, F., Breton, N., Moreno-Tabarez, U., Delgado, J., Rua, M., de-Graft Aikins, A., & Hodgetts, D. (2023). Participatory action research. *Nature Reviews Methods Primers*, 3, 34. https://doi. org/10.1038/s43586-023-00214-1

Cowan, N. (2015). George Miller's magical number of immediate memory in retrospect: Observations on the faltering progression of science. *Psychological Review*, 122(3), 536–541. https://doi. org/10.1037/a0039035

Damasio, A. (1994). *Descartes' error: Emotion, reason, and the human brain.* G. P. Putnam.

Fordham Institute. (2021). *Children learn best when they feel safe and valued.* https://fordhaminstitute.org/national/commentary/children-learn-best-when-they-feel-safe-and-valued

Hamasaki, H. (2020). Effects of diaphragmatic breathing on health: A narrative review. *Medicines (Basel)*, 7(10), 65. www.ncbi.nlm.nih.gov/pmc/articles/PMC7602530/

Hausfather, S. J. (1996). Vygotsky and schooling: Creating a social contest for learning. *Action in Teacher Education*, 18, 1–10.

hooks, b. (1994). *Teaching to transgress.* Routledge.

hooks, b. (1997). *Cultural criticism & transformation interview transcript* (M. Patierno, S. Jhally, & H. Hirshorn, Eds.). www.mediaed.org/transcripts/Bell-Hooks-Transcript.pdf

hooks, b. (2015). *Talking back: Thinking feminist, thinking black* (2nd ed.). Routledge.

Intimacy Directors and Coordinators. (2023). *Defining consent: From FRIES to CRISP* (blog). www.idcprofessionals.com/blog/defining-consent-from-fries-to-crisp#:~:text=In%20the%20 past%2C%20many%20intimacy,Informed%2C%20Enthusiastic%2C%20and%20Specific

Joëls, M., Pu, Z., Wiegert, O., Oitzl, M. S., & Krugers, H. J. (2006). Learning under stress: How does it work? *Trends in Cognitive Sciences*, 10(4), 152–158. https://doi.org/10.1016/j.tics. 2006.02.002

Johnson, N. D. (2022). *DEI&A resources: Boundaries & consent. Artists heal.* Workshop resource. www.artistsheal.org/about

Kirschner, P. A., Sweller, J., & Clark, R. E. (2006). Why minimal guidance during instruction does not work: An analysis of the failure of constructivist, discovery, problem-based, experiential, and inquiry-based teaching. *Educational Psychologist*, 41(2), 75–86. https://doi.org/10.1207/ s15326985ep4102_1

Lieberman, L., & Shankman, S. (2016). Fear of the unknown common to many anxiety disorders. *Neuroscience News.* https://neurosciencenews.com/anxiety-disorders-unknown-fear-5558/

Pace, C. (2020). *Best practices.* Theatrical Intimacy Education, Online Workshop. http://www.chelsea pace.com/theatrical-intimacy-education

Pace, C., with contributions from Rikard, L. (2020). *Staging sex: Best practices, tools, and techniques for theatrical intimacy.* Routledge.

Rikard, L., & Villarreal, A. (2023). Focus on impact, not intention: Moving from "safe" spaces to spaces of acceptable risk. *The Journal of Consent-Based Performance*, 2(1).

The Second City. (2023). *How to say "yes, and".* www.secondcity.com/how-to-say-yes-and/

Shah, T., & Rashid, S. (2017). *Applying Vygotsky to adult learning.* www.researchgate.net/publication/322517416

Sigman-Marx, A. (2022). *Building a culture of consent.* Thumbprint Studios, Workshop. https://www.thumbprintstudios.org/events

Skulmowski, A., & Rey, G. D. (2017). Measuring cognitive load in embodied learning settings. *Frontiers in Psychology, 8,* 1–6. https://doi.org/10.3389/fpsyg.2017.01191

Stamatiou, E. (2022). Pierre Bourdieu and actor training: Towards decolonizing and decentering actor training pedagogies. *Theatre, Dance and Performance Training, 13.* https://doi.org/10.1080/19443927.2021.1943509

van de Pol, J., Volman, M., & Beishuizen, J. (2010). Scaffolding in teacher – student interaction: A decade of research. *Educational Psychology Review, 22,* 271–296. https://doi.org/10.1007/s10648-010-9127-6

van Merriënboer, J. J. G., Kirschner, P. A., & Kester, L. (2003). Taking the load off a learner's mind: Instructional design for complex learning. *Educational Psychologist, 38*(1), 5–13. https://doi.org/10.1207/S15326985EP3801_2

Zak, P. (2014). Why your brain loves good storytelling. *Harvard Business Review.* https://hbr.org/2014/10/why-your-brain-loves-good-storytelling

Zingela, Z., Stroud, L., Cronje, J., Fink, M., & van Wyk, S. (2022). The psychological and subjective experience of catatonia: A qualitative study. *BMC Psychology, 10*(1), 173. https://doi.org/10.1186/s40359-022-00885-7. PMID: 35841077; PMCID: PMC9287913.

15 A *Neurocosmopolitan* Approach to Actor Training

Learning from Neurodivergent Ways-of-doing

Zoë Glen

Introduction

This is a proposition of what I view to be a necessary paradigm shift in how we approach neurodiversity within actor training and the inclusion of neurominority students. By this, I refer to students who identify with one or more neurodivergences, such as dyslexia, dyspraxia, autism, attention deficit and hyperactivity disorder (ADHD), dyscalculia, or dysgraphia. I approach this question from the perspective of my own neurodivergence. My neurodivergence encompasses multiple diagnoses, overlapping with each other and fitting in several boxes but also neatly into none. My neurodivergence informs my experience of the roles I take on. It informs my past experiences of being a performance student in a drama school, and my current experience of being a PhD student at a university. It informs my experience as an actor trainer navigating my own neurodivergence as a practitioner within institutions. It amplifies my ability to notice the issues at play for neurodivergent students and informs the questions I ask as an academic.

Academic research around neurodivergence is historically contentious and problematic given that

> [r]esearch regarding atypical development has traditionally been conducted within the framework of the medical model, which assumes that disabilities are pathological in nature: that they are medical diseases and disorders of the body and mind which lead individuals to have deficits and experience functional limitations.
>
> (Dwyer, 2022, p. 91)

Most of the research operates within a deficit model and is conducted by neurotypical researchers and positions neurodivergent people as 'other'. It creates a dominant narrative that neurocognitive differences are something that should be categorised as conditions to be treated and problems to be fixed. This, in my view, leads to the strengths that neurodiversity brings not being given the same weight as its challenges. It has been noted that 'the current balance of research appears overwhelmingly biased towards studying – and treating – individual "deficits" rather than exploring the role that environments, contexts, and society play in disabling individuals' (Dwyer, 2022, p. 91). These assumptions around disability as a deficit have a significant impact on the way that research is conducted surrounding neurodivergence, and the result of this is an idea of disabled people as 'less-than' and as 'other'. Disabled people experience the consequences of this in many aspects of their day-to-day lives, including in educational settings.

My own experiences as a neurodivergent drama school student led me to pursue research on how to better the experiences of neurodivergent students in drama school. Among

DOI: 10.4324/9781003393672-20

several challenging experiences, my reflective writing on one directed production in my training ended up being about my exclusion from it, as this was the only thing I could focus on. In attempting to contextualise this for myself, I came across the work by Daron Oram (2018a; 2018b) on equitable training for dyspraxic and dyslexic students. In this moment, I was struck by both the richness of this emerging body of research and how it validated one part of my neurodivergent identity and acknowledged its challenges. That said, I also noted a research gap concerning how many perspectives on neurodivergent experiences of acting were absent from the literature. Writing on the needs of autistic students and students with ADHD was completely missing, as was writing on other neurodivergences, and the co-occurrences and intersections of these neurotypes.

This chapter builds on some of my previous work on neurodivergence and actor training. In 'Improving Access for Autistic Student Actors: Interrogating the Use of Empathy in Actor-Training Methods' (Glen, 2023), I propose that we take a 'maximising approach' to neurodivergence and actor training and explore how autistic ways of understanding others' emotions could be used to make adaptations to acting exercises that make them more beneficial for all students. This idea of 'maximising' is drawn from Shaun May's writing exploring stand-up comedy with autistic young people and was originally coined by autistic artist Penni Winter (May, 2017). In this context, maximisation is the opposite of normalisation. Normalisation is what I believe to be currently happening within drama schools; with adaptations being focused on how students can fit into environments that were not designed with them in mind.

I now build further on this idea, framing it with neurodiversity theorist Nick Walker's similar concept of *neurocosmopolitanism* to explore the access implications for actor training. This research was presented at the Theatre and Performance Research Association's annual conference in 2022 as part of the performer training working group, where I spoke specifically about the imagination and access within actor training. In this chapter, I further the idea, broadening it to encompass a wider range of neurodivergences and elements of training.

Within my positions as a student, teacher, actor, and academic, I encounter daily reminders of the need for this research. I am reminded when I am speaking with tutors about struggling students and they defend the practices instead of considering adapting them according to student needs. I am reminded when I am listening, as someone who is also sensitive to sound, as access requests of sound-sensitive students are dismissed by programme directors saying 'It's a drama school. You can't expect it not to be noisy'. I am reminded when I notice how a student who does not hide their autistic traits on stage gets feedback that they are 'disrupting the rhythm of the scene'.

These incidents are the product of years of drama schools establishing narrow ideas of what 'acting' looks like and the way it should be done. Such ideas then become the default and lead to students who do not fit this essentially being trained to pretend they do. In this chapter, I am guided by how I have experienced my neurodivergence within various spaces, and by accounts from current and former students who identify as neurodivergent. I frame these with ideas from neurodiversity theory to explore how we can engage with neurodiversity in actor training in a way that aligns with the ideas of the neurodiversity movement, rather than one which aligns with deficit models while using the language of the neurodiversity movement.

In addition to taking an autoethnographic stance to talk broadly about how neurodiversity theory can be applied to actor training, I also draw on semi-structured interviews with neurodivergent drama students to propose ways that this could work in practice. These interviews were conducted in a multi-modal way, with some done through written communication and some through spoken conversation. The responses detailed in this chapter came from eight interviewees, all of whom had different neurodivergent identities. In the conversations, the participants were asked about the challenges they encountered within their training, the examples of accessible practice they encountered, and most significantly how they feel their neurodivergence contributes to their interest and skills as an actor. The questions were structured in a way designed to encourage the sharing of experiences.

Because '[p]henomenology is concerned with the study of experience from the perspective of the individual' (Lester, 1999, p. 1), a phenomenological approach to analysing the interviews seemed productive. Phenomenological approaches 'are powerful for understanding subjective experience, gaining insights into people's motivations and actions, and cutting through the clutter of taken-for-granted assumptions and conventional wisdom' (ibid). This resonated with my interest in neurodivergent students' experiences of their world view, body–mind and training, rather than on prescribed ideas of their 'conditions' or how others perceive them.

In keeping with unpacking 'taken-for-granted assumptions and conventional wisdom', this research is rooted in standpoint epistemology. Ginny Russell writes:

> Standpoint theorists support the idea that people with lived experience have expertise in their own area. This is the theoretical epistemic stance that underpins this volume. It assumes standpoints are relative and cannot be evaluated by any absolute criteria, but makes the assumption that the oppressed (autistic people) are less biased (or more impartial) than the privileged (NT people).
>
> (Russell in Kapp, 2020, p. 287)

Standpoint epistemology's recognition of the value of subjective knowledge based on lived experience is pertinent to this enquiry. Viewing neurodivergent lived experience as a valuable source of knowledge is particularly useful as many experiences of neurodivergent people are poorly documented or missing from published literature.

The Research Gap

Drama schools have high levels of neurodivergent students. On the BA Acting: collaborative and devised theatre programme at The Royal Central School of Speech and Drama in the United Kingdom, 'after auditioning around 5000 students each year, the course can have a cohort of students that sometimes has 70% with some sort of learning difference' (Oram, 2018b, p. 56). For comparison, it is estimated that around 15–20% of the general population are neurodivergent. This is reflected in my experience as a practitioner. In any cohort of students I encounter, there is a high percentage of the cohort who are neurodivergent, even without accounting for those who are undiagnosed or who haven't disclosed their needs.

Despite this, research into the intersection of neurodivergence and actor training is very much still an emerging field. Work has been published investigating the issues for dyslexic actors when working with text and how this might be addressed (Leveroy, 2012, 2013; Whitfield, 2013, 2019). Oram has also published work on the experience of actors with dyslexia and dyspraxia learning psychophysical voice training methods (2018a, 2018b) and on equitable online actor training for neurodivergent students (2020). Tanya Zybutz and Colin Farquharson have also written on the support needs of dyspraxic acting students (2016).

The last two decades have seen higher education programmes designed specifically for autistic and learning-disabled artists. Disability-led arts organisations Graeae, Access All Areas and Mind the Gap have all partnered with universities or conservatoires to deliver this specific training, and some literature exists about training learning-disabled artists (Gee & Hargrave, 2011). Further research on learning disability and acting also includes 'The Silent Approach' as developed by Vanessa Brooks, artistic director of Separate Doors, a company which is a 'platform for the work of vocational actors in the United Kingdom with learning disabilities and neuro-diversities' (Separate Doors, 2023). Brooks' approach is based on 'Stanislavskian precepts of action, objective, given circumstances and character' and is described as 'a dynamic way to direct general audience-facing theatre to standard timescales with casts with all kinds of neuro-divergencies' (Brooks, n.d.). It came about to work with non-verbal learning-disabled artists in text-based plays (ibid). Academic literature also writes on approaches to working with learning-disabled actors (Palmer & Hayhow, 2009; Hayhow in Whitfield, 2021) but it focuses on working with learning-disabled artists in specific provision, not in mainstream/neurodiverse settings.

In *Inclusivity and Equality in Performer Training* (Whitfield, 2021), various chapters explore neurodiversity and actor training. Dyslexia and dyspraxia in actor training are well covered here in a range of chapters. Strategies are given for using actioning to work with text for dyslexic actors; using digital technology to support dyslexic students with Shakespeare, and how the use of imagery, sound, and somatic approaches can be effective when working with dyslexic students, both in practical and essay writing context. These essays provide significant guidance on teaching performance students who are dyslexic and dyspraxic, with significant recurring themes of working with classical text and using mediums other than language to access text.

This collection also offers a chapter on Aphantasia in the Theatre Classroom (Black in Whitfield, 2021, pp. 43–61) and on Steps toward an Anti-discriminatory Approach to Neurodivergence in Actor Training (Oram in Whitfield, 2021, pp. 61–77). This edited collection is currently the only one of its kind. Given the lack of knowledge in the field previously, it makes a considerable contribution to advancing the information available on training neurodivergent actors.

That said, this field of research is still sparse, and I want to highlight two critiques of the current body of knowledge, especially in relation to the multiplicity and intersectionality of neurodivergent identities. For example, the aforementioned research by Oram, Whitfield, and Leveroy focuses on dyslexia and dyspraxia, inviting further research on other neurodivergences. This may be due to both higher incidences, or diagnosis rates of these neurotypes, which are diagnosed in around 10% of the population; and to their existing association with creativity. This disproportionate emphasis on dyslexia and dyspraxia sidelines the needs of students who are autistic or have ADHD or other neurodivergences, such as dysgraphia, dyscalculia, Tourette's syndrome, and sensory processing disorder. It also plays into the stigma that certain neurodivergences, such as autism, are associated with lower levels of creativity (Baron, 2008; Quirici, 2015). This is not necessarily the fault of the individual pieces of literature, but instead a reflection of the gaps in neurodivergent representation in the arts and academia overall. Some neurominority groups are more accepted than others within these fields, and this shows in the literature that is available.

Also, with the focus being so specifically on dyslexia and dyspraxia, the idea of neurodiversity as a spectrum and the intersections between these diagnostic categories is also lost. For example, students diagnosed as autistic have an 85% chance of also being dyspraxic (Kilroy et al., 2022, p. 1), students diagnosed as dyspraxic have a 40% chance of also having ADHD (Kirby & Sugden, 2007, p. 3), and students diagnosed as being autistic have a 50–57% chance of also having ADHD (Hours et al., 2022, p. 4). It is also possible to experience certain traits of neurodivergence without meeting the clinical threshold for a particular diagnosis. Current research leaves a gap in knowledge regarding students who experience a co-occurrence of multiple neurodivergences, or whose neurodivergent experience and identity does not fit neatly into a diagnostic box.

Furthermore, my second critique of the current literature in the field is that it primarily focuses on adaptation/reasonable adjustment. The current set-up of drama school curricula contextualises this angle that the existing research takes. Reasonable adjustments are part of the frameworks of UK higher education that drama schools fall within. As Oram writes, '[t]he predominant theoretical model of learning difference within tertiary education is the psycho-medical model of learning difference, which seeks to objectify dyslexia [and dyspraxia] as a condition' (2018a, p. 281). However, adapting practices based in neurotypical processes to allow neurodivergent students to undertake them, is still ultimately a way of bringing neurodivergent students into neurotypical ways-of-doing, rather than allowing neurodivergent ways-of-doing to inform what is done. We are adapting methods so that neurodivergent students can act like neurotypical students. So that they can do, or *appear to be doing*, the same processes as their neurotypical peers.

In this, we focus on what neurodivergent students cannot do, and how we can support them to do those things, rather than focusing on what they can do. We make reasonable adjustments to neurotypical ways-of-doing so that neurodivergent students can seem to be doing them, but we do not do the opposite. We do not consider what neurotypical students can learn from neurodivergent ways-of-doing. In other words, even though such reasonable adjustments have improved the experience of neurodivergent students, they might still stigmatise them and distract from the opportunities for actor training to learn from neurodivergent students.

It is important, especially when considering actor training within drama schools, that we acknowledge the complexity of neurodivergence, and the tensions present with viewing it as a set of diagnostic categories that are neatly separated. This is particularly true in a higher education setting, as many students only realise they are neurodivergent during their studies, and embark on the process of formal diagnosis mid-way through their training. There are also significant barriers to professional diagnosis within the UK healthcare system and this raises issues when institutional structures require proof of formal diagnosis to give accommodations.

Therefore, there is a need for an approach that shifts beyond typical inclusivity interventions that adjust training based on individual conditions and that can supplement understanding of different neurotypes by providing a space that is designed for a neurodiverse group and can accommodate all students. I propose that an important next step in this research is to approach the topic through theory from the neurodiversity paradigm.

Bringing the Neurodiversity Paradigm to Actor Training

The neurodiversity movement takes as its core idea the premise that neurocognitive variability between humans is a natural form of diversity, the same as any other and that it should be treated as such rather than pathologised (Singer, 1998). The neurodiversity movement has developed on these ideas, positioning autism and other neurodivergences as natural forms of human diversity, rather than medical deficits. Judy Singer notes that this is not a scientific term, but a political one, stating that 'it simply names an indisputable fact about our planet, that no two human minds are exactly alike, and uses it to name a paradigm for social change' (Singer, 1998, p. 3).

Jacqueline den Houting offers a further summary of the ideas of the neurodiversity paradigm, noting that 'all forms of neurological diversity are valuable, and that such diversity should be respected as a natural form of human variation' (2019, p. 272). The paradigm acknowledges that neurodiversity is subject to societal power structures in the same way that other forms of diversity are. Therefore, under this paradigm, neurodivergent refers to anyone whose neurological function is different to what is deemed acceptable by these power structures. We can consider that these power structures are also present in actor training environments and that some ways-of-doing and skillsets are privileged over others.

A key theorist in this area is Nick Walker, whose writing on neurodiversity follows from Singer and others to both give an overview of current terminology and its working definitions and to propose new concepts. Walker writes:

> When it comes to human neurodiversity, the dominant paradigm in the world today is what I refer to as the pathology paradigm. The long term wellbeing and empowerment of autistics and members of other neurocognitive minority groups hinges on our ability to create a paradigm shift – a shift from the pathology paradigm to the neurodiversity paradigm. Such a shift must happen internally, within the consciousness of individuals, and must also be propagated in the cultures in which we live.
>
> (2021, p. 16)

As I have noted above, while the ways we currently discuss neurodiversity in actor training use the language of the neurodiversity paradigm, they are in many ways in line with the pathology paradigm in ideas. The culture shift that Walker suggests is yet to happen within actor training.

In *Neuroqueer Heresies* (2021), Walker explores definitions of neurodiversity, language, and its relationship to autistic empowerment. She discusses the idea of *neurocosmopolitanism*, which means that embracing neurodivergent strengths, processes, and ways-of-doing has the potential to teach and enhance society overall (2021, p. 73). She also suggests the term neuroqueer which suggests positing neurodivergence as a form of neurological queerness in line with queer theory and recognising the intersection of neurodivergent and queer identities. Neurocosmopolitanism is a term that was coined by both Walker and Ralph Savarese (Walker, 2021; Savarese, 2014) independently of each other, applying the ideas of cosmopolitanism to neurodiversity. Walker gives the following definition:

> [T]he open minded embracing of human diversity . . . traditionally used in regard to the diversity of cultures, ethnicities and nationalities; cosmopolite literally translated as citizen of the world. The cosmopolite regards all of humanity as ultimately part of a single global community – an essential unity which is in no way invalidated by the differences among us, and which in fact has the potential to be greatly enriched by those differences when we engage with them in a spirit of humility, respect and openness to learning.
>
> (Walker, 2021, p. 73)

The benefits of applying these ideas of cosmopolitanism to neurodiversity theory are described by Walker:

> Neurocosmopolitanism goes beyond this baseline of acceptance, just as cosmopolitanism goes beyond mere tolerance of cultural differences. The Neurocosmopolitan seeks

to actively engage with and preserve human neurodiversity, and to honour, explore and cultivate its creative potentials.

(2021, p. 75)

Another key aspect of this idea is that 'A neurocosmopolitan perspective privileges no body-mind as the "natural" default way of being, nor as more "normal" or intrinsically correct than any other' (ibid). Given this, I suggest that a *neurocosmopolitan* lens is a useful one to apply to training methods, particularly those from practitioners such as Konstantin Stanislavski, Michael Chekhov, or Sanford Meisner, whose practices are so ingrained in the Western actor training canon. I explore how the processes of neurominority actors can be incorporated into them, with a dual function of celebrating neurodiversity and enhancing the training method for everyone. I propose that to move towards a more neuroinclusive version of actor training, we must take a *neurocosmopolitan* approach to acting and consider how the processing styles of neurominorities can open new possibilities within actor training. A *neurocosmopolitan* approach asks how neurodivergent strengths, experiences, and ways-of-doing can inform curriculums and pedagogies; how this can enrich actor-training environments for all students, and; how the idea of a default, normal ways of acting can be left behind altogether.

Application in Practice

To consider how this may work in practice, I conducted qualitative interviews with eight neurodivergent participants about the challenges and positives of their training experience. In these descriptions of challenges, strengths, and experiences, several common themes emerged. Some of these were particular to a specific neurodivergent identity, and some were a commonality across multiple neurodivergences. These form the basis of this research, filtered through my own autoethnographic stance, allowing for examples to be given of how a *neurocosmopolitan* approach to acting could work in practice. Within the participant group, four students identified as having ADHD; two identified as being autistic and ADHD; one identified as autistic, and one identified as dyslexic and dyspraxic. Four students studied at Rose Bruford College, two at The Royal Central School of Speech and Drama, one at East 15 Acting School, and one at Trinity Laban Conservatoire of Music and Dance. Participants responded to an open call on social media to discuss their experiences with me.

Challenges

It is important to consider the challenges that neurodivergent students currently experience alongside considering their strengths. A *neurocosmopolitan* approach to actor training requires systemic barriers to first be removed. I wish to exemplify that neurodivergent people have skill profiles of strengths and challenges, just as neurotypical people do – the difference is that neurodivergent skill profiles are not supported by societal or institutional structures.

The challenges of their training that interviewees described are laid out in this section in correspondence to the neurodivergent identities of the students who described them, but I have also endeavoured to show clearly where there are overlaps of experience.

The three out of eight students who identified as autistic noted difficulty with 'lots of last-minute changes to scheduling' that were justified as part of 'learning to adapt' (Participant A, personal communication, 2023)[1] to survive in the industry. Autistic students also noted inaccessibility of communication and the social environment, describing difficulty with 'rehearsal room hierarchies and relationships', 'difficulty understanding feedback, sometimes feeling like rejection', and 'finding it difficult understanding when I have space to speak in a group discussion' (Participant B, personal communication, 2023).

The rejection-sensitive dysphoria noted in the difficulties with receiving feedback described above was also a challenge faced by students with ADHD. 'Rejection-sensitive dysphoria' is an experience that is part of Autism and ADHD, described as 'when you experience severe emotional pain because of a failure or feeling rejected. This condition is linked to ADHD and experts suspect it happens due to differences in brain structure' (Cleveland Clinic, 2022). Students noted 'feeling kinda stupid' (Participant H, personal communication, 2023); 'feeling anxious and more self-conscious that I couldn't focus' (Participant E, personal communication, 2023) and finding training 'very hard on (my) self-esteem and confidence' (Participant C, personal communication, 2023). Difficulties with confidence also are noted by dyslexic and dyspraxic students. A dyslexic actor (Participant D, personal communication, 2023) described that 'it messed up my confidence as an actor because I have to put so much more effort to focus on reading, instead of putting it in my performance'. This is echoed by the current literature on dyslexia and acting. Oram writes of noticing a 'self-conscious disengagement from the work' (2018a, p. 278) from his dyslexic and dyspraxic students, and Leveroy notes effective support as being essential to dyslexic students having positive identity (2013, p. 2). This existing literature aligns with what was disclosed by participants in this research regarding the challenges with confidence and self-esteem experienced by neurodivergent students.

A further challenge faced by both autistic students and students with ADHD was sensory inaccessibility. The two most described issues were lots of overlapping noise in the space, and strobe lights being used in productions. Participant C noted 'having to miss lessons due to overstimulation' (personal communication, 2023).

Another challenge experienced generally had to do with a lack of awareness from the teaching staff. Students noted not being able to 'take a break from the space to recover' (Participant B, personal communication, 2023) and that 'with various external directors to the school can often be tricky translating my learning needs to them in a way they understand/ respect as valid' (Participant C, personal communication, 2023). One student mentioned 'several occasions where ableist language has been used without content warning or any sensitivity' (Participant A, personal communication, 2023). When discussing what would have made their training better, answers included: 'An all-round improved understanding from staff and students of neurodivergence' (Participant B, personal communication, 2023) and there being 'any discourse around access/accommodations' (Participant A, personal communication, 2023). Disability awareness training for staff was suggested among interventions that would have improved students' experience of their training, alongside 'having better ways to deal with my own internalised ableism' (Participant H, personal communication, 2023).

These challenges provide insight into some of the barriers to learning that students experience within the current set-up of actor training. These can be viewed as examples of normalisation. Expecting students to fit themselves into unsuitable sensory environments, excusing inaccessible practice as 'training for the industry', and a lack of education and awareness from staff are all factors that put neurodivergent students in a position of having to normalise themselves to hide their distress at the environment, or to hide neurodivergent traits around staff who lack awareness.

Positives and Strengths

Participants were also asked to contribute positive experiences they had during their training experience, allowing the identification of good practices and opportunities that can be taken forward by other actor trainers. Many noted enjoying the practical nature of their training. For example, participant C wrote that 'the practical side to actor training has often meant I've felt engaged and able to express my left-of-field creativity' (Participant C, personal communication, 2023). Another wrote 'I think actor-training appeals to the part of me that needs to move, to be in my body' (Participant B, personal communication, 2023). Similarly, Participant E testified that 'the rehearsal room felt like my safe space to be able to have shoes off and fidget and move my body' (Participant E, personal communication, 2023).

A key part of these conversations around experiences of neurodivergence in actor training focused on how neurodivergent strengths can contribute to skills and interest in acting. Students with ADHD experienced their levels of energy and hyperfocus as being contributors to their performance skills, as is demonstrated with observations such as '[c]onstant energy is always a plus. The hyper focus also makes me incredibly alive and present onstage' (Participant F, personal communication, 2023) and 'the state of such full focus but still being able to play and react in real-time' (Participant G, personal communication, 2023). A *neurocosmopolitan* approach could embrace this, incorporating higher energy and engagement activities into warm-up or preparatory activities where stillness and mindfulness are often favoured. This would validate the idea that being ready for performance may look different for everyone and encourage student awareness of their own individual preferences.

Autistic students also noted the benefits of hyperfocus, or of having a 'special interest in theatre' (Participant B, personal communication, 2023). The autistic students who contributed also noted how their experience of masking had contributed to the development of their skills. Among autistic communities, masking can be described as 'the suppression of aspects of self and identity to "fly under the radar" or "appear normal," using conscious (i.e. mimicking facial expressions) or unconscious (i.e. unintentionally suppressing aspects of one's identity) means' (Miller et al., 2021, p. 331).

Autistic students made observations such as 'I think my fascination with characters is related to my exploration of masking and how I present myself around different people' (Participant A, personal communication, 2023) and 'my acting abilities are helped by my desire to understand people better' (Participant B, personal communication, 2023). Autistic students also noted enjoying alternative ways of communicating, with one student observing: 'I enjoy communicating in styles other than speech' (Participant B, personal communication, 2023). By validating these ways-of-doing, we can open a range of possibilities for communication on stage and beyond.

Both autistic students and students with ADHD noted being 'able to think outside of the box and overcome obstacles in ways no one would think' (Participant F, personal communication, 2023), 'seeing things differently' (Participant C, personal communication, 2023) and 'having different thought patterns to other people' (Participant B, personal communication, 2023) as useful to their performance abilities. These strengths align with those noted in the existing literature on neurodivergence. Oram notes that positive attributes often recognised in dyslexic learners, such as creative thinking skills and big-picture problem-solving, are aligned with ideal traits for a student on an acting course (Oram, 2018a, p. 279). Whitfield also notes the visual thinking strengths of dyslexic students (2018a, p. 2). So, from these existing sources in combination with these participant contributions, we can consider that strengths in creative thinking are observed across multiple neurodivergences.

Other ways that students experience their neurodivergence as a strength during their training include 'My organisational skills are definitely attributable to my autism, as are my skills in written communication (e.g. emails to industry professionals and staff, essay writing)' (Participant A, personal communication, 2023) and 'my own pleasure and understanding of the sensory world has led me to focus on creating/directing/performing in sensory participant led work' (Participant E, personal communication, 2023). The strengths that these students have self-attributed to their neurodivergence show the wide range of skills that neurodivergence can bring to acting. Therefore, a training space that takes a *neurocosmopolitan* approach, and which allows equal validation of both neurodivergent and neurotypical skills profiles, can illuminate how acknowledging the multiplicity and intersectionality of abilities in the training space invites the multifaceted development of all trainees.

Applying A *Neurocosmopolitan* Approach to the Canon

Having explored the range of strengths that neurodivergent students bring to their performance training, I now move to contextualise why considering both strengths and challenges simultaneously is so important, giving some broad examples of the difference between adaptation, or reasonable adjustment, and a *neurocosmopolitan* approach to acting. In this, I refer to various practitioners whose ideas are commonly taught within Western actor-training settings.

To begin with a better-documented neurodivergence, dyslexic students have noted difficulties working with text when exploring methods that advocate for a lot of textual analysis before exploring the material practically. These students prefer to learn through kinaesthetic means. Reasonable adjustments to this have been noted within research, including the breaking of the text down into chunks, and thinking about the overall (holistic) sense of the text first (Leveroy, 2013) A *neurocosmopolitan* approach would take the angle of using the dyslexic impulse to work things out kinaesthetically as a key part of practice and curriculum, rather than supporting dyslexic students to engage with text just as non-dyslexic students are doing. Therefore, this would mean that the whole group, not only the dyslexic students, would explore the material kinaesthetically. This would have the potential to teach non-dyslexic students skills in exploring and understanding material through the body, meaning they get to learn from dyslexic ways of processing.

To give a further example, I now draw on the autistic strengths that respondents described to invite actor trainers to explore new approaches to characterisation. Autistic students reported how their ability to mask enhanced their acting abilities. As noted above, masking, or 'camouflaging', is a common behaviour in autistic people, described as 'behaviours that hide or mask aspects of oneself from others, or to 'pass' everyday social interactions' (Cage & Troxell-Whitman, 2019, 1900).

Many autistic people observe that through constant masking they are very knowledgeable about the behaviours of others. In 'Stim: An Autistic Anthology', one contributor notes of growing up autistic:

> [y]ou study the people around you like the smallest anthropologist in the world. There is a secret language that lives in people's bodies, in the air that hangs around them. You take it apart and you piece it back together like a puzzle.
>
> (SM in Huxley-Jones, 2020, p. 188)

In a YouTube video on autistic masking, actress and autism advocate Paige Layle states that 'acting to me made sense because that's how life was like, except someone else told me what to do instead of me trying to figure it out' (Layle, 2021, 8:10–8:42) Autistic actress Chloé Hayden has also spoken on how growing up feeling as if she was always performing developed her acting skills (2023, pp. 208–213).

Autistic students echo these sentiments when they note how masking, and the analytical observation of others they do to achieve this enhances their acting skills. This is due to reasons such as feeling as though they are performing all the time by masking to be accepted by others and as a result, having developed skills in this area, and spending a lot of time observing others' body language and behaviour to understand social dynamics.

Some practices that are commonly taught in drama schools take a very different approach to this. The ability to instinctively understand what another is thinking or feeling is highly privileged within actor training. A useful example to demonstrate this is the Meisner technique, with its basis in the idea that actors should act before they think' (Hart in Bartow, 2008, p. 54).

In the repetition exercise, actors are asked to sit opposite each other and to, after a series of back-and-forth objective observations, make statements about their scene partners' emotional state based on an instinctive reading of changes in body language. This is to be done spontaneously, without thinking about it. I found this to be challenging in my experience as an autistic student whose experience of understanding other people comes from an analytical thought process.

In this instance, one way to take a *neurocosmopolitan* approach to acting would be to listen to how autistic students experience reading others and to take their methods of analysing others' behaviour and then performing it into training. I have previously written on how this could be used to adapt and enhance practices such as Meisner, suggesting adaptations to the repetition exercise. In the following extract, I explain what this exercise could look like if more analytical ways of 'reading' others were welcomed into the technique:

For this exercise to accommodate this, autistic ways of empathising, the exercise would need to change to be something like this:

- Before beginning the exercise, the actors decide on a simple scenario that they can draw on during the observations, giving the interaction a set of given circumstances.
- Next, the actors sit opposite each other, or can be in a different configuration if it better suits the circumstances and begin the objective observations as in the original exercise.
- In this new version of the exercise, the need for instantaneous response without thought is removed. Providing the actors follow the rule that the observations must be what they believe to be accurate and that the parameters of each stage of the exercise (i.e., moving from objective into subjective observations), then they are welcome to achieve this task as they wish.

(Glen, 2023, p. 12)

This is an example of applying autistic processes to improving existing practice, and I note from workshopping this exercise with a neurodiverse group that this can reduce the risk of personal tensions coming into the exercise for all students, due to the parameters of a specific scenario being added. It also has the effect of opening new options of ways of relating to each other, giving all actors an element of choice, and the chance to figure out what works best for them. Here, autistic ways-of-doing allow non-autistic students to learn a way of working with emotion that is not reliant on feeling the feelings of other people, or on summoning intangible states of empathy.

A further area that a *neurocosmopolitan* approach could be applied to is focus. Autistic students and students with ADHD reported that the ability to hyperfocus improved their 'stage presence' and allowed them to give a lot to the work. Hyperfocus has been described within the medical model as '[a] clinical phenomenon of 'locking on' to a task in patients with ADHD who have a difficulty of shifting their attention from one subject to another, especially if the subject is about their interests' (Conner in Ashinoff & Abu-Akel, 2021, p. 4.) In other words, hyperfocus can be understood as

> a more specific (and perhaps extreme) type of sustained attention in which the individual's behaviour is controlled for a long period of time by a task which is 'non-routine' or of interest to him/her, to the point that his/her awareness of the environment is considerably diminished.
>
> (Sklar, 2013, p. 20)

The links between ADHD/autistic hyperfocus and acting skills have not been previously researched, and would benefit from further exploration. This is an interesting area to explore due to its links to ideas of 'flow state'. The benefits of flow state in actor training have been explored by Aphrodite Evangelatou who comments on their use for finding pleasure in training even when negative emotions are activated (2021, pp. 21–39) and Marc Silberschatz who notes the parallels between flow state and Stanislavski's practice (Silberschatz, 2013, pp. 13–23).

Hyperfocus can be entered when a neurodivergent student is engaged in something that is interesting to them and at a particular level of stimulation. While often elusive and hard to initiate at will, I have found in my own experiences of ADHD and while working with ADHD students, it is often helpful to consider how to construct an idea of what factors lead to hyperfocus. For example, to find hyperfocus in a moment of performance, I may give myself a certain number of small tasks, such as physical or vocal choices, selecting an amount that is achievable but that provides the level of mental stimulation to find a state of hyperfocus and the presence that comes with it.

To take a *neurocosmopolitan* approach to this could be to encourage students to explore the factors that affect their focus while performing. In other words, to experiment with how much they need to be doing internally to enter the state of hyperfocus, or the similar 'flow state'. This approach is aligned with Phillip Zarrilli's phenomenology of acting (2019) and we can consider generally that a phenomenology of acting may be a strong basis for a *neurocosmopolitan* actor training, due to the focus on individual experience. The benefits of this for all students are that they gain a greater awareness of themselves as a performer by considering focus in a similar way to how someone with ADHD may and that through this, they can develop focus as a skill, rather than as an intangible, and therefore unreliable, thing. One respondent with ADHD said: 'I also think that because I've had to learn how to force certain levels of focus/alertness, I can do that on stage easier' Participant E, (personal communication, 2023), indicating the possibility of focus as a skill that can be learnt.

As demonstrated in these ideas, the overarching implication is that we can consider how alongside adjusting practices created for neurotypical thought processes, we can use neurodivergent processes and strengths to lead us in both adapting and creating practice. While the outcomes may still be changes to components of existing exercises, there is a crucial difference with this approach. *Neurocosmopolitanism* moves us away from focusing on what neurodivergent students can't do and removing that element from the training, and into a space where we are adding. A *neurocosmopolitan* approach asks what neurodivergent students excel at, adds that to the training, and invites everyone else in the space to also engage in it. This provides us opportunity to discover new ways to approach acting and leads to more accessible and flexible training.

These examples provided are beginning points: provocations of things to explore with a neurodiverse cohort of students. It is important to note that taking a *neurocosmopolitan* approach is not about ranking existing practices on a scale of least to most *neurocosmopolitan*. Neurodivergent access is not one-size-fits-all, and two neurodivergent people may have completely different profiles of strengths and challenges. Instead, *neurocosmopolitanism* allows us to respond to the array of different needs that arise because of the intersectional neurodivergent identities in the room; knowing that the resulting changes to the practice may be different with every different group of students and finding celebration and curiosity in that.

For this approach to create a long-term shift, first there must be an increase in the knowledge about neurodiversity that staff have identified in interviews as lacking. If institutions were to advocate for a *neurocosmopolitan* approach to be taken overall, this would require staff to be able to discuss neurodiversity using language that does not belong to the deficit model and considering the varying strengths and challenges of a neurodiverse cohort as something to be explored. We must approach neurodiversity as a fact of any group of students, or indeed of any group of people, rather than adjusting canonical practice through a lens of deficit when we encounter neurodivergent students.

A *neurocosmopolitan* approach necessitates a shift to a more collaborative, facilitated environment where we ask each other questions about our experiences and processes: 'How are you approaching this? What makes this easy for you? What makes this hard for you? How can we learn from each other? How are we all approaching this task differently? Where is the joy and potential in that?' There is also the potential for this to benefit understanding of each other across all intersectional identities, functioning as an invitation to celebrate what different experiences and skills can add to a space.

With this, we open new possibilities, and through a student-centred approach overhaul the deficit-model-based approach that actor training has taken so far, embracing both the range of neurodivergent identities, and identities in general, that are present in any group, and those whose experiences do not fit neatly into the boxes created by the medical model.

Note

1 As described in the introduction to this chapter, communications with participants took various forms, including emails, voice messages, and conversations. The format of conversation was chosen by each participant in line with their personal communication needs and preferences.

References

Anonymous personal communication. (2023). Conducted January – March, London UK.

Ashinoff, B. K., & Abu-Akel, A. (2021). Hyperfocus: The forgotten frontier of attention. *Psychological Research*, *85*(1), 1–19. https://doi.org/10.1007/s00426-019-01245-8

Baron, M. (2008). Autism – a creative process? Poetry, poets, imagination. *Popular Narrative Media*, *1*(1), 103–113. https://doi.org/10.3828/pnm.1.1.11

Bartow, A. (2008). *Handbook of acting techniques*. Nick Hern.

Brooks, V. (n.d.). *Vanessa Brooks: Producer writer & director* [Professional Portfolio]. Vanessa Brooks. Retrieved October 23, 2023, from https://vanessabrooks2020.com/

Cage, E., & Troxell-Whitman, Z. (2019). Understanding the reasons, contexts and costs of camouflaging for autistic adults. *Journal of Autism and Developmental Disorders*, 49(5), 1899–1911. https://doi.org/10.1007/s10803-018-03878-x

Cleveland Clinic. (2022). *Rejection sensitive dysphoria (RSD): Symptoms & treatment*. Retrieved October 30, 2023, from https://my.clevelandclinic.org/health/diseases/24099-rejection-sensitive-dysphoria-rsd

den Houting, J. (2019). Neurodiversity: An insider's perspective. *Autism*, 23(2), 271–273. https://doi.org/10.1177/1362361318820762

Dwyer, P. (2022). The neurodiversity approach(es): What are they and what do they mean for researchers? *Human Development*, 66(2), 73–92. https://doi.org/10.1159/000523723

Evangelatou, A. (2021). Konstantin Stanislavski and Michael Chekhov: Tracing the two practitioners' "lures" for emotional activation. *Stanislavski Studies*, 9(1), 21–39.

Gee, E., & Hargrave, M. (2011). A proper actor? The politics of training for learning disabled actors. *Theatre, Dance and Performance Training*, 2(1), 34–53. https://doi.org/10.1080/19443927.2011.545252

Glen, Z. (2023). Access for autistic student-actors: Interrogating the role of empathy within actor-training methods. *Theatre, Dance and Performance Training*, 14(1), 57–73. https://doi.org/10.1080/19443927.2022.2095428

Hayden, C. (2022). *Different, not less: A neurodivergent's guide to embracing your true self and finding your happily ever after*. Allen & Unwin.

Hours, C., Recasens, C., Baleyte, J. M. (2022, February 28). ASD and ADHD comorbidity: What are we talking about? *Front Psychiatry*, 13, 837424. https://doi.org/10.3389/fpsyt.2022.837424. PMID: 35295773; PMCID: PMC8918663.

Huxley-Jones, L. (2020). *Stim: An autism anthology*. Retrieved October 5, 2021, from https://unbound.com/books/stim/

Kilroy, E., Ring, P., Hossain, A., Nalbach, A., Butera, C., Harrison, L., Jayashankar, A., Vigen, C., Aziz-Zadeh, L., & Cermak, S. A. (2022). Motor performance, praxis, and social skills in autism spectrum disorder and developmental coordination disorder. *Autism Research: Official Journal of the International Society for Autism Research*, 15(9), 1649–1664. https://doi.org/10.1002/aur.2774

Kirby, A., & Sugden, D. A. (2007, April). Children with developmental coordination disorders. *Journal of the Royal Society of Medicine*, 100(4), 182–186. https://doi.org/10.1177/014107680710011414. PMID: 17404341; PMCID: PMC1847727.

Layle, P. (2021). *What is masking? | Autism & how masking makes me feel* [Video]. https://neurodivergentinsights.com/blog/what-is-masking-in-autism

Lester, S. (1999). *An introduction to phenomenological research*. Stan Lester Developments.

Leveroy, D. C. (2013). Enabling performance: Dyslexia, (dis) ability and "reasonable adjustment". *Theatre, Dance and Performance Training*, 4(1), 87–101. https://doi.org/10.1080/19443927.2012.748687

May, S. (2017). Autism and comedy: Using theatre workshops to explore humour with adolescents on the spectrum. *Research in Drama Education: The Journal of Applied Theatre and Performance*, 22(3), 436–445.

Miller, D., Rees, J., & Pearson, A. (2021). "Masking is life": Experiences of masking in autistic and nonautistic adults. *Autism in Adulthood: Challenges and Management*, 3(4), 330–338. https://doi.org/10.1089/aut.2020.0083

Oram, D. (2018a). Finding a way: More tales of dyslexia and dyspraxia in psychophysical actor training. *Voice and Speech Review*, 12(3), 276–294. https://doi.org/10.1080/23268263.2018.1518375

Oram, D. (2018b). Losing sight of land: Tales of dyslexia and dyspraxia in psychophysical actor training. *Theatre, Dance and Performance Training*, 9(1), 53–67. https://doi.org/10.1080/19443927.2017.1415955

Oram, D. (2020). The heuristic pedagogue: Navigating myths and truths in pursuit of an equitable approach to voice training. *Theatre, Dance and Performance Training*, 11(3), 300–309. https://doi.org/10.1080/19443927.2020.1788272

Palmer, J., & Hayhow, R. (2009). *Learning disability and contemporary theatre: Devised theatre, physical theatre, radical theatre*. Full Body and the Voice.

Quirici, M. (2015). Geniuses without imagination: Discourses of autism, ability, and achievement. *Journal of Literary & Cultural Disability Studies*, 9(1), 71–88, 121. www.proquest.com/docview/1664941063/abstract/203814352ADD441EPQ/1

Russell, G. (2020). Critiques of the neurodiversity movement. In S. K. Kapp (Ed.), *Autistic community and the neurodiversity movement: Stories from the frontline* (pp. 287–303). Springer. https://doi.org/10.1007/978-981-13-8437-0_21

Savarese, R. (2014). *What some autistics can teach us about poetry: A neurocosmopolitan approach.* Oxford University Press. Retrieved May 4, 2023.

Silberschatz, M. (2013). Creative state/flow state: Flow theory in Stanislavsky's practice. *New Theatre Quarterly*, 29(1), 13–23. https://doi.org/10.1017/S0266464X1300002X

Separate Doors. (2016). *Separate doors.* Vanessa Brooks. Retrieved April 17, 2023, from https://vanessabrooks2020.com/separate-doors/

Singer, J. (1998). *Neurodiversity: The birth of an idea.* https://www.worldcat.org/oclc/1039095077

Sklar, R. H. (2013). *Hyperfocus in adult ADHD: An EEG study of the differences in cortical activity in resting and arousal states* [Thesis]. http://ujdigispace.uj.ac.za/handle/10210/8640

Walker, N. (2021). *Neuroqueer heresies: Notes on the neurodiversity paradigm, autistic empowerment, and postnormal possibilities.* Autonomous Press.

Whitfield, P. (2013). Shakespeare, pedagogy and dyslexia. *Voice and Speech Review*, 6(1), 254–262.

Whitfield, P. (2019). *Teaching strategies for neurodiversity and dyslexia in actor training: Sensing Shakespeare.* Routledge.

Whitfield, P. (Ed.). (2021). *Inclusivity and equality in performer training.* Routledge.

Zarrilli, P. (2019). *(Toward) a phenomenology of acting.* Routledge.

Zybutz, T., & Farquharson, C. (2016). Psychophysical performance and the dyspraxic actor. *Journal of Neurodiversity in Higher Education*, 2, 76–87.

Afterword

Dear Reader,

Stan Brown invites us to notice 'How do I feel? What do I think? What do I believe?' (Chapter 5).

How do you feel?
What do you think?
What do you believe?

I am thinking about that old improvisation adage: *Listening as a willingness to change.* In what ways are you, dear reader, willing to invite change in from these chapters?

And in order to change, what might you need to let go of?

This collection centres on the need for critical approaches to intersectional actor pedagogies. Criticality is often connected to a breaking down, a deconstruction, or a picking apart. It can be painful and terrifying; there is a vulnerability to it. Especially when our identities are entwined in generative work like artmaking and teaching. I invite you to see both things as necessary: two sides of the same coin.

In what ways does the humbling messiness of criticality within these chapters reside in your body? Can you breathe through those spaces with a willingness to change?

In what ways can you acknowledge that your body, your classroom, studio, rehearsal space, conservatoire, or university-at-large is a 'type of organism – intersecting and in a constant state of becoming?' (Chapter 10). These spaces are also breathing, expanding, and contracting with all the fear and courage we muster.

In what ways might your heart mind, in all its biases, experiences, and harm (both caused and lived through) – be in a constant state of becoming?

In their chapter, Kristine Landon-Smith and Chris Hay remind us that 'we cannot move forward until the actor is ignited' (Chapter 2). So much of actor training has extinguished our students' light. My wish is for you to take what you learned here as combustible energy that will burn through what you thought you knew and give heat to new, bright pedagogies. May we all ignite and be a light for one another.

In solidarity,
Amy Mihyang Ginther

Index

Note: Page numbers in *italic* indicate a figure and page numbers in **bold** indicate a table on the corresponding page.